D0583552

Statutory Interpretation

Cases, Text and Materials

Randal N. Graham

Faculty of Law
University of Western Ontario

2002
EMOND MONTGOMERY PUBLICATIONS LIMITED
TORONTO, CANADA

Copyright © 2002 Emond Montgomery Publications Limited. All rights reserved. No part of this publication may be reproduced, stored in a retrieval system, or transmitted, in any form or by any means, photocopying, electronic, mechanical, recording, or otherwise, without the prior written permission of the copyright holder.

Printed in Canada.

Edited, designed, and typeset by WordsWorth Communications of Toronto, Canada.

We acknowledge the financial support of the Government of Canada through the Book Publishing Industry Development Program (BPIDP) for our publishing activities.

National Library of Canada Cataloguing in Publication

Graham, Randal N.
    Statutory interpretation : cases, text and materials / Randal N. Graham.

Companion for Statutory Interpretation : theory and practice.
ISBN 1-55239-091-8

    1. Law—Canada—Interpretation and construction—Cases.   I. Title

KE482.S84G73 2001 Suppl.   348.71′02   C2002-902859-0

Preface

This casebook is designed as a companion for *Statutory Interpretation: Theory and Practice* (Toronto: Emond Montgomery, 2001) (*"Theory and Practice"*). While *Theory and Practice* deals with the theoretical underpinnings of statutory construction, this casebook is designed to demonstrate the "nuts and bolts" of the subject. The cases found in the present work have been selected for the purpose of introducing students to basic interpretive arguments and "rules," which will help students build upon the interpretive theories developed in *Theory and Practice*.

Together, the present work and *Theory and Practice* are designed to constitute a complete set of materials for a course on statutory interpretation. This casebook should be regarded as the primary source of readings for such a course. At the beginning of each chapter of this casebook, students are directed to a set of required readings from *Theory and Practice*. Those readings explain the competing interpretive theories that informed the decisions found in the relevant chapters of this book. By combining the theories developed in *Theory and Practice* with the selection of cases presented in this book, students will develop a high degree of skill in the interpretation of legislative language: a skill that will assist students throughout the remainder of their legal studies and their subsequent careers.

It is often difficult to evaluate student progress in a course combining practical skills with complex legal theory. In order to assist instructors, each chapter of this casebook concludes with a series of exercises designed to test student progress. Instructors should feel free to pick and choose from these assignments when designing their own courses. The best way to develop skills in the interpretation of statutes is to practise interpreting legislative text. As a result, most of the exercises found in this book require students to apply the text of legislative provisions to concrete fact scenarios. Through these exercises, students should come to appreciate the difficulty involved in applying interpretive theory to real-life situations. More importantly, students will hone the analytical and rhetorical skills that are critical for success in the legal profession.

A secondary purpose of this book is to demonstrate the current relevance of statutory construction. While the phrase "statutory interpretation" tends to conjure up images of dusty legal tomes with little relevance for current legal scholars, the truth of the matter is that many of the most controversial legal decisions in recent years have centred on problems of statutory interpretation. In order to emphasize this point, this book features cases dealing with controversial topics including abortion, pornography, same-sex marriages, gun control, and the sex industry. While cases of this nature tend to hold student interest, they also emphasize the increasing importance of legislative language in the regulation of deeply personal choices. Students will come to realize that whatever controversial legal issues they encounter, the debate will eventually turn on matters of statutory construction. By honing their own interpretive skills, students will enhance their ability to participate in the legal debates that shape every field of human endeavour.

The materials in this book were selected, in part, according to the input of students I taught at Osgoode Hall Law School, York University, and the University of New Brunswick. I am grateful to all of the students who provided me with their comments. In particular, I would like to thank Matthew Letson, LLB 2002, for the valuable research assistance that he provided throughout the preparation of this text. I would also like to thank Joanne Levison and Wanda Bailey for their indispensable administrative support. Finally, I would like to thank my partner, Stephanie Montgomery, for all of the help and inspiration that she never fails to provide.

Randal N. Graham
March 2002

Table of Contents

Preface iii
Detailed Table of Contents vii
Table of Cases xiii

CHAPTER ONE   JUDICIAL APPROACHES TO STATUTORY INTERPRETATION 1
    I. Introduction 1
    II. The Mushroom Case 1
    III. EGALE Canada Inc. v. Canada 12
    IV. Quebec v. Boisbriand 21
    V. Roe v. Wade 31
    VI. R v. Mara 51
  VII. Exercises 56

CHAPTER TWO   THE MAXIMS OF INTERPRETATION 61
    I. Introduction 61
    II. Noscitur a Sociis 62
    III. Ejusdem Generis 70
    IV. Reddendo Singula Singulis 82
    V. Expressio Unius Est Exclusio Alterius 85
    VI. Casus Omissus 91
  VII. Exercises 96

CHAPTER THREE   THE RULES OF INTERPRETATION 99
    I. Introduction 99
    II. The Literal Rule and the Golden Rule 100
    III. The Mischief Rule 124
    IV. Exercises 140

CHAPTER FOUR   EVIDENCE OF THE STATUTE'S MEANING 145
    I. Introduction 145
    II. Title 146
    III. Preamble 150
    IV. Headings 152
    V. Marginal Notes 157

VI. Punctuation 162
VII. Previous Versions of the Statute 166
VIII. Debates and Parliamentary Materials 176
IX. Exercises 182

CHAPTER FIVE   INTERPRETING CRIMINAL LEGISLATION 187
I. Introduction 187
II. R v. Mac 187
III. R v. Russell 196
IV. Caron v. United States 202
V. Other Cases 208
VI. Exercises 208

CHAPTER SIX   INTERPRETING TAX LAWS 213
I. Introduction 213
II. Will-Kare Paving & Contracting 213
III. Ludco Enterprises Ltd. v. Canada 229
IV. O'Gilvie v. United States 239
V. Exercise 250

Detailed Table of Contents

Preface iii
Table of Contents v
Table of Cases xiii

CHAPTER ONE   JUDICIAL APPROACHES TO STATUTORY INTERPRETATION   1
  I. Introduction   1
    A. Purpose   1
    B. Required Readings   1
  II. The Mushroom Case   1
    A. Introduction   1
    B. The Court's Decision   2
      Re Ontario Mushroom Co. Ltd. and Learie   2
      Notes and Questions   9
  III. EGALE Canada Inc. v. Canada   12
    A. Introduction   12
    B. The Court's Decision   12
      EGALE Canada Inc. v. Canada (Attorney General)   12
      Notes and Questions   18
  IV. Quebec v. Boisbriand   21
    A. Introduction   21
    B. The Court's Decision   21
      Quebec (Commission des droits de la personne et des droits
      de la jeunesse) v. Montreal (City); Quebec (Commission
      des droits de la personne et des droits de la jeunesse) v.
      Boisbriand (City)   21
      Notes and Questions   30
  V. Roe v. Wade   31
    A. Introduction   31
    B. The Court's Decision   32
      Roe et al. v. Wade, District Attorney of Dallas County   32
      Notes and Questions   48

VI.   R v. Mara 51
      A. Introduction 51
      B. The Court's Decision 51
          R v. Mara 51
          Notes and Questions 55
VII. Exercises 56
      A. The Moral Propriety Code 56
      B. EGALE Canada Inc. Revisited 57
      C. The Bait Shop 57

CHAPTER TWO   THE MAXIMS OF INTERPRETATION 61
   I.   Introduction 61
        A. Purpose 61
        B. Required Readings 61
   II. Noscitur a Sociis 62
        A. Introduction 62
        B. Koskolos Realty 62
            R v. A.N. Koskolos Realty Ltd. 62
            Notes and Questions 65
        C. Gutierrez v. Ada 66
            Gutierrez and Bordallo v. Ada and Camacho 66
            Notes and Questions 70
   III. Ejusdem Generis 70
        A. Introduction 70
        B. Nanaimo v. Rascal Trucking 71
            Nanaimo (City) v. Rascal Trucking Ltd. 71
            Notes and Questions 74
        C. Circuit City Stores v. Saint Clair Adams 75
            Circuit City Stores, Inc. v. Saint Clair Adams 75
            Notes and Questions 78
        D. Grini v. Grini 79
            Grini v. Grini 79
            Notes and Questions 82
   IV. Reddendo Singula Singulis 82
        A. Introduction 82
        B. The Lobster Case 83
            Commonwealth v. William A. Barber 83
            Notes and Questions 84
        C. Quinn v. Lowell Electric 84
            Hugh Quinn v. Lowell Electric Light Corporation 84
            Notes and Questions 84
   V.   Expressio Unius Est Exclusio Alterius 85
        A. Introduction 85

      B. Morgan v. Crawshay 85
          George Morgan and Others Plaintiffs in Error; and Henry Crawshay
            Defendant in Error 85
          Notes and Questions 90
  VI. Casus Omissus 91
      A. Introduction 91
      B. US v. Sheldon 91
          United States v. Sheldon 91
          Notes and Questions 92
      C. Ex Parte Brown 93
          Ex Parte Brown 93
          Notes and Questions 96
 VII. Exercises 96
      A. The Farm Offences Act 96
      B. The Prize Fight 97
      C. Originalism and Dynamism 98

CHAPTER THREE   THE RULES OF INTERPRETATION 99
   I. Introduction 99
      A. The Three Rules 99
      B. Required Readings 100
  II. The Literal Rule and the Golden Rule 100
      A. Introduction 100
      B. Smith v. United States 101
          Smith v. United States 101
          Notes and Questions 106
      C. R v. McIntosh 107
          R v. McIntosh 107
          Notes and Questions 122
 III. The Mischief Rule 124
      A. Introduction 124
      B. Legislation 125
      C. R v. Sharpe 125
          R v. Sharpe 126
          Notes and Questions 133
      D. Rizzo & Rizzo Shoes 134
      E. R v. Egger 135
          R v. Egger 135
          Notes and Questions 139
  IV. Exercises 140
      A. Auditions 140
      B. Subway Repair 141
      C. Current Judicial Approaches 144

CHAPTER FOUR   EVIDENCE OF THE STATUTE'S MEANING 145

  I. Introduction 145

  II. Title 146

    A. Legislation 146

    B. R v. Lane 146

        R v. Lane, Ex p. Gould 146

        Notes and Questions 148

    C. Committee for the Commonwealth of Canada 148

        Committee for the Commonwealth of Canada v. Canada 148

        Notes and Questions 150

  III. Preamble 150

    A. Introduction 150

    B. Legislation 150

    C. The Anti-Inflation Act 151

        Re Anti-Inflation Act 151

        Notes and Questions 152

  IV. Headings 152

    A. Legislation 152

    B. R v. Lohnes 153

        R v. Lohnes 153

        Notes and Questions 156

  V. Marginal Notes 157

    A. Legislation 157

    B. R v. Basaraba 158

        R v. Basaraba 158

        Notes and Questions 158

    C. R v. Wigglesworth 159

        R v. Wigglesworth 159

        Notes and Questions 162

  VI. Punctuation 162

    A. Introduction 162

    B. R v. Jaagusta 163

        R v. Jaagusta 163

        Notes and Questions 164

    C. R v. Popoff 165

        R v. Popoff 165

        Notes and Questions 165

  VII. Previous Versions of the Statute 166

    A. Introduction 166

    B. Legislation 167

    C. Re Simon Fraser University 168

        Re Simon Fraser University and District of Burnaby 168

        Notes and Questions 171

D. R v. Ulybel Enterprises Ltd. 172
    R v. Ulybel Enterprises Ltd. 172
    Notes and Questions 175
E. R v. McIntosh 176
VIII. Debates and Parliamentary Materials 176
A. Introduction 176
B. Re Rizzo & Rizzo Shoes Ltd. 178
    Re Rizzo & Rizzo Shoes Ltd. 178
    Notes and Questions 179
C. The Firearms Reference 180
    Reference re Firearms Act (Can.) 180
    Notes and Questions 181
IX. Exercises 182
A. Spy Mission 182
B. Human Rights Legislation 184
C. Dynamism and Evidentiary Rules 185

CHAPTER FIVE   INTERPRETING CRIMINAL LEGISLATION 187
I. Introduction 187
II. R v. Mac 187
A. Introduction 187
B. The Court's Decision 188
    R v. Mac 188
    Notes and Questions 195
III. R v. Russell 196
A. The Court's Decision 196
    R v. Russell 196
    Notes and Questions 201
IV. Caron v. United States 202
A. The Court's Decision 202
    Caron v. United States 202
    Notes and Questions 207
V. Other Cases 208
VI. Exercises 208
A. The Roller Coaster 208
B. Firearms Prohibitions 209
C. Originalism, Dynamism, and Criminal Legislation 211

CHAPTER SIX   INTERPRETING TAX LAWS 213
I. Introduction 213
II. Will-Kare Paving & Contracting 213
A. Introduction 213

B. The Court's Decision 214
        Will-Kare Paving & Contracting Ltd. v. Canada 214
        Notes and Questions 227
III. Ludco Enterprises Ltd. v. Canada 229
    A. Introduction 229
    B. The Court's Decision 230
        Ludco Enterprises Ltd. v. Canada 230
        Notes and Questions 238
IV. O'Gilvie v. United States 239
    A. The Court's Decision 239
        O'Gilvie v. United States 239
        Notes and Questions 249
    V. Exercise 250

Table of Cases

A page number in boldface type indicates that the text of the case or a portion thereof is reproduced. A page number in lightface type indicates that the case is merely quoted briefly or discussed by the authors. Cases mentioned within excerpts are not listed.

A.N. Koskolos Realty Ltd., R v. (1995), 27 WCB (2d) 162 (NS Prov. Ct.) **62**, 65, 125

Abley v. Dale, 11 CB 391 100

Anti-Inflation Act, Re, [1976] 2 SCR 373 .... **151**, 152

Barber, William A., Commonwealth v., 143 Mass. 560 (SJC 1887) **83**, 84

Basaraba, R v., [1975] 3 WWR 481 (Man. QB) 157, **158**, 159

Bathurst Paper Ltd. v. New Brunswick Minister of Municipal Affairs,
    [1972] SCR 471 167

Big M Drug Mart, R v., [1985] 1 SCR 295 177

Brown, Ex Parte, 21 SD 515 (SD SC 1907) **93**, 96

Cardinal v. R, [1980] 1 FC 149 165

Caron v. United States, 524 US 308 (1998) **202**, 207

Circuit City Stores, Inc. v. Saint Clair Adams, 532 US 105 (2001) **75**, 78

Committee for the Commonwealth of Canada v. Canada, [1991] 1 SCR 139 .... **148**, 150

Crown Zellerbach Canada Ltd., R v., [1988] 1 SCR 401 20

EGALE Canada Inc. v. Canada (Attorney General)
    (2001), CRDJ 642 (BC SC) **12**, 18-20, 49, 50, 56, 57, 90

Egger, R v., [1993] 2 SCR 451 .... **135**, 139

Estabrooks Pontiac Buick Ltd., New Brunswick v.
    (1982), 44 NBR (2d) 201 (CA) 123

Firearms Act (Can.), Reference re, [2000] 1 SCR 783 .... **180**, 181-82

Goulis, R v. (1981), 125 DLR (3d) 137 (Ont. CA) 62

Grand Trunk Pacific Railway Co. v. Dearborn (1919), 58 SCR 315 123

Gravel v. City of St. Leonard, [1978] 1 SCR 660 166

Grey v. Pearson (1857), 6 HL Cas. 60 123

Grini v. Grini (1969), 5 DLR (3d) 640 (Man. QB) 78, **79**, 82

Gutierrez and Bordallo v. Ada and Camacho, 528 US 250 (2000) **66**, 70

Hasselwander, R v., [1993] 2 SCR 398 .... 166, 195-96

Heydon's Case (1584), 3 Co. Rep. 7a; 76 ER 637 124

Hyde v. Hyde and Woodmansee (1866), LR 1 P & D 130 19

Jaagusta, R v., [1974] 3 WWR 766 .... **162** 164

Landauer v. Conklin, 3 SD 462; 54 NW 322 96

Lane, R v., Ex p. Gould, [1937] 1 DLR 212 (NB SC, App. Div.) **146**, 148

Lohnes, R v., [1992] 1 SCR 167 .... **153**

Ludco Enterprises Ltd. v. Canada, 2001 SCC 62 .... 229, **230**, 238-39, 250

Mac, R v. (2001), 152 CCC (3d) 1 (Ont. CA) 187, **188**, 195-96

Mara, R v., [1997] 2 SCR 630 .... **51**, 55-56, 65

McIntosh, R v., [1995] 1 SCR 686 .... 12, **107**, 122-24, 134,
                                                                      139, 162, 176, 208

Moore, R v., [1999] 3 SCR 250 162

Morgan, George, and Others Plaintiffs in Error; and Henry Crawshay
   Defendant in Error (1871), 5 HL 304 .... 19, **85**, 90

Morgentaler, R v., [1993] 3 SCR 463 .... 177, 179

Nanaimo (City) v. Rascal Trucking Ltd., [2001] 1 SCR 342 .... **71**, 74, 78

O'Gilvie v. United States, 519 US 79 (1996) **239**, 249-50

Ontario Mushroom Co. Ltd. et al. and Learie et al., Re
   (1977), 15 OR (2d) 639 (HC) 1, **2**, 9-12, 19, 30, 31, 49

Popoff, R v. (1985), 14 WCB 290 (BC Co. Ct.) **165**

Quebec (Commission des droits de la personne et des droits
   de la jeunesse) v. Montreal (City); Quebec (Commissions
   des droits de la personne et des droits de la jeunesse) v.
   Boisbriand (City), [2001] 1 SCR 665 .... **21**, 30-31, 49, 70, 150, 180, 185

Quinn, Hugh v. Lowell Electric Light Company,
   140 Mass. 106 (SJC 1885) **84**

Rizzo & Rizzo Shoes Ltd., Re, [1998] 1 SCR 27 .... 134, **178**, 179-80

Roe et al. v. Wade, District Attorney of Dallas County,
   410 US 113 (1973) 31, **32**, 48-50, 51, 56

Russell, R. v., [2001] SCJ no. 53 .... **196**, 201

Sharpe, R v., [2001] 1 SCR 45 .... 125, **126**, 133-34

Sheldon, United States v., 15 US 119 (1817) **91**, 92-93

Simon Fraser University and District of Burnaby, Re (1968), 67 DLR
   (2d) 638 (BC SC), aff'd. 1 DLR (3d) 427 (BC CA) **168**, 171-72

Skapinker, Law Society v., [1984] 1 SCR 357 156-57

Smith v. United States, 508 US 223 (1993) **101**, 106-7, 208

Ulybel Enterprises Ltd., R., [2001] SCJ no. 55 .... **172**, 175

Wellesley Hospital v. Lawson, [1978] 1 SCR 893 123

Wigglesworth, R v., [1987] 2 SCR 541 .... 157, **159**, 162

Will-Kare Paving & Contracting Ltd. v. Canada,
   [2000] 1 SCR 915 .... 213, **214**, 227-29, 250

CHAPTER ONE

Judicial Approaches to Statutory Interpretation

I. INTRODUCTION

A. Purpose

The purpose of this chapter is to provide an introduction to the process of statutory interpretation. The cases presented in this chapter demonstrate a wide variety of interpretive techniques, ranging from remarkably sensible, contextual readings of legislation to bizarre interpretations that have little or no basis in the legislative text. When reading the cases that follow, consider each of the following questions: (1) Does the interpretive technique adopted by a particular judge control the outcome of the case, or does the judge select an outcome based on other concerns and then use interpretation as a means of justifying that decision? (2) What do judges mean when they purport to base their decisions on the "intention" of a legislative body? (3) Is interpretation nothing but a stylized form of rhetoric that makes reference to textual clues, or does interpretation involve the application of fixed, knowable rules to legislative text? (4) If the legislature writes the law, but the court has the power to interpret the law's meaning, who really has the lawmaking power? and (5) What forms of interpretive reasoning do you find the most convincing? These questions will be developed and explored in the notes and questions following each decision in this chapter.

B. Required Readings

Before reading the cases in this chapter, students should review chapter 1 of Randal N. Graham, *Statutory Interpretation: Theory and Practice* (Toronto: Emond Montgomery, 2001) ("*Theory and Practice*").

II. THE MUSHROOM CASE

A. Introduction

The decision of the Ontario High Court of Justice in *Re Ontario Mushroom Co. Ltd. and Learie* (1977), 15 OR (2d) 639 (HC), provides an excellent introduction to the process of statutory interpretation. The decisions of the majority and the dissent demonstrate tension between the ideas of plain meaning and accurate meaning, and reveal the role of a judge's personal opinion in construing the language of statutory provisions. The decision also settles a question that has plagued philosophers for countless generations—can a mushroom be regarded as a vegetable?

B. The Court's Decision

Re Ontario Mushroom Co. Ltd. and Learie
(1977), 15 OR (2d) 639 (HC)

SOUTHEY, J (orally) (dissenting):[1] This is an appeal by Ontario Mushroom Co. Ltd. and Meadowglen Mushroom Growers Ltd. from the decision of Mr. Sharman Learie, QC, given as a designee under s. 34 of the *Employment Standards Act*, RSO 1970, c. 147. ... The issue before Mr. Learie was whether the appellants were required to pay vacation pay and were bound by the minimum wages provisions of the *Employment Standards Act*.

Section 6 of Regulation, RRO 1970, Reg. 244 [now repealed and replaced by O Reg. 803/75, s. 17] under the *Employment Standards Act* exempts certain work from the minimum wages provisions of the statute. The relevant subsection reads as follows:

> "MINIMUM WAGES
>   6. Sections 6 to 16 apply to every establishment, on and after the 1st day of January, 1969, but do not apply to work performed by,
>
>   . . .
>
>   (f) a person employed on a farm whose employment is directly related to the primary production of eggs, milk, grain, seeds, fruit, vegetables, maple products, honey, tobacco, pigs, cattle, sheep and poultry;"

The issue is whether persons employed by the appellants in connection with the production of mushrooms are exempted from the minimum wages provisions of the statute, because they are employed in the production of vegetables.

The designee held that such employees were not exempted by s. 6(f). His reasoning was that it could not have been intended in the Regulations to include persons engaged in mushroom growing in s. 6(f) because, in other exempting provisions in which the exemption is stated in terms similar to s. 6(f), there is also included a specific exemption covering persons engaged in mushroom growing. For example s. 5(k) of the Regulations relating to overtime pay exempts from the overtime pay provisions persons employed on a farm in terms identical with s. 6(f). Section 5(d) of the Regulations, however, contains the following exemption:

[1   In the official reporter, the judgment of Reid J appears before that of Southey J. The order of judgments has been altered in this casebook in order to promote clarity.]

"(d) a person employed in the business, trade or activity of,
- (i) landscape gardening,
- (ii) mushroom growing,
- (iii) the growing of flowers for the retail and wholesale trade, or
- (iv) the growing, transporting and laying of sod;"

I interpret the designee as saying that if persons employed in mushroom growing had been included in the exemption of persons employed in the production of vegetables, it would be unnecessary to have a specific exemption dealing with mushroom growing and therefore "vegetables" must be given a meaning which excludes "mushrooms." The designee did not develop his reasoning in any detail and it is impossible to be certain as to what he meant.

In my judgment, if the word "vegetables," properly interpreted, does include mushrooms, then persons engaged in mushroom growing are exempt from the relevant provisions of the statute or Regulations even though the legislators went on to exclude them in a specific exemption dealing with mushroom growing.

The real question in this appeal, therefore, is whether the proper interpretation of the word "vegetables," in the Regulations, includes mushrooms. A great deal of evidence was led by the appellants before the designee to show that mushrooms are considered by persons engaged in the cultivation and marketing of mushrooms as being vegetables. The appellants relied, for instance, on evidence that mushroom growers are members of the Ontario Fruit and Vegetables Growers Association. One of the witnesses, when asked why he considered mushrooms to be a vegetable, gave as his reason that it was an edible food and had all the qualifications that any other food that is grown has. I refer to the evidence of the witness Gahm.

In my view, however, none of this evidence really came to grips with the question as to the accurate meaning of the word "vegetables." Furthermore, I am unable to accept the submission that a mushroom is generally regarded as being a vegetable. It is likely that many people have never directed their mind to the question, but when one does consider the meaning of vegetable and the definition of a mushroom the only conclusion that I can draw is that a mushroom, in strict parlance, is not a vegetable.

I turn first to the meaning of the word "vegetable" and I am using *Webster's New World Dictionary of the American Language*, 2nd ed., printed in 1976. The first meaning given for vegetable is "of, or having the nature of, plants in general (the vegetable kingdom)." That meaning is the one that is used by persons playing the old children's game of "Animal, Vegetable or Mineral." Anything that is not animal or mineral is vegetable. In my judgment, that is much too broad a meaning to give to the word in this Regulation because it would then include trees, sod, indeed anything that grows in the nature of a plant.

The preferable meaning to be used in connection with this Regulation, in my judgment, is this one: (a) "Any herbaceous plant that is eaten whole or in part, raw or cooked, generally with an entree or in a salad but not as a dessert, (b) the edible part of such a plant, as the root (e.g., a carrot), tuber (a potato), seed (a pea), fruit (a tomato), stem (celery), leaf (lettuce), etc." Thus, in order to be a "vegetable," using this meaning, it must be shown that a mushroom is an herbaceous plant or a part of an herbaceous plant.

The meanings of herbaceous are "(1) of, or having the nature of, an herb or herbs, (2) like a green leaf in texture, colour, shape, etc." A herb is defined as any seed plant whose stem withers away to the ground after each season's growth, as distinguished from a tree or shrub whose woody stem lives from year to year.

A mushroom does not have a woody stem and it withers at the end of its life cycle, but, in my judgment, it cannot for that reason alone be regarded as an herbaceous plant. The definition of mushroom contained in the dictionary is "any of various rapid-growing, fleshy fungi ... typically having a stalk capped with an umbrellalike top." The dictionary meaning of fungus is "any of a large group of thallophytes, including moulds, mildews, mushrooms, rusts and smuts, which are parasites on living organisms or feed upon dead organic material, lack chlorophyll, true roots, stems, and leaves, and reproduce by means of spores." A fungus, in my judgment, is not an herbaceous growth, because it does not have leaves or chlorophyll and does not utilize food from the soil with sunlight to manufacture tissue.

Accordingly, in my judgment, a mushroom is not, strictly speaking, a vegetable. It is apparent from the evidence that "vegetable" is often used with a meaning broad enough to include mushrooms and I now look at the Regulations as a whole to see if they contain any indication as to whether the word was used in its strict, correct meaning, or with a more general meaning. The conclusion that it was used in the strict, correct meaning is indicated by those sections of the Regulations to which the designee referred, containing specific references to mushroom growing. It will be seen that those sections contain a specific exemption of persons employed in mushroom growing, despite the fact that they contain a general exemption of persons employed in the production of vegetables. This indicates to me that the word "vegetables" is used in the Regulations in its strict meaning, which does not include mushrooms.

Accordingly, I would affirm the interpretation given by the designee as to the meaning of the minimum wages provision of the Regulations.

REID, J (orally): ... Turning to the merits of the appeal, I find no real issue arising out of the reasons of Mr. Learie on the question whether a mushroom is a vegetable. Mr. Learie said ... that having heard witnesses (and, presumably, the arguments)—these witnesses gave evidence that: "(2) All levels of government regarded a mushroom as a vegetable." He then went on to deal with the cross-examination wherein an attempt was made, as he said, to "take from this general evidence." He said further on p. 5: "However, the evidence in chief was overwhelming that all levels of government in Canada regarded mushrooms as vegetables." I take that to mean that he drew the conclusion that all levels of Government in Canada regarded mushroom growing as farming and mushrooms as vegetables. He went on in that same vein on p. 6 of his reasons to refer to "... the uncontradicted evidence that all 3 levels of government in Canada in all situations treat mushroom growing in Canada as farming." And so it does appear to me that he accepted the evidence as amounting to this: that it was uncontradicted before him that a mushroom was a vegetable; and that he was satisfied that, generally speaking, mushroom growing in Canada was regarded as farming. His concluding paragraph may give the key to his decision to an opposite effect. It says:

"However the fact that in Parts III & IV of the Act, a "mushroom growing" exception is added to a "farming" exception makes it clear that the "farming" exception does not include mushroom growing."

By that I take him to mean that, notwithstanding a general acceptance of farming as including mushroom growing, because s. 4 of the Regulation ... created specific exemptions for mushroom growing and employment on a farm growing vegetables from Part III of the Act, and s. 5 of the Regulation did the same for Part IV of the Act, the exemption of employment on a farm growing vegetables created by s. 6(f) of the Regulation should be read so as not to include mushroom growing. The reason for this was apparently that in ss. 4 and 5 the word "farm" did not imply mushroom growing because a specific exemption was made for mushroom growing.

That is the way I read his reasons and that is why I say it does not seem to me that the issue in this Court is whether the term "vegetable" includes the term "mushroom." That seemed to be accepted by Mr. Learie and, indeed, no real attack is made on that in this Court. We invited Mr. Fleming to comment on that, to ask whether he accepted that "mushroom" was included in the term "vegetable" in s. 6(f). As I interpreted his response it was that it was unnecessary to face that question since his argument depended upon the force of the wording of ss. 4 and 5 of the Regulation to the effect that one should read the term "farm" in s. 6 as excluding the activity of mushroom growing. If I am wrong in this appraisal, I should deal with the question whether "vegetable" includes "mushroom." I do so particularly out of deference to my brother Southey who has given it prominence in his reasons. I agree that a statute should normally be interpreted in its popular sense. The texts on statute interpretation are fairly uniform to the effect that general statutes should prima facie be interpreted in general terms. In *Maxwell on Interpretation of Statutes*, 12th ed. (1969), the following occurs at p. 81, under the heading "Words Used In Popular Sense":

"In dealing with matters relating to the general public, statutes are presumed to use words in their popular, rather than their narrowly legal or technical sense: "loquitur ut vulgus, that is, according to the common understanding and acceptation of the terms." The Fusilier (1865) Br. & L 341, per Dr. Lushington at p. 393. If an "Act is directed to dealing with matters affecting everybody generally, the words used have the meaning attached to them in the common and ordinary use of language." *Unwin v. Hanson*, [1891] 2 QB 115, per Lord Esher MR at p. 119."

Citations are given by the author to support those propositions. I subscribe to them and I look at this statute in the light of those observations: see also *36 Hals.*, 3rd ed., p. 392, and *Stephens v. Cuckfield Rural District Council*, [1960] 2 QB 373 at p. 383 (CA). It seems to me that this is a general statute directed to people generally and that therefore the meaning attached should be the common and ordinary meaning of the words. The statute obviously applies to a broad segment of the public, which includes employers and employees in a very wide variety of kinds of employment. The section we are concerned with deals with farms and farming. I would not think that the language was used with any other intention than it should be comprehensible to persons engaged in the kind of occupations that are covered. These include sales-men, superintendents, students employed at a camp for children, persons employed on farms, etc. It seems to me, therefore, that the statute should be interpreted in accordance with the common understanding of terms in common use. Thus if there is a plain meaning arising out of the common understanding of those terms, I would think it would be preferable to accept that meaning rather than to reject it and search elsewhere for a meaning.

With respect to the word "mushroom," the testimony was virtually uniform that, in the understanding of those who were called before the designee, "vegetable" included "mushroom." I am impressed with the breadth of the public represented by those witnesses and, particularly, with the fact that these witnesses obviously had a close association with mushroom growing, in some cases for many years. But apart from that, a member of the Canadian Horticultural Council, that, according to Mr. Learie, co-ordinates all agriculture in Canada except grain, dairy and poultry, also supported the general view that a mushroom was a vegetable. These witnesses are described very briefly in Mr. Learie's reasons. I need go no further than say that they included Mr. D. F. Gahm, the President of the Ontario Mushroom Co. Ltd., a man with training in bacteriology, botany and microbiology and with 35 years of mushroom business in Canada; Mr. Scrow was the managing director of Meadowglen, the other company involved. Mr. Loughton, a research scientist in charge of mushroom research in Vineland, Ontario, for the Ministry of Agriculture also testified. He was a Bachelor of Science in Horticulture, University of Nottingham, England, and a Master of Science. Mr. Lepresti had been in the mushroom business for 20 years and was the general manager of the Maple Leaf Mushroom Farm and president at some time of the Cana-dian Mushroom Grower's Association. Mr. R. H. Taylor was the executive secretary of the Canadian Horticultural Council. He was called to give evidence and said at p. 90:

"Q. Now, finally, you have indicated the representation at the Canadian Horticultural Council, including the provincial representatives, has it ever been suggested that a mush-room is not a fruit or vegetable.

A. No, it has never been considered because all areas of federal government, every branch of federal government going right through customs, finance, everything, in their farm section they classify mushroom growing as a farm operation, and most provincial bodies are the same."

I select that merely as an example of what appears was the kind of evidence that Mr. Learie referred to when he concluded that it was overwhelming on the evidence that a mushroom was a vegetable.

On the basis of that evidence, which, in my respectful opinion, is entitled to con-sideration, because it is evidence from those persons who are not only knowledge-able on the subject of mushroom and vegetable growing, but are also the kind of persons to whom the Act appears to be directed. Therefore, it is useful to hear what they have to say. No attempt was made to contradict their evidence. Mr. Fleming did not call evidence intended to contradict evidence that amounted to the acceptance that a mushroom was a vegetable. And so, on the basis of that evidence, one might reasonably conclude that a mushroom is commonly understood to be a vegetable. Not a word was said to gainsay this. If we are to interpret the Act in accordance with the common understanding of mankind, then s. 6(f) should be interpreted consistently with that evidence, in my respectful opinion.

That, however, is not the only possible source of common meanings. A number of dictionaries were referred to. My brother referred to Webster's. I need not repeat the parts that he has read, but it is plain that the first meaning given to "vegetable" is a meaning of very wide import indeed, and that is any plant. I would have thought that it was open to the applicants before Mr. Learie, if they needed to go further than rely on the evidence given by witnesses, to refer to that very general meaning, as being support for that evidence. That meaning is reflected in other dictionaries. He could, in my opinion, rest his case there, leaving it to anyone who contended for a different interpretation to call evidence or to refer to authorities that would show that that prima facie meaning should not be accepted in the circumstances of this case.

I am personally a little reluctant to refer to dictionaries for the purpose of contradicting the common understanding of a common term. I am not surprised at the evidence given before Mr. Learie to the effect that a mushroom was accepted as a vegetable. That accords with my own experience. While that might not govern, and I do not go so far as to say that it is open to Judges simply to rely on their own experience and treat that as a proper subject of judicial notice, nevertheless, I would have been surprised, based on my experience with the terms "vegetable" and "mushroom," if any other conclusion had been reached. I do not entirely set aside my own understanding but, of course, I do not rely on it. What I would do with reluctance is set aside a common understanding by reference only to dictionary definitions. It seems to me that, first of all, it is unnecessary to go to the dictionary when we have evidence of the type that we have here and when we have, indeed, a prima facie meaning given by the dictionaries that is in accord with that interpretation. Dictionaries can, in my experience, be somewhat misleading. I have thought over the lunch hour of the extent to which that might be the case. I have thought, for instance, of the word "Fall," which in the common understanding of people in Ontario, and I need no evidence at all on this to satisfy myself, can mean the season "Autumn." Yet, in the *Oxford English Dictionary*, the 10-volume work originally called *Murray's New English Dictionary*, I fail to find the word "Fall" at all nor does the word "Fall" appear there as having that meaning save "in the US," I would not be willing to abandon my understanding of the meaning of the word "Fall," as including the season "Autumn" simply because it is not written down in the *Oxford English Dictionary*. In some other rather superficial research over the lunch hour, I looked at the word "bonnet" in the *Concise Oxford Dictionary*, and I find that one of the meanings given is a "hinged cover over the motor of a car." I do not require evidence to satisfy myself that in Ontario that is not a common nor an accepted meaning for the word "bonnet." I would not accept the meaning given in that dictionary, and we can assume that that is contained in the greater versions of that work, as an appropriate meaning if the word "bonnet" occurred in an Ontario statute and it was argued that, in the context of that statute, it should be interpreted to mean the hinged cover over the motor of a car. One need not look very much further for another example. The word "boot" comes to mind. In the dictionary I have just referred to, "boot" is given a number of meanings; first of all, an outer foot covering, and I would accept that. It is also, however, given a meaning which I quote: "the luggage receptacle in a coach under the guard's and coachman's seat" and it is my own experience that English people in England commonly refer to what we call the trunk of a car as the boot. Again, if the word "boot" appeared in a statute relating to affairs or things in Ontario, I would not lightly accept the meaning given in the *Oxford Dictionary*, if it were suggested that "boot" was to be interpreted as the trunk of a car, in the face of my entire experience to the contrary. So, therefore, I have the view that it is dangerous, and unnecessary, to apply to dictionaries when the meaning of a common word has been shown to have been commonly understood by the persons towards whom legislation is directed. I would not accept a secondary dictionary meaning for "vegetable" that would exclude "mushroom" when a primary meaning includes it.

It is, therefore, my respectful view that it is not only unnecessary to resort to other parts of the statute, but it is probably wrong to resort to other parts of the statute if the plain meaning has been shown to be accepted. Mr. Learie, while not disagreeing that the commonly accepted meaning of "vegetable" includes "mushroom," nevertheless, denied himself that choice of interpretation because of other language used in other sections. That seems to me to be engaging in a backwards method of statutory interpretation. To defeat the plain meaning by resorting to other parts of the statute, dealing with other matters, seems to me to be getting it backwards. The right approach to me is that resort should be had to other parts of the statute only where there is some need for it, as where a plain meaning has not otherwise been elicited. Secondly, it seems to me that the general rule that one should examine the general context of the statute as a course of interpretation is one that has to be considered in the light of each statute. This statute seems to me to be not one statute but really a series of statutes, and I can say the same for the Regulations. While, generally speaking, the statute deals with employment standards, so-called, it, and the Regulation, really deal individually with a number of separate subjects. Thus "hours of work" are covered by Part III of the Act and s. 4 of the Regulation; "overtime pay" by Part IV of the Act and s. 5 of the Regulation, and "minimum wages" (our concern) by Part V of the Act and s. 6 of the Regulation.

Therefore, it seems to me that one should first look at the part and section that constitutes, in effect, a code or little statute in relation to its general heading. Thus, in relation to overtime pay, one would look first at Part IV and s. 5. The terms used in each part or section may be taken to be deliberately chosen to achieve the object of this particular part or section, and directed to its application.

In this case, the issue is the exemption from the statutory provision for minimum wages. There is nothing in the other parts or sections that relates to the exemption from minimum wages. One would surely look at the sections of the Regulation and part of the statute that relate to overtime pay and try to interpret those first without going to what almost amounts to a different statute, that is a different part relating to a different subject-matter, in search of assistance. So it seems to me, therefore, that it is inappropriate, where a clear and accepted meaning exists for a word in one section, to refer to other sections and parts. Therefore, the general concept that one should look at a word in the general context of the statute has to be modified in the light of the fact that this legislation amounts really to a series of small codes or statutes.

Therefore, I think, with respect, that the designee fell into error by defeating the common understanding of the word "vegetable" through the device of referring to other parts of the statute dealing with other subjects, and that that was an inappropriate way of proceeding and is what led to what, in my respectful view, is an error in his decision.

I would therefore have set aside and reversed the decision in respect of his interpretation of s. 6(f).

MALONEY, J (orally): I find myself not satisfied that a mushroom is necessarily excluded from the term "vegetable" on the basis of the definition set forth in the dictionary referred to by my brother Southey. It seems to me that, bearing in mind the definitions set forth in other dictionaries, such as, for example, Funk and Wagnall, which was referred to in argument, one might conclude that a mushroom is a vegetable or, at least, be left in doubt. Certainly, it appears that governmental authorities at all levels and in various jurisdictions consider mushrooms to be vegetables and mushroom growers to be vegetable farmers for purposes relating to control and taxation. In any event, as a matter of statutory interpretation of this particular enactment, I prefer the approach adopted by my brother Reid as to the meaning of the terminology used and I therefore agree that the appeal should be allowed.

Appeal allowed.

NOTES AND QUESTIONS

1. As Southey J points out at the beginning of his dissent, Mr. Learie (the designee who interpreted the *Employment Standards Act* (ESA) at first instance) based his interpretation of the relevant language upon a comparison between two provisions of the ESA's regulations. Specifically, the designee compared s. 6(f) (which contains an exemption for "vegetable" farming) and s. 5 of the regulation, which contains separate exemptions for "vegetable" farming and "mushroom growing." Consider the following questions:

   a. If the legislature intended to include "mushroom growing" within the phrase "vegetable farming," why would the legislature feel the need to list both items separately in s. 5 of the regulation?
   b. Assuming that the legislature did intend to distinguish "vegetable farming" from "mushroom growing" in s. 5 of the regulation, is it safe to assume that the term "vegetable farming," as it appears in s. 6(f) of the regulation, carries the same meaning as it does in s. 5? In other words, is it safe to assume that words are used consistently in different sections of a single enactment?[2]

---

2   The type of reasoning used by the designee is encapsulated by the legal maxim *expressio unius est exclusio alterius*, which is dealt with at 104-9 of *Theory and Practice*. That section of *Theory and Practice* also explains the role of the "presumption of consistent expression" in the interpretation of legal language.

2. In *The Interpretation of Legislation in Canada* (Cowansville, QC: Yvon Blais, 1992), Pierre-André Côté deals with the assumption (relied upon by Mr. Learie) that words are used consistently in different parts of the same enactment. According to Côté (at 279-80):

> Legislative drafters are supposed to respect the principle of uniformity of expression. Each term should have one and only one meaning, wherever it appears in the statute or regulation. An idea should be expressed in the same terms throughout the enactment. ... This rule of drafting leads to a principle of interpretation deeming a word to maintain the same meaning throughout. Similarly, a different expression implies a different concept: different terms, different meanings. ... The principle of uniformity of expression is not an infallible guide to interpretation, however.

3. Southey J noted that much of the evidence presented in the appeal dealt with the fact that "mushrooms are regarded by persons engaged in the cultivation and marketing of mushrooms as being vegetables." In the interpretation of a document written by members of a legislative assembly (very few of whom, presumably, have ever been mushroom growers), why would we concern ourselves with the intentions and views of persons employed in the mushroom industry? Would the views of mushroom growers become more relevant if the evidence established that mushroom growers were consulted when the relevant statutory language was being drafted?

4. Which is more relevant in the interpretation of legislation—the meaning intended by the author (that is, Parliament or a legislative assembly) or the meaning that will likely be attributed to the text by its primary audience? How are these two potential meanings related?

5. Southey J focuses on the "accurate" meaning of the word "vegetables" rather than on the meaning intended by the legislature or the meaning that would be given to the relevant term by mushroom growers.[3] Is it fair to assume that the legislature intended to use the word "vegetables" accurately? What if the so-called accurate meaning is obscure, or conflicts with the average person's usage of the relevant word?

6. Compare Southey J's decision with that of Reid J, where "ordinary meaning" is preferred over "accurate" meaning. Which approach is more persuasive?

7. If you were to order a pizza with no vegetables, would you be surprised to discover mushrooms on your pizza? Would you have been relying upon an "accurate meaning" of the word "vegetables"? Would the average person be surprised to find mushrooms in the vegetable section of a grocery store? Do these considerations matter in the construction of legislation, or should we expect language to be used more formally in a statute?

8. Southey J makes reference to a number of dictionaries when interpreting the words "mushroom" and "vegetable." What is the evidentiary value of a dictionary? Is it likely that the drafters of legislation rely heavily on dictionary meanings when preparing legislation? What happens when two dictionaries point toward different meanings for a

---

3   See, for example, where Southey J states that "the only conclusion that I can draw is that a mushroom, in strict parlance, is not a vegetable," and that the evidence led at trial did not come to grips "with the question as to the *accurate* meaning of the word 'vegetables' " (emphasis added).

particular word? Should a judge prefer a meaning found in the *Oxford English Dictionary* (for example) to one found in an online dictionary service?

9. According to Southey J, the term "vegetable" (as it is used in the Regulations) refers to "any herbaceous plant ... whose stem withers away to the ground after each season's growth." Is it likely that, when enacting the relevant statute, the legislature thought that it was enacting legislation dealing with "herbaceous plants"? Would this definition bring grapes within the meaning of the term "vegetable"? If so, are grapes "vegetables" for the purposes of the ESA?[4]

10. Reid J relies on the "fact" that "all levels of Government in Canada [regard] mushrooms as vegetables." If this is true, does it matter that, scientifically speaking, all levels of government are *wrong*?

11. If, as Southey J contends, a mushroom is not embraced by the "accurate" meaning of the word "vegetable," is it likely that all members of every legislature, at every level of government in Canada, regard mushrooms as vegetables? If not, what did Reid J mean by the statement that "all levels of Government in Canada [regard] mushrooms as vegetables"? What evidence could be used to establish that the government thinks of mushrooms as vegetables?

12. Reid J relied heavily on the testimony of witnesses who appeared before the designee. Each of the relevant witnesses claimed that the ordinary meaning of "vegetable" included mushrooms. By relying on this evidence, Reid J claimed to be "impressed with the breadth of the public represented by these witnesses." Does it matter that most of the witnesses cited by Reid J were involved in the management of mushroom companies, and that (presumably) if the phrase "vegetable farming" was found *not* to include mushroom growing, these mushroom companies would be bound by the ESA's minimum wage provisions?

13. Should "ordinary meaning" be established through the testimony of "ordinary people"? Can judges simply rely on their own experiences regarding the usual meaning of a particular term? Consider the following portion of Reid J's decision:

> I am not surprised at the evidence given before Mr. Learie to the effect that a mushroom was accepted as a vegetable. That accords with my own experience. While that might not govern, and I do not go so far as to say that it is open to Judges simply to rely on their own experience and treat that as a proper subject of judicial notice, nevertheless, I would have been surprised, based on my experience with the terms "vegetable" and "mushroom," if any other conclusion had been reached.

14. Reid J claims to be "a little reluctant to refer to dictionaries for the purpose of contradicting the common understanding of a common term." What are dictionaries, if not catalogues of "the common understanding" of common terms?

15. According to Reid J:

> It is, therefore, my respectful view that it is not only unnecessary to resort to other parts of the statute, but it is probably wrong to resort to other parts of the statute if the plain meaning

---

4   Of course, the question whether grapes count as "vegetables" in the ESA regulations is purely academic—both fruits and vegetables are addressed by the relevant regulations, so grape growers will be entitled to the relevant exemptions regardless of whether their crop is classified as a "fruit" or a "vegetable."

has been shown to be accepted. ... The right approach to me is that resort should be had to other parts of the statute only where there is some need for it, as where a plain meaning has not otherwise been elicited.

Note that this view of interpretation is opposed by the bulk of interpretive jurisprudence and academic commentary. Generally speaking, it is *always* important to look to other provisions within an enactment when interpreting the language of one section. See, for example, *R v. McIntosh*, [1995] 1 SCR 686 (reported in chapter 3 of this text), as well as E.A. Driedger, *Driedger on the Construction of Statutes*, 3d ed., Ruth Sullivan, ed. (Toronto: Butterworths, 1994), at 131, where Driedger writes: "There is only one rule in modern interpretation, namely, courts are obliged to determine the meaning of legislation in its total context."

III. EGALE CANADA INC. v. CANADA

A. Introduction

Not all judicial decisions turn on issues as controversial as the question of whether mushrooms are vegetables. The next decision discussed in this chapter deals with a much more mundane issue: does s. 91(26) of the *Constitution Act, 1867*, which gives Parliament the right to legislate in the area of "Marriage and Divorce," give Parliament the authority to approve of same-sex marriages? The court approached this question as a problem of statutory interpretation: does the term "Marriage," as it appears in the constitution, include unions between people of the same sex? The court in *EGALE Canada Inc. v. Canada* (2001), CRDJ 642 (BC SC), dealt with this highly charged political and interpretive issue.

B. The Court's Decision

EGALE Canada Inc. v. Canada (Attorney General)
(2001), CRDJ 642 (BC SC)

PITFIELD, J: ...

I. Introduction

The petitioners, other than EGALE Canada Inc., are same-sex couples who wish to marry. Each couple applied to the British Columbia Director of Vital Statistics for a marriage licence. Each request was refused on the basis that the common law governing the question of capacity to marry did not recognize the marriage of two persons of the same sex and, because the capacity to marry was within federal constitutional jurisdiction, only the federal government could enact legislation to redefine marriage or change the rules on capacity.

The petitioners apply for a declaration that the marriage of two persons of the same sex is not prohibited at common law or by statute; a declaration that the Director is entitled to issue marriage licences to same-sex couples; and an order requiring the Director to issue marriage licences to them. In the alternative, the petitioners apply for a declaration that any common law or statutory provision prohibiting the marriage of same-sex couples infringes, denies and is inconsistent with the rights and freedoms guaranteed by the *Canadian Charter of Rights and Freedoms* and is, therefore, of no force and effect.

It is obvious that the petitioners seek state, and therefore public, recognition of the legitimacy of same-sex relationships. The individual petitioners are supported by EGALE Canada Inc., an organization engaged in the national pursuit of equality for gay and lesbian individuals. ...

V. "Marriage" and the Common Law

"Marriage" is not defined by federal statute but two Acts touch upon the substance of the relationship.

Section 1.1 of the *Modernization of Benefits and Obligations Act*, provides as follows:

> 1.1. For greater certainty, the amendments made by the Act do not affect the meaning of the word "marriage," that is, the lawful union of one man and one woman to the exclusion of all others.

The *Marriage (Prohibited Degrees) Act*, SC 1990, c. 46 prohibits one person from marrying another in the event they are related by lineal consanguinity, affinity or adoption, or related as brother and sister by blood, half-blood or adoption, but does not define marriage.

In the absence of a statutory definition, marriage is a legal construct or relationship defined by common, or judge-made, law. It must be understood that saying marriage is a common law construct does not mean it is similar to what is called, in the vernacular, "living common-law," a term applied to unmarried, opposite sex couples living in a conjugal relationship.

The earliest relevant judicial discussion of marriage as a legal relationship to which I was referred is that in *Hyde v. Hyde and Woodmansee* (1866), LR 1 P & D 130, at p. 130, a decision of the English House of Lords. The court described marriage in the following terms:

> Marriage has been well said to be something more than a contract, either religious or civil—to be an Institution. It creates mutual rights and obligations, as all contracts do, but beyond that it confers a status. The position or status of "husband" and "wife" is a recognised one throughout Christendom: the laws of all Christian nations throw about that status a variety of legal incidents during the lives of the parties, and induce definite rights upon their offspring. What, then, is the nature of this institution as understood in Christendom? Its incidents vary in different countries, but what are its essential elements and invariable features? If it be of common acceptance and existence, it must needs ... have some pervading identity and universal basis. I conceive that marriage, as understood in Christendom, may for this purpose be defined as the voluntary union for life of one man and one woman, to the exclusion of all others. ...

. . .

Counsel for EGALE urged that the definition of marriage appearing in *Hyde* is not binding on this court as it was not necessary to the ruling in that case, concerned as it was with the monogamous nature of marriage and not its opposite-sex character.

Hyde was concerned with the question whether a court in England would grant a matrimonial remedy, namely divorce, to the petitioner when, at the time of marriage in Utah which was then part of the territory of the United States, the petitioner and the respondent were adherents to the Mormon faith which permitted polygamous marriages. The petitioner and respondent had separated and, without divorcing the petitioner, the respondent married a second man in accordance with then accepted Mormon practice. The second relationship subsisted when the petitioner's application for divorce was heard.

In *Hyde* the court ruled that a marriage that was not subject to the same strictures as a marriage in England would not be recognized as a marriage to which a matrimonial remedy would be afforded. Because it was of that view, the court was required to state its opinion of the nature of marriage in England at that time. In that sense, the requirements of heterosexuality and monogamy were material parts of the reasoning.

Although *Hyde* was concerned with polygamy and not gender, I cannot accede to the petitioners' claim that the case should be interpreted to describe the construct of marriage as a monogamous relationship between any two individuals regardless of sex. The reference to "man" and "woman" in the definition cited by court is as important as the reference to the requirement that, during the currency of the marriage, each spouse not be married to, or capable of being married to, another person.

I do not construe *Hyde* to create any new judicial characterization of the construct of marriage but to accurately state the law as it was before 1866 and, in the absence of any indication to the contrary, as it was at November 19, 1858.

Section 6 of the *Marriage Act*, RSBC 1996, c. 282 provides that the law of British Columbia with respect to the validity of marriage is the common law of England at November 19, 1858 until that law is changed by statute. Because no legislative body has attempted to change the common law of England as it was at the relevant date, "marriage" in British Columbia in 2001 is a relationship that may only subsist between one man and one woman. ...

The judicial construct of marriage is endorsed in common parlance. The *Oxford English Dictionary* was compiled over several decades. Volume VI was published in 1908. The dictionary offered various definitions of marriage, the first two of which were the following:

> 1. The condition of being a husband or wife; the relation between married persons; spousehood, wedlock.
> 2. Entrance into wedlock; the action, or an act, of marrying; the ceremony or procedure by which two persons are made husband and wife.

The dictionary definition that appeared in 1908 has been carried forward, unchanged in substance, to this day. I was referred to no dictionary definition of marriage which contemplates the union of two persons of the same sex.

I conclude that the common law in Canada and the province of British Columbia is that a marriage is a lawful and monogamous union of two persons of opposite sex.

· · ·

VII. The Constitutional Question

The Canadian Constitution divides the entire range of legislative authority between Parliament and the provincial legislatures under ss. 91 and 92 of the *Constitution Act, 1867*. As a result there is no doubt the Canadian constitutional framework permits one or other, but not both, of Parliament or the provincial legislatures to enact legislation that will publicly sanction and recognize same-sex relationships, should either wish to do so. The difficult question is where the authority to provide state sanction and recognition of those relationships resides.

Under s. 91, Parliament has the authority to make laws for the "peace, order, and good government of Canada." Under s. 91(26), Parliament has the exclusive authority to legislate in relation to "Marriage and Divorce." Section 91 excludes matters that are assigned exclusively to the provinces under s. 92 from Parliament's legislative authority. Section 92(13) assigns exclusive authority to legislate in relation to "Property and Civil Rights in the Province" to the provinces.

In my opinion, a question that arises in the context of these petitions is whether same-sex relationships fall within the class of "Marriage and Divorce" so as to be subject to governance by Parliament. ... This answer to the question is important because the petitioners seek remedies that presuppose the meaning of "marriage" can be changed by Parliament. As I see it, the assumption around which the debate before me has been framed is that Parliament is empowered to enact legislation to define a head of power as opposed to enacting legislation under the authority of a head of power. The distinction is important.

In order to find that Parliament has the power to define same-sex relationships as marriage, the word "marriage" in s. 91(26) must be construed to mean a legal relationship between two persons regardless of sex, or to include "marriage-like" relationships. There is nothing to suggest that "marriage," in s. 91(26), was used in any context other than its legal context as understood in 1867, namely, a monogamous, opposite-sex relationship. That being the case, if Parliament were to enact legislation saying that "marriage" means a relationship solemnized between two persons without reference to sex, it would be attempting to change the meaning of the head of power and thereby unilaterally amend the Constitution.

It is noteworthy that the petitioners do not want same-sex relationships to be characterized as "marriage-like" relationships because that would permit Parliament to sanction same-sex relationships without equating them to the legal construct of marriage. The affidavit evidence in these proceedings makes it absolutely clear that the petitioners want legal recognition without distinction from opposite-sex marriages. The only way the objective can be achieved is by changing the legal definition of marriage.

The petitioners say that s. 91(26) should be construed to permit Parliament to provide legislative endorsement of same-sex relationships. Their arguments and my response to them are these. The petitioners say that the Constitution must be interpreted in a broad and liberal manner consistent with the social and cultural times. In saying that the meaning of words in the Constitution may be modified to conform to current societal values the petitioners rely principally on the judgment of the Privy Council in *Edwards v. Attorney General for Canada*, [1930] AC 124, a case concerned with the question whether women were "persons" within the meaning of s. 24 of the *Constitution Act, 1867* who could be appointed to the senate of Canada. The issue in *Edwards* was not whether women were persons, which they were, but whether they were persons under some legal disability that prevented them from being appointed to the Senate. The Privy Council held that s. 24 of the Act should be construed in a manner that did not impose any legal disability on women. In the course of its reasons, the Privy Council said this at p. 136:

> The British North America Act planted in Canada a living tree capable of growth and expansion within its natural limits. ...
>
> Their Lordships do not conceive it to be the duty of this Board—it is certainly not their desire—to cut down the provisions of the Act by a narrow and technical construction, but rather to give it a large and liberal interpretation so that the Dominion to a great extent, but within certain fixed limits, may be mistress in her own house, as the Provinces to a great extent, but within certain fixed limits, are mistresses in theirs.

The Privy Council agreed with the submission that the *Constitution Act, 1867* should be interpreted in a large, liberal and comprehensive spirit given the magnitude of the subjects with which it purports to deal in very few words, but said "the question is not what may be supposed to have been intended but what was said."

Because the Privy Council was concerned with the question whether women were persons who were denied the legal capacity to be appointed to the Senate of Canada, it took care to point out at page 137 that it was not concerned with the meaning or scope of heads of power under ss. 91 and 92:

> It must be remembered, too, that their Lordships are not here considering the question of the legislative competence either of the Dominion or its Provinces which arise under ss. 91 and 92 of the Act providing for the distribution of legislative powers and assigning to the Dominion and its Provinces their respective spheres of Government.

As examples of the manner in which the *Constitution Act, 1867* has been liberally and progressively interpreted, the petitioners point to the interpretation of the word "banking" in s. 91(15) which was extended to financial institutions of a kind proposed by the government of Alberta in the era of social credit and not restricted to the kinds of financial institutions regarded as banks in 1867; the phrase "criminal law" in s. 91(27) which has not limited the range of criminal offences to those offences identified in the law of England in 1867; the phrase "inter-provincial undertaking" appearing in s. 91(10) which has been construed to permit Parliament to legislate in relation to telephones although such instruments were unknown in 1867; and the words "direct taxation within the province" used in s. 92(2) which have been construed to extend to a personal tax, the nature of which did not exist in 1867.

In *Edwards* the Privy Council observed that there was ambiguity surrounding the question of which persons could serve as senators. The general words "banking," "criminal law," "inter-provincial undertaking" and "direct taxation within the province" are equally ambiguous. The general nature of the words has permitted flexibility and fluid interpretation in order to give effect to the Constitution as the needs of Canadian society have changed over the years.

None of the words that have been construed in a liberal manner were legal relationships created by the common law. Indeed, "marriage" is the only word in either s. 91
or 92 that refers to a legally defined relationship or construct. The meaning and legal
character of the word are not ambiguous. The word is not generic as would be, for
instance, the word "family" had that word been used in s. 91(26). I do not construe
the reasoning in *Edwards* to permit the legal construct of marriage to be unilaterally
changed by Parliament.

In the course of argument, it was suggested that the *Indian Act*, RSC 1985, c. I-5,
provides support the proposition that Parliament can define a head of power. The
argument is that in accordance with the exclusive authority conferred by s. 91(24) of the
Constitution Act, 1867 with respect to "Indians, and lands reserved for the Indians,"
Parliament enacted the *Indian Act* that defines "Indian" to mean "a person who pursuant
to this Act is registered as an Indian or is entitled to be registered as an Indian," thereby
suggesting that those who do not meet the criteria are not Indians.

I am not persuaded by the argument. The Supreme Court of Canada has ruled that
the reference to "Indian" in s. 91(24) is a reference to the aboriginal peoples of Canada.
If an individual is aboriginal, the character cannot be taken away by registration or
entitlement to register. The definition in the *Indian Act* does nothing more than ensure
that, of all persons who are Indian, only those who register or are entitled to register
will be entitled to the benefits or obligations imposed by the Act. That is far different
from attempting to define who is or is not "Indian" or what is or is not marriage.

. . .

In my opinion, the fact that persons of the same sex may not legally marry is not a
question of capacity. Rather the inability of same-sex couples to marry results from the
fact that, by its legal nature, marriage is a relationship which only persons of opposite sex
may formalize. The requirement that parties to a legal marriage be of opposite sex goes
to the core of the relationship and has nothing to do with capacity.

The Attorney General of Canada relies on the case of *Egan v. Canada*, [1995] 2
SCR 513 in support of her claim that Parliament may enact legislation under s. 91(26)
to define marriage to include same-sex relationships. In *Egan*, the Supreme Court of Canada
held that the provisions of the *Old Age Security Act*, RSC 1985, c. O-9, excluding
same-sex partners from the definition of spouse, did not violate the Charter. The case
was not concerned with marriage but La Forest J, speaking for four of nine judges,
said the following at p. 536:

> My colleague Gonthier J in *Miron v. Trudel* has been at pains to discuss the fundamental
> importance of marriage as a social institution, and I need not repeat his analysis at
> length or refer to the authorities he cites. Suffice it to say that marriage has from time
> immemorial been firmly grounded in our legal tradition, one that is itself a reflection of
> long-standing philosophical and religious traditions. But its ultimate raison d'etre tran-
> scends all of these and is firmly anchored in the biological and social realities that
> heterosexual couples have the unique ability to procreate, that most children are the
> product of these relationships, and that they are generally cared for and nurtured by
> those who live in that relationship. In this sense, marriage is by nature heterosexual. It
> would be possible to legally define marriage to include homosexual couples, but this
> would not change the biological and social realities that underlie the traditional marriage.

Counsel for the petitioners and the Attorney General of Canada say that the comments of the learned La Forest J in *Egan* are authority for the proposition that Parliament can redefine "marriage." With the greatest of respect, I interpret the learned judge to be saying nothing more than that the definition of marriage might be changed, a proposition with which one can readily agree. That observation does not answer the question whether the meaning of the word as it appears is s. 91(26) can be changed and if so, by whom and in what manner.

In conclusion on this point, I am persuaded that same-sex relationships do not fall within the meaning of marriage in s. 91(26). ... Since Parliament cannot amend the meaning of marriage within s. 91(26) of the *Constitution Act, 1867*, the relationship will persist as a monogamous, opposite-sex relationship. That being the nature of marriage for purposes of s. 91(26), differentiation between those who can legally marry and those who cannot must inevitably occur. The Charter cannot be used to override the reality of differentiation. As Wilson J stated in *Reference Re Bill 30, an Act to Amend the Education Act*, [1987] 1 SCR 1148, at p. 1197 "it was never intended ... the *Charter* could be used to invalidate other provisions of the Constitution." The principle was adapted and applied by the Supreme Court of Canada in *Adler v. Ontario*, [1996] 3 SCR 609, at p. 648.

The relief sought, namely the characterization of same-sex relationships as marriages, cannot be delivered by Parliament under s. 91(26) of the Constitution of Canada without an amendment to the Constitution procured with the agreement of the provinces in the manner contemplated by the *Constitution Act, 1982*. In my opinion the petitions must be dismissed.

NOTES AND QUESTIONS

1. In determining the meaning of "marriage" for the purposes of the *Constitution Act, 1867*, Pitfield J relies on an 1866 common law definition of marriage. That definition explicitly relies on "the laws of all Christian nations," and refers to the institution of marriage "as understood in Christendom." Should a court be permitted, under the guise of interpretation, to interpret the constitution by reference to values enshrined by a particular religion (in this case, Christianity)? Is this what Pitfield J is doing? Does it matter that the values of "Christendom" have evolved such that some sects of Christians now accept same-sex unions?

2. The definitions of "marriage" adopted by Pitfield J are based on judicial decisions handed down at (or near) the time that the language of the *Constitution Act, 1867* was enacted. Generally, judicial interpretations rendered at or near the time that a particular word was used in a legislative text are preferred to those that are handed down years later. This view is encapsulated in the maxim *contemporanea expositio*, which is discussed by Reed Dickerson in *The Interpretation and Application of Statutes* (Boston: Little, Brown, 1975), 125-31. Dickerson writes (at 125):

> Suppose the customary meaning of a statutory word changes after the statute is enacted. Is the word now to be read in the light of current usage or in the light of the original usage? The question extends also to changes in general context. ... According to Craies, "The sense

must be that which the words used ordinarily bore at the time when the statute was passed."
Gény agrees. Craies then refers to the doctrine of *contemporanea expositio*, "that is, seeing
how the statutory words were understood at the time they were passed." [Citations omitted.]

Note that *contemporanea expositio* is a purely evidentiary rule: it simply means that
where older statutes are concerned, the best evidence of their meaning resides in interpretations rendered at or near the time of enactment. Does this make sense in the interpretation of a constitution? What is the difference between the evidentiary rule *contemporanea
expositio* and the substantive rule of originalism (or the "original meaning rule") discussed in chapter 1 of *Theory and Practice*? (See also *Morgan v. Crawshay* (1871), 5 HL
304, discussed in chapter 2 of this casebook.)

3. Would Pitfield J's definition of "marriage," which is based on Christian laws,
recognize Hindu marriages, Jewish marriages, or marriages recognized by a newer
religion (founded, say, in the mid-1900s)? Would Parliament be competent to enact
legislation recognizing such marriages?

4. Would Pitfield J's definition of "marriage" recognize marriages between two individuals
who were incapable of having children?

5. The facts of *Hyde* (discussed in Pitfield J's judgment) make it clear that polygamous
marriage was a known phenomenon in 1867, when the *Constitution Act, 1867* was
enacted. Could an interpreter rely on this fact to hold that in 1867 "marriage" was recognized as a "shifting" term—a term that was capable of evolution over time, or as a term
that embraced different meanings for different social groups? Could the interpreter then
hold that the original drafters of s. 91(26) recognized that the word "marriage" would
continue to evolve (as it had shifted and evolved in the past) along with changing social
conditions? Note that a similar approach has been taken with the "right to bear arms" in
the American *Bill of Rights*: see *Theory and Practice*, at 78-84.

6. Like Southey J in the *Mushroom* case (see above), Pitfield J relies on dictionary
definitions in arriving at his decision. In particular, Pitfield J notes that the court "was
referred to no dictionary definition of marriage which contemplates the union of two
persons of the same sex." Is it likely that Pitfield J's decision would have been markedly
different had the judge been directed to a dictionary that *did* contain such a definition, or
to a dictionary that failed to mention the "opposite-sex" requirement? Is it appropriate for
judges like Southey and Pitfield JJ to determine the meaning of statutes and constitutions
by reference to dictionaries, the quality and comprehensiveness of which may vary? Is it
likely that parliamentarians (or the constitution's framers) intended to give statutory
force to the definitions contained in dictionaries?

7. Pitfield J's definition of "marriage" for the purposes of s. 91(26) is remarkably originalist
in nature, in that it (a) relies on the meaning of "marriage" as it was understood at the
time that s. 91(26) was first enacted, and (b) refuses to acknowledge the possibility that
the framers of the *Constitution Act, 1867* were content to permit the meaning of "marriage"
to evolve with changing social conditions. Is Pitfield J's analysis convincing? Note that
"originalist construction" has generally been rejected as a method of interpreting the
language of Canada's constitution: see *Theory and Practice*, at 34-37.

8. Consider the following quotation from Pitfield J's decision: "If Parliament were to
enact legislation saying that 'marriage' means a relationship between two persons without

reference to sex, it would be attempting to change the meaning of a head of power and thereby unilaterally amend the Constitution." If Parliament were to enact legislation recognizing marriage between 12-year-old children (of the opposite sex), would it be changing the meaning of the "head of power"? What if Parliament enacted legislation recognizing marriage between siblings? Or marriages between corporations? Are any of these questions comparable to the question of marriage between same-sex individuals? Why or why not?

9. Pitfield J acknowledges that Parliament has the authority to create new crimes and, arguably, the authority to enlarge the scope of the phrase "criminal law" as it appears in s. 91(27) of the *Constitution Act, 1867*. Pitfield J declines to allow Parliament to expand the meaning of "marriage" in s. 91(26). The court justifies this decision on the grounds that "criminal law" is an ambiguous phrase, while "marriage" had a settled definition in 1867. Is this analysis convincing? Is it likely that Pitfield J's decision would have been different if someone had pointed out a settled definition of "criminal law" dating from 1867?

10. Much of Pitfield J's decision turns on the notion that Parliament lacks the power to alter the scope of a "head of power" in s. 91 of the *Constitution Act, 1867*. In *R v. Crown Zellerbach Canada Ltd.*, [1988] 1 SCR 401, the Supreme Court of Canada redefined Parliament's power over "peace, order and good government" in a rather detailed way that was unlikely to have been predicted by the constitution's framers. Does this mean that, while Parliament lacks the authority to redefine a head of power in ways that conflict with the framers' intentions, the judiciary *has* that power? What does this say for the distribution of power between the legislative branch of government and the judiciary?

11. If Pitfield J was confronted with evidence that one of the drafters (or perhaps a majority of the drafters) of the *Constitution Act, 1867* was in favour of same-sex marriages, would his decision have changed? Given that we have little or no conclusive evidence concerning the sexual preferences or attitudes of the framers, is reliance on historical "legislative intention" sensible in cases like *EGALE*?

12. According to Pitfield J:

> In my opinion, the fact that persons of the same sex may not legally marry is not a question of capacity. Rather the inability of same-sex couples to marry results from the fact that, by its legal nature, marriage is a relationship which only persons of opposite sex may formalize. The requirement that parties to a legal marriage be of opposite sex goes to the core of the relationship and has nothing to do with capacity.

What does this passage mean? Is this analysis convincing?

13. Is it likely that a judge who favoured same-sex marriages would have felt constrained by the factors mentioned in Pitfield J's decision to interpret "marriage" in a way that excluded same-sex unions?

14. Is it possible to write an "originalist" interpretation of s. 91(26) that recognizes same-sex marriages? Is it possible to write a "dynamic" judgment that does not? Can a judge's commitment to a specific interpretive theory truly preclude any specific result in a given case, or does it merely change the manner in which the judge must justify his or her decision?

IV. QUEBEC v. BOISBRIAND

A. Introduction

In *Boisbriand* the Supreme Court of Canada was asked to interpret s. 10 of Quebec's *Charter of Human Rights and Freedoms*, RSQ, c. C-12. Specifically, the court was asked to determine whether the prohibition of discrimination based on a "handicap" extended to prohibit discrimination based on health conditions that create no functional limitations for the person suffering from the relevant condition. Note that, throughout the court's decision, references to "the Charter" refer to the Quebec *Charter of Human Rights and Freedoms*, while references to "the Canadian Charter" refer to the *Charter of Rights and Freedoms* as entrenched in the *Constitution Act, 1982*.

When reading *Boisbriand*, pay particular attention to the manner in which L'Heureux-Dubé J establishes the meaning of the word "handicap": what is considered admissible evidence of the term's true meaning? This question will become particularly relevant in chapter 4, which deals with evidence of a statute's meaning.

B. The Court's Decision

Quebec (Commission des droits de la personne et des droits de la jeunesse) v. Montreal (City); Quebec (Commission des droits de la personne et des droits de la jeunesse) v. Boisbriand (City)
[2000] 1 SCR 665

L'HEUREUX-DUBÉ J: ...

I. Facts

... The facts, which were uncontested, were set out by Mr. Justice Jacques Philippon, who delivered the unanimous judgment of the Quebec Court of Appeal. I quote:

> "[TRANSLATION] ... In February 1990, after successfully completing the pre-employment medical exam, Palmerino Troilo (hereinafter the "complainant") was hired as a police officer by the municipality of Boisbriand (hereinafter "Boisbriand"), subject to a probationary period of 12 months. He performed his duties very well indeed, with excellent results until May 22, when he was absent for a period of time because of an acute attack of ileitis followed by a fistula (perforation of the intestine), which was treated surgically.
>
> It was then discovered that the complainant has a chronic inflammation of the intestine, known as "Crohn's disease." For unknown reasons, this disease affects certain parts of the digestive tract; it is a chronic disease which is aggravated by stress, among other factors. The severity varies for each individual; for some it may remain benign while others may require several operations.
>
> All of the medical reports written after the complainant's recovery attest that he is in good health and that, as he is asymptomatic, the complainant is able to perform the

short and medium term duties of a police officer. Boisbriand nevertheless dismissed him in August 1990. It preferred, instead, to minimize potential costs by filling its complement of permanent employees with police officers who present the lowest risk of absenteeism.

The Commission is therefore appealing on the ground that Boisbriand discriminated against the complainant on the basis of handicap. The complainant has been working as a police officer for the City of Boucherville since January 1991." ...

II. Statutory Provisions

The following provisions are relevant to this appeal:

Charter of Human Rights and Freedoms, RSQ, c. C-12
"10. Every person has a right to full and equal recognition and exercise of his human rights and freedoms, without distinction, exclusion or preference based on race, colour, sex, pregnancy, sexual orientation, civil status, age except as provided by law, religion, political convictions, language, ethnic or national origin, social condition, a handicap or the use of any means to palliate a handicap.

Discrimination exists where such a distinction, exclusion or preference has the effect of nullifying or impairing such right." ...

Canadian Charter of Rights and Freedoms
"15(1) Every individual is equal before and under the law and has the right to the equal protection and equal benefit of the law without discrimination and, in particular, without discrimination based on race, national or ethnic origin, colour, religion, sex, age or mental or physical disability." ...

. . .

V. Analysis

(a) Principles of Interpretation

The Charter does not define the term "handicap" and the word's ordinary meaning is not clear from the various dictionary definitions. It seems that "handicap" can have a vague or very broad meaning. Therefore, as this appeal is essentially an exercise in interpretation, we must first review certain principles that apply in this situation.

As Philippon J pointed out, given its fundamental and quasi-constitutional status, human rights legislation prevails over other legislation. That principle has been reiterated by this Court on several occasions. ... The Court has also held that because of its quasi-constitutional status, the Charter must be interpreted in light of both its context and objectives. ... Accordingly, in *Beliveau St-Jacques v. Fédération des employées et employés de services publics inc.*, [1996] 2 SCR 345, at para. 116, Gonthier J wrote the following on the subject of the Quebec Charter:

"Like the statutes that are its counterparts in the other provinces, the Charter, which was enacted in 1975, has a special quasi-constitutional status. Certain of its provisions thus have relative primacy, resulting from s. 52. By its very nature, such a statute calls for a large and liberal interpretation that allows its objectives to be achieved as far as possible. In this sense, not only the provisions at issue but the entire statute must be examined (see in this regard *Ontario Human Rights Commission and O'Malley v. Simpsons-Sears Ltd.*, [1985] 2 SCR 536, at p. 547)."

More generally, in *Driedger on the Construction of Statutes* (3rd ed. 1994), at pp. 383-84, Professor R. Sullivan summarized as follows the rules of interpretation that apply to human rights legislation:

> "(1) Human rights legislation is given a liberal and purposive interpretation. Protected rights receive a broad interpretation, while exceptions and defences are narrowly construed.
>
> (2) In responding to general terms and concepts, the approach is organic and flexible. The key provisions of the legislation are adapted not only to changing social conditions but also to evolving conceptions of human rights."
>
> ...

This Court has repeatedly stressed that it is inappropriate to rely solely on a strictly grammatical analysis, particularly with respect to the interpretation of legislation which is constitutional or quasi-constitutional in nature. ... The courts are increasingly recognizing that all statutes, whether or not they are constitutional in nature, must be interpreted contextually. P.-A. Côté, *Interpretation des lois* (3rd ed. 1999), stated at pp. 355-56:

> "[TRANSLATION] Without going so far as to say that words have no intrinsic meaning, their dependence on context for real meaning must be recognized. A dictionary provides a limited assortment of potential meanings, but only within the context is the effective meaning revealed." ...

Thus, as this Court stated in *Rizzo & Rizzo Shoes Ltd. (Re)*, [1998] 1 SCR 27, at para. 21-23, it is appropriate to consider the legislative context. According to Côté, *supra*, at pp. 355-56, the context of a law includes the other provisions of the law, related statutes, the objective of both the law and the specific provision, as well as the circumstances which led to the drafting of the text.

(i) Objectives of the Charter

The preamble of a statute often provides a good indication of that statute's objectives: *Ontario Human Rights Commission and O'Malley v. Simpsons-Sears Ltd.*, *supra*; *Interpretation Act*, RSQ, c. I-16, s. 40. Thus, in the case at bar, it is helpful to examine the following three paragraphs of the preamble to the Charter:

> "WHEREAS every human being possesses intrinsic rights and freedoms designed to ensure his protection and development;
>
> Whereas all human beings are equal in worth and dignity, and are entitled to equal protection of the law;
>
> Whereas respect for the dignity of the human being and recognition of his rights and freedoms constitute the foundation of justice and peace;"

The preamble suggests that the Charter's objective is to protect the dignity and equality rights of all human beings and, by logical extension, to eliminate discrimination. McIntyre J first made the connection between these concepts in *Andrews v. Law Society of British Columbia*, [1989] 1 SCR 143, at p. 172, when he said, "Discrimination is unacceptable in a democratic society because it epitomizes the worst effects of the denial of equality ... ."

It was also in *Andrews v. Law Society of British Columbia*, at pp. 174-75, that McIntyre J described discrimination as follows:

> "... [it is] a distinction, whether intentional or not but based on grounds relating to personal characteristics of the individual or group, which has the effect of imposing burdens, obligations, or disadvantages on such individual or group not imposed upon others, or which withholds or limits access to opportunities, benefits, and advantages available to other members of society. Distinctions based on personal characteristics attributed to an individual solely on the basis of association with a group will rarely escape the charge of discrimination, while those based on an individual's merits and capacities will rarely be so classed." ...

The purpose of Canadian human rights legislation is to protect against discrimination and to guarantee rights and freedoms. With respect to employment, its more specific objective is to eliminate exclusion that is arbitrary and based on preconceived ideas concerning personal characteristics which, when the duty to accommodate is taken into account, do not affect a person's ability to do a job.

In the following passage from the Report of the Commission on Equality in Employment (1984) (also called the "Abella Report"), at p. 2, the Commission eloquently explained that:

> "Equality in employment means that no one is denied opportunities for reasons that have nothing to do with inherent ability. It means equal access free from arbitrary obstructions. Discrimination means that an arbitrary barrier stands between a person's ability and his or her opportunity to demonstrate it. If the access is genuinely available in a way that permits everyone who so wishes the opportunity to fully develop his or her potential, we have achieved a kind of equality. It is equality defined as equal freedom from discrimination.
>
> Discrimination in this context means practices or attitudes that have, whether by design or impact, the effect of limiting an individual's or group's right to the opportunities generally available because of attributed rather than actual characteristics. What is impeding the full development of the potential is not the individual's capacity but an external barrier that artificially inhibits growth." ...

The objectives of the Charter, namely the right to equality and protection against discrimination, cannot be achieved unless we recognize that discriminatory acts may be based as much on perception and myths and stereotypes as on the existence of actual functional limitations. Since the very nature of discrimination is often subjective, assigning the burden of proving the objective existence of functional limitations to a victim of discrimination would be to give that person a virtually impossible task. Functional limitations often exist only in the mind of other people, in this case that of the employer.

It would be strange indeed if the legislature had intended to enable persons with handicaps that result in functional limitations to integrate into the job market, while excluding persons whose handicaps do not lead to functional limitations. Such an approach appears to undermine the very essence of discrimination.

I am, therefore, of the view that the Charter's objective of prohibiting discrimination requires that "handicap" be interpreted so as to recognize its subjective component. A "handicap," therefore, includes ailments which do not in fact give rise to any limitation or functional disability.

(ii) Related Legislation

Philippon J correctly noted that human rights legislation must conform to constitutional norms, including those set out in the Canadian Charter. While there is no requirement that the provisions of the Charter mirror those of the Canadian Charter, they must nevertheless be interpreted in light of the Canadian Charter: *Vriend v. Alberta, supra,* and *British Columbia (Public Service Employee Relations Commission) v. BCGSEU, supra.* Thus, when a statutory provision is open to more than one interpretation, it must be interpreted in a manner consistent with the provisions of the Canadian Charter. [Citations omitted.]

Section 10 of the Charter must also be examined in light of other federal and provincial human rights legislation. The parties noted that the terminology used in human rights legislation varies from one jurisdiction to another. In fact, words such as "handicap" and "disability" are used in English, while words such as "handicap," "déficience," "incapacité" and "invalidité" are used in French. See, for example, *Canadian Charter,* s. 15(1); *Canadian Human Rights Act,* RSC, 1985, c. H-6, s. 3(1); *Human Rights Act,* RSPEI 1988, c. H-12, s. 1(1)(1); *Fair Practices Act,* RSNWT 1988, c. F-2, s. 3; *Human Rights Code,* SM 1987-88, c. 45, CCSM, c. H175, s. 9(2)(1); *Human Rights Act,* RSNS 1989, c. 214, s. 3(1); *Human Rights Code,* RSO 1990, c. H.19, s. 2.

Judge Brossard held that it was not necessary to compare the ground "handicap" in the Charter with words used in other legislation since federal statutes and those of the majority of Canadian provinces prohibit discrimination on the basis of expressions other than "handicap." According to Judge Brossard, such a comparison would not facilitate the interpretation of the word "handicap" as it is used in s. 10 of the Charter.

As Philippon J observed, different human rights laws share a common objective and this has often prompted Canadian courts to ascribe a common meaning to similar provisions. In this way, courts have minimized the importance of minor differences in terminology. See *Andrews v. Law Society of British Columbia, supra; Brossard (Town) v. Quebec (Commission des droits de la personne),* [1988] 2 SCR 279; *Central Alberta Dairy Pool v. Alberta (Human Rights Commission),* [1990] 2 SCR 489.

This Court has often stressed that mere differences in terminology do not support a conclusion that there are fundamental differences in the objectives of human rights statutes. In *University of British Columbia v. Berg,* [1993] 2 SCR 353, at p. 373, Lamer CJ, speaking for the majority, stated the following:

"If human rights legislation is to be interpreted in a purposive manner, differences in wording between provinces should not obscure the essentially similar purposes of such provisions, unless the wording clearly evinces a different purpose on behalf of a particular provincial legislature."

Because the Charter must be interpreted in light of the Canadian Charter and other human rights legislation, we are faced with the question of whether the ground of discrimination found in s. 15(1) of the Canadian Charter and in other human rights statutes includes disabilities which do not give rise to any functional limitation.

Whatever the wording of the definitions used in human rights legislation, Canadian courts tend to consider not only the objective basis for certain exclusionary practices (i.e. the actual existence of functional limitations), but also the subjective and erroneous perceptions regarding the existence of such limitations. Thus, tribunals and courts have recognized that even though they do not result in functional limitations, various ailments such as congenital physical malformations, asthma, speech impediments, obesity, acne and, more recently, being HIV positive, may constitute grounds of discrimination. [Citations omitted.]

With respect to the Canadian Charter, M. D. Lepofsky and J. E. Bickenbach, "Equality Rights and the Physically Handicapped," in A. F. Bayefsky and M. Eberts, eds., *Equality Rights and the Canadian Charter of Rights and Freedoms* (1985), 323, at p. 346, submit that a "disability" within the meaning of s. 15 includes an actual or perceived "disability":

> "... the context of section 15 reveals that a Charter plaintiff can bring a complaint under section 15 whether or not he or she actually has a physical disability, so long as the Charter defendant ... believed the plaintiff to have a physical disability. If, for example, a federal civil servant was fired from her job because she was allegedly an epileptic, that civil servant could frame an action under section 15 even if she was not in fact an epileptic. ... Section 15(1) confers rights on "every individual" not "every physically or mentally disabled individual" and points to "discrimination because of disability" instead of "discrimination against disabled persons." This clearly suggests that perceived, as well as actual, disability is included in section 15."

In *Bahlsen v. Canada (Minister of Transport)*, [1997] 1 FC 800, the Federal Court of Appeal held that a diabetic able to control hypoglycemic episodes before they become incapacitating, has a "disability" for the purposes of s. 15(1) of the Canadian Charter.

Similarly, in *Cinq-Mars v. Transports Provost Inc.* (1988), 9 CHRR D/4704, the Canadian Human Rights Tribunal agreed that bilateral spondylolisis which does not cause any functional limitation constitutes a "disability" under the *Canadian Human Rights Act*.

Thus, by confining the availability of remedies to persons suffering from limitations in the performance of everyday activities, Judge Brossard imposed considerably narrower criteria than those applied under related legislation, including the term "mental or physical disability" in s. 15 of the Canadian Charter. It is therefore my view that Judge Brossard interpreted s. 10 of the Charter too narrowly.

(iii) Legislative History

As Philippon J of the Court of Appeal stated, with respect to legislative interpretation, the importance of legislative history is well established: "... prior enactments may throw some light on the intention of the legislature in repealing, amending, replacing or adding to it": *Gravel v. City of St-Leonard*, [1978] 1 SCR 660, at p. 667. It is, therefore, useful to review the legislative history which Philippon J also examined.

The first version of the Charter which dates from 1975, offered no protection against discrimination based on disability or handicap. In 1978, s. 10 of the Charter was amended to include a ground defined as *"the fact* that he is a handicapped person or that he uses any means to palliate his handicap" (emphasis added). See s. 112 of An Act to secure the handicapped in the exercise of their rights.

At that time, courts regularly interpreted the term "handicapped person" in a manner consistent with the following definition, found in s. 1(g) of An Act to secure the handicapped in the exercise of their rights, which I reproduce again:

> " "handicapped person," or "the handicapped" in the plural, means a person limited in the performance of normal activities who is suffering, significantly and permanently, from a physical or mental deficiency, or who regularly uses a prosthesis or an orthopedic device or any other means of palliating his handicap."

According to the courts' interpretation, this ground of discrimination offers protection against discrimination only to persons suffering from actual limitations in the performance of everyday activities. In *Commission des droits de la personne du Quebec v. Ville de Laval*, [1983] CS 961, at p. 966, Benoit J of the Superior Court, dismissing an application by a police officer whose employment was terminated because of an ankle fracture, explained the scope of the protection as follows:

> "[TRANSLATION] When an employer refuses to hire someone because it considers the candidate's skin to be too brown, regardless of whether the candidate actually has brown skin or whether the employer subjectively perceives it as such, the employer has engaged in discriminatory practices on the basis of colour and it must then justify the exclusion as a requirement of the employment. Thus, whether the exclusion is based on race, colour, sex, sexual orientation, civil status, religion, political convictions, language, ethnic or national origin or social condition, discrimination exists whether the employer's identification of that race, colour, sex, or sexual orientation is objective or purely subjective."

As to the ground of "handicap," Benoit J pointed out that subjective perceptions were not relevant considerations (at p. 966):

> "[TRANSLATION] The wording of s. 10 forces us to conclude that the ground of exclusion based on a person's handicap cannot be a matter of perception, since the Charter protects a person who is a handicapped person."

Thus, the case law from that period indicates that courts rejected subjective perception in the case of handicap, although they did take it into account when considering other grounds of discrimination in s. 10. ...

In 1982, the legislature again amended s. 10 of the Charter, replacing "the fact that he is a handicapped person or that he uses any means to palliate his handicap" with "handicap or the use of any means to palliate a handicap": An Act to amend the Charter of Human Rights and Freedoms, SQ 1982, c. 61, s. 3.

According to Professor Côté, *supra*, at pp. 530-31, a statutory amendment is presumed to have been made in order to change the meaning of the text. In fact, in the present case, there is an indication that the substantive change intended by the legislature was the expansion of the protection against discrimination. In discussions leading up to the passage of the bill to amend the Charter, by the Hon. Marc-André Bédard, then Minister of Justice, made the following statement:

> "[TRANSLATION] In addition to being less unwieldy, the proposed wording will cover all handicapped persons and not only, as the courts have interpreted it to date, those handicapped persons contemplated by the Act to secure the handicapped in the exercise of their rights. ... the court's interpretation ... indicated that it only covered the severely handicapped. However, this amendment ... will allow us to include all handicapped persons." [Citations omitted.]

In *Droit constitutionnel* (3rd ed. 1997), at p. 1083, Professors H. Brun and G. Tremblay confirm that the purpose of the amendment of s. 10 [TRANSLATION] "was apparently to move away from the line of cases based on the 1978 Act."

A clear trend has developed in the case law following the 1982 amendment. Courts have consistently recognized that discrimination based on "handicap" includes a subjective component. ... In contrast with this trend, the interpretation proposed by Judge Brossard and by the appellants does not take into account the statutory amendment and the legislature's clear objective in this regard. The legislative history, the extrinsic evidence and the manner in which the new wording of s. 10 of the Charter has been interpreted by a majority of Quebec courts all support a broad interpretation of the ground of "handicap," which does not require functional limitations.

(iv) Other Provisions of the Charter

A statute is presumed to form a coherent whole. Therefore, according to the principles of contextual interpretation, s. 10 and the ground of "handicap" should be interpreted in light of the other provisions of the Charter. In this regard, s. 20 is particularly relevant.

As Philippon J correctly pointed out, the Charter contemplates a two-step process for analysing discrimination. The first step, set out in s. 10, attempts to eliminate discrimination and requires that the applicant produce prima facie evidence of the discrimination. At this stage, the burden on the applicant is limited to showing prejudice and its connection to a prohibited ground of discrimination. There is no onus on the applicant to establish that his or her capacity is limited.

It is only at the second step, under s. 20 of the Charter, that the employer has the onus of showing that the measure taken is justified because it is based on aptitudes or qualifications required for the job. Evidence of actual limitations becomes relevant only at this second step.

In light of this allocation of the burden or proof, s. 10 of the Charter should not be interpreted as requiring evidence of justification, since this relates instead to s. 20

and the second part of the analysis. Requiring the applicant to prove that he or she has functional limitations under s. 10 would have the effect of reversing the burden of proof. I adopt the analysis of Professor Proulx, *supra*, at p. 420, where he says:

> "[TRANSLATION] Under this structure, the question of whether an anomaly involves limitations which are likely to interfere with the safe and efficient performance of the work cannot be asked in order to determine whether the employer was justified, within the meaning of s. 20, in excluding or being unfair to an employee. At the s. 10 stage, the only relevant question is whether the employer based its decision, in whole or in part, on the fact or presumption that the individual had a physical or mental anomaly which constitutes a handicap. ... The question of whether or not functional limitations exist and whether they are relevant or important are thus central to the justification process. These considerations are unrelated to the proof of discrimination and the ground on which is it based, which the applicant must establish under s. 10 (combined with s. 16 in the case of employment)."

Section 20.1 of the Charter also helps clarify the notion of handicap. That section, which was added in 1996, creates an exemption which applies, inter alia, to insurance contracts and social benefits plans. I reproduce that section again:

> "20.1 In an insurance or pension contract, a social benefits plan, a retirement, pension or insurance plan, or a public pension or public insurance plan, a distinction, exclusion or preference based on age, sex or civil status is deemed non-discriminatory where the use thereof is warranted and the basis therefor is a risk determination factor based on actuarial data.
>
> In such contracts or plans, the use of health as a risk determination factor does not constitute discrimination within the meaning of section 10."

Given the presumption that the legislature does not speak in vain, it is my view that if the legislature has expressly provided an exemption based on health, it must be because, outside the context of insurance contracts and plans, health may constitute a prohibited ground of discrimination. This argument is particularly persuasive in that s. 10 establishes an exhaustive list of grounds of discrimination, and handicap is the only listed ground that can be connected to health. We must, therefore, conclude that the legislature has established a connection between the concepts of "health" and "handicap," which supports an interpretation of the word "handicap" that includes ailments related to health.

In short, to require proof of functional limitations under s. 10 would create contradictions between s. 10 and s. 20. It follows that the Act, considered in its entirety, and the presumption of coherence support a broad interpretation of the word "handicap" that does not require anomalies involving functional limitations and that could include ailments related to health.

(v) Conclusion

The rules of interpretation do not support the appellants' argument that the word "handicap" must mean a physical or mental anomaly that necessarily results in functional limitations. The liberal and purposive method of interpretation along with the contextual approach, which includes an analysis of the objectives of human rights legislation, the way in which the word "handicap" and other similar terms have been interpreted elsewhere in Canada, the legislative history, the intention of the legislature and the other provisions of the Charter, support a broad definition of the word "handicap," which does not necessitate the presence of functional limitations and which recognizes the subjective component of any discrimination based on this ground.

(b) Meaning and Scope of "Handicap"

From our analysis of these principles of interpretation, it is clear that "handicap" as it is used in the Charter can include both an ailment, even one with no resulting functional limitation, as well as the perception of such an ailment. ...

VI. Disposition

Based on the foregoing analysis, and given the facts in the cases at bar, I find that there was discrimination against ... Mr. Troilo based on handicap for the purposes of s. 10 of the Charter. Accordingly, I would dismiss the appeal and affirm the judgments of the Quebec Court of Appeal.

NOTES AND QUESTIONS

1. L'Heureux-Dubé J notes that all statutes must be interpreted contextually, and that "the context of a law includes the other provisions of the law, related statutes, the objective of both the law and the specific provision, as well as the circumstances which led to the drafting of the text." Compare this holding with the decisions of Reid and Southey JJ in the *Mushroom* case. Do the decisions in the *Mushroom* case conform to the interpretive method described by the Supreme Court of Canada in *Boisbriand*?

2. L'Heureux-Dubé J focuses on the *purpose* of the relevant statutory language when discerning the statute's meaning. Note that this form of analysis is required by interpretation acts found in various Canadian jurisdictions: see *Theory and Practice*, at 21-23. Do the previous decisions in this chapter conform to the "purposive" method of analysis?

3. L'Heureux-Dubé J points out the consequences of the interpretation put forward by the city of Boisbriand. In particular, L'Heureux-Dubé notes that "it would be strange indeed if the legislature had intended to enable persons with handicaps that result in functional limitations to integrate into the job market, while excluding persons whose handicaps do not lead to functional limitations." This form of interpretation is known as "consequential analysis." Generally speaking, a court will adopt an interpretation that leads to sensible consequences over an interpretation that leads to consequences that are surprising, absurd, or impractical. This method of construction is discussed at length in chapter 3, under the heading "The Literal Rule and the Golden Rule."

4. Why should the language of Quebec's Charter be interpreted in light of human rights enactments from other provinces? Is it sensible to allow the meaning of Quebec legislation to be influenced by language used in acts from Manitoba or PEI? If one of the central ideas of federalism is the notion that provinces should be allowed to use differing methods to address local concerns and social conditions, does it make sense to interpret enactments from different provinces in a way that promotes uniformity or eliminates local differences? Is this a legitimate goal of statutory interpretation?

5. When interpreting the meaning of "handicap" in the Quebec Charter or "disability" in the Canadian Charter, the court in *Boisbriand* makes it clear that the meaning ascribed to legislation should conform with the current values concerning the protection and fulfillment of disabled individuals. The court extracts these values from (among other sources) academic commentaries concerning the protection of the disabled. Is it legitimate for a court to interpret legislative language by reference values put forward in "non-legislative" materials such as academic articles? What if these articles are written after the enactment of the relevant language?

6. Is it legitimate for a judge to determine the nature of "current social values" that should inform the interpretation of obscure legislative language?

7. In the *Mushroom* case, Reid J looked only to "plain meaning" or "common under-standing" in arriving at the court's interpretation of "vegetable farming." Reid J held that it was inappropriate to look at other sections of the relevant statute in a manner that might displace "plain meaning." In contrast, the court in *Boisbriand* looks to many sources, including (a) the statute's preamble, (b) the constitution, (c) similar statutes in other jurisdictions, (d) other operative provisions of the relevant legislation, and (e) previous versions of the same enactment. Assuming that an enactment does have a "plain meaning" (in the sense that a specific meaning would "jump out" at a typical reader), is it legitimate for a court to displace that meaning by referring to the other sources of meaning listed above? What if the reader has limited access to those sources of meaning? Will a typical reader of legislation be able to refer back to previous versions of the same enactment?

8. Does L'Heureux-Dubé J appear to be concerned with what the author meant by adding the word "handicap" to the statute, or with what the author *ought to have meant* when enacting the relevant language? Which approach is more appropriate? Which approach provides greater certainty for individuals charged with administering the statute? Which approach promotes justice?

9. L'Heureux-Dubé J refers to the presumption that the legislature "does not speak in vain." This is also known as the "no extraneous words" presumption, which is discussed at 92-97 (and again at 107) of *Theory and Practice*. Note that this presumption also formed the basis for the "designee's" decision in the *Mushroom* case.

V. ROE v. WADE

A. Introduction

The decision of the US Supreme Court in *Roe v. Wade* is among the most famous (or infamous) judicial decisions of the last century. Those who know of the decision know that *Roe v. Wade* deals with abortion. What most people fail to recognize, however, is that the key issues of *Roe v. Wade* turn on questions of statutory interpretation. Indeed, Blackmun J (who delivered the opinion of the majority in *Roe v. Wade*) seems to forget this as well, and rarely makes reference to the constitutional language being interpreted.[5]

---

5   The minority judgments (concurring and dissenting) do a far better job of dealing with the text of the constitution.

The language being construed in *Roe v. Wade* is the "due process clause" of the 14th Amendment to the US Constitution. The 14th Amendment provides (in part) as follows:

All persons born or naturalized in the United States, and subject to the jurisdiction thereof, are citizens of the United States and of the State wherein they reside. No State shall make or enforce any law which shall abridge the privileges or immunities of citizens of the United States; *nor shall any State deprive any person of life, liberty, or property, without due process of law*; nor deny to any person within its jurisdiction the equal protection of the laws. [Emphasis added.]

The key question in *Roe v. Wade* was whether the due process clause (seen in the italicized language above) prohibited the states from interfering with a woman's choice to procure an abortion. The answer to this question depended upon the meaning of the word "liberty" (that is, whether "liberty" includes the freedom to procure an abortion) and the meaning of "due process of law." A subordinate issue was whether the word "person" at the beginning of the 14th Amendment included an "unborn" person.

Owing to the complexity of the interpretive issues facing the court in *Roe v. Wade*, the court's decision is rather long. Large portions of the court's decision are reproduced below. When reviewing this decision, consider the following questions: (1) Is the court in *Roe v. Wade* actually concerned with the "meaning" of the text of the due process clause, or is the court simply grafting its own ideas of sound public policy onto the text of the US Constitution? (2) Is the court's decision originalist or dynamic in nature? and (3) Was the court compelled to reach its decision by the text of the Constitution or by non-textual factors?

B. The Court's Decision

Roe et al. v. Wade, District Attorney of Dallas County
410 US 113 (1973)

BLACKMUN J: This Texas federal appeal and its Georgia companion, *Doe v. Bolton*, *post*, p. 179, present constitutional challenges to state criminal abortion legislation. The Texas statutes under attack here are typical of those that have been in effect in many States for approximately a century. The Georgia statutes, in contrast, have a modern cast and are a legislative product that, to an extent at least, obviously reflects the influences of recent attitudinal change, of advancing medical knowledge and techniques, and of new thinking about an old issue.

We forthwith acknowledge our awareness of the sensitive and emotional nature of the abortion controversy, of the vigorous opposing views, even among physicians, and of the deep and seemingly absolute convictions that the subject inspires. One's philosophy, one's experiences, one's exposure to the raw edges of human existence, one's religious training, one's attitudes toward life and family and their values, and the moral standards one establishes and seeks to observe, are all likely to influence and to color one's thinking and conclusions about abortion. In addition, population growth, pollution, poverty, and racial overtones tend to complicate and not to simplify the problem.

Our task, of course, is to resolve the issue by constitutional measurement, free of emotion and of predilection. We seek earnestly to do this, and, because we do, we have inquired into, and in this opinion place some emphasis upon, medical and medical-legal history and what that history reveals about man's attitudes toward the abortion procedure over the centuries. We bear in mind, too, Mr. Justice Holmes' admonition in his now-vindicated dissent in *Lochner v. New York*, 198 US 45, 76 (1905):

> "[The Constitution] is made for people of fundamentally differing views, and the accident of our finding certain opinions natural and familiar or novel and even shocking ought not to conclude our judgment upon the question whether statutes embodying them conflict with the Constitution of the United States."

I

The Texas statutes that concern us here are Arts. 1191-1194 and 1196 of the State's Penal Code. These make it a crime to "procure an abortion," as therein defined, or to attempt one, except with respect to "an abortion procured or attempted by medical advice for the purpose of saving the life of the mother." Similar statutes are in existence in a majority of the States.

Texas first enacted a criminal abortion statute in 1854. Texas Laws 1854, c. 49, § 1, set forth in 3 H. Gammel, Laws of Texas 1502 (1898). This was soon modified into language that has remained substantially unchanged to the present time. See Texas Penal Code of 1857, c. 7, Arts. 531-536; G. Paschal, Laws of Texas, Arts. 2192-2197 (1866); Texas Rev. Stat., c. 8, Arts. 536-541 (1879); Texas Rev. Crim. Stat., Arts. 1071-1076 (1911). The final article in each of these compilations provided the same exception, as does the present Article 1196, for an abortion by "medical advice for the purpose of saving the life of the mother."

II

Jane Roe, a single woman who was residing in Dallas County, Texas, instituted this federal action in March 1970 against the District Attorney of the county. She sought a declaratory judgment that the Texas criminal abortion statutes were unconstitutional on their face, and an injunction restraining the defendant from enforcing the statutes.

Roe alleged that she was unmarried and pregnant; that she wished to terminate her pregnancy by an abortion "performed by a competent, licensed physician, under safe, clinical conditions"; that she was unable to get a "legal" abortion in Texas because her life did not appear to be threatened by the continuation of her pregnancy; and that she could not afford to travel to another jurisdiction in order to secure a legal abortion under safe conditions. She claimed that the Texas statutes were unconstitutionally vague and that they abridged her right of personal privacy, protected by the First, Fourth, Fifth, Ninth, and Fourteenth Amendments. By an amendment to her complaint Roe purported to sue "on behalf of herself and all other women" similarly situated.

James Hubert Hallford, a licensed physician, sought and was granted leave to intervene in Roe's action. In his complaint he alleged that he had been arrested previously for violations of the Texas abortion statutes and that two such prosecutions were pending against him. He described conditions of patients who came to him seeking abortions, and he claimed that for many cases he, as a physician, was unable to determine whether they fell within or outside the exception recognized by Article 1196. He alleged that, as a consequence, the statutes were vague and uncertain, in violation of the Fourteenth Amendment, and that they violated his own and his patients' rights to privacy in the doctor-patient relationship and his own right to practice medicine, rights he claimed were guaranteed by the First, Fourth, Fifth, Ninth, and Fourteenth Amendments.

. . .

V

The principal thrust of appellant's attack on the Texas statutes is that they improperly invade a right, said to be possessed by the pregnant woman, to choose to terminate her pregnancy. Appellant would discover this right in the concept of personal "liberty" embodied in the Fourteenth Amendment's Due Process Clause; or in personal, marital, familial, and sexual privacy said to be protected by the Bill of Rights or its penumbras, see *Griswold v. Connecticut*, 381 US 479 (1965); *Eisenstadt v. Baird*, 405 US 438 (1972); *id.*, at 460 (White, J, concurring in result); or among those rights reserved to the people by the Ninth Amendment, *Griswold v. Connecticut*, 381 US, at 486 (Goldberg, J, concurring). Before addressing this claim, we feel it desirable briefly to survey, in several aspects, the history of abortion, for such insight as that history may afford us, and then to examine the state purposes and interests behind the criminal abortion laws.

VI

It perhaps is not generally appreciated that the restrictive criminal abortion laws in effect in a majority of States today are of relatively recent vintage. Those laws, generally proscribing abortion or its attempt at any time during pregnancy except when necessary to preserve the pregnant woman's life, are not of ancient or even of common-law origin. Instead, they derive from statutory changes effected, for the most part, in the latter half of the 19th century.

1. *Ancient attitudes.* These are not capable of precise determination. We are told that at the time of the Persian Empire abortifacients were known and that criminal abortions were severely punished. We are also told, however, that abortion was practiced in Greek times as well as in the Roman Era, and that "it was resorted to without scruple." The Ephesian, Soranos, often described as the greatest of the ancient gynecologists, appears to have been generally opposed to Rome's prevailing free-abortion practices. He found it necessary to think first of the life of the mother, and he resorted to abortion when, upon this standard, he felt the procedure advisable. Greek and Roman law afforded little protection to the unborn. If abortion was prosecuted in some places, it seems to have been based on a concept of a violation of the father's right to his offspring. Ancient religion did not bar abortion.

2. *The Hippocratic Oath.* What then of the famous Oath that has stood so long as the ethical guide of the medical profession and that bears the name of the great Greek (460(?)-377(?) BC), who has been described as the Father of Medicine, the "wisest

and the greatest practitioner of his art," and the "most important and most complete medical personality of antiquity," who dominated the medical schools of his time, and who typified the sum of the medical knowledge of the past? The Oath varies somewhat according to the particular translation, but in any translation the content is clear: "I will give no deadly medicine to anyone if asked, nor suggest any such counsel; and in like manner I will not give to a woman a pessary to produce abortion," or "I will neither give a deadly drug to anybody if asked for it, nor will I make a suggestion to this effect. Similarly, I will not give to a woman an abortive remedy."

Although the Oath is not mentioned in any of the principal briefs in this case or in *Doe v. Bolton, post*, p. 179, it represents the apex of the development of strict ethical concepts in medicine, and its influence endures to this day. Why did not the authority of Hippocrates dissuade abortion practice in his time and that of Rome? The late Dr. Edelstein provides us with a theory: The Oath was not uncontested even in Hippocrates' day; only the Pythagorean school of philosophers frowned upon the related act of suicide. Most Greek thinkers, on the other hand, commended abortion, at least prior to viability. See Plato, *Republic*, V, 461; Aristotle, *Politics*, VII, 1335b 25. For the Pythagoreans, however, it was a matter of dogma. For them the embryo was animate from the moment of conception, and abortion meant destruction of a living being. The abortion clause of the Oath, therefore, "echoes Pythagorean doctrines," and "in no other stratum of Greek opinion were such views held or proposed in the same spirit of uncompromising austerity."

Dr. Edelstein then concludes that the Oath originated in a group representing only a small segment of Greek opinion and that it certainly was not accepted by all ancient physicians. He points out that medical writings down to Galen (AD 130-200) "give evidence of the violation of almost every one of its injunctions." But with the end of antiquity a decided change took place. Resistance against suicide and against abortion became common. The Oath came to be popular. The emerging teachings of Christianity were in agreement with the Pythagorean ethic. The Oath "became the nucleus of all medical ethics" and "was applauded as the embodiment of truth." Thus, suggests Dr. Edelstein, it is "a Pythagorean manifesto and not the expression of an absolute standard of medical conduct."

This, it seems to us, is a satisfactory and acceptable explanation of the Hippocratic Oath's apparent rigidity. It enables us to understand, in historical context, a long-accepted and revered statement of medical ethics.

3. *The common law*. It is undisputed that at common law, abortion performed *before* "quickening"—the first recognizable movement of the fetus *in utero*, appearing usually from the 16th to the 18th week of pregnancy—was not an indictable offense. The absence of a common-law crime for pre-quickening abortion appears to have developed from a confluence of earlier philosophical, theological, and civil and canon law concepts of when life begins. These disciplines variously approached the question in terms of the point at which the embryo or fetus became "formed" or recognizably human, or in terms of when a "person" came into being, that is, infused with a "soul" or "animated." A loose consensus evolved in early English law that these events occurred at some point between conception and live birth. This was "mediate animation." Although Christian theology and the canon law came to fix the

point of animation at 40 days for a male and 80 days for a female, a view that persisted until the 19th century, there was otherwise little agreement about the precise time of formation or animation. There was agreement, however, that prior to this point the fetus was to be regarded as part of the mother, and its destruction, therefore, was not homicide. Due to continued uncertainty about the precise time when animation occurred, to the lack of any empirical basis for the 40-80-day view, and perhaps to Aquinas' definition of movement as one of the two first principles of life, Bracton focused upon quickening as the critical point. The significance of quickening was echoed by later common-law scholars and found its way into the received common law in this country.

Whether abortion of a *quick* fetus was a felony at common law, or even a lesser crime, is still disputed. Bracton, writing early in the 13th century, thought it homicide. But the later and predominant view, following the great common-law scholars, has been that it was, at most, a lesser offense. In a frequently cited passage, Coke took the position that abortion of a woman "quick with child" is "a great misprision, and no murder." Blackstone followed, saying that while abortion after quickening had once been considered manslaughter (though not murder), "modern law" took a less severe view. A recent review of the common-law precedents argues, however, that those precedents contradict Coke and that even post-quickening abortion was never established as a common-law crime. This is of some importance because while most American courts ruled, in holding or dictum, that abortion of an unquickened fetus was not criminal under their received common law, others followed Coke in stating that abortion of a quick fetus was a "misprision," a term they translated to mean "misdemeanor." That their reliance on Coke on this aspect of the law was uncritical and, apparently in all the reported cases, dictum (due probably to the paucity of common-law prosecutions for post-quickening abortion), makes it now appear doubtful that abortion was ever firmly established as a common-law crime even with respect to the destruction of a quick fetus. ...

5. *The American law.* In this country, the law in effect in all but a few States until mid-19th century was the pre-existing English common law. Connecticut, the first State to enact abortion legislation, adopted in 1821 that part of Lord Ellenborough's Act that related to a woman "quick with child." The death penalty was not imposed. Abortion before quickening was made a crime in that State only in 1860. In 1828, New York enacted legislation that, in two respects, was to serve as a model for early anti-abortion statutes. First, while barring destruction of an unquickened fetus as well as a quick fetus, it made the former only a misdemeanor, but the latter second-degree manslaughter. Second, it incorporated a concept of therapeutic abortion by providing that an abortion was excused if it "shall have been necessary to preserve the life of such mother, or shall have been advised by two physicians to be necessary for such purpose." By 1840, when Texas had received the common law, only eight American States had statutes dealing with abortion. It was not until after the War Between the States that legislation began generally to replace the common law. Most of these initial statutes dealt severely with abortion after quickening but were lenient with it before quickening. Most punished attempts equally with completed abortions. While many statutes included the exception for an abortion thought by one or more physicians

to be necessary to save the mother's life, that provision soon disappeared and the typical law required that the procedure actually be necessary for that purpose.

Gradually, in the middle and late 19th century the quickening distinction disappeared from the statutory law of most States and the degree of the offense and the penalties were increased. By the end of the 1950's, a large majority of the jurisdictions banned abortion, however and whenever performed, unless done to save or preserve the life of the mother. The exceptions, Alabama and the District of Columbia, permitted abortion to preserve the mother's health. Three States permitted abortions that were not "unlawfully" performed or that were not "without lawful justification," leaving interpretation of those standards to the courts. In the past several years, however, a trend toward liberalization of abortion statutes has resulted in adoption, by about one-third of the States, of less stringent laws, most of them patterned after the ALI Model Penal Code, § 230.3. ...

It is thus apparent that at common law, at the time of the adoption of our Constitution, and throughout the major portion of the 19th century, abortion was viewed with less disfavor than under most American statutes currently in effect. Phrasing it another way, a woman enjoyed a substantially broader right to terminate a pregnancy than she does in most States today. At least with respect to the early stage of pregnancy, and very possibly without such a limitation, the opportunity to make this choice was present in this country well into the 19th century. Even later, the law continued for some time to treat less punitively an abortion procured in early pregnancy.

6. *The position of the American Medical Association.* The anti-abortion mood prevalent in this country in the late 19th century was shared by the medical profession. Indeed, the attitude of the profession may have played a significant role in the enactment of stringent criminal abortion legislation during that period.

An AMA Committee on Criminal Abortion was appointed in May 1857. It presented its report ... to the Twelfth Annual Meeting. That report observed that the Committee had been appointed to investigate criminal abortion "with a view to its general suppression." It deplored abortion and its frequency and it listed three causes of "this general demoralization":

> "The first of these causes is a wide-spread popular ignorance of the true character of the crime—a belief, even among mothers themselves, that the foetus is not alive till after the period of quickening.
>
> "The second of the agents alluded to is the fact that the profession themselves are frequently supposed careless of foetal life. ...
>
> "The third reason of the frightful extent of this crime is found in the grave defects of our laws, both common and statute, as regards the independent and actual existence of the child before birth, as a living being. These errors, which are sufficient in most instances to prevent conviction, are based, and only based, upon mistaken and exploded medical dogmas. With strange inconsistency, the law fully acknowledges the foetus in utero and its inherent rights, for civil purposes; while personally and as criminally affected, it fails to recognize it, and to its life as yet denies all protection." *Id.*, at 75-76.

The Committee then offered, and the Association adopted, resolutions protesting "against such unwarrantable destruction of human life," calling upon state legislatures to revise their abortion laws, and requesting the cooperation of state medical societies "in pressing the subject." *Id.*, at 28, 78.

In 1871 a long and vivid report was submitted by the Committee on Criminal
Abortion. It ended with the observation, "We had to deal with human life. In a matter
of less importance we could entertain no compromise. An honest judge on the bench
would call things by their proper names. We could do no less." 22 Trans. of the Am.
Med. Assn. 258 (1871). It proffered resolutions, adopted by the Association, *id.*, at
38-39, recommending, among other things, that it "be unlawful and unprofessional
for any physician to induce abortion or premature labor, without the concurrent
opinion of at least one respectable consulting physician, and then always with a view
to the safety of the child—if that be possible," and calling "the attention of the clergy
of all denominations to the perverted views of morality entertained by a large class of
females—aye, and men also, on this important question."

Except for periodic condemnation of the criminal abortionist, no further formal
AMA action took place until 1967. In that year, the Committee on Human Reproduction urged the adoption of a stated policy of opposition to induced abortion, except
when there is "documented medical evidence" of a threat to the health or life of the
mother, or that the child "may be born with incapacitating physical deformity or
mental deficiency," or that a pregnancy "resulting from legally established statutory
or forcible rape or incest may constitute a threat to the mental or physical health of
the patient," two other physicians "chosen because of their recognized professional
competence have examined the patient and have concurred in writing," and the
procedure "is performed in a hospital accredited by the Joint Commission on Accreditation of Hospitals." The providing of medical information by physicians to state
legislatures in their consideration of legislation regarding therapeutic abortion was
"to be considered consistent with the principles of ethics of the American Medical
Association." This recommendation was adopted by the House of Delegates. Proceedings of the AMA House of Delegates 40-51 (June 1967).

In 1970, after the introduction of a variety of proposed resolutions, and of a report
from its Board of Trustees, a reference committee noted "polarization of the medical
profession on this controversial issue"; division among those who had testified; a
difference of opinion among AMA councils and committees; "the remarkable shift in
testimony" in six months, felt to be influenced "by the rapid changes in state laws
and by the judicial decisions which tend to make abortion more freely available;" and
a feeling "that this trend will continue." On June 25, 1970, the House of Delegates
adopted preambles and most of the resolutions proposed by the reference committee.
The preambles emphasized "the best interests of the patient," "sound clinical judgment,"
and "informed patient consent," in contrast to "mere acquiescence to the patient's
demand." The resolutions asserted that abortion is a medical procedure that should
be performed by a licensed physician in an accredited hospital only after consultation
with two other physicians and in conformity with state law, and that no party to
the procedure should be required to violate personally held moral principles. Proceedings of the AMA House of Delegates 220 (June 1970). The AMA Judicial Council
rendered a complementary opinion.

7. *The position of the American Public Health Association.* In October 1970, the Executive Board of the APHA adopted Standards for Abortion Services. These were five in number:

"a. Rapid and simple abortion referral must be readily available through state and local public health departments, medical societies, or other nonprofit organizations.

"b. An important function of counseling should be to simplify and expedite the provision of abortion services; it should not delay the obtaining of these services.

"c. Psychiatric consultation should not be mandatory. As in the case of other special-ized medical services, psychiatric consultation should be sought for definite indications and not on a routine basis.

"d. A wide range of individuals from appropriately trained, sympathetic volunteers to highly skilled physicians may qualify as abortion counselors.

"e. Contraception and/or sterilization should be discussed with each abortion patient." Recommended Standards for Abortion Services, 61 Am. J Pub. Health 396 (1971).

Among factors pertinent to life and health risks associated with abortion were three that "are recognized as important":

"a. the skill of the physician,

"b. the environment in which the abortion is performed, and above all

"c. the duration of pregnancy, as determined by uterine size and confirmed by menstrual history." *Id.*, at 397.

It was said that "a well-equipped hospital" offers more protection "to cope with unforeseen difficulties than an office or clinic without such resources. ... The factor of gestational age is of overriding importance." Thus, it was recommended that abortions in the second trimester and early abortions in the presence of existing medical complications be performed in hospitals as inpatient procedures. For pregnancies in the first trimester, abortion in the hospital with or without overnight stay "is probably the safest practice." An abortion in an extramural facility, however, is an acceptable alternative "provided arrangements exist in advance to admit patients promptly if unforeseen complications develop." Standards for an abortion facility were listed. It was said that at present abortions should be performed by physicians or osteopaths who are licensed to practice and who have "adequate training." *Id.*, at 398.

8. *The position of the American Bar Association.* At its meeting in February 1972 the ABA House of Delegates approved, with 17 opposing votes, the Uniform Abor-tion Act that had been drafted and approved the preceding August by the Conference of Commissioners on Uniform State Laws. 58 ABAJ 380 (1972). ...

VII

Three reasons have been advanced to explain historically the enactment of criminal abortion laws in the 19th century and to justify their continued existence.

It has been argued occasionally that these laws were the product of a Victorian social concern to discourage illicit sexual conduct. Texas, however, does not advance this justification in the present case, and it appears that no court or commentator has taken the argument seriously. The appellants and *amici* contend, moreover, that this is not a proper state purpose at all and suggest that, if it were, the Texas statutes are overbroad in protecting it since the law fails to distinguish between married and unwed mothers.

A second reason is concerned with abortion as a medical procedure. When most criminal abortion laws were first enacted, the procedure was a hazardous one for the woman. This was particularly true prior to the development of antisepsis. Antiseptic techniques, of course, were based on discoveries by Lister, Pasteur, and others first announced in 1867, but were not generally accepted and employed until about the turn of the century. Abortion mortality was high. Even after 1900, and perhaps until as late as the development of antibiotics in the 1940's, standard modern techniques such as dilation and curettage were not nearly so safe as they are today. Thus, it has been argued that a State's real concern in enacting a criminal abortion law was to protect the pregnant woman, that is, to restrain her from submitting to a procedure that placed her life in serious jeopardy.

Modern medical techniques have altered this situation. Appellants and various *amici* refer to medical data indicating that abortion in early pregnancy, that is, prior to the end of the first trimester, although not without its risk, is now relatively safe. Mortality rates for women undergoing early abortions, where the procedure is legal, appear to be as low as or lower than the rates for normal childbirth. Consequently, any interest of the State in protecting the woman from an inherently hazardous procedure, except when it would be equally dangerous for her to forgo it, has largely disappeared. Of course, important state interests in the areas of health and medical standards do remain. The State has a legitimate interest in seeing to it that abortion, like any other medical procedure, is performed under circumstances that insure maximum safety for the patient. This interest obviously extends at least to the performing physician and his staff, to the facilities involved, to the availability of after-care, and to adequate provision for any complication or emergency that might arise. The prevalence of high mortality rates at illegal "abortion mills" strengthens, rather than weakens, the State's interest in regulating the conditions under which abortions are performed. Moreover, the risk to the woman increases as her pregnancy continues. Thus, the State retains a definite interest in protecting the woman's own health and safety when an abortion is proposed at a late stage of pregnancy.

The third reason is the State's interest—some phrase it in terms of duty—in protecting prenatal life. Some of the argument for this justification rests on the theory that a new human life is present from the moment of conception. The State's interest and general obligation to protect life then extends, it is argued, to prenatal life. Only when the life of the pregnant mother herself is at stake, balanced against the life she carries within her, should the interest of the embryo or fetus not prevail. Logically, of course, a legitimate state interest in this area need not stand or fall on acceptance of the belief that life begins at conception or at some other point prior to live birth. In assessing the State's interest, recognition may be given to the less rigid claim that as long as at least *potential* life is involved, the State may assert interests beyond the protection of the pregnant woman alone.

Parties challenging state abortion laws have sharply disputed in some courts the contention that a purpose of these laws, when enacted, was to protect prenatal life.

Pointing to the absence of legislative history to support the contention, they claim that most state laws were designed solely to protect the woman. Because medical advances have lessened this concern, at least with respect to abortion in early pregnancy, they argue that with respect to such abortions the laws can no longer be justified by any state interest. There is some scholarly support for this view of original purpose. The few state courts called upon to interpret their laws in the late 19th and early 20th centuries did focus on the State's interest in protecting the woman's health rather than in preserving the embryo and fetus. Proponents of this view point out that in many States, including Texas, by statute or judicial interpretation, the pregnant woman herself could not be prosecuted for self-abortion or for cooperating in an abortion performed upon her by another. They claim that adoption of the "quickening" distinction through received common law and state statutes tacitly recognizes the greater health hazards inherent in late abortion and impliedly repudiates the theory that life begins at conception.

It is with these interests, and the weight to be attached to them, that this case is concerned.

VIII

The Constitution does not explicitly mention any right of privacy. In a line of decisions, however, going back perhaps as far as *Union Pacific R Co. v. Botsford*, 141 US 250, 251 (1891), the Court has recognized that a right of personal privacy, or a guarantee of certain areas or zones of privacy, does exist under the Constitution. ... This right of privacy, whether it be founded in the Fourteenth Amendment's concept of personal liberty and restrictions upon state action, as we feel it is, or, as the District Court determined, in the Ninth Amendment's reservation of rights to the people, is broad enough to encompass a woman's decision whether or not to terminate her pregnancy. The detriment that the State would impose upon the pregnant woman by denying this choice altogether is apparent. Specific and direct harm medically diagnosable even in early pregnancy may be involved. Maternity, or additional offspring, may force upon the woman a distressful life and future. Psychological harm may be imminent. Mental and physical health may be taxed by child care. There is also the distress, for all concerned, associated with the unwanted child, and there is the problem of bringing a child into a family already unable, psychologically and otherwise, to care for it. In other cases, as in this one, the additional difficulties and continuing stigma of unwed motherhood may be involved. All these are factors the woman and her responsible physician necessarily will consider in consultation.

On the basis of elements such as these, appellant and some *amici* argue that the woman's right is absolute and that she is entitled to terminate her pregnancy at whatever time, in whatever way, and for whatever reason she alone chooses. With this we do not agree. Appellant's arguments that Texas either has no valid interest at all in regulating the abortion decision, or no interest strong enough to support any limitation upon the woman's sole determination, are unpersuasive. The Court's decisions recognizing a right of privacy also acknowledge that some state regulation in areas protected by that right is appropriate. As noted above, a State may properly assert important interests in safeguarding health, in maintaining medical standards, and in protecting potential life. At some point in pregnancy, these respective interests become sufficiently compelling to sustain regulation of the factors that govern the abortion decision. The privacy right involved, therefore, cannot be said to be absolute. In fact, it is not clear to us that the claim asserted by some *amici* that one has an unlimited right to do with one's body as one pleases bears a close relationship to the right of privacy previously articulated in the Court's decisions. The Court has refused to recognize an unlimited right of this kind in the past. *Jacobson v. Massachusetts*, 197 US 11 (1905) (vaccination); *Buck v. Bell*, 274 US 200 (1927) (sterilization).

We, therefore, conclude that the right of personal privacy includes the abortion decision, but that this right is not unqualified and must be considered against important state interests in regulation.

We note that those federal and state courts that have recently considered abortion law challenges have reached the same conclusion. A majority, in addition to the District Court in the present case, have held state laws unconstitutional, at least in part, because of vagueness or because of overbreadth and abridgment of rights. ... Others have sustained state statutes. ... Although the results are divided, most of these courts have agreed that the right of privacy, however based, is broad enough to cover the abortion decision; that the right, nonetheless, is not absolute and is subject to some limitations; and that at some point the state interests as to protection of health, medical standards, and prenatal life, become dominant. We agree with this approach.

Where certain "fundamental rights" are involved, the Court has held that regulation limiting these rights may be justified only by a "compelling state interest," ... and that legislative enactments must be narrowly drawn to express only the legitimate state interests at stake. ...

IX

The District Court held that the appellee failed to meet his burden of demonstrating that the Texas statute's infringement upon Roe's rights was necessary to support a compelling state interest, and that, although the appellee presented "several compelling justifications for state presence in the area of abortions," the statutes outstripped these justifications and swept "far beyond any areas of compelling state interest." 314 F Supp., at 1222-1223. Appellant and appellee both contest that holding. Appellant, as has been indicated, claims an absolute right that bars any state imposition of criminal penalties in the area. Appellee argues that the State's determination to recognize and protect prenatal life from and after conception constitutes a compelling state interest. As noted above, we do not agree fully with either formulation.

A. The appellee and certain *amici* argue that the fetus is a "person" within the language and meaning of the Fourteenth Amendment. In support of this, they outline at length and in detail the well-known facts of fetal development. If this suggestion of personhood is established, the appellant's case, of course, collapses, for the fetus' right to life would then be guaranteed specifically by the Amendment. The appellant conceded as much on reargument. On the other hand, the appellee conceded on reargument that no case could be cited that holds that a fetus is a person within the meaning of the Fourteenth Amendment.

The Constitution does not define "person" in so many words. Section 1 of the Fourteenth Amendment contains three references to "person." The first, in defining "citizens," speaks of "persons born or naturalized in the United States." The word also appears both in the Due Process Clause and in the Equal Protection Clause. "Person" is used in other places in the Constitution: in the listing of qualifications for Representatives and Senators, ... in the Apportionment Clause, ... in the Migration and Importation provision, ... in the Emolument Clause ... in the Electors provisions, ... and the superseded cl. 3; in the provision outlining qualifications for the office of President. ... But in nearly all these instances, the use of the word is such that it has application only postnatally. None indicates, with any assurance, that it has any possible pre-natal application.

All this, together with our observation, *supra*, that throughout the major portion of the 19th century prevailing legal abortion practices were far freer than they are today, persuades us that the word "person," as used in the Fourteenth Amendment, does not include the unborn. This is in accord with the results reached in those few cases where the issue has been squarely presented. ... Indeed, our decision in *United States v. Vuitch*, 402 US 62 (1971), inferentially is to the same effect, for we there would not have indulged in statutory interpretation favorable to abortion in specified circumstances if the necessary consequence was the termination of life entitled to Fourteenth Amendment protection.

This conclusion, however, does not of itself fully answer the contentions raised by Texas, and we pass on to other considerations.

B. The pregnant woman cannot be isolated in her privacy. She carries an embryo and, later, a fetus, if one accepts the medical definitions of the developing young in the human uterus. See Dorland's Illustrated Medical Dictionary 478-479, 547 (24th ed. 1965). The situation therefore is inherently different from marital intimacy, or bedroom possession of obscene material, or marriage, or procreation, or education, with which *Eisenstadt* and *Griswold, Stanley, Loving, Skinner*, and *Pierce* and *Meyer* were respectively concerned. As we have intimated above, it is reasonable and appropriate for a State to decide that at some point in time another interest, that of health of the mother or that of potential human life, becomes significantly involved. The woman's privacy is no longer sole and any right of privacy she possesses must be measured accordingly.

Texas urges that, apart from the Fourteenth Amendment, life begins at conception and is present throughout pregnancy, and that, therefore, the State has a compelling interest in protecting that life from and after conception. We need not resolve the difficult question of when life begins. When those trained in the respective disciplines of medicine, philosophy, and theology are unable to arrive at any consensus, the judiciary, at this point in the development of man's knowledge, is not in a position to speculate as to the answer.

It should be sufficient to note briefly the wide divergence of thinking on this most sensitive and difficult question. There has always been strong support for the view that life does not begin until live birth. This was the belief of the Stoics. It appears to be the predominant, though not the unanimous, attitude of the Jewish faith. It may be taken to represent also the position of a large segment of the Protestant community, insofar as that can be ascertained; organized groups that have taken a formal position on the abortion issue have generally regarded abortion as a matter for the conscience of the individual and her family. As we have noted, the common law found greater significance in quickening. Physicians and their scientific colleagues have regarded that event with less interest and have tended to focus either upon conception, upon live birth, or upon the interim point at which the fetus becomes "viable," that is, potentially able to live outside the mother's womb, albeit with artificial aid. Viability is usually placed at about seven months (28 weeks) but may occur earlier, even at 24 weeks. The Aristotelian theory of "mediate animation," that held sway throughout the Middle Ages and the Renaissance in Europe, continued to be official Roman Catholic dogma until the 19th century, despite opposition to this "ensoulment" theory from those in the Church who would recognize the existence of life from the moment of conception. The latter is now, of course, the official belief of the Catholic Church. As one brief *amicus* discloses, this is a view strongly held by many non-Catholics as well, and by many physicians. Substantial problems for precise definition of this view are posed, however, by new embryological data that purport to indicate that conception is a "process" over time, rather than an event, and by new medical techniques such as menstrual extraction, the "morning-after" pill, implantation of embryos, artificial insemination, and even artificial wombs.

In areas other than criminal abortion, the law has been reluctant to endorse any theory that life, as we recognize it, begins before live birth or to accord legal rights to the unborn except in narrowly defined situations and except when the rights are contingent upon live birth. For example, the traditional rule of tort law denied recovery for pre-natal injuries even though the child was born alive. That rule has been changed in almost every jurisdiction. In most States, recovery is said to be permitted only if the fetus was viable, or at least quick, when the injuries were sustained, though few courts have squarely so held. In a recent development, generally opposed by the commentators, some States permit the parents of a stillborn child to maintain an action for wrongful death because of prenatal injuries. Such an action, however, would appear to be one to vindicate the parents' interest and is thus consistent with the view that the fetus, at most, represents only the potentiality of life. Similarly, unborn children have been recognized as acquiring rights or interests by way of inheritance or other devolution of property, and have been represented by guardians *ad litem*. Perfection of the interests involved, again, has generally been contingent upon live birth. In short, the unborn have never been recognized in the law as persons in the whole sense.

X

In view of all this, we do not agree that, by adopting one theory of life, Texas may override the rights of the pregnant woman that are at stake. We repeat, however, that the State does have an important and legitimate interest in preserving and protecting the health of the pregnant woman, whether she be a resident of the State or a nonresident who seeks medical consultation and treatment there, and that it has still *another* important and legitimate interest in protecting the potentiality of human life. These interests are separate and distinct. Each grows in substantiality as the woman approaches term and, at a point during pregnancy, each becomes "compelling."

With respect to the State's important and legitimate interest in the health of the mother, the "compelling" point, in the light of present medical knowledge, is at approximately the end of the first trimester. This is so because of the now-established medical fact, referred to above at 149, that until the end of the first trimester mortality in abortion may be less than mortality in normal childbirth. It follows that, from and after this point, a State may regulate the abortion procedure to the extent that the regulation reasonably relates to the preservation and protection of maternal health. Examples of permissible state regulation in this area are requirements as to the qualifications of the person who is to perform the abortion; as to the licensure of that person; as to the facility in which the procedure is to be performed, that is, whether it must be a hospital or may be a clinic or some other place of less-than-hospital status; as to the licensing of the facility; and the like.

This means, on the other hand, that, for the period of pregnancy prior to this "compelling" point, the attending physician, in consultation with his patient, is free to determine, without regulation by the State, that, in his medical judgment, the patient's pregnancy should be terminated. If that decision is reached, the judgment may be effectuated by an abortion free of interference by the State.

With respect to the State's important and legitimate interest in potential life, the "compelling" point is at viability. This is so because the fetus then presumably has the capability of meaningful life outside the mother's womb. State regulation protective of fetal life after viability thus has both logical and biological justifications. If the State is interested in protecting fetal life after viability, it may go so far as to proscribe abortion during that period, except when it is necessary to preserve the life or health of the mother.

Measured against these standards, Art. 1196 of the Texas Penal Code, in restricting legal abortions to those "procured or attempted by medical advice for the purpose of saving the life of the mother," sweeps too broadly. The statute makes no distinction between abortions performed early in pregnancy and those performed later, and it limits to a single reason, "saving" the mother's life, the legal justification for the procedure. The statute, therefore, cannot survive the constitutional attack made upon it here.

This conclusion makes it unnecessary for us to consider the additional challenge to the Texas statute asserted on grounds of vagueness. See *United States v. Vuitch*, 402 US, at 67-72.

XI

To summarize and to repeat:

1. A state criminal abortion statute of the current Texas type, that excepts from criminality only a *lifesaving* procedure on behalf of the mother, without regard to pregnancy stage and without recognition of the other interests involved, is violative of the Due Process Clause of the Fourteenth Amendment.

(a) For the stage prior to approximately the end of the first trimester, the abortion decision and its effectuation must be left to the medical judgment of the pregnant woman's attending physician.

(b) For the stage subsequent to approximately the end of the first trimester, the State, in promoting its interest in the health of the mother, may, if it chooses, regulate the abortion procedure in ways that are reasonably related to maternal health.

(c) For the stage subsequent to viability, the State in promoting its interest in the potentiality of human life may, if it chooses, regulate, and even proscribe, abortion except where it is necessary, in appropriate medical judgment, for the preservation of the life or health of the mother.

2. The State may define the term "physician," as it has been employed in the preceding paragraphs of this Part XI of this opinion, to mean only a physician currently licensed by the State, and may proscribe any abortion by a person who is not a physician as so defined. ...

This holding, we feel, is consistent with the relative weights of the respective interests involved, with the lessons and examples of medical and legal history, with the lenity of the common law, and with the demands of the profound problems of the present day. The decision leaves the State free to place increasing restrictions on abortion as the period of pregnancy lengthens, so long as those restrictions are tailored to the recognized state interests. The decision vindicates the right of the physician to administer medical treatment according to his professional judgment up to the points where important state interests provide compelling justifications for intervention. Up to those points, the abortion decision in all its aspects is inherently, and primarily, a medical decision, and basic responsibility for it must rest with the physician. If an individual practitioner abuses the privilege of exercising proper medical judgment, the usual remedies, judicial and intra-professional, are available. ...

STEWART, J (concurring): In 1963, this Court, in *Ferguson v. Skrupa*, 372 US 726, purported to sound the death knell for the doctrine of substantive due process, a doctrine under which many state laws had in the past been held to violate the Fourteenth Amendment. As Mr. Justice Black's opinion for the Court in *Skrupa* put it: "We have returned to the original constitutional proposition that courts do not substitute their social and economic beliefs for the judgment of legislative bodies, who are elected to pass laws." *Id.*, at 730.

Barely two years later, in *Griswold v. Connecticut*, 381 US 479, the Court held a Connecticut birth control law unconstitutional. In view of what had been so recently said in *Skrupa*, the Court's opinion in *Griswold* understandably did its best to avoid reliance on the Due Process Clause of the Fourteenth Amendment as the ground for decision. Yet, the Connecticut law did not violate any provision of the Bill of Rights, nor any other specific provision of the Constitution. So it was clear to me then, and it is equally clear to me now, that the *Griswold* decision can be rationally understood only as a holding that the Connecticut statute substantively invaded the "liberty" that is protected by the Due Process Clause of the Fourteenth Amendment. As so understood, *Griswold* stands as one in a long line of pre-*Skrupa* cases decided under the doctrine of substantive due process, and I now accept it as such.

"In a Constitution for a free people, there can be no doubt that the meaning of 'liberty' must be broad indeed." *Board of Regents v. Roth*, 408 US 564, 572. The Constitution nowhere mentions a specific right of personal choice in matters of marriage and family life, but the "liberty" protected by the Due Process Clause of the Fourteenth Amendment covers more than those freedoms explicitly named in the Bill of Rights. ... As Mr. Justice Harlan once wrote: "The full scope of the liberty guaranteed by the Due Process Clause cannot be found in or limited by the precise terms of the specific guarantees elsewhere provided in the Constitution. This 'liberty' is not a series of isolated points pricked out in terms of the taking of property; the freedom of speech, press, and religion; the right to keep and bear arms; the freedom from unreasonable searches and seizures; and so on. It is a rational continuum which, broadly speaking, includes a freedom from all substantial arbitrary impositions and purposeless restraints ... and which also recognizes, what a reasonable and sensitive judgment must, that certain interests require particularly careful scrutiny of the state needs asserted to justify their abridgment." *Poe v. Ullman*, 367 US 497, 543 (opinion dissenting from dismissal of appeal) (citations omitted). In the words of Mr. Justice Frankfurter, "Great concepts like ... 'liberty' ... were purposely left to gather meaning from experience. For they relate to the whole domain of social and economic fact, and the statesmen who founded this Nation knew too well that only a stagnant society remains unchanged." *National Mutual Ins. Co. v. Tidewater Transfer Co.*, 337 US 582, 646 (dissenting opinion).

Several decisions of this Court make clear that freedom of personal choice in matters of marriage and family life is one of the liberties protected by the Due Process Clause of the Fourteenth Amendment. ... As recently as last Term, in *Eisenstadt v. Baird*, 405 US 438, 453, we recognized "the right of the *individual*, married or single, to be free from unwarranted governmental intrusion into matters so fundamentally affecting a person as the decision whether to bear or beget a child." That right necessarily includes the right of a woman to decide whether or not to terminate her pregnancy. "Certainly the interests of a woman in giving of her physical and emotional self during pregnancy and the interests that will be affected throughout her life by the birth and raising of a child are of a far greater degree of significance and personal intimacy than the right to send a child to private school protected in *Pierce v. Society of Sisters*, 268 US 510 (1925), or the right to teach a foreign language protected in *Meyer v. Nebraska*, 262 US 390 (1923)." *Abele v. Markle*, 351 F Supp. 224, 227 (Conn. 1972).

Clearly, therefore, the Court today is correct in holding that the right asserted by Jane Roe is embraced within the personal liberty protected by the Due Process Clause of the Fourteenth Amendment.

It is evident that the Texas abortion statute infringes that right directly. Indeed, it is difficult to imagine a more complete abridgment of a constitutional freedom than that worked by the inflexible criminal statute now in force in Texas. ...

REHNQUIST, J (dissenting): The Court's opinion brings to the decision of this troubling question both extensive historical fact and a wealth of legal scholarship. While the opinion thus commands my respect, I find myself nonetheless in fundamental disagreement with those parts of it that invalidate the Texas statute in question, and therefore dissent. ...

While the Court's opinion quotes from the dissent of Mr. Justice Holmes in *Lochner v. New York*, 198 US 45, 74 (1905), the result it reaches is more closely attuned to the majority opinion of Mr. Justice Peckham in that case. As in *Lochner* and similar cases applying substantive due process standards to economic and social welfare legislation, the adoption of the compelling state interest standard will inevitably require this Court to examine the legislative policies and pass on the wisdom of these policies in the very process of deciding whether a particular state interest put forward may or may not be "compelling." The decision here to break pregnancy into three distinct terms and to outline the permissible restrictions the State may impose in each one, for example, partakes more of judicial legislation than it does of a determination of the intent of the drafters of the Fourteenth Amendment.

The fact that a majority of the States reflecting, after all, the majority sentiment in those States, have had restrictions on abortions for at least a century is a strong indication, it seems to me, that the asserted right to an abortion is not "so rooted in the traditions and conscience of our people as to be ranked as fundamental," *Snyder v. Massachusetts*, 291 US 97, 105 (1934). Even today, when society's views on abortion are changing, the very existence of the debate is evidence that the "right" to an abortion is not so universally accepted as the appellant would have us believe.

To reach its result, the Court necessarily has had to find within the scope of the Fourteenth Amendment a right that was apparently completely unknown to the drafters of the Amendment. As early as 1821, the first state law dealing directly with abortion was enacted by the Connecticut Legislature. Conn. Stat., Tit. 20, §§ 14, 16. By the time of the adoption of the Fourteenth Amendment in 1868, there were at least 36 laws enacted by state or territorial legislatures limiting abortion. While many States have amended or updated their laws, 21 of the laws on the books in 1868 remain in effect today. Indeed, the Texas statute struck down today was, as the majority notes, first enacted in 1857 and "has remained substantially unchanged to the present time." *Ante*, at 119.

There apparently was no question concerning the validity of this provision or of any of the other state statutes when the Fourteenth Amendment was adopted. The only conclusion possible from this history is that the drafters did not intend to have the Fourteenth Amendment withdraw from the States the power to legislate with respect to this matter.

NOTES AND QUESTIONS

1. At the outset of its decision, the court in *Roe* acknowledges that "[o]ne's philosophy, one's experiences, one's exposure to the raw edges of human existence, one's religious training, one's attitudes toward life and family and their values, and the moral standards one establishes and seeks to observe, are all likely to influence and to color one's thinking and conclusions about abortion. ... In addition, population growth, pollution, poverty, and racial overtones tend to complicate and not to simplify the problem." Are these statements relevant to an originalist inquiry into the meaning of the due process clause? Why or why not?

2. Are the considerations quoted in question (1), above, relevant only to a decision concerning abortion, or are they also relevant to questions involving euthanasia, criminal

justice, hospital administration, taxation, etc.? Are there many "legislative" issues that do not carry implications for one's religious, cultural, moral, or philosophical opinions? What does this say about the interpretive process? Why does the court invoke these values, rather than relying simply on the intention of the constitution's framers?

3. The court attempts to describe what "history reveals about man's attitudes toward the abortion procedure over the centuries." Why would the court embark upon such an inquiry? Would it be permissible for a court to render its decision based on its own views about "the abortion procedure"? Is it possible for a court to set aside its own views when determining the legality of abortion legislation?

4. In light of the decisions in the *Mushroom* case, *EGALE*, *Boisbriand*, and *Roe*, is there any way of predicting when a court will confine itself to "textual" or "linguistic" issues and when the court will inquire into "value-laden" questions? Does it depend solely upon the nature of the question before the court (i.e., is the question "political," like the question in *Roe v. Wade*, or "mundane," like the question in the *Mushroom* case)?[6] Does it depend on the language of the provision being construed? Does the court in *Roe* focus on "values" and "public policy" simply because the text of the 14th Amendment gives the court insufficient guidance to embark upon a textual inquiry?

5. Are the views of ancient Greeks relevant in determining the meaning of the word "liberty" in the due process clause? Why does the court in *Roe* spend so much time dealing with this issue? Are the reasons rhetorical, stylistic, political, or interpretive? Are there differences between "political" reasons and "interpretive" reasons?

6. The court in *Roe* seems concerned with the probable views of the people involved in the drafting of the US constitution. For example, the court undertakes a lengthy discussion in order to prove that "at the time of the adoption of our Constitution, and throughout the major portion of the 19th century, abortion was viewed with less disfavor than under most American statutes currently in effect." Why should the views of the constitution's framers continue to control the meaning of the constitution's language? Is the court in *Roe* applying the same interpretive method adopted by the court in *EGALE*?

7. If the court's decision in *Roe* is properly characterized as an "originalist" decision, is the court saying that:

a. The constitution's framers specifically considered the question whether the 14th Amendment guaranteed the right to an abortion, and
b. The framers intended the words "due process" to imply that a state would have *some* freedom to regulate or prohibit abortions, but only during the second and third trimesters of a pregnancy?

8. Is it likely that the framers of the constitution considered the "abortion question"? If not, does that mean that the constitution cannot be applied to the "abortion question" until the constitutional text is amended? Would that be a practical solution?

9. When courts rely on "legislative intention," are the courts actually attributing specific thoughts to the legislative drafters, or are the courts simply trying to balance

---

6   Students should consider whether it is truly possible to draw a line between "mundane" and "political" questions. Are all legal questions inherently political?

competing rights based on the courts' own views of what a particular provision is *capable* of meaning? What is the court doing in *Roe v. Wade*?

10. The majority in *Roe* considers arguments concerning the original purpose of state abortion laws. How did the litigants in *Roe v. Wade* demonstrate the laws' purposes? What evidence would be useful in determining the purpose of a law? In *Boisbriand*, above, the court looked to a law's preamble and legislative history in determining a statute's purpose. These issues will become particularly relevant in chapter 3, under the heading "The Mischief Rule," and chapter 4, which deals with evidence of a statute's meaning.

11. The court in *Roe* notes that "[t]he Constitution does not explicitly mention any right of privacy." Nonetheless, the court determines that a right of privacy is found within "the Fourteenth Amendment's concept of personal liberty and restrictions upon state action." Subsequent to that holding, the court holds that this unwritten right of privacy "is broad enough to encompass a woman's decision whether or not to terminate her pregnancy." The court effectively "reads" a "right to procure abortions" into an unwritten guarantee of privacy, which it previously read into the word "liberty" within the 14th Amendment. Is this asking too much of the word "liberty"? Conversely, is it possible that the framers of the constitution selected the broad, malleable word "liberty" so that the courts could adjust the constitution's meaning in order to deal with evolving social attitudes and new public policies?

12. When the court determines that an unborn fetus is not a "person" within the meaning of the 14th Amendment, is the court's decision based on the legislators' historical intentions? How do we know? If medical science established that a fetus became self-aware at some specific time before birth, would we still feel bound by the constitution's framers' original intentions? What if science determined that babies do not become self-aware until the second month *following* their birth?

13. Why does the majority make only passing references to the language of the 14th Amendment? Why do the minority judges (concurring and dissenting) feel the need to focus more intently on this language?

14. Would the decision in *Roe* be easier to justify on openly dynamic grounds? Is the decision in *Roe* an instance of dynamic interpretation, despite the repeated references to historical intention?

15. Note that Rehnquist J (in dissent) states that the court's decision "partakes more of judicial legislation than it does of a determination of the intent of the drafters of the Fourteenth Amendment."[7] Would this criticism lose its force if the majority simply admitted that it was using dynamic construction as a method of imposing current views on the language of the constitution?

---

7   See also Rehnquist J's claim that the majority has found "within the scope of the Fourteenth Amendment a right that was apparently completely unknown to the drafters of the Amendment."

VI. R v. MARA

A. Introduction

One of the key features of *Roe v. Wade* was its focus on the evolution of public opinion—as "society's views" changed, so too did the meaning of the constitution's language. The debate in *Roe* accordingly underscored the tension between originalist and dynamic construction.

Like the decision in *Roe v. Wade*, the decision of the Supreme Court of Canada in *R v. Mara*, [1997] 2 SCR 630 dealt (in part) with the evolution of public opinion. Specifically, the court in *Mara* was asked to determine the way in which modern, erotic "dancing" was dealt with by a statute, originally enacted in 1892, that prohibited "indecent" perform-ances. When reviewing the court's decision, recall the tension between originalist and dynamic construction revealed in chapter 1 of *Theory and Practice*. Pay particular attention to the nature of the "erotic performances" described in *Mara*, and consider whether a statutory drafter writing in 1892 would consider such acts "indecent." More importantly, consider the extent to which that drafter's opinion should be relevant to a modern court faced with interpretive questions.

B. The Court's Decision

R v. Mara
[1997] 2 SCR 630

SOPINKA J: This appeal concerns the criminal liability of the appellants for allowing an indecent performance. The performances in question involved varying degrees of sexual contact between "dancers" and patrons at Cheaters Tavern in Toronto. ... In my view, as a matter of law, the performances in question went beyond community standards of tolerance and were therefore indecent. ...

I. Facts

Cheaters Tavern in midtown Toronto was licensed to sell alcoholic beverages and food and presented "adult entertainment." The appellant, Patrick Mara, was the owner and operator of the tavern and the appellant, Allan East, was the manager in charge of entertainment.

Undercover police attended at the tavern on several days in March and April 1991. The officers testified about the adult entertainment being presented. Women performed exotic dances on stage, for which there was no charge. For a fee, the entertainer per-formed a "table dance" in which she would be nude, save for a long, unbuttoned blouse. The dancer would lower her chest to the patron's face, allowing the patron to suck and lick her breasts. For a larger fee, the dancer performed a "special dance" called a "lap dance." The dancer would sit on the patron's lap with her back to the patron and her bare buttocks on the patron's groin area. The trial judge summarized the sexual activity as follows:

"The conduct of each dancer with the customer is clearly detailed in the evidence, and includes: (a) being nude except for wearing an open shirt or blouse; (b) fondling her own breasts, buttocks, thighs and genitals while close to the customer; (c) sitting on a customer's lap and grinding her bare buttocks into his lap; (d) sitting on a customer's lap, reaching into his crotch and apparently masturbating the customer; (e) permitting the customer to touch and fondle her breasts, buttocks, thighs and genitals; (f) permitting the customer to kiss, lick and suck their breasts; (g) permitting what appeared to be cunnilingus." ...

II. Relevant Statutory Provision

Criminal Code, RSC, 1985, c. C-46

"167(1) Every one commits an offence who, being the lessee, manager, agent or person in charge of a theatre, presents or gives or allows to be presented or given therein an immoral, indecent or obscene performance, entertainment or representation."

• • •

IV. Analysis

• • •

B. Indecency

The trial judge found that the tavern constituted a theatre for the purposes of s. 167, and that the "dances" in question constituted performances. Given these findings, aside from the question of intent, conviction or acquittal turns only on whether the performances were indecent.

As set out in *Tremblay* ... the appropriate test to determine indecency is the community standard of tolerance. Dickson CJ stated in *Towne Cinema*, *supra*, at p. 508:

"The cases all emphasize that it is a standard of *tolerance* not taste, that is relevant. What matters is not what Canadians think is right for themselves to see. **What matters is what Canadians would not abide other Canadians seeing because it would be beyond the contemporary Canadian standard of tolerance to allow them to see it.**"
[Italics in original; emphasis added.]

As discussed above, *Butler* set out that harm is the principle underlying the notion of what Canadians would tolerate. The majority stated in that case at p. 485:

"The courts must determine as best they can what the community would tolerate others being exposed to on the basis of the degree of harm that may flow from such exposure. Harm in this context means that it predisposes persons to act in an anti-social manner as, for example, the physical or mental mistreatment of women by men, or, what is perhaps debatable, the reverse. Anti-social conduct for this purpose is conduct which society formally recognizes as incompatible with its proper functioning."

While *Butler* concerned the obscenity of particular pornographic materials, the present case concerns the indecency of live performances. The tolerance basis of the community standards test is the same in indecency cases as in obscenity cases (see *Tremblay*), but indecency, unlike obscenity, entails an assessment of the surrounding circumstances in applying the community standards test. As the majority stated in *Tremblay* at p. 960:

> "In any consideration of the indecency of an act, the circumstances which surround the performance of the act must be taken into account. Acts do not take place in a vacuum. The community standard of tolerance is that of the whole community. However just what the community will tolerate will vary with the place in which the acts take place and the composition of the audience."

Putting the above observations together, a performance is indecent if the social harm engendered by the performance, having reference to the circumstances in which it took place, is such that the community would not tolerate it taking place. I agree with the Court of Appeal that the activities in the present case were such that the community would not tolerate them and thus were indecent.

The relevant social harm to be considered pursuant to s. 167 is the attitudinal harm on those watching the performance as perceived by the community as a whole. In the present case, as outlined in the facts, the patrons of Cheaters could, for a fee, fondle and touch women and be fondled in an intimately sexual manner, including mutual masturbation and apparent cunnilingus, in a public tavern. In effect, men, along with drinks, could pay for a public, sexual experience for their own gratification and those of others. In my view, such activities gave rise to a social harm that indicates that the performances were indecent. I agree with the Court of Appeal, which stated (at p. 650 OR):

> "The conduct in issue in this case in the context in which it takes place is harmful to society in many ways. It degrades and dehumanizes women and publicly portrays them in a servile and humiliating manner, as sexual objects, with a loss of their dignity. It dehumanizes and desensitizes sexuality and is incompatible with the recognition of the dignity and equality of each human being. It predisposes persons to act in an antisocial manner, as if the treatment of women in this way is socially acceptable and is normal conduct, and as if we live in a society without any moral values."

Any finding of indecency must depend on all the circumstances. I am satisfied that the activities in the present case were indecent insofar as they involved sexual touching between dancer and patron. Thus, the fondling and sucking of breasts, as well as contact between the dancer or patron and the other person's genitals, in circumstances such as the present case gave rise to an indecent performance. It is unacceptably degrading to women to permit such uses of their bodies in the context of a public performance in a tavern. Insofar as the activities were consensual, as the appellants stressed, this does not alter their degrading character. Moreover, as I stated in *Butler*, at p. 479, "sometimes the very appearance of consent makes the depicted acts even more degrading or dehumanizing."

This analysis, in my view, is sufficient to ground the finding that the performances were indecent. However, I agree with the Court of Appeal that it is also relevant that the Municipality of metropolitan Toronto recently passed a by-law prohibiting contact between anyone who provides services designed to appeal to erotic or sexual appetites or inclinations at an adult entertainment parlour from [*sic*] touching or having physical contact with any other person in any manner whatsoever involving any part of that person's body, and prohibits the owner from permitting such conduct. While the by-law has been challenged unsuccessfully as being ultra vires the municipality, I agree with the Court of Appeal that, aside from its validity, the by-law is instructive in the present case as evidence confirming that community standards of tolerance were exceeded by the activities in question.

The Court of Appeal considered two other factors which I view as only marginally relevant to a determination of indecency. A finding of an indecent performance depends on a finding of harm to the spectators of the performance as perceived by the community as a whole. The potential harm to the performers themselves, while obviously regrettable, is not a central consideration under s. 167. The Court of Appeal, however, appeared to treat the risk of sexually transmitted diseases and the harms associated with prostitution as significant factors in finding indecency in the present case. In my view, the risk of harm to the performers is only relevant insofar as that risk exacerbates the social harm resulting from the degradation and objectification of women. Thus, if there is increased degradation of women, and therefore an increased likelihood of social harm, because the performances in question posed risk to the performers, then these factors are relevant. In the present case, these additional factors are not necessary to my conclusion that the performances in question were indecent. Aside from the risks of harm from sexually transmitted diseases and from the activities' similarity to prostitution, the social harm resulting from the performances in the context in which they took place is sufficient to find them indecent. Women were degraded and objectified in a socially unacceptable manner, whether or not the additional harms associated with prostitution and sexually transmitted diseases were associated with the performances.

· · ·

The Court of Appeal, in assessing indecency, provided a further reason to conclude that the acts in question were indecent. Dubin CJO observed (at pp. 651-52 OR) that:

"Both [Mara and East] denied knowledge of the acts described. However, the following exchange took place during cross-examination of the respondent East by Crown counsel:

Q. And for a woman to be masturbating herself in the presence and within view of the male patron, would you consider that to be improper?

A. Improper, whether she was in view or not. Highly improper.

Q. And would that warrant dismissal, as far as you would be concerned?

A. Yes, of course.

Q. And for the patrons to be fondling the breasts of the dancers at Cheaters?

A. If they were to do that also, I would eject the customer and the dancer.

Q. Why?

A. Why?

Q. Why? Yes.

A. Because it—I would consider it improper.

Q. And for the dancers to be masturbating the [male] customers through their clothing?

A. Need you ask? Of course. It would be very improper. Instant, total dismissal for life."

Thus, the appellant East himself acknowledged that the acts described by the police were "improper," which lends further support to the conclusion that the performances in question were indecent.

In summary, on the undisputed facts as described by the trial judge in the facts set out above, the performances in the present case were indecent. By finding them to be otherwise, in my view the trial judge erred in law and the Court of Appeal was correct to overturn this finding. ... With respect to consideration of the risk of sexually transmitted diseases, given that I place little or no weight on this factor, I will decline to consider whether it was proper for the Court of Appeal to examine those risks in assessing indecency even though they were not a factor discussed by the trial judge. In my view, the undisputed facts outside of the risk of sexually transmitted diseases were sufficient to ground a finding of indecency.

NOTES AND QUESTIONS

1. The original version of s. 167 of the *Criminal Code* was found in *An Act To Amend the Criminal Code, 1892*, which received royal assent on June 25, 1903. At the time of its original enactment, the section provided as follows:

> Every person who, being the lessee, agent or person in charge or manager of a theatre, presents or gives or allows to be presented or given therein any immoral, indecent or obscene play, opera, concert, acrobatic, variety, or vaudeville performance, or other entertainment or representation is guilty of an indictable offence and liable, if convicted upon indictment, to one year's imprisonment with or without hard labour, or to a fine of five hundred dollars, or to both, and, on summary conviction, to six months' imprisonment, or to a fine of fifty dollars, or to both.

When this provision was first drafted (in 1892) or assented to, would there have been any question of whether or not a public display of "apparent cunnilingus" would count as "indecent" for the purposes of the Act?

2. Note that it was the mutual touching of dancers and patrons that gave rise to the court's holding that the activities in *Mara* stepped beyond the "community standard of tolerance." In *Tremblay* (discussed in *Mara*, above), the court held that a nude dance involving the use of a vibrator by the dancer, while a patron masturbated, did not violate the "community standard of tolerance." Would the framers of s. 167 have supported the decision in *Tremblay*? Would they have drawn the "line of indecency" at the point of mutual touching, as the court did in *Mara*?

3. The court in *Mara* repeatedly asserts that a "contemporary Canadian standard of tolerance" controls the meaning of "indecent" in s. 167. Why are "contemporary"

standards relevant? Should the court be concerned with the intention of the statute's original authors, rather than with the morals of contemporary Canadians?

4. It seems sensible to conclude that one of the objectives of the original version of s. 167 was to prevent "moral decline." Assuming that this was one of the statute's original purposes, does it make sense to determine the meaning of "indecent" by reference to current moral standards, rather than by reference to the standards that applied when the law was drafted? Doesn't the court's use of "contemporary standards" defeat the ultimate purpose of the legislation in question?

5. What would be the consequences of an originalist construction of s. 167? Would all lap dancing be illegal? Stripping? Blasphemous jokes? Wet T-shirt contests? R-rated movies? If the original drafters would have prohibited such theatrical performances in 1892, does it necessarily follow that their intention would be to continue to prohibit those performances, regardless of any changes in public opinion? Does the language require (or permit) that result?

6. The court in *Roe v. Wade*, like the court in *EGALE*, placed a great deal of emphasis on the intention of legislative authors. The court in *Mara*, in contrast, seems to pay little attention to such concerns. What justifies the difference between *Mara* on the one hand, and *Roe* and *EGALE* on the other? Is it the fact that *Mara* deals with an "ordinary" statute while both *Roe* and *EGALE* deal with a constitution? Note that in Canada, courts and academic commentators typically state the constitution should be interpreted dynamically (or progressively), with little or no attention paid to the constitution's framers, while ordinary statutes should be interpreted in accordance with legislative intent. (See also the cases and authors cited at 34-37 of *Theory and Practice*.) Did the courts in *Mara*, *EGALE*, and *Roe* get it backward?

7. The court in *Mara* found that the conduct taking place at Cheater's violated the "community standard of tolerance" because it "degrades and dehumanizes women and publicly portrays them in a servile ... manner." Would the original drafters of s. 167 have been concerned with the portrayal of women as "servile"?

8. Assume that the original drafters would not have been concerned with the portrayal of women as "servile" (see question (7), above). If the framers of old statutes had values or ideals that conflict with current public policies, should we *ever* pay attention to the framers' expectations? Should American courts interpret the constitution by reference to the expectations or values of drafters who may have owned slaves?

VII. EXERCISES

A. The Moral Propriety Code

Suggested length: 2-5 pages

Section 36 of the *Moral Propriety Code* (a fictional piece of legislation) provides as follows:

(1) Any person who exhibits an illicit film to minors is guilty of an offence punishable by six months in prison or a fine of up to three thousand dollars.

(2) For the purposes of subsection (1), an "illicit film" includes any film having sexuality as its dominant characteristic.

On January 6, 1997, Sheila Thompson (a high school science teacher) presented a slide show entitled *Mating Habits of the Yellow-Throated Condor* to her grade 10 biology class. The main focus of the slide show was the strange sexual behaviour exhibited by the yellow-throated condor during its mating season. All of the students in Ms Thompson's class were "minors" within the meaning of the relevant legislation.

Unfortunately for Ms Thompson, one of the students in the biology class was Patrick Smith, the son of famed moral activist Prudence Merriwether. Patrick reported Ms Thompson's activities to his mother, who in turn raised a complaint with the Moral Defence League. As a result of the league's incessant lobbying, Ms Thompson was charged under s. 36 of the *Moral Propriety Code* (reproduced above).

At trial, Ms Thompson was convicted under s. 36 of the Code and sentenced to six months in prison. In addition, Ms Thompson was ordered to pay a fine of $250.

Ms Thompson has appealed her conviction (and, in the alternative, her sentence) to you, a judge of the Appellate Division. Prepare a short judgment dismissing or allowing Ms Thompson's appeal. Regardless of your disposition of the appeal as to conviction, you should also address the propriety of the sentence imposed at trial. Be sure that your judgment deals only with "interpretive issues" (that is, issues relating to the meaning of words or phrases in the legislation and the application of those words or phrases to the facts at hand).

B. EGALE Canada Inc. Revisited

Suggested length: 7-12 pages

Revisit the court's decision in *EGALE Canada Inc.* (above). Prepare a Court of Appeal judgment overturning or affirming the court's decision with respect to the meaning of "marriage" in s. 91(26) of the *Constitution Act, 1867*. Be sure that your decision addresses the strengths, weaknesses, and interaction of originalist construction and dynamic interpretation.

C. The Bait Shop

Suggested length: 5-10 pages

Old Henry Bower has a bait shop located in picturesque Peterborough, Ontario. The shop, known as Bower's Baitery, is found on the Old Mill Road, 50 metres from Lisa Ruckpaul's hobby farm.

Lisa and Henry are not the closest of neighbours. Lisa purchased her hobby farm three months ago for the purpose of enjoying the peace and quiet of the rural Peterborough (as well as for the tax writeoff that often accompanies farming property). Just days after purchasing the property, however, Lisa realized that the setting was not as peaceful as it seemed.

In recent months, Bower's Baitery has become a hub of activity. Bower has a fully stocked trout pond on his property, and visitors to the baitery have become fond of spending their afternoons trying out their new bait in Bower's pond. Bower replenishes his stock of trout weekly, ensuring that his customers will catch plenty of trout, demonstrating the efficacy of Bower's specialty baits. The fun atmosphere and plentiful fish have attracted hundreds of visitors in recent months, many of whom have brought their children to teach them the art of fishing. Needless to say, the constant stream of patrons and small children to Bower's shop has significantly diminished the "peace and quiet" sought by Lisa.

To make matters worse, Bower has recently added a petting zoo to his property, where his customers' children can play with Bower's assortment of sheep, horses, and poultry. The addition of the petting zoo has substantially increased the popularity of Bower's shop.

Not surprisingly, Lisa was annoyed at Bower's success. The more customers Bower had, the more noise and general "hubbub" there was to interrupt Lisa's rest. Lisa accordingly hatched a plan to crush Bower's business and restore peace and quiet to her neighbourhood.

Around midnight on October 12, 1998, Lisa snuck onto Bower's property and poured five doses of Drowz-all Cold Suppressant into Bower's trout pond. Lisa hoped that this potent sleep-aid would pacify Bower's fish, making them sleep throughout the day, substantially decreasing the daily catch of Bower's patrons. While on Bower's property, Lisa also poured some Drowz-all into the troughs at the petting zoo. Lisa snickered at the thought of Bower's customers and their children, disappointed at the sight of sleeping horses and drunken chickens. News of Bower's lame attractions would spread like wildfire, destroying Bower's business and restoring the peaceful atmosphere at the neighbouring Ruckpaul farm.

Lisa's plan went off without a hitch. Early on the morning of October 13, Bower awoke to find his horses, sheep, chicken, and trout fast asleep, unable to be awakened from their drug-induced stupor. As Bower's customers arrived, they were appalled at the condition of Bower's animals. Indeed, one of Bower's customers went so far as to launch a complaint with the local Humane Society, claiming that Bower's animals appeared to have been mistreated.

As a result of the customer's complaint, Melissa Mason (the lead investigator of the Peterborough Society for the Protection of Animals) came to Bower's farm to investigate the allegations of animal mistreatment. Being a rather thorough investigator, Melissa performed an exemplary investigation and discovered traces of Drowz-all in the animal troughs and in the pond.

Laboratory tests confirmed that the Drowz-all came from a lot that had been purchased by Lisa Ruckpaul on October 11. When confronted with this evidence, Lisa quickly admitted to her heinous actions.

Lisa was charged with offences under ss. 444 and 445 of the *Criminal Code* (entitled "Cattle and Other Animals"), which provide as follows:

> 444. Everyone who wilfully
>> 1. kills, maims, wounds, poisons or injures cattle, or
>> 2. places poison in such a position that it may easily be consumed by cattle,
> is guilty of an indictable offence and liable to imprisonment for a term not exceeding five years.

> 445. Everyone who wilfully and without lawful excuse
>> 1. kills, maims, wounds, poisons or injures dogs, birds or animals that are not cattle and are kept for a lawful purpose, or

2. places poison in such a position that it may easily be consumed by dogs, birds
or animals that are not cattle and are kept for a lawful purpose,
is guilty of an offence punishable on summary conviction.

Prepare a judgment convicting or acquitting Lisa of the offences with which she has
been charged. In preparing this assignment, you must address acquittal or conviction with
respect to: (1) the trout, (2) the horses, and (3) the chickens, all of which fell victim to
the Drowz-all.

Note that the *Criminal Code* is a real statute. As a result, you should consult the
Criminal Code in order to determine (for example) whether any of the terms used in the
relevant sections have been defined elsewhere in the Code.

Horses   Sheep   Chicken?   trout.

Cattle: neat cattle or animal from the
Bovine species. by whatever technical or
familiar name it is known – including
any horse, mule, ass, pig, sheep or goat.

CHAPTER TWO

The Maxims of Interpretation

I. INTRODUCTION

A. Purpose

The purpose of this chapter is to introduce students to the maxims of statutory construction. By the end of this chapter, students should be capable of using (and counteracting) several maxims of interpretation including *noscitur a sociis, ejusdem generis, reddendo singula singulis, expressio unius est exclusio alterius*, and *casus omissus*. While this is only a small sampling of the maxims that can be found in Canadian, American, and English jurisprudence, an understanding of these basic maxims will allow students to hone their interpretive skills and develop an appreciation of the role of careful, textual reading in the interpretation of legislative language.

B. Required Readings

The maxims are discussed in detail in chapter 3 of Randal N. Graham, *Statutory Interpretation: Theory and Practice* (Toronto: Emond Montgomery, 2001) (*"Theory and Practice"*). Students should review that portion of *Theory and Practice* before reading the cases in this chapter.

As noted above, one of the virtues of maxims is their ability to demonstrate the importance of careful reading in the construction of legislation. One result of careful reading is the ability to identify typical language patterns that give rise to problems of statutory construction. The four language patterns that most frequently give rise to interpretive problems are known as "vagueness," "ambiguity," "subtext," and "analogy." Vagueness and ambiguity are described in chapter 4 of *Theory and Practice*, while subtext and analogy are described in chapter 5. Students should read chapters 4 and 5 of *Theory and Practice* while reviewing the cases found in this chapter. When studying the cases that follow, students should attempt to classify each case's key "interpretive problem" by identifying the relevant pattern of language as an instance of vagueness, ambiguity, subtext, or analogy.

II. NOSCITUR A SOCIIS

A. Introduction

Roughly translated, the phrase *noscitur a sociis* means "to know a thing by its associates." Distilled to its basic elements, the maxim encapsulates a process that takes place automatically in the minds of most readers: the maxim calls upon the reader to determine the meaning of words by reference to any other words or phrases with which the contentious text is associated. For example, when reading a passage dealing with "sickness or injury," the reader should interpret the word "injury" by reference to the word "sickness." Since "sickness" clearly deals with health-related ailments, the word "injury," when accompanying the word "sickness," should be understood in a similar sense. The reader should therefore presume that "injury" deals with bodily injuries, rather than injuries of an economic nature.

Noscitur a sociis is dealt with at 87-91 of *Theory and Practice*. When reviewing that portion of *Theory and Practice*, students should pay particular attention to the decision of the Ontario Court of Appeal in *R v. Goulis* (1981), 125 DLR (3d) 137 (Ont. CA), which is dealt with at 90-91.

B. Koskolos Realty

R v. A.N. Koskolos Realty Ltd.
(1995), 27 WCB (2d) 162 (NS Prov. Ct.)

OXNER J:

Introduction

A.N. Koskolos Realty Limited is charged that it did on or about the 6th of June, 1994, at, or near Halifax in the Province of Nova Scotia, being the owner of a property [in] Halifax, unlawfully permit the said premises to be unsightly, to wit: due to the manner in which the said building has been painted, after receipt on May 31, 1994, of a request to remove the unsightly condition, contrary to Section 363 (7) of the *Halifax City Charter*, SNS 1963, c. 52. ...

The issues to be determined by the Court are:

1. is the manner of painting the properties a violation of Section 363 of the *Halifax City Charter*, and
2. if so, does the *Halifax City Charter* thereby violate the *Canadian Charter of Rights and Freedoms*.

Evidence led by City witnesses ... established that the Defendant had these properties painted with a variety of colours. For instance, the evidence of the building inspector is that the paint on 1958 Robie Street included the colours red, blue, yellow, green, white, pink, mauve, purple and grey. The Crown witnesses all gave evidence that the paint was applied very sloppily "without rhyme or reason" and "haphazardly." In the words of witness Linda McAlpine, "some of it is done in zig zag, some of it is done in horizontal lines, some of the shingles are painted up to a certain point and some other colour takes on."

The buildings had been previously painted grey. They were repainted in the manner at issue shortly after City Council refused the Defendant's application for an amendment to the Municipal Development Plan to allow the construction of a high density apartment building on the property on which the subject houses are located. City Council refused the application for amendment despite a positive recommendation in the Defendant's favour by the Development and Planning staff of the City of Halifax.

Crown witnesses were of the view that the colouration and manner of application of the paint were acts of revenge by the Defendant for their successful opposition to its application to City Council. The Defence evidence contended that the acts were a political statement made to draw attention to the Defendant's unhappiness with the Council's decision and the process which allowed City Council to disregard the City staff's recommendation in its favour.

The facts of the colouration and uneven application of the paint are not in dispute. I accept the evidence of the Crown witnesses that they found the buildings, as repainted by the Defendant, to be in their opinion "unsightly." I accept they were of the honest opinion that the attention getting style of painting of the Koskolos Realty Limited properties detracted from their pride in their neighbourhood and their enjoyment of the view of their neighbourhood from their homes.

In my opinion, the Defendant had the buildings painted to attract attention to its dissatisfaction with the action of City Council and used this means in conjunction with a sign and media interviews to convey that dissatisfaction to the Halifax public. The properties, as painted, attracted public and media attention.

The Statute

The Crown submits that the City's authority for the present charge is pursuant to Section 363 (3) of the *Halifax City Charter*. The substantive Subsections are as follows:

"(1) The owner or occupier of a property shall keep the property free from any accumulation of wood shavings, paper, sawdust, dry and inflammable grass or weeds or other combustible material.

(2) No person shall permit any grass, bush or hedge located on property owned by that person to become *unsightly in relation to neighbouring properties*.

(3) *No person shall permit a property owned or occupied by that person to be unsightly* or in a state of disrepair, or shall permit to remain on any part of the property ashes, junk, rubbish, refuse, a derelict vehicle, or bodies or parts of, a vehicle, machine or equipment or dilapidated boat, or any thing of any nature whatsoever that by reason of being on the property causes the property to be unsightly or offensive.

(4) No person shall permit property owned by that person to be *unsightly in relation to neighbouring properties* by reason of the failure to maintain a walkway, driveway or parking area to the standard common to the neighbourhood.

(5) No person shall permit property owned by that person to be *unsightly in relation to the neighboring properties* by reason of lack of ground covering or other surfacing.

(6) No person shall permit a building owned by that person to become *unsightly in relation to neighbouring properties* by reason of the failure to maintain the exterior finish of the building." (emphasis added)

Reference may be made to the *Interpretation Act*, RSNS 1989, c. 235:

"9(5) Every enactment shall be deemed remedial and interpreted to insure the attainment of its objects by considering among other matters
  (a) the occasion and necessity for the enactment;
  (b) the circumstances existing at the time it was passed;
  (c) the mischief to be remedied;
  (d) the object to be attained;
  (e) the former law, including other enactments upon the same or similar subjects;
  (f) the consequences of a particular interpretation;
  (g) the history of legislation on the subject." ...

One ordinary principle of language is that the meaning of a word is influenced by the words with which it is associated. In the words of Mr. Justice A. Martin of the Ontario Court of Appeal in *R v. Goulis*, (1981), 33 OR (2d) 55:

"It is an ancient rule of statutory construction commonly expressed by the Latin maxim *"noscitur a sociis"* that the meaning of a doubtful word may be ascertained by reference to the meaning of words associated with it." ...

A reading of Section 363 shows that Subsection 1 deals with the accumulation of specific material. Subsections 2, 4, 5 and 6 deal with specific unsightly conditions in relation to neighbouring properties. Subsection 3, the one in issue, appears to include a prohibition against all unspecified unsightly conditions on property.

The *Shorter Oxford English Dictionary* defines "unsightly" as "unpleasing to look at; ugly." (It has a second meaning "applied to immaterial things ..." which is clearly not the meaning intended here.) Subsection 3, therefore, creates an offence of permitting property to be unsightly, unpleasing to look at or ugly. There is no further specific guidance as to the standard to be used to determine unsightliness or ugliness. Subsection 3 does not even provide the standard of "in relation to neighbouring properties" which limits the word "unsightly" when used elsewhere in Section 163. I think I may take into account the fact notorious in the community and within the knowledge of the average juror that beauty is a value judgement in the eye of the beholder and that what is "ugly" to one is often attractive to another.

This vague sweeping provision would give the City extraordinary powers in derogation of common law rights including the power to charge property owners or occupiers for using an unpopular colour of paint.

In my view, the use of the value judgement word "unsightly" in the context of Subsection 3 where it is found without any expressed standards to define or limit it causes an ambiguity in the meaning of the word that calls for the statutory interpretation aids referred to above. I agree with the Defence submission that the meaning of "unsightly" in Subsection 3 must be ascertained by reference to the words associated with it,—"a state of disrepair or the accumulation of physical debris." In my opinion, this would exclude the manner in which the properties are painted from the operation of the Statute. I would, therefore, enter an acquittal.

On the view I take of the law, it is not necessary for me to make a decision on the facts. I should mention that in my understanding any standard to be read into the provision if this is to be done, would be an objective one. This would put the burden on the City of proving beyond a reasonable doubt by the evidence of witnesses guided not by their subjective interests or aesthetic values, but by an objective City-wide standard that the subject properties are unsightly. [The discussion of Charter issues is omitted.]

NOTES AND QUESTIONS

1. If a person without legal training wished to order his or her affairs in accordance with s. 363(3) of the *Halifax City Charter*, could that person safely rely on the "plain meaning" of the word "unsightly"? Would a person consulting the statute need to be familiar with *noscitur a sociis* in order to understand the relevant language? Is this asking too much of the "typical reader," or does the maxim simply reflect the manner in which a typical reader will automatically read the text?

2. The word "unsightly" is an instance of vague language. Consider the "implications of vagueness" described at 126-38 of *Theory and Practice*. What was the legislator's purpose in employing the vague term "unsightly" in the *Halifax City Charter*? Why didn't the drafter specify every type of condition that could render a property "unsightly"?

3. If the *Halifax City Charter* prohibits "unsightly" property, and a court determines (as it appears to have determined, above) that a particular property *would* be considered unsightly by most people, should that not be enough for a conviction? Why or why not?

4. Is it likely that the authors of s. 363(3) intended the provision to be construed by reference to *noscitur a sociis*? Does a legislature have to be aware of a Latin maxim before we can safely apply it to a legislative text?

5. Is the court's decision in *Koskolos* an instance of originalist or dynamic interpretation?

6. Note that s. 9(5) of the Nova Scotia *Interpretation Act* (relied on in *Koskolos*) requires courts to determine a statute's purpose by reference to "the occasion and necessity for the enactment ... the circumstances existing at the time that it was passed ... the mischief to be remedied ... the object to be attained ... the former law, including other enactments upon the same or similar subjects ... the consequences of a particular interpretation [and] the history of legislation on the subject." Does the interpretive approach advocated by this *Interpretation Act* conform to the approaches developed by the courts in chapter 1?

7. Is the meaning of "unsightly" likely to remain static over time, or is it likely to evolve (like the term "indecent" in the *Mara* decision, discussed in chapter 1)? Is a maxim such as *noscitur a sociis* sufficiently flexible to allow the meaning of the word "unsightly" to change in accordance with evolving standards of beauty? Why or why not?

8. Does the use of maxims preclude or conflict with reliance on a statute's purpose as the key to statutory interpretation?

C. Gutierrez v. Ada

Gutierrez and Bordallo v. Ada and Camacho
528 US 250 (2000)

SOUTER J: The question here is whether the statute governing elections for Governor and Lieutenant Governor of the Territory of Guam compels a runoff election when a candidate slate has received a majority of the votes cast for Governor and Lieutenant Governor, but not a majority of the number of ballots cast in the simultaneous general election. We hold that the statute requires no runoff.

I

In the November 3, 1998, Guam general election, petitioners Carl T. C. Gutierrez and Madeleine Z. Bordallo were candidates running on one slate for Governor and Lieutenant Governor, opposed by the slate of respondents Joseph F. Ada and Felix P. Camacho. Gutierrez received 24,250 votes, as against 21,200 for Ada. *Ada v. Guam*, 179 F3d 672, 675 (CA9 1999); App. 16. One thousand and two hundred ninety-four voted for write-in candidates; 1,313 persons who cast ballots did not vote for either slate or any write-in candidate; and 609 voted for both slates. 179 F3d at 675; App. 16. The total number of ballots cast in the general election was thus 48,666, and the Gutierrez slate's votes represented 49.83 percent of that total. The Guam Election Commission certified the Gutierrez slate as the winner, finding it had received 51.21 percent of the vote, as calculated by deducting the 1,313 ballots left blank as to the gubernatorial election from the total number of ballots cast. 179 F3d at 675. Respondents Ada and Camacho sued in the United States District Court for a writ of mandamus ordering a runoff election, contending that Gutierrez and Bordallo had not received a majority of the votes cast, as required by the Organic Act of Guam, 64 Stat. 384, as amended, 48 USC § 1421 *et seq.* (1994 ed. and Supp. III).

So far as relevant, the Organic Act provides that:

> "the executive power of Guam shall be vested in an executive officer whose official title shall be the 'Governor of Guam.' The Governor of Guam, together with the Lieutenant Governor, shall be elected by a majority of the votes cast by the people who are qualified to vote for the members of the Legislature of Guam. The Governor and Lieutenant Governor shall be chosen jointly, by the casting by each voter of a single vote applicable to both offices. If no candidates receive a majority of the votes cast in any election, on the fourteenth day thereafter a runoff election shall be held between the candidates for Governor and Lieutenant Governor receiving the highest and second highest number of votes cast. The first election for Governor and Lieutenant Governor shall be held on November 3, 1970. Thereafter, beginning with the year 1974, the Governor and Lieutenant Governor shall be elected every four years at the general election. The Governor and Lieutenant Governor shall hold office for a term of four years and until their successors are elected and qualified." 48 USC § 1422.

Respondents' position boils down to the claim that the phrase "majority of the votes cast in any election" requires that a slate of candidates for Governor and Lieutenant

Governor receive a majority of the total number of ballots cast in the general election, regardless of the number of votes for all gubernatorial slates by those casting ballots. If this is the correct reading of the phrase, the parties agree that a runoff was required. If, however, the phrase refers only to votes cast for gubernatorial slates, no runoff was in order, and petitioners were elected Governor and Lieutenant Governor.

The United States District Court for the District of Guam read the statute to require a majority of the total number of voters casting ballots in the general election and so ruled that the Gutierrez slate had not received "a majority of the votes cast in any election." The court accordingly issued a writ of mandamus for a runoff election to be held on December 19, 1998, *Ada v. Guam*, No. Civ. 98-00066 (Dec. 9, 1998), App. to Pet. for Cert. A-25, A-55.

Although the Court of Appeals for the Ninth Circuit issued an emergency stay of the District Court's order pending appeal, 179 F3d at 676, it ultimately affirmed. The Court of Appeals understood the reference to "majority of the votes cast" as meaning "all votes cast at the general election, for Congress presumably would not have included the phrase 'in any election,' if it meant to refer only to the votes cast in the single election for governor and lieutenant governor." 179 F3d at 677. The court thought that any other reading would render the phrase "in any election" a "nullity." *Ibid.* The Court of Appeals also relied on a comparison of § 1422, with 48 USC § 1712, which provides that a candidate for Guam's Delegate to Congress must receive "a majority of the votes cast for the office of Delegate" in order to be elected. The Ninth Circuit reasoned that Congress could have used similar language of limitation if it had intended the election of a Governor and Lieutenant Governor to require only a majority of votes cast for gubernatorial slates. 179 F3d at 678. The Ninth Circuit stayed its mandate pending disposition of petitioners' petition for a writ of certiorari.

We granted certiorari ... to resolve a split between the Ninth Circuit's interpretation of the Organic Act of Guam and the Third Circuit's reading of identical language in the Revised Organic Act of the Virgin Islands. See 68 Stat. 503, as amended, 48 USC § 1591 (providing for a runoff election for Governor and Lieutenant Governor of the Virgin Islands "if no candidates receive a majority of the votes cast in any election"); *Todman v. Boschulte*, 694 F2d 939 (CA3 1982). We reverse.

II

The key to understanding what the phrase "in any election" means is also the most salient feature of the provision in which it occurs. The section contains six express references to an election for Governor and Lieutenant Governor: "The Governor of Guam, together with the Lieutenant Governor, shall be elected ..."; "the Governor and Lieutenant Governor shall be chosen jointly, by the casting by each voter of a single vote ..."; "a runoff election shall be held between the candidates for Governor and Lieutenant Governor ..."; "the first election for Governor and Lieutenant Governor shall be held ..."; "the Governor and Lieutenant Governor shall be elected every four years ..."; "the Governor and Lieutenant Governor shall hold office ... until their successors are elected. ..." 48 USC § 1422. The reference to "any election" is preceded by two references to gubernatorial election and followed by four. With "any election" so surrounded, what could it refer to except an election for Governor and Lieutenant Governor, the subject of such relentless repetition? To ask the question is merely to apply an interpretive rule as familiar outside the law as it is within, for words and people are known by their companions. See *Gustafson v. Alloyd Co.*, 513 US 561, 575, 131 L Ed. 2d 1, 115 S Ct. 1061 (1995) ("[A] word is known by the company it keeps"); *Jarecki v. G. D. Searle & Co.*, 367 US 303, 307, 6 L Ed. 2d 859, 81 S Ct. 1579 (1961) ("The maxim *noscitur a sociis*, ... while not an inescapable rule, is often wisely applied where a word is capable of many meanings in order to avoid the giving of unintended breadth to the Acts of Congress"). Cf. *Foster v. Love*, 522 US 67, 71, 139 L Ed. 2d 369, 118 S Ct. 464 (1997) ("When the federal statutes speak of 'the election' of a Senator or Representative, they plainly refer to the combined actions of voters and officials meant to make a final selection of an officeholder (subject only to the possibility of a later run-off...)").

Other clues confirm that Congress did not shift its attention when it used "any election" unadorned by a gubernatorial reference or other definite modifier. Later on in the same provision, Congress did vary the specific modifier when it spoke of the "general election" at which the gubernatorial election would occur; it is thus significant that Congress did not peg the majority-vote requirement to "votes cast in any [general] election." Congress would hardly have used "any election" to mean "general election," only to mention "general election" a few lines further on.

It would be equally odd to think that after repeatedly using "votes" or "vote" to mean an expression of choice for the gubernatorial slate, Congress suddenly used "votes cast in any election" to mean "ballots cast." And yet that is just what would be required if we were to treat the phrase respondents' way, for they read "votes cast in any election" as referring to "ballots containing a vote for any office." Surely a Congress that meant to refer to ballots, midway through a statute repeatedly referring to "votes" for gubernatorial slates, would have said "ballots." To argue otherwise is to tag Congress with an extravagant preference for the opaque when the use of a clear adjective or noun would have worked nicely. But even aside from that, Congress has shown that it recognizes the difference between ballots and votes in the very context of Guamanian elections. From 1972 until 1998, 48 USC § 1712 expressly required that the Guam Delegate be elected "by separate ballot and by a majority of the votes cast for the office of Delegate." There is simply no reason to think that Congress meant "ballots" when it said "votes" in § 1422.

To accept respondents' reading would also impute to the Congress a strange preference for making it hard to select a Governor. On respondents' reading the statute could require a runoff (as it would in this case) even though one slate already had a majority of all those who cared to make any choice among gubernatorial candidates. Respondents try to counter the unreality of their position by emphasizing state cases holding that passing a referendum requires a majority of voters going to the polls, not a mere majority of persons voting on a particular referendum issue. Cf. *Allen v. Burkhart*, 377 P2d 821 (Okla. 1963); *Thurston County Farm Bureau v. Thurston County*, 136 Neb. 575, 287 NW 180 (1939); *Missouri v. Winkelmeier*, 35 Mo. 103 (1864). But there is no uniform rule, see, *e.g.*, *Wooley v. Sterrett*, 387 SW 2d 734, 739-740 (Tex. Civ. App. 1965); *Munce v. O'Hara*, 340 Pa. 209, 16 A2d 532

(1940); *State ex rel. Short v. Clausen*, 72 Wash. 409, 130 P 479 (1913), and even if there were, treatment of referendums would not be a plausible model for elections of officials. Referendums are exceptions to the normal legislative process, and passage of a referendum is not itself essential to the functioning of government. If a ballot-majority requirement makes it impossible to pass a referendum measure, nothing need be done except record the failure. The same requirement to elect an official, on the other hand, would necessitate further action, the trouble and expense of which would not make any apparent sense when those who expressed any preference among candidates had already given a majority to one of them.

As a final confirmation of the obvious reading, we note that requiring a majority of the total number of voters on election day would be in some tension with § 1422a, which provides for recall elections for Governor and Lieutenant Governor. Section 1422a(b) provides that "any Governor, Lieutenant Governor, or member of the legislature of Guam may be removed from office by a referendum election in which at least two-thirds of the number of persons voting for such official in the last preceding general election at which such official was elected vote in favor of recall and in which those so voting constitute a majority of all those participating in such referendum election." The recall provision thus looks to the total number of persons who actually voted for Governor, not the total number who went to the polls. In a rational world, we would not expect the vote required to oust a Governor to be pegged to a lower number than it would take to elect one.

If all these considerations confirm the reading according to the rule of meaning by association, respondents nevertheless emphasize two considerations said to point the other way. First, as we noted before, § 1712 includes a specific statement that "a majority of the votes cast for the office of Delegate" is necessary and presumably sufficient to elect a Delegate. Without a comparably clear modifier in § 1422 referring to votes sufficient to elect gubernatorial slates, respondents argue, "a majority of the votes cast in any election" must refer to a majority of all those voting for any office. But the drafting difference supports no such inference. Congress adopted the language in § 1712 four years after enacting the phrase at issue in this case, and there is no affirmative indication in § 1712 that Congress gave any thought to differentiating the terms of Delegate and gubernatorial elections. Hence, as we have said before, later laws that "do not seek to clarify an earlier enacted general term" and "do not depend for their effectiveness upon clarification, or a change in the meaning of an earlier statute," are "beside the point" in reading the first enactment. *Almendarez-Torres v. United States*, 523 US 224, 237, 140 L Ed. 2d 350, 118 S Ct. 1219 (1998). Congress may have spoken with explicit clarity when it passed § 1712, but we can say no more than that.

The second argument supposedly undermining the meaning naturally suggested by association was stressed by the Court of Appeals, which thought that reading "any election" to mean gubernatorial election would render the phrase a nullity and thus offend the rule against attributing redundancy to Congress, see *Kungys v. United States*, 485 US 759, 778, 99 L Ed. 2d 839, 108 S Ct. 1537 (1988). The fact is that this argument has some force, but not enough. There is no question that the statute would be read as we read it even if the phrase were missing. But as one rule of construction among many, albeit an important one, the rule against redundancy does not necessarily have the strength to turn a tide of good cause to come out the other way. Besides, there is even a reason for thinking the phrase in question has some clarifying value. Section 1422 provides specifically for an initial gubernatorial election in 1970, and generally for successive elections every four years thereafter. "Any election," therefore may be read to make it clear that the runoff requirement applies equally to the initial election and to those periodically scheduled in the future. That may not be very heavy work for the phrase to perform, but a job is a job, and enough to bar the rule against redundancy from disqualifying an otherwise sensible reading.

The judgment of the Court of Appeals is reversed, and the case is remanded for proceedings consistent with this opinion.

It is so ordered.

NOTES AND QUESTIONS

1. Did Gutierrez and Bordallo receive a "majority of the votes cast in [the] election," as is required by the *Organic Act*? Since Gutierrez received only 49.83 percent of the votes cast in the general election, must one give an unusual reading to the word "majority" in order to declare Gutierrez the winner by "majority vote"?

2. The court in *Gutierrez* makes it clear that it is attempting to determine what Congress meant (that is, the intention of the enacting body) when enacting the *Organic Act* of Guam. The court employs *noscitur a sociis* to discover this meaning. Does this imply that, generally speaking, *noscitur a sociis* is an "originalist" tool?

3. Note the court's use of consequential analysis. According to the court:

> To accept respondents' reading would also impute to the Congress a strange preference for making it hard to select a Governor. On respondents' reading the statute could require a runoff (as it would in this case) even though one slate already had a majority of all those who cared to make any choice among gubernatorial candidates.

Does it matter that a particular interpretation of a law would give rise to "strange" consequences? Is Congress prohibited from enacting strange laws? If not, why would the court pay attention to the consequences of a particular reading of statutory text? This form of consequential analysis is discussed in greater detail in chapter 3, section II, under the heading "The Literal Rule and the Golden Rule."

4. The court in *Gutierrez* notes that its reading of the *Organic Act* might deprive the words "any election" of any purpose in the provision. According to the court, this offends "the rule against attributing redundancy to Congress." This presumption is also known as the "no extraneous words" rule, and is dealt with at 92-97 of *Theory and Practice*. See also the notes and questions following the *Boisbriand* decision in chapter 1 of this text.

III. EJUSDEM GENERIS

A. Introduction

Ejusdem generis is a specialized form of *noscitur a sociis*. This specialized version of *noscitur* applies wherever a list of specific items is accompanied by general words that embrace those specific items. Consider the phrase "pens, paper, paper clips, and other office supplies." In this example, the words "pens, paper, and paper clips" are a specific list, and the words "other office supplies" are general words that embrace those specific items (in other words, pens, paper, and paper clips are all specific kinds of "office supplies"). When *ejusdem generis* applies, it counsels the reader not to interpret the general words in their broadest possible sense, but instead to "read them down" or "construe them narrowly" such that they embrace only items that are *similar in nature* to the specifically listed items. Thus, in a provision dealing with "pens, paper, paper clips, and other office supplies," the phrase "office supplies" should be read down to include items that are similar in nature to pens, paper, and paper clips. Pencils, staples, and "sticky notes" would probably be included, but computers, chairs, and desks would probably not. While desks and computers may *sometimes* qualify as "office supplies" (in that they are each "supplied" to one's "office"), the term "office supplies," when associated with the words "pens, paper, and paper clips," must be understood more narrowly, such that it excludes any items that have very little in common with the specifically listed items.

The application and rationale of *ejusdem generis* (together with several critiques of that maxim) are explained at 91-98 of *Theory and Practice*. Students should review that portion of *Theory and Practice* before continuing with the cases in this section.

B. Nanaimo v. Rascal Trucking

Nanaimo (City) v. Rascal Trucking Ltd.
[2000] 1 SCR 342

MAJOR J: This appeal engages an interpretation of s. 936 of the *Municipal Act*, RSBC 1979, c. 290 (now RSBC 1996, c. 323, s. 727). As well, it raises the standard of judicial review applicable to municipal bodies, previously visited by this Court in *Shell Canada Products Ltd. v. Vancouver (City)*, [1994] 1 SCR 231.

I. Factual Background

The respondent, Rascal Trucking Ltd. ("Rascal"), leased a parcel of land located within the City of Nanaimo ("Nanaimo" or the "City") from Kismet Enterprises Inc. ("Kismet"). In April 1996, Rascal applied for and received a permit from the appellant Nanaimo to deposit approximately 15,000 cubic yards of soil on its site with the intent to conduct soil processing operations, an activity permitted by the applicable zoning classification.

Shortly after Rascal started delivering soil to the site, neighbouring residents raised complaints about dust and noise emissions. A city inspector inspected the site and recommended that an order be issued compelling the owner to remove the pile of soil.

On July 3, 1996, Nanaimo held a public meeting where it heard from local residents and the respondent. It received a professional engineer's report analysing the noise emissions from the property, and an opinion from its legal counsel. The Nanaimo council deliberated and ultimately passed a resolution declaring the pile of soil a nuisance pursuant to s. 936 of the *Municipal Act*, and ordered Kismet to remove it within 30 days. It did not comply.

On August 19, 1996, Nanaimo passed a second resolution ordering the respondent to remove the topsoil within 15 days, in default of which it would be removed by the City at the respondent's or owner's cost. Neither the owner Kismet nor the respondent Rascal obeyed. On September 6, 1996, Rascal denied access for removal purposes to agents of the City.

These events precipitated two applications before the Supreme Court of British Columbia. Nanaimo brought the first, asking for a declaration that it was entitled to access the property and remove the offending pile of soil. Maczko J granted the petition on the basis that Nanaimo had the jurisdiction both to declare the dirt pile a nuisance and order its removal.

Kismet and Rascal brought the second petition, requesting that the resolutions be quashed. Rowan J dismissed the petition.

The British Columbia Court of Appeal allowed Rascal's appeal, set aside the orders and quashed the July 3rd and August 19th resolutions: (1998), 49 BCLR (3d) 164.

II. Relevant Statutory Provisions

Municipal Act, RSBC 1979, c. 290 ...

> Removal of dangerous erections
>
> 936(1) The council may declare a building, structure or erection of any kind, or a drain, ditch, watercourse, pond, surface water or other matter or thing, in or on private land or a highway, or in or about a building or structure, a nuisance, and may direct and order that it be removed, pulled down, filled up or otherwise dealt with by its owner, agent, lessee or occupier, as the council may determine and within the time after service of the order that may be named in it. ...

V. Analysis

(1) *Did s. 936 of the Municipal Act Empower the Appellant to Pass the Resolutions Declaring the Pile of Soil a Nuisance and Ordering Its Removal?*

Nanaimo relied upon s. 936 of the *Municipal Act* as its authority to declare Rascal's pile of soil a nuisance and to order its removal. The appellant submitted that a "broad and benevolent" rule of statutory construction be adopted in ascertaining its jurisdiction under s. 936 rather than the narrow view adopted by the Court of Appeal. Nanaimo argued that s. 936's reference to "or other matter or thing" cannot be limited to the genus of constructed things and watercourses preceding it. To the contrary, Nanaimo said this phrase is meant to stand alone and apart from the preceding items. Therefore, the power to declare "other matter or thing" a nuisance referred to the municipality's jurisdiction to abate nuisances and health hazards generally.

In support of this conclusion Nanaimo pointed out that prior to the 1979 revision of the *Municipal Act*, the predecessor equivalent of s. 936 (*Municipal Act*, RSBC

1960, c. 255, s. 873) contained an additional comma prior to "or other matter or thing," which it was argued was included to set this phrase off as a stand alone grant of general power. Although this comma was removed in the 1979 revision, Nanaimo claims s. 8 of the *Statute Revision Act* required the Court to interpret s. 936 as if the comma remained, should the inclusion of a comma have the substantive effect of setting off this phrase as a general grant of jurisdiction over nuisances.

The respondent argued that this Court should not subscribe a priori to either a benevolent or strict approach, but rather seek to discern the "true intent" of s. 936. In the respondent's submission, such an analysis, aided by the *ejusdem generis* or limited class rule, forces the conclusion that s. 936 empowered Nanaimo to address only two classes of potential nuisance—constructed things and things associated with the handling, transit, or storage of water. To ascribe greater meaning to the phrase "or other matter or thing" it was said would run contrary to the intent of listing specific items before it, as well as deprive those words of meaning. In light of the specific items enumerated, the respondent company said it would be anomalous to conclude that reference to "or other matter or thing" permits a municipality to, in effect, declare anything to be a nuisance.

The first step is to consider the approach the courts should take when construing municipal legislation. As noted by Iacobucci J in *R v. Sharma*, [1993] 1 SCR 650, at p. 668:

> "... as statutory bodies, municipalities 'may exercise only those powers expressly conferred by statute, those powers necessarily or fairly implied by the expressed power in the statute, and those indispensable powers essential and not merely convenient to the effectuation of the purposes of the corporation.'"

The process of delineating municipal jurisdiction is an exercise in statutory construction. There is ample authority, on the interpretation of statutes generally and of municipal statutes specifically, to support a broad and purposive approach.

While *R v. Greenbaum*, [1993] 1 SCR 674, favoured restricting a municipality's jurisdiction to those powers expressly conferred upon it by the legislature, the Court noted that a purposive interpretation should be used in determining what the scope of those powers are. ...

This conclusion follows recent authorities dictating that statutes be construed purposively in their entire context and in light of the scheme of the Act as a whole with a view to ascertaining the legislature's true intent. See *Rizzo & Rizzo Shoes Ltd. (Re)*, [1998] 1 SCR 27, at paras. 21-23, *M & D Farm Ltd. v. Manitoba Agricultural Credit Corp.*, [1999] 2 SCR 961, at para. 25, and the BC *Interpretation Act*, s. 8.

It is my opinion that the legislature, by including the phrase "or other matter or thing," did not intend to expand the scope of s. 936 to allow municipalities to declare almost anything to be a nuisance. I accept the respondent's submission that to construe that phrase as creating a third class of potential nuisance would effectively negate the purpose of including rather specific preceding language.

The phrase "or other matter or thing" extends the two classes of nuisances outlined before it, that is constructed or erected things, and watercourses. This interpretation follows from both a purposive interpretation and the application of the *ejusdem generis*

limited class rule. It is not reasonable to believe that the legislature intended to subscribe such importance to the missing comma, namely that such minor punctuation
should render null the specific items listed before. ...

The fact that s. 936 empowers municipalities to declare only two classes of thing
to be a nuisance does not foreclose the possibility that a pile of soil may fall within
one of those categories. It is clear that a pile of soil does not fall within any of the
water-related items constituting the second class. However, does a pile of soil fall
within the first class of constructed or erected things? Specifically, does it fall within
the phrase "building, structure or erection of any kind"? I conclude that it does. A pile
of soil does not materialize on its own. It must at least be erected presumably by
piling or dumping. As well, a pile of soil clearly may be a "hazardous erection" within
the wording of s. 936's heading, either in the sense of reducing air quality through
dust pollution, or by posing a serious risk to curious children.

Rizzo & Rizzo Shoes, supra, at para. 27, noted "it is a well established principle of
statutory interpretation that the legislature does not intend to produce absurd consequences." In this sense, an absurdity would result if s. 936 did not extend to a pile of
soil. It would mean a building, structure or pond could be declared a nuisance, but the
soil excavated to create them could not.

It is my opinion that s. 936 empowered the appellant to issue resolutions declaring
Rascal's pile of soil a nuisance and ordering its removal. ...

NOTES AND QUESTIONS

1. Does the court's application of *ejusdem generis* in the *Rascal Trucking* decision
accord with the presumption of "no extraneous words"? Why or why not?

2. Does the application of a Latin maxim accord with the "broad and purposive
approach" advocated by Major J in his decision?

3. Do you agree with Major J's contention that a pile of dirt may constitute a "dangerous
erection," given the two classes of nuisances suggested by *ejusdem generis*?

4. Note that Major J repeatedly refers to *ejusdem generis* as the "limited class rule." It
is important to bear in mind that, by whichever name it is known, *ejusdem generis* is not,
in fact, a "rule." A court is never bound to apply *ejusdem generis*: it is simply one method
of analysis designed to reveal interpretive possibilities within a piece of legislation.

5. Is the linguistic problem at issue in *Rascal Trucking* attributable to vagueness,
ambiguity, subtext, or analogy (as those terms are defined in chapters 4 and 5 of *Theory
and Practice*)? Is it possible to determine the legislator's reason for employing the
drafting pattern that is exhibited in this case?

6. Major J notes that it would be "absurd" if a pile of dirt could not be declared a
nuisance. Is this persuasive? Given that the heading above the relevant section is "removal
of dangerous erections," is it "absurd" to presume that the legislature did not think of a
dirt pile as an "erection"?

7. What was the "typical case" envisioned by legislative drafters when they enacted
the words "erection of any kind"? Did they envision dirt piles? If not, can it be said that a pile
of dirt comes within the "legislature's intention"? Does it matter that the drafters *would
have* intended to catch dirt piles (and may have amended the language accordingly) if the
potential hazard of dirt piles had been drawn to their attention?

C. Circuit City Stores v. Saint Clair Adams

Circuit City Stores, Inc. v. Saint Clair Adams
532 US 105 (2001)

KENNEDY J: Section 1 of the Federal Arbitration Act (FAA) excludes from the Act's coverage "contracts of employment of seamen, railroad employees, or any other class of workers engaged in foreign or interstate commerce." 9 USC § 1. All but one of the Courts of Appeals which have addressed the issue interpret this provision as exempting contracts of employment of transportation workers, but not other employment contracts, from the FAA's coverage. A different interpretation has been adopted by the Court of Appeals for the Ninth Circuit, which construes the exemption so that all contracts of employment are beyond the FAA's reach, whether or not the worker is engaged in transportation. It applied that rule to the instant case. We now decide that the better interpretation is to construe the statute, as most of the Courts of Appeals have done, to confine the exemption to transportation workers.

I

In October 1995, respondent Saint Clair Adams applied for a job at petitioner Circuit City Stores, Inc., a national retailer of consumer electronics. Adams signed an employment application which included the following provision:

> "I agree that I will settle any and all previously unasserted claims, disputes or controversies arising out of or relating to my application or candidacy for employment, employment and/or cessation of employment with Circuit City, *exclusively* by final and binding *arbitration* before a neutral Arbitrator. By way of example only, such claims include claims under federal, state, and local statutory or common law, such as the Age Discrimination in Employment Act, Title VII of the Civil Rights Act of 1964, as amended, including the amendments of the Civil Rights Act of 1991, the Americans with Disabilities Act, the law of contract and the law of tort." App. 13 (emphasis in original).

Adams was hired as a sales counselor in Circuit City's store in Santa Rosa, California.

Two years later, Adams filed an employment discrimination lawsuit against Circuit City in state court, asserting claims under California's Fair Employment and Housing Act, Cal. Govt. Code Ann. § 12900 *et seq.* (West 1992 and Supp. 1997), and other claims based on general tort theories under California law. Circuit City filed suit in the United States District Court for the Northern District of California, seeking to enjoin the state-court action and to compel arbitration of respondent's claims pursuant to the FAA, 9 USC §§ 1-16. The District Court entered the requested order. Respondent, the court concluded, was obligated by the arbitration agreement to submit his claims against the employer to binding arbitration. An appeal followed.

While respondent's appeal was pending in the Court of Appeals for the Ninth Circuit, the court ruled on the key issue in an unrelated case. The court held the FAA does not apply to contracts of employment. See *Craft v. Campbell Soup Co.*, 177 F3d 1083 (1999). In the instant case, following the rule announced in *Craft*, the Court of Appeals held the arbitration agreement between Adams and Circuit City was contained in a "contract of employment," and so was not subject to the FAA. 194 F3d 1070 (1999). Circuit City petitioned this Court, noting that the Ninth Circuit's conclusion that all employment contracts are excluded from the FAA conflicts with every other Court of Appeals to have addressed the question [citations omitted].

II

A

Congress enacted the FAA in 1925. As the Court has explained, the FAA was a response to hostility of American courts to the enforcement of arbitration agreements, a judicial disposition inherited from then-longstanding English practice. ... To give effect to this purpose, the FAA compels judicial enforcement of a wide range of written arbitration agreements. ...

The instant case, of course, involves not the basic coverage authorization under § 2 of the Act, but the exemption from coverage under § 1. The exemption clause provides the Act shall not apply "to contracts of employment of seamen, railroad employees, or any other class of workers engaged in foreign or interstate commerce." 9 USC § 1. Most Courts of Appeals conclude the exclusion provision is limited to transportation workers, defined, for instance, as those workers "actually engaged in the movement of goods in interstate commerce." *Cole, supra*, at 1471. As we stated at the outset, the Court of Appeals for the Ninth Circuit takes a different view and interprets the § 1 exception to exclude all contracts of employment from the reach of the FAA. ...

B

...

Respondent, endorsing the reasoning of the Court of Appeals for the Ninth Circuit that the provision excludes all employment contracts, relies on the asserted breadth of the words "contracts of employment of ... any other class of workers engaged in ... commerce." Referring to our construction of § 2's coverage provision in *Allied-Bruce*—concluding that the words "involving commerce" evidence the congressional intent to regulate to the full extent of its commerce power—respondent contends § 1's interpretation should have a like reach, thus exempting all employment contracts. The two provisions, it is argued, are coterminous; under this view the "involving commerce" provision brings within the FAA's scope all contracts within the Congress' commerce power, and the "engaged in ... commerce" language in § 1 in turn exempts from the FAA all employment contracts falling within that authority.

This reading of § 1, however, runs into an immediate and, in our view, insurmountable textual obstacle. Unlike the "involving commerce" language in § 2, the words "any other class of workers engaged in ... commerce" constitute a residual phrase, following, in the same sentence, explicit reference to "seamen" and "railroad employees." Construing the residual phrase to exclude all employment contracts fails to give independent effect to the statute's enumeration of the specific categories of workers which precedes it; there would be no need for Congress to use the phrases "seamen" and "railroad employees" if those same classes of workers were subsumed within the meaning of the "engaged in … commerce" residual clause. The wording of § 1 calls for the application of the maxim *ejusdem generis*, the statutory canon that "where general words follow specific words in a statutory enumeration, the general words are construed to embrace only objects similar in nature to those objects enumerated by the preceding specific words." N. Singer, *Sutherland on Statutes and Statutory Construction* § 47.17 (1991); see also *Norfolk & Western R Co. v. Train Dispatchers*, 499 US 117, 129, 113 L Ed. 2d 95, 111 S Ct. 1156 (1991). Under this rule of construction the residual clause should be read to give effect to the terms "seamen" and "railroad employees," and should itself be controlled and defined by reference to the enumerated categories of workers which are recited just before it; the interpretation of the clause pressed by respondent fails to produce these results.

Canons of construction need not be conclusive and are often countered, of course, by some maxim pointing in a different direction. The application of the rule *ejusdem generis* in this case, however, is in full accord with other sound considerations bearing upon the proper interpretation of the clause. For even if the term "engaged in commerce" stood alone in § 1, we would not construe the provision to exclude all contracts of employment from the FAA. Congress uses different modifiers to the word "commerce" in the design and enactment of its statutes. The phrase "affecting commerce" indicates Congress' intent to regulate to the outer limits of its authority under the Commerce Clause. See, *e.g.*, *Allied-Bruce*, 513 US at 277. The "involving commerce" phrase, the operative words for the reach of the basic coverage provision in § 2, was at issue in *Allied-Bruce*. That particular phrase had not been interpreted before by this Court. Considering the usual meaning of the word "involving," and the pro-arbitration purposes of the FAA, *Allied-Bruce* held the "word 'involving,' like 'affecting,' signals an intent to exercise Congress' commerce power to the full." *Ibid*. Unlike those phrases, however, the general words "in commerce" and the specific phrase "engaged in commerce" are understood to have a more limited reach. In *Allied-Bruce* itself the Court said the words "in commerce" are "often-found words of art" that we have not read as expressing congressional intent to regulate to the outer limits of authority under the Commerce Clause. *Id.* at 273; see also *United States v. American Building Maintenance Industries*, 422 US 271, 279-280, 45 L Ed. 2d 177, 95 S Ct. 2150 (1975) (the phrase "engaged in commerce" is "a term of art, indicating a limited assertion of federal jurisdiction"); *Jones v. United States*, 529 US 848, 855, 146 L Ed. 2d 902, 120 S Ct. 1904 (2000) (phrase "used in commerce" "is most sensibly read to mean active employment for commercial purposes, and not merely a passive, passing, or past connection to commerce"). …

In sum, the text of the FAA forecloses the construction of § 1 followed by the Court of Appeals in the case under review, a construction which would exclude all employment contracts from the FAA. While the historical arguments respecting Congress' understanding of its power in 1925 are not insubstantial, this fact alone does not give us basis to adopt, "by judicial decision rather than amendatory legislation," *Gulf Oil, supra*, at 202, an expansive construction of the FAA's exclusion provision that goes beyond the meaning of the words Congress used. While it is of course

possible to speculate that Congress might have chosen a different jurisdictional formulation had it known that the Court would soon embrace a less restrictive reading
of the Commerce Clause, the text of § 1 precludes interpreting the exclusion provision
to defeat the language of § 2 as to all employment contracts. Section 1 exempts from
the FAA only contracts of employment of transportation workers. ... As the conclusion
we reach today is directed by the text of § 1, we need not assess the legislative history
of the exclusion provision. See *Ratzlaf v. United States*, 510 US 135, 147-148, 126
L Ed. 2d 615, 114 S Ct. 655 (1994) ("We do not resort to legislative history to cloud a
statutory text that is clear"). ...

NOTES AND QUESTIONS

1. Does the court's interpretation of the phrase "any other class of workers" comply
with the "no extraneous words" principle? Note that the court explicitly addresses this
problem. According to the court:

> Construing the residual phrase to exclude all employment contracts fails to give independent
> effect to the statute's enumeration of the specific categories of workers which precedes it;
> there would be no need for Congress to use the phrases "seamen" and "railroad employees" if
> those same classes of workers were subsumed within the meaning of the "engaged in ...
> commerce" residual clause.

2. Like the Supreme Court of Canada in *Rascal Trucking*, the United States Supreme
Court refers to *ejusdem generis* as a "rule of construction." As noted above, *ejusdem
generis* should not be regarded as a mandatory "rule," despite any judicial dicta to the
contrary. As chapter 3 of *Theory and Practice* points out, there are as many cases
refusing to apply these so-called rules as there are cases that actually apply them. The
court in *Circuit City* acknowledges this when it states that "[c]anons of construction need
not be conclusive and are often countered, of course, by some maxim pointing in a
different direction."

3. What if the statute at issue in *Circuit City*, instead of applying to "seamen,
railroad employees, or any other ... workers" applied to "seamen, airline employees,
employees working in overland transport, or any other workers"? In the new formulation of the section, *all* employees in the transportation industry are apparently caught
by the specific list of items (that is, seamen, airline employees, and employees working
in overland transport). If there were no additional types of transportation employees
beyond those listed in the language of the section, would it still be possible to construe
"any other workers" as referring only to "transportation employees"? The answer is no:
if the only genus suggested by a specific list of items is completely exhausted by the
items mentioned in the list, any general words accompanying that list cannot be
narrowed by reference to the *ejusdem generis* maxim. This exception to *ejusdem
generis*, known as the "exhausting the genus" exception, is discussed at 96-97 of
Theory and Practice. It is also the topic of *Grini v. Grini*, which is discussed in the next
section of this chapter.

D. Grini v. Grini

Grini v. Grini
(1969), 5 DLR (3d) 640 (Man. QB)

WILSON, J: The parties were married at Winnipeg on April 18, 1942, and separated by agreement about mid-June, 1958. There was one child, a daughter Corolie born March 30, 1952, and so over the age of 16 years when these proceedings for divorce were begun in July, 1968. Petitioner rests his case on s. 4(1)(e) of the *Divorce Act*, 1967-68 (Can.), c. 24, namely, their separation for at least three years.

In fact, they have been apart for almost 11 years, and certainly there has been a permanent breakdown of the marriage. Petitioner wishes to marry someone else with whom, quite obviously, he has been acquainted for several years; respondent says that as husband and father, petitioner was never better than a failure. Throughout the hearing she stared at him with a look of keen dislike, and her evidence was given in a hostile tone.

Respondent, however, protests that dissolution of the marriage will prejudicially affect the making of reasonable arrangements for maintenance of their daughter, and would be unduly harsh or unjust to the respondent herself, whereby the decree ought to be refused, and she points to s. 9(1)(e) and (f) of the Act. The crux of the matter is the separation agreement, ex. 4, executed when they parted in June, 1958.

That agreement was signed by way of compromise of differences then about to be aired in Court following the laying of an information by the respondent, in which she alleged persistent cruelty and desertion by the petitioner. By para. 2(g) of the agreement, petitioner specifically maintained his denial of such complaints and reserved the right to test their validity in the event of further proceedings in any Court.

To the extent the case before me was intended to be a definition of the guilty party, I can only say that, hearing only the parties themselves, I am unable to say which of them was chiefly at fault so many years ago. They were married during the war, the husband went overseas shortly afterwards, and he was away four years. Each of them says the other changed for the worse during that interval, so that the resumed cohabitation after the war was unhappy, and that as the years went by these changes worsened to the point of utter exasperation and loss of affection.

Although married in wartime, theirs was not a whirlwind affair; they had been going together for a year or more and ought to have known each other's nature and interests. Perhaps theirs was, like many others, a case of a wife who expected that marriage would change the husband, and he expecting it would not change the wife, so that both were disappointed. The extent of give and take needed to save their marriage at the time cannot now be fixed; in all likelihood both were at fault in allowing their differences to spread and become an irreconcilable and continuous quarrel.

By their agreement, Corolie was to remain with the respondent, and petitioner was to pay for their joint maintenance and support $175 per month *"while the marriage subsists*" (my italics). In fact, he has been paying $200. But while seemingly he would like to assist his daughter, petitioner insists on his right to terminate payments in any amount to the respondent, should the divorce be granted; at the same time, he denies any legal obligation to maintain Corolie, who, he says, is not a child of the marriage within the meaning of s. 2(b) of the Act. ...

What of Corolie? Now aged 17, she is in good health and is taking a commercial course (grade 11) in public school. Respondent expects she will pass her June examinations and hopes she will be able to find employment at a salary level and with prospects for advancement such as will persuade her to accept this as a career. Else, she says, Corolie would like to attend business college for a year to better her opportunities for employment. ...

Before any award can be made in Corolie's favour under the *Divorce Act*, however (and that is the case before me), she must come within s. 2(b)(ii) of the *Divorce Act* as being unable "by reason of illness, disability or other cause," to withdraw herself from parental charge or provide herself with the necessaries of life. ...

On the face of it, Corolie's attendance at school is sufficient explanation and reason for her inability to support herself. And while under the *Public Schools Act*, RSM 1954, c. 215, of this Province, the "school leaving age" is 16 years, by s. 237 the right to attend free public school extends to everyone between the ages of six and 21 years. Indeed, unless we are to ignore the exhortations of teachers, school boards, and provincial and federal departments of Government alike as being insincere, the pattern of today's society is that every boy or girl who reasonably can, ought to continue in school beyond the 16 year age level. And, particular cases apart, while attending school students are unable to provide their own "necessaries of life," a phrase which must embrace shelter, food, clothing and school supplies, which last may well include something for recreation.

However that may be, says petitioner, because of the *ejusdem generis* rule, s. 2(b)(ii) of the *Divorce Act* may not be interpreted to authorize an award of maintenance for a child of the full age of sixteen years simply because that child is attending school. If that is correct, the education of many a child whose attendance at school depends absolutely upon the receipt of maintenance will be cut off in mid-term because of the unfortunate accident of a sixteenth birthday. I find it hard to believe that is what Parliament intended.

The *ejusdem generis* rule (or principle of construction) as it is described in *Craies on Statute Law*, 6th ed., p. 179, requires that where in a statute there are general words following particular and specific words, the general words must be confined to things of the same kind as those specified; and see *Maxwell on Interpretation of Statutes*, 11th ed., p. 327, and Odgers, *Construction of Deeds and Statutes*, 5th ed., p. 184. For the rule to apply there must of course be a genus, or group of associated expressions, the general nature of which is spelled out by the particular or specific words which in fact appear in the legislation under review.

And here, urges plaintiff's counsel, the phrase "other cause" where this appears in the expression "by reason of illness, disability or other cause" in s. 2(b)(ii) is to be restricted to causes akin to illness or disability.

For the lawyer, of course, "disability" may refer to the absence of legal capacity to do certain acts or enjoy certain benefits, such as disability, to sue, to enter into contracts, to alienate property, etc. As used in the above context, however, the word must be given its other meaning, which refers rather to want of physical or mental ability, either native or by reason of intervening cause; and see s. 4(1)(d) of the Act, which speaks of non-consummation of a marriage "by reason of illness or disability."

There, the expression "illness or disability" imports the notion of personal incapacity, the physical inability of the respondent to consummate the marriage, willingness apart. The phrase exhaustively describes the situation, and to extend the expression to include the phrase "or other cause" would add nothing more. Had Parliament, in s. 4(1)(d), adopted the expression "illness, disability, or other cause," the last phrase would have been redundant. Likewise in s. 2(b)(ii), the inability of a child to support himself by his own efforts due to incapacity arising from physical or mental shortcoming is sufficiently expressed as one caused by illness or disability. What other physical or mental disablement might there be, pray, which that phrase would not embrace?

And where—as I believe to be here the case—the particular words exhaust the whole genus, the general words which follow must refer to some larger genus and are not to be construed as restrictive, and see Odgers, *Principles of Pleading and Practice*, 19th ed., p. 188; *Fenwick v. Schmalz* (1868), LR 3 CP 313, Willes, J, at p. 315; *R v. Morris*, [1923] 1 DLR 541, 38 CCC 370, 56 NSR 1, Rogers, J, p. 544; *City of Calgary v. Reed and Vincent* (1959), 17 DLR (2d) 198, 27 WWR 193, Johnson, JA, p. 214 DLR.

It is, after all, a question of the presumed intention of the statute, something emphasized by each of the learned authors mentioned above. In *Allen v. Emmerson*, [1944] KB 362 at p. 367, Asquith, J, said that the tendency of the more modern authorities is to attenuate the application of the rule, and he referred to *Anderson v. Anderson*, [1895] 1 QB 749, where at p. 753, Esher, MR, said:

> Nothing can well be plainer than that to shew that *prima facie* general words are to be taken in their larger sense, unless you can find that in the particular case the true construction of the instrument requires you to conclude that they are intended to be used in a sense limited to things *ejusdem generis* with those which have been specifically mentioned before.

And more recently in *Chandris v. Isbrandsten-Moller Co. Inc.*, [1951] 1 KB 240 at p. 244, Devlin, J, said:

> The *ejusdem generis* rule means that there is implied into the language which the parties have used words of restriction which are not there. It cannot be right to approach a document with the presumption that there should be such an implication.

And so, I reject the notion that I may not consider attendance at school as a reason whereby a child, issue of the parties to divorce proceedings, may properly look to a parent for maintenance even though that child be of the full age of 16 years. In every case, of course, the decision to award or deny maintenance must depend on all the circumstances of the case, no less the ability of the concerned student to benefit from the education in question than the ability of the parent to bear the expense of the award demanded. ... In the result, there will be a decree of divorce, with custody of the child Corolie awarded to the respondent. Petitioner will pay to the respondent maintenance for herself at the rate of $150 per month and for Corolie at the rate of $40 per month, payments for Corolie to cease on June 30, 1970. In the event Corolie takes employment before that date, the matter may be spoken to again. Respondent will have her costs.

Petition granted.

NOTES AND QUESTIONS

1. Was Corolie unable to withdraw from parental charge "by reason of illness, disability or other cause"? How did the court approach this interpretive problem?

2. Does the court's application (or non-application) of *ejusdem generis* respect the presumption of "no extraneous words"? What "independent meaning" is given to the words "illness" and "disability" as a result of the court's decision? Why would Parliament have added the words "illness" and "disability," presuming that Parliament intended the words "other cause" to be interpreted in the manner proposed by the court in *Grini*?

3. If the court had determined that the "other causes" mentioned in the *Divorce Act* *were* limited to "physical or mental disablements," what independent meaning would be given to the words "other cause"? Is there *any* way to interpret the relevant section without somehow violating the "no extraneous words" principle?

4. What was more important to the court in *Grini v. Grini*: the "exhausting the genus" exception from the *ejusdem generis* maxim, or the consequences of the interpretation put forward by Corolie's father? When answering this question, refer to the court's statement:

> "If [Corolie's father's] view is correct, the education of many a child whose attendance at school depends absolutely upon the receipt of maintenance will be cut off in mid-term because of the unfortunate accident of a sixteenth birthday. I find it hard to believe that is what Parliament intended."

5. What "linguistic problem" (among the typical patterns of drafting set out in chapters 4 and 5 of *Theory and Practice*) gave rise to the problem at issue in *Grini v. Grini*? Should the statute at issue in this case be interpreted in an originalist or a dynamic manner?

IV. REDDENDO SINGULA SINGULIS

A. Introduction

This rarely invoked maxim, literally translated, means "referring each to each," and is explained at 98-103 of *Theory and Practice*. As you will see from the cases that follow, the maxim is sometimes referred to as "*reddenda singula singulis*."[1]

---

1   Because the maxim is sometimes known as *reddendo* and sometimes as *reddenda*, it is important to look for *both* formulations when searching for occurrences of the maxim in judicial decisions.

B. The Lobster Case

Commonwealth v. William A. Barber
143 Mass. 560 (SJC 1887)

DEVENS, J: This is a complaint under the Pub. Sts. c. 91, § 84, as amended by the St. of 1884, c. 212, § 1. The original section imposing a penalty upon one for selling or offering for sale, or having in his possession "with intent to sell, either directly or indirectly," a lobster of less than a prescribed size, was amended by striking out the words "with intent to sell, either directly or indirectly." As thus amended, it reads as follows: "Whoever sells or offers for sale, or has in his possession, a lobster less than ten and one half inches in length, measuring from one extreme of the body extended to the other, exclusive of claws or feelers, shall forfeit five dollars for every such lobster; and in all prosecutions under this section the possession of any lobster not of the required length shall be *prima facie* evidence to convict."

The contention of the defendant is, that no prosecutions can be maintained upon propositions which can be read *uno flatu*, declaring that possession shall cause a penalty to be incurred, and that possession shall be *prima facie* evidence to convict; that these two propositions became law at the same instant of time; and that there is no resource except to declare the whole section, so far as it relates to the offence of possession, as unmeaning and incapable of enforcement. ...

[I]f we assume, in favor of the defendant's contention, that the possession which is visited by the section with a penalty is applicable whether the lobsters be taken within or without the Commonwealth, the section appears susceptible of an intelligible interpretation entirely in accordance with well-settled rules of construction. There are set forth in the earlier clause three offences, selling, offering for sale, and having in possession. To the first two of these the latter clause is certainly applicable, but to the third it is not. The intent of the legislation is to make possession *prima facie* evidence of the offence, where the offence consists in something more than possession. Artificial force is often thus given by special provisions of statutes to particular facts when offered in evidence. *Commonwealth v. Williams*, 6 Gray 1. *Holmes v. Hunt*, 122 Mass. 505.

But where the whole offence consists in possession, the latter clause has no application to it, and the offence must be proved in the ordinary way. Although, in terms, the clause applies to "all prosecutions under this section," when the context shows that this cannot be followed literally without reaching an absurdity, it is reasonable to hold that such was not the intent of the legislation, and that such an interpretation should be rejected. *Commonwealth v. Kimball*, 24 Pick. 366. If possible, all parts of a statute should be viewed in connection with the whole, and made to harmonize so as to give a sensible effect to each. The different portions of a sentence, or different sentences, are to be referred respectively to the other portions or sentences to which we can see they respectively relate, even if strict grammatical construction should demand otherwise. The maxim of construction, *reddenda singula singulis*, is well established, and, if the latter clause be construed *respective et distributive*, it will be found that it relates to the first two offences described in the section, and not to the third. *Coffin v. Hussey*, 12 Pick. 289. *Commonwealth v. Jordan*, 18 Pick. 228.

Nor, even if the latter clause must of necessity be applied to the offence of having in possession, should we be prepared to hold that the statute was in this regard incapable of enforcement, and that there could be no prosecution for this offence. While the clause, as applied to it, would be superfluous and absurd, it would not be more than this. The government would still have upon it the burden of proving its case of possession beyond reasonable doubt, and the defendant could not contend that such proof, if made, was mere *prima facie* evidence. ...

NOTES AND QUESTIONS

1. Would it really be "absurd" (as the court suggests) to hold that "possession" constitutes *prima facie* proof of possession? Why or why not?

2. Does the court's application of *reddendo* successfully overcome the literal text of the section, which states that "*in all prosecutions* under this section the possession of any lobster ... shall be *prima facie* evidence to convict"?

3. Does the court's application of *reddendo* follow the pattern demonstrated in *Theory and Practice*, or is this case merely an instance of a "quasi-*reddendo*" problem?

C. Quinn v. Lowell Electric

Hugh Quinn v. Lowell Electric Light Corporation
140 Mass. 106 (SJC 1885)

W. ALLEN, J: The license was under the Pub. Sts. c. 102, §§ 40, 47, which prohibit the erection of a stationary engine within five hundred feet of a dwelling-house or public building, without a license, in any city or town in which the St. of 1862, c. 74, has been adopted "at a legal meeting of the city council of the city or the inhabitants of the town called for that purpose." The St. of 1862, c. 74, was adopted at a regular meeting of the city council, and not at a special meeting called for the purpose. We think that the requirement that the adoption shall be at a meeting called for the purpose is limited to an adoption by the inhabitants of a town, and does not apply to the action of a city council, which is usually composed of different bodies, acting at regular meetings and under prescribed rules of procedure. ...

NOTES AND QUESTIONS

1. How would you redraft the "town meeting" clause in order to eliminate the ambiguity discovered in *Quinn v. Lowell Electric*?

2. What pattern of language gives rise to the interpretive problem at issue in this case? Is it an instance of vagueness, ambiguity, subtext, or analogy? What are the implications of the relevant pattern of language?

3. Should the provision at issue in *Quinn* be interpreted in an "originalist" manner, or through the application of dynamic interpretation?

V. EXPRESSIO UNIUS EST EXCLUSIO ALTERIUS

A. Introduction

Literally translated, this maxim means that "the expression of one thing implies the exclusion of another." This maxim, together with its logical basis, is described in detail at 104-9 of *Theory and Practice*. Students should review that section of *Theory and Practice* before reading the cases below.

B. Morgan v. Crawshay

The *Poor Law Act* of 1601 allowed the local "overseers of the poor" to collect a "poverty relief tax" from local mine owners. The language of the Act imposed taxes (or "rates") on "coal mines," but failed to mention whether any other mines were taxable under the relevant legislation. The plaintiff, Mr. Morgan, was the overseer of the poor in Gloucester. He sought to levy a tax on an iron mine belonging[2] to the Defendant, Mr. Crawshay. The decision of the House of Lords, below, focuses on the question of whether the statute's explicit reference to "coal mines" (without mentioning other specific types of mines) precludes the statute's application to "iron mines" as well.

George Morgan and Others Plaintiffs in Error; and Henry Crawshay Defendant in Error
(1871), 5 HL 304

Introduction

This was a proceeding in Error against a judgment of the Court of Exchequer Chamber, which had affirmed a previous judgment of the Court of Queen's Bench.

The Plaintiffs in Error were the overseers of the poor of the township of *East Dean*, in the county of *Gloucester*. The Defendant in Error was interested in certain iron mines in the township. What was the legal character of his interest therein was one of the questions presented for consideration. The other was, whether iron mines were rateable to the relief of the poor under the 43 Eliz. c. 2, s. 1. ...

The first question here is whether iron mines are rateable under the provisions of the Statute of *Elizabeth*; and the second, if they are so, whether the Respondent in this case is rateable as an occupier.

As to the first of these questions, the claim of exemption is that the statute only mentions coal mines, which it is said shews that mines were in the contemplation of

---

2   The question of Mr. Crawshay's "interest" in the mine was actually before the court. It was not established that Mr. Crawshay was the iron mine's owner, but that he was simply the mine's "galee." Because of the manner in which the court determined the *expressio unius* question, it was not necessary to consider whether the "galee" of a mine was responsible to pay the poor tax.

the Legislature, but that it deemed no other mines except coal mines ought to be rated, and that this construction must be put upon the Act in accordance with the principle *expressio unius est exclusio alterius*. But it is doubtful if this opinion is warranted by the authorities. It is true that in *The Lead Smelting Company v. Richardson*, which was the first case where the rateability of mines, not coal mines, was discussed, Lord Mansfield adopted this principle as the ground of his decision, observing that, at the time of the statute, "there were other mines in this country." But then he goes on to shew why he considered these other mines to have been excluded from the operation of the statute, and refers that exclusion to their nature and condition, the way in which they were worked, and the risk attending the working of them. Having referred to what he supposes may have been a sufficient reason to except them out of the Act, he says: "As there *may be* a reason for the strict letter of the statute, and nolle appears for extending it beyond the letter, we have no ground for giving it that extended construction." The decision, therefore, of that case depended on the idea of what had been the motives of the Legislature, and not upon the simple application of the rule of *expressio unius*. Now it is clear that the reasons which at that time influenced the mind of the Court did not, or do not any longer, exist, for all such mines may be worked with at least as little risk or difficulty, and with quite as much certainty of profit, as coal mines. The reasons given by Lord Mansfield have often since been remarked on, and not always with approval, by subsequent Judges. In *Rex v. Cunningham*, where coal and iron mines had been included in one rate, the rate was quashed, Lord Ellenborough assuming that iron mines could not be rated, and quashing the rate because being bad as to part it could not be sustained. But he gave no opinion in favour of the assumed statutory ground of exemption. In *Rex v. Sedgley*, Lord Tenterden having said that he took it to be now established that the expression of coal mines in the Statute of *Elizabeth* had the effect of excluding all other mines, went on to observe on the reasons given by the Judges in preceding cases, and said: "I must confess that much that has been said is by no means satisfactory to my own mind, and I feel great difficulty in endeavouring to reconcile the several *dicta* with each other;" yet because the rule had been established for a long time he thought it must be adhered to. The disinclination which he felt to overrule the decisions of his predecessors in his own Court is, of course, not applicable to this House, where the principles of those decisions can be authoritatively considered. Again, in *Rex v. Brettell* where clay pits were, from the manner of working them, held to be clay mines, and therefore not rateable, the Court adhered to the precedent afforded by *Rex v. Sedgley*. So far, therefore, the rule appeared to have been acted on, but with a clear expression, in one case at least, of doubt as to the correctness of the reasoning by which that rule was established. …

BARON MARTIN: In answer to the question proposed to the Judges by your Lordships, I have to state their unanimous opinion that the Defendant in Error being galee of certain mines of iron ore in the township of *East Dean*, in the manner stated in the special case, is not liable to be rated to the relief of the poor.

Your Lordships' question depends upon the construction of the 1st section of the original *Poor Law Act*, 43 Eliz. c. 2. This Act was passed in the year 1601, and the point now in dispute, viz., whether any other mines except coal mines are rateable to poor-rate, has been the subject of very many decisions reported in the books, and from the time of its enactment, 270 years ago, to the present time, the practice has been uniform, that no mines except coal mines have ever been rated, and although the reported cases do not commence so early, yet so far as they are known, there has been one unvariable, uniform, and constant flow of decisions all one way, that except coal mines no other mines are rateable.

Very many cases were cited on the argument. I mean to refer to three only. The first is the case of *The Governor and Company for Smelting Lead v. Richardson*. This was in Lord Mansfield's time, in the year 1762. It was twice argued, and by the direction of the Court inquiry was made as to what mines were in fact rated, and the answer seems to have been that none other than coal mines had been. In the result Lord Mansfield and the other Judges delivered most decided judgments that no other mines except coal mines were rateable.

The next case to which I desire to refer is *Rex v. The Inhabitants of Sedgley*. This case was decided in 1831. It was argued at great length, and Lord Tenterden delivered the judgment of the Court. He stated it to be established law that the expression of "coal mines" in the statute had the effect of excluding all other mines. He expressed himself as by no means satisfied in his own mind with that construction, but he said that the rule had been established and acted upon for so long a time that it ought to be adhered to, unless it could be positively said that it was wrong, and productive of inconvenience. I need not tell your Lordships that no inconvenience was pointed out in the argument before you; which was rather directed against some reasons which former Judges had given in some of the old cases. This case is important, because it shews that Lord Tenterden and the Court of King's Bench forty years ago thought that if there had been error in the construction of the statute, it was too late to remedy it.

The next case, the third and last case to which I propose to refer, is *Crease v. Sawle*, in the Exchequer Chamber. The question there was not the same as the present, although it arose upon the same section of the Act as to the poor; but the late Chief Justice Tindal, in delivering the judgment of the Court, said: "Important as it is in all branches of the law to abide by previous decisions, in none is it more important than in this. The rules which apply to the rateability of property are everywhere daily acted upon in the management of parochial affairs, and materially affect the value of estates."

This case was decided in 1842, and the Court of Exchequer Chamber acted in conformity with the opinion of the Court of King's Bench in 1831.

The question depends upon the construction of language used considerably more than two centuries ago. One uniform construction has been put upon it ever since, and no doubt very many persons have entered into contracts, and are now in the occupation of property, in the belief that what has been held to be law so long shall continue to be so until altered by the Legislature. If we were to set up our own opinions against such a long-continued contemporaneous exposition, where are we to stop? If we go back to give a new construction to a writing nearly 300 years old, why may we not go back 500 years and give a new construction to the statute "*Quia Emptores*" or "*De Donis*," or the *Statute of Uses*, because we do not feel satisfied that the language in which they are expressed properly bears the meaning attributed to it by Lord Coke and the other old authorities in the law.

In construing old statutes it has been usual to pay great regard to the construction put upon them by the Judges who lived at or soon after the time when they were made, because they were best able to judge of the intention of the makers at the time. The uniform practice for 170 years after the Act of Elizabeth passed, not to rate any mines but coal mines, shews what the contemporaneous exposition of the Act was. "*Contemporanea expositio est fortissima in lege*" is a favourite maxim of Coke's as applied to statutes: See 2nd Institute, 11 and 136; 4th Institute, 138.

It is almost superfluous to add that at the time when the Act was passed other mines were known and worked as well as coal mines. Coke speaks of a grant to the Duke of Bedford, when Regent of France, of all mines of gold and silver in England, rendering a certain portion to the King and a certain portion to the owner of the soil: 4th Institute, 360.

The reason for excluding all mines but coal mines from the Act may possibly have been that other mines were regarded rather as in the nature of manufactures or commercial enterprises carried on by means of the ores than as things in their natural state capable of occupation; and if this was wrong, and so wrong as to demand a remedy, it may be redressed by the Legislature in such manner and with such regulations as to rating as may be deemed just.

But we do not consider ourselves at liberty now to enter into a critical examination of the words of the Act. We think its meaning is absolutely and conclusively settled by authority. …

LORD CHELMSFORD: My Lords, the questions raised by this proceeding in Error are, whether mines of iron ore are rateable to the relief of the poor under the statute of the 43 Eliz. c. 2; and if they are, whether galees of such mines are liable to be rated as occupiers? …

The six learned Judges whose assistance your Lordships desired, in answer to the question put to them, have now delivered their unanimous opinion that the Defendant in Error was not liable to be rated to the relief of the poor.

After these uniform judicial decisions, after more than two centuries and a half of practical acquiescence in the construction of the Statute of *Elizabeth*, there not being a single instance of any other mines than coal mines having been rated to the relief of the poor during this long period, unless it clearly appeared that the decisions had commenced and had been continued in error, your Lordships would be very reluctant to disturb what has invariably been regarded as the settled law upon the subject. But the highest point to which the argument against the construction put upon the statute can be carried is only to the suggestion of a doubt. It may be difficult to explain why coal mines alone should have been specified in the Statute of *Elizabeth*, when other mines existed and were profitable to the workers. The reasons assigned by Lord Mansfield and the other Judges in the case of *The Lead Company v. Richardson*, for the statute having confined the liability of taxation for the relief of the poor to one species of mines, may not be satisfactory; but the statute must speak for itself; and when, in particularizing the various descriptions of property from which the money for the relief of the poor is to be raised, it comes to mines, and mentions coal mines only, it must be taken to mean that these alone shall be taxable. The well-known rule of construction *expressio unius est exclusio alterius* is here applicable. And the intention to exclude other mines from the operation of the statute which it implies is strongly fortified by contemporaneous exposition in the uniform practice which has prevailed from the passing of the statute to the present time.

Nor are there wanting decisions upon the very point. The first which is reported is that which has been already mentioned, *The Lead Company v. Richardson*, which was decided more than a century ago, namely, in the year 1762. That was a case as to the rateability of lead mines, and the Court caused inquiry to be made with respect to the rating of other mines besides coal mines, and learnt that at that time (160 years after the passing of the Statute of *Elizabeth*) lead mines throughout England and tin mines in Cornwall had never been rated. The Court of King's Bench held that the Plaintiffs, lessees of lead mines, who paid no rent, but only a certain part of the ore raised, were not liable in respect thereof to be rated to the relief of the poor. ...

The case of *Rex v. The Inhabitants of Sedgley*, was decided in the year 1831; all the cases upon the subject of the rateability of mines, from that of *The Lead Company v. Richardson* downwards, were cited there in the course of the argument; and it was held that the express mention of coal mines in the Statute of *Elizabeth* was a virtual exclusion of all other mines, and consequently that other mines were not rateable to the relief of the poor. Lord Tenterden, in adverting to the *dicta* and opinions of Judges before whom questions of this nature had been brought, said: "I must confess that much that has been thus said is by no means satisfactory to my own mind, and that I feel great difficulty in an endeavour to reconcile the several *dicta* with each other. But it is not necessary to do this. The rule of construction has been established and acted upon for a long time and ought to be adhered to, unless we could say positively that it is wrong and productive of inconvenience." After this long-continued course of *dicta* and decisions, unless your Lordships entertained the strongest opinion that the first decision on the subject was erroneous, and all the cases that followed were merely echoes of the first, you would be most unwilling to pronounce a condemnation of the judgments which have been given, and of the practice which has uniformly prevailed for so long a period, for the exemption of all other mines except coal mines from liability to be rated for the relief of the poor. But if the question had been one which had to be considered for the first time, although I am unable to satisfy my mind why the statute mentions coal mines alone as subjects of taxation, I should, in acting upon the ordinary rules for the construction of statutes, have been unable to gather an implied intention on the part of the Legislature beyond what it has expressed. If it was intended that all mines should be taxable towards the objects of the statute, it is not easy to explain why this intention was not made plain, by simply expressing it; or if, with this existing intention, coal mines for some reason or other were to be specially mentioned, it could hardly fail to have occurred to the Legislature to bring the rest of the mines expressly within the liability to taxation by the words "coal and other mines."

I submit to your Lordships that the judgment of the Court of Exchequer ought to be affirmed. ...

NOTES AND QUESTIONS

1. The House of Lords suggests that it would have to go beyond "the strict letter of the statute" in order to permit the taxation of iron mines. Why is this an important consideration? If the statute's objective was to obtain revenue in order to provide relief to the poor, isn't it sensible to construe the statute in a way that *maximizes* the revenue available to the poor, regardless of the statute's "strict letter"? What problems might such an approach create?

2. The Law Lords note that the original reason for confining the Act to "coal mines" may have been that other mines (such as iron mines) were relatively unsafe, creating great risks for their owners and operators. Presumably, the Act failed to impose a tax on such mines in order to minimize the disincentives facing iron miners and to encourage others to enter the dangerous iron-mining business (which was surely a valuable industry for England). The court goes on to note, however, that at the time of the decision in *Morgan*, iron mines could "be worked with at least as little risk or difficulty, and with quite as much certainty of profit, as coal mines." If the reason for the Act's exclusive reference to "coal mines" has disappeared, should the court now be permitted to give an expansive reading to the Act, allowing the taxation of other mines as well? Would this amount to a "judicial amendment" of the relevant legislation? Is this permissible under either originalist or dynamic interpretation?

3. At the outset of his judgment, Baron Martin notes that earlier cases had decided that the *expressio unius* construction could be avoided if it was "productive of inconvenience." Should mere "inconvenience" be enough to permit the court to apply the statute to "iron mines," when the statute mentions only "coal mines"? To what kinds of "inconvenience" might the court be referring?

4. Throughout its decision, the House of Lords repeatedly mentions that the *expressio unius* construction (which held that all mines other than "coal mines" were excluded from the statute) had been "acted upon" for many years. Why was this a relevant consideration? Doesn't a statute "mean what it means" regardless of whether people have acted upon an incorrect interpretation of the statute's terms?[3]

5. The House of Lords refers to the doctrine of "contemporaneous exposition." This rule is also mentioned (under its Latin name *contemporanea expositio*) in the notes to *EGALE Canada Inc. v. Canada* (2001) CRDJ 642 (BC SC) (discussed in chapter 1). In *Morgan*, the court describes the doctrine as follows: "in construing old statutes it has been usual to pay great regard to the construction put upon them by the Judges who lived at or soon after the time when they were made, because they were best able to judge the intention of the makers at the time." Is *contemporanea expositio* simply another name for "originalist construction," or is there a difference between these two ideas?

---

3   See, for example, where the court notes that "no doubt very many persons have entered into contracts, and are now in the occupation of property, in the belief that what has been held to be law so long shall continue to be so until altered by the Legislature."

VI. CASUS OMISSUS

A. Introduction

This maxim is mentioned only briefly in *Theory and Practice* at 105 and 198. Literally translated, the maxim means "a case omitted." This maxim may be applied wherever the literal language of an enactment fails to embrace a particular subject (or "case") to which it seems the Act was probably meant to apply. Where it seems likely that the lawgiver (if asked) would have intended to have the Act apply to a particular fact scenario, but the literal language of the Act fails to reach that fact scenario, that scenario is said to be a "case omitted" (a *casus omissus*). When courts invoke *casus omissus*, they generally refuse to extend the statute's terms to catch the "omitted case."

B. US v. Sheldon

United States v. Sheldon
15 US 119 (1817)

WASHINGTON J: The defendant, George Sheldon, was indicted in the circuit court for the district of Vermont, for transporting, over land, in November, 1813, a certain number of fat oxen, cows, steers, and heifers, from a place in the United States to the province of Lower Canada. A special verdict was found which submitted to the court the questions, whether living fat oxen, cows, steers, and heifers, are articles of provision and munitions of war, and whether driving living fat oxen, cows, steers, and heifers, on foot, is a transportation thereof, within the true intent and meaning of the act of Congress then in force. The judges being opposed in opinion upon both these questions, the cause comes before this court upon a certificate of such disagreement.

This indictment was founded on the act of the 6th of July, 1812; the second section of which declares "that if any citizen of the United States, or person inhabiting the same, shall transport, or attempt to transport, over land or otherwise, in any waggon, cart, sleigh, boat, or otherwise, naval or military stores, arms or munitions of war, or any articles of provision from the United States to Canada, &c., the waggon, cart, sleigh, boat, or the thing by which the said articles are transported, or attempted to be transported, together with the articles themselves, shall be forfeited; and the person aiding, or privy to the same, shall forfeit to the United States a sum equal in value to the waggon, &c. or thing by which the said articles were transported, and shall moreover be considered as guilty of a misdemeanor and liable to fine and imprisonment."

In answer to the first question submitted to this court, we are unanimously of opinion that living fat oxen, &c. are articles of provision and munitions of war, within the true intent and meaning of the above-recited act.

The second question is attended with much more difficulty: Is the driving of living fat oxen, &c. a transportation of them within the true intent and meaning of the law?

There is no doubt but that the word transport, correctly interpreted as well as in its ordinary acceptation, means to carry, to convey; and in this sense it seems to a majority of the court the legislature intended to use it. The offence is made to consist in transporting in any waggon, cart, sleigh, boat, or otherwise, the prohibited articles. Had the words "or otherwise" been omitted, it would scarcely admit of a doubt, that unless the prohibited articles had been conveyed on some one of the enumerated vehicles, no offence would have been committed within the words or the meaning of the law. What then is the correct interpretation of these expressions, taken in connection with the other parts of the section? To transport an article in a waggon, or otherwise, would seem necessarily to mean to carry or convey it in that or in some other vehicle, by whatever name it might be distinguished. If these words are construed to mean, a removal of the article from one place to another otherwise than in a vehicle, it might well admit of a doubt, whether a removal in a vehicle, other than one of those which are enumerated, would be a case within the law.

But so far from this matter being left a doubt by the law, we find, that when the punishment by way of forfeiture is prescribed, the words "or otherwise" are very plainly construed to mean the thing by which the articles are transported; thus distinguishing between the thing which transports, and the thing which is transported.

It may be admitted, that the mischief is the same, whether the enemy be supplied with provisions in the one way or the other; but this affords no good reason for construing a penal law by equity, so as to extend it to cases not within the correct and ordinary meaning of the expressions of the law, particularly when it is confirmed by the interpretation which the legislature has given to the same expressions in the same law. If it were impossible to satisfy the words "or otherwise," except in the way contended for on the part of the United States, there would be some reason for giving that interpretation to them. But it has been shown that this is not the case.

It was contended by the Attorney General, that these questions were in effect settled in the case of the *United States v. Barber*. But this is clearly a mistake. The only question in that case which was referred to this court, was, "whether fat cattle are provisions or munitions of war?" The decision of this court was in the affirmative. But whether the fat cattle were dead or alive, and if the latter was to be intended, whether they were driven or transported in some vehicle did not appear, and, of course, the law arising out of that state of facts was not, and could not be decided.

Upon the whole, it is the opinion of a majority of this court, that driving living fat oxen, &c. on foot, is not a transportation thereof, within the true intent and meaning of the above-recited act of Congress.

NOTES AND QUESTIONS

1. As noted above, the legislation at issue in *Sheldon* provided that no citizen could "transport, or attempt to transport, over land or otherwise, in any waggon, cart, sleigh, boat, or otherwise, naval or military stores, arms or munitions of war, or any articles of provision from the United States to Canada." The court construed this passage by invoking the reasoning that underlies the *casus omissus* maxim. Could the court have applied *ejusdem generis* or *noscitur a sociis* in order to resolve the same problem? How would those maxims apply to this section?

2. Is the linguistic problem at issue in *Sheldon* an instance of vagueness, ambiguity, subtext, or analogy? How should the court have addressed the relevant problem?

3. Note that the reasoning underlying *casus omissus* is found in the following passage of the court's judgment: "[i]t may be admitted, that the mischief is the same, whether the enemy be supplied with provisions in the one way or the other; but this affords no good reason for construing a penal law by equity, so as to extend it to cases not within the correct and ordinary meaning of the expressions of the law." In other words, the "case" of a man leading cattle into Canada is probably one that the legislature would have tried to catch had that case been drawn to the lawmaker's attention. Unfortunately, the literal language of the law fails to catch the case in question. As a result, the case is a "case omitted" that will escape the reach of the law—the court will not expand the reach of the Act beyond its literal terms.

C. Ex Parte Brown

Ex Parte Brown
21 SD 515 (SD SC 1907)

FULLER, PJ: ... the supposed public offense is described as follows: "That on the 2d day of December, AD 1907, at the city of Sioux Falls, in said county R. F. Brown did he then and there being, and being then and there a druggist engaged in the business of selling drugs and medicines, wilfully, wrongfully, and unlawfully offer, expose for sale, and unlawfully sell to the said A. H. Wheaton certain prepared medicines, towit, one bottle of Peruna, one bottle of Hamburger's Drops, one bottle of Chamberlain's Diarrhoea Remedy, one bottle of Piso's Cure for Consumption, one bottle of Kodol for dyspepsia, and one bottle of Dr. King's New Discovery, all of said prepared medicines being then and there misbranded, in that none of the said medicines bore a qualitative statement of what it was composed, and each and all of said medicines not being then and there such drugs as are recognized in the United States Pharmacopoe and the National Formulary." Whether the act complained of constitutes a public offense depends upon judicial powers to supply certain terms claimed to have been inadvertently omitted by the Legislature, and which subject the petitioner to the operation of a penal statute in which the word "druggist" does not appear.

To sustain the assertion that a druggist who has sold prepared medicines containing no qualitative statement or analysis of contents is guilty of a misdemeanor, punishable by fine or imprisonment, we are directed to what is commonly called the "pure food law," being chapter 151, p. 322, Laws 1907, entitled, "An act to provide for a state food and dairy commission; to prevent the adulteration, misbranding and imitation of foods, beverages and condiments, candies, drugs and medicines, meats and fish, and to regulate the manufacture and sale thereof, and of dairy products." Section 1 of the act creates the food and dairy department, and empowers the Governor, by and with the consent of the Senate, to appoint a commissioner to take charge of the office at a salary of $1,600 per annum. ... section 10, which reads as follows ... is measurably relied upon to sustain this prosecution:

> "It shall be unlawful for any person acting for himself or as the servant or agent of any
> other person, firm or corporation, to manufacture, sell, offer or expose for sale any

article of food which is adulterated or misbranded within the meaning of this act. The
possession by an innkeeper, hotel keeper, restaurant keeper, or boarding house keeper
of any food or drug which is adulterated or misbranded within the meaning of this act
shall be deemed to be the keeping of such food or drug for sale."

Neither the term "druggist" nor "medicine" was employed by the Legislature in this
provision, and the unlawful possession of the adulterated or misbranded "drug,"
mentioned only in the final sentence, is unaccountably limited to the dispensers of
food. The 23 sections of the statute immediately following the provision above quoted
are devoted to dairy products and various articles of food, and the word "drug" as
used in the act is first defined in section 34. Section 35, consisting of eight subdivisions, is declarative merely of what conditions are essential to constitute misbranded
or adulterated drugs or articles of food; but no language is used therein tending in the
slightest degree to evidence a legislative intent to make anything unlawful or justify
the infliction of a penalty for the sale or offering for sale of prepared medicine "bearing no qualitative statement of what it is composed." While this section regulates
nothing, and is merely descriptive of the articles of food and medicine mentioned
therein and is incapable of transgression by any person, the provision immediately
following, being section 36, declares that "any person violating any of the provisions
of the preceding section of this act shall be deemed guilty of a misdemeanor and
upon conviction thereof shall be punished by a fine of not less than ten nor more than
one hundred dollars or by imprisonment in the county jail not to exceed thirty days or
by both such fine and imprisonment for each offense." Were it to be assumed, as
contended by counsel for the food and dairy commissioner, that the expression "preceding section" might authoritatively be changed to "preceding sections," this
prosecution would not be maintainable, for the reason that there is nothing in section
10 nor in any other provision of the "pure food law" authorizing the arrest of a druggist
or making anything that is charged in the complaint a penal offense. According to an
elementary rule of construction, the statutory enumeration of persons of the same
class by specific terms, such as the keeper of an inn, hotel, restaurant, or boarding
house, must be restricted to that class of individuals, and no consideration of the
mischief to be remedied by the passage of the act is sufficient to justify the
interpolation required to bring within its operation another class of persons whose
business is distinctly different

It was orally argued and urged in the brief of counsel for the food and dairy commissioner that to carry out the intention of section 10, and make it broad enough to
justify this prosecution, we should insert the phrase "or drugs" in the first sentence
thereof, but that would require a most glaring invasion of the legislative prerogative,
and amount to a judicial attempt to amend a statute definitely expressed in words of
common speech. The headnote prepared by this court in *Landauer v. Conklin*, 3 SD 462,
54 NW 322, is as follows: "A fundamental rule of interpretation applied to statutes,
mandatory as well as directory, is that words in a statute, if of common use, are to be
taken in their natural and ordinary sense, without any forced or subtle construction
either to limit or extend their import." Delivering the opinion of the court in *United
States v. Wiltberger*, 18 US 76, 5 Wheat. (US) 76, 5 L Ed. 37, Chief Justice Marshall

said: "The intention of the Legislature is to be collected from the words they employ. Where there is no ambiguity in the words, there is no room for construction. The case must be a strong one, indeed, which would justify a court in departing from the plain meaning of words, especially in a penal act, in search of an intention which the words themselves did not suggest. To determine that a case is within the intention of a statute its language must authorize us to say so. It would be dangerous, indeed, to carry the principle that a case which is within the reason or mischief of a statute is within its provisions so far as to punish a crime not enumerated in the statute, because it is of equal atrocity, or of kindred character, with those which are enumerated." The case of *United States v. Sheldon*, 15 US 119, 2 Wheat. (US) 119, 4 L Ed. 199, was a prosecution under an indictment of the accused for transporting articles of provision and munitions of war overland from Vermont to Lower Canada, and the question of law presented was "whether driving living fat oxen, cows, steers, and heifers on foot is a transportation thereof" within the meaning of an act of Congress to prohibit trading with the enemy in time of war. The section of the statute upon which such prosecution was based made it a misdemeanor punishable by a fine and imprisonment for any citizen to "transport, or attempt to transport, overland or otherwise, in any wagon, cart, sleigh, boat or otherwise, … any articles of provision, from the United States to Canada." In deciding that the means employed to transfer such animals from the United States to Canada did not amount to transportation within congressional meaning, the court said: "It may be admitted that the mischief is the same, whether the enemy be supplied with provisions in the one way or the other; but this affords no good reason for construing a penal law by equity, so as to extend it to cases not within the correct and ordinary meaning of the expressions of the law." While it is the duty of the court to seek for and give effect to the meaning of the lawmakers, its research must not extend beyond legislative language when couched in words that are free from any ambiguity. Consequently it is not within judicial power to create a public offense by supplying words necessary to subject the accused druggist to the penalties of a statute which in plain terms relates only to a class of persons to which he does not belong. However inconsistent with the general policy of the enactment, it must be presumed that the words required to bring him within its operation were omitted in conformity with the legislative will. To thus supply terms, in whatever manner omitted from a statute that is penal in its nature, would be contrary to the prevailing doctrine, based upon a sound legal maxim and stated generally by Prof. Black as follows: "When a statute makes specific provisions in regard to several enumerated cases or objects, but omits to make any provision for a case or object which is analogous to those enumerated, or which stands upon the same reason, and is therefore within the general scope of the statute, and it appears that such case or object was omitted by inadvertence or because it was overlooked or unforeseen, it is called a 'casus omissus.' Such omissions or defects cannot be supplied by the courts." *Black on Interpretation of Laws*, 57.

   There being no legal authority for the process under which the petitioner is restrained of his liberty nor general law to justify a conviction, his application to this court for a discharge on *habeas corpus* is granted.

NOTES AND QUESTIONS

1. What was the "mischief" (or social problem) that motivated the legislature to enact s. 10 of the *Pure Food Law*? Is it clear that the legislature intended to catch people in Mr. Brown's position when they enacted the relevant language? If so, is *casus omissus* designed to thwart "purposive readings" of legislation?

2. What was the typical case that the legislature sought to penalize when it enacted s. 10? Is Mr. Brown's situation similar?

3. Does it seem sensible to conclude that the legislature meant to prohibit "restaurant keepers" from administering "drugs" or "keeping drugs for sale"? Does the statute's explicit reference to "drugs" make it clear that the legislature intended to apply the law to druggists?

4. What is the linguistic problem at the heart of the *Brown* decision? Does it involve an occurrence of vagueness, ambiguity, subtext, or analogy?

5. According to the court in *Brown*, "no consideration of the mischief to be remedied by the passage of the act is sufficient to justify the interpolation required to bring within its operation another class of persons whose business is distinctly different." What policy rationale might underlie this "rule" of construction? What does this rule say about the division of legislative and judicial power?

6. The court in *Brown* cites *Landauer v. Conklin*, in which it was held that "[a] fundamental rule of interpretation applied to statutes, mandatory as well as directory, is that words in a statute, if of common use, are to be taken in their natural and ordinary sense, without any forced or subtle construction either to limit or extend their import." Do the cases discussed in chapters 1 and 2 of this text comply with this "fundamental rule" of construction?

VII. EXERCISES

A. The Farm Offences Act

Suggested length: 2-4 pages

Section 12 of the *Farm Offences Act* (a fictional piece of legislation) provides as follows:

> 12(a) Every one who trespasses upon a farm and commits a theft of livestock is guilty of an indictable offence and liable to imprisonment for a term not exceeding 4 years.
>
> (b) For the purposes of this section, a "farm" includes any real property used for the purpose of agriculture or animal husbandry.

On September 5, 1997, Phil Hufnagel decided to spend an evening fishing at his favourite fishing hole in Lakefield, Ontario. After fishing for several hours without any luck, Phil decided to change his tactics by using live bait.

Phil wandered around his fishing hole for over an hour looking for worms, and was just about to give up when he happened to notice several people picking worms in the backyard of Wally's Wigglers, a local bait shop specializing in worms and crickets. Apparently, the land behind the bait shop was particularly "wormy" due to the special fertilizer that Wally used on his lawn, a fertilizer that Wally developed for the express purpose of attracting worms.

After the worm pickers had finished their work and left the area, Phil hopped the fence behind Wally's Wigglers and picked a handful of worms from Wally's lawn. Armed with a fresh supply of bait, Phil headed back toward his fishing hole to try his luck again.

Unfortunately for Phil, the new bait didn't make a difference; he fished for over an hour without any success. Phil eventually gave up and decided to head for home.

Phil was tired from his long evening of fishing and wanted to get home quickly. He decided to take a shortcut across a cornfield on Emily Bower's farm. As Phil crossed the field, he noticed some trout jumping in a pond on Bower's property. Phil walked over to the pond and caught several trout with some left over worms that he had in his pocket.

Unfortunately for Phil, one of the bait pickers at Wally's Wigglers had observed Phil picking worms in Wally's yard and called the local sheriff. The sheriff found Phil on Bower's farm and Phil was arrested and charged with two violations of s. 12 of the *Farm Offences Act* (one count with respect to the worms, one count with respect to the trout).

Will Phil be convicted on either count? Address only "interpretive issues" (that is, those issues relating to the meaning of words or phrases found in the legislation) when preparing your decision.

B. The Prize Fight

Suggested length: 9-12 pages

Murray Dupuis was a local ruffian attending Prince Albert High School in Fredericton, New Brunswick. One afternoon when Murray was in a rather surly mood, he walked up to local nerd, Roger Boyko, and challenged him to a fight. Not wanting to appear to be a "wimp" in front of his friends, Roger reluctantly agreed. Roger and Murray decided that the fight was to take place after school (at 4:00 p.m.) in the parking lot beside the smoking area.

As four o'clock approached, the school's principal, Annette Nguyen, learned of the impending fight between Roger and Murray. Although her first impulse was to put a stop to the altercation, Principal Nguyen decided against intervening: Nguyen had never particularly liked Murray Dupuis, and was aware that Roger Boyko, unbeknownst to most of his classmates, had secretly been studying tae kwon do for several years. Principal Nguyen looked forward to seeing Dupuis learn his lesson.

As the clock struck four, most of the students of Prince Albert High found their way into the parking lot and prepared to watch the fight. The group expected the fight to be short-lived, as very few people knew of Roger's skills as a martial artist, and most expected the much larger Murray to prove victorious with little or no effort. Principal Nguyen, who could hardly wait to see Murray beaten by a nerd, secretly hid in some nearby bushes to watch the fight.

Murray and Roger arrived at the parking lot at the appointed time. Murray removed his leather jacket and handed it to his girlfriend Gillian Nickle, who also agreed to hold Roger's windbreaker and spectacles during the fight. Murray assumed a traditional "boxing stance" and prepared for battle.

As Gillian cried out, "Kill him, Murray!" she was amazed to see Roger leap across several parking spaces and kick Murray squarely between the eyes, sending him to the ground like a sack full of jelly. As Murray struggled to regain his feet, local constable

Luther Crough happened to stumble by the scene of the fight, whereupon he arrested Murray, Roger, and Gillian. Since Constable Crough was particularly observant, he also spotted Principal Nguyen hiding in the bushes, and arrested her as well. All four of the "arrestees" were charged with offences under s. 83 of the *Criminal Code*, which provides (in part) as follows:

> 83(1) Every one who
> a. engages as a principal in a prize fight,
> b. advises, encourages or promotes a prize fight, or
> c. is present at a prize fight as an aid, second, surgeon, umpire, backer or reporter,
> is guilty of an offence punishable on summary conviction.

Should any or all of the four accused persons be convicted under any provision of s. 83?

Notes: Despite the high school setting, assume that all of the accused are at least 18 years of age. When completing this assignment, address only "interpretive issues" (that is, issues that relate to the meaning of words or phrases found in the legislation). Finally, note that this provision is drawn from an actual piece of legislation (the *Criminal Code*). Feel free to avail yourself of any interpretive assistance that you can draw from other relevant portions of the Code.

C. Originalism and Dynamism

Suggested length: 12-15 pages

Discuss the following statement:

> The interpretation of legislation involves nothing more than a search for the legislator's intention. Any attempt to move beyond the parameters of the lawgiver's intention is an exercise in "judicial legislation," which violates the fundamental division of powers between the judiciary and democratically accountable lawmaking bodies. As a result, in the interpretation of legislative language, courts must restrict themselves to the use of textual tools (such as maxims of construction) that are designed to ferret out the legislator's historical, static intent.

CHAPTER THREE

The Rules of Interpretation

I. INTRODUCTION

A. The Three Rules

In his seminal article entitled "Statute Interpretation in a Nutshell" (1938), 16 *Canadian Bar Review* 1, John Willis described three basic rules of statutory interpretation. According to Willis (at 9-10):

> "Every school boy knows" that our law recognizes three main approaches to all statutes: their usual names are (1) the "literal (plain meaning) rule"; (2) the "golden rule"; (3) the "mischief (Heydon's Case) rule." Any one of these three approaches may legitimately be adopted by your court in the interpretation of any statute: which it does in fact adopt, and the manner of its application, will, if your case is a close one, be decisive of the result.

Of course, if a court can "legitimately" adopt any one of the three approaches, it is a little misleading to refer to the three approaches as "rules"; surely the word "rule" implies that the court *must* adopt the relevant form of interpretation. However, the literal rule, the golden rule, and the mischief rule are nothing more than optional approaches to statutory construction that may or may not feature prominently in decisions involving the meaning of a legislative text.

All three of Willis's rules continue to be relied upon by judges faced with problems involving statutory construction. Indeed, a judge's personal commitment to one of the three rules may be the core feature of that judge's interpretive decisions. It is important to note, however, that the rules may or may not have any impact on the *result* of a case involving a statute's meaning: in many cases, a judge can justify a wide array of results even if he or she is committed to using one particular "rule." If the judge is deeply committed to the golden rule, for example, the judge may still be able to justify several different (and contradictory) results on the basis of that rule. While the golden rule will not control the result of the judge's decision, it will have a significant impact upon the manner in which the judge expresses (or justifies) the outcome of the case. As a result, students should be skeptical of any claim that a judge's commitment to a particular rule of construction compels the judge to reach a particular result.

B. Required Readings

The three "rules" of interpretation are not dealt with in a separate chapter of Randal N. Graham, *Statutory Interpretation: Theory and Practice* (Toronto: Emond Montgomery, 2001) (*"Theory and Practice"*). Instead, they appear throughout the text wherever they are relevant to a particular interpretive doctrine or decision. The literal rule is generally called the "plain meaning rule," and is given special prominence in cases involving criminal law and taxation. This can be seen throughout chapter 7 of *Theory and Practice*.[1] The golden rule is often referred to as "consequential analysis," and is discussed at length at 166-71 of *Theory and Practice*. Finally, the mischief rule is generally looked upon as a component of "purposive interpretation," and is addressed at 21-31 of *Theory and Practice*.

At this stage, students should have already reviewed chapters 4 and 5 of *Theory and Practice*, which deal with typical problems of legislative language. Students should now review chapter 6 of *Theory and Practice*, which describes the manner in which courts may use these typical language problems in the creation of a consistent method of statutory construction. When reading the cases below, students should consider the manner in which the theory of construction proposed in chapter 6 of *Theory and Practice* (known as the "unified theory") would address the linguistic problems facing the courts.

II. THE LITERAL RULE AND THE GOLDEN RULE

A. Introduction

The literal rule and the golden rule are dealt with together in this section in order to emphasize their significant similarities and differences. According to John Willis ("Statutory Interpretation in a Nutshell," at 10, citing *Abley v. Dale*, 11 CB 391, per Jervis CJ), the literal rule

> directs that "if the precise words used are plain and unambiguous ... we are bound to construe them in their ordinary sense, even though it leads ... to an absurdity or a manifest injustice." If it follows this rule your court will clear its mind of any knowledge it has about the social purpose of the Act before it, will disregard both context and subject matter, and will confine its attention strictly to the actual words it is asked to construe.

As a result, the literal rule can be summarized as follows:

> **The Literal Rule:** The words of a statute should be interpreted in their plain, ordinary, and literal sense, regardless of any hardship, inconvenience, or absurdity caused by that plain, ordinary, and literal meaning.

As noted above, the literal rule continues to feature prominently in many current judicial decisions, generally under the rubric of the "plain meaning rule."

---

1   Students need not read chapter 7 of *Theory and Practice* at this time—that chapter can be saved for the
     units on criminal statutes and tax legislation, which will be addressed in chapters 5 and 6 of this book.

The golden rule can be expressed in terms that are strikingly similar to the foregoing formulation of the literal rule, with some very significant differences. The golden rule can be summarized as follows:

> **The Golden Rule:** The words of a statute should be given their plain, ordinary and literal meaning *except where doing so* would give rise to some hardship, inconvenience, or absurdity. Where the literal meaning of a statute gives rise to results that are harsh, inconvenient, or absurd, the court may *depart from the statute's literal meaning to the extent required to avoid the hardship, inconvenience, or absurdity.*

While the literal rule suggests that the courts should *ignore* bizarre consequences that flow from a statute's "literal meaning," the golden rule suggests that such consequences may justify a departure from the statute's literal terms. Because of its sensitivity to the consequences of specific interpretations, the golden rule is often referred to as a form of "consequential analysis." The operation of the golden rule is described at 166-71 of *Theory and Practice* (students should read that section before progressing through the cases discussed below).

Note that consequential analysis need not conform strictly to the foregoing formulation of the golden rule. Indeed, most references to consequential analysis do not involve an application of the golden rule at all. Where the golden rule is properly reserved for cases in which the court is asked to "override" a statute's literal language, most cases involving consequential analysis do not involve departures from a statute's literal terms. In most instances of consequential analysis, a court explores the consequences of two or more plausible interpretations of a given statute's language, and then explores the consequences of adopting each competing possibility. Interpretations that give rise to sensible or laudable consequences are (for obvious reasons) preferred over interpretations that give rise to consequences that are bizarre, absurd, impolitic, or harsh. This form of consequential analysis relies on legislative intention, in that the court is loath to presume that a legislature intended to enact a law that gave rise to absurd consequences. It should be noted that, even where courts engage in this form of consequential analysis (that is, to select one interpretation or another, rather than to depart from the statute's literal language), the courts may still purport to be relying on the golden rule of statutory construction.

B. Smith v. United States

Smith v. United States
508 US 223 (1993)

O'CONNOR J: ... Petitioner John Angus Smith and his companion went from Tennessee to Florida to buy cocaine; they hoped to resell it at a profit. While in Florida, they met petitioner's acquaintance, Deborah Hoag. Hoag agreed to, and in fact did, purchase cocaine for petitioner. She then accompanied petitioner and his friend to her motel room, where they were joined by a drug dealer. While Hoag listened, petitioner and the dealer discussed petitioner's MAC-10 firearm, which had been modified to operate as an automatic. The MAC-10 apparently is a favorite among criminals. It is small and compact, lightweight, and can be equipped with a silencer. Most important of all, it can be devastating: A fully automatic MAC-10 can fire more than 1,000 rounds per minute. The dealer expressed his interest in becoming the owner of a MAC-10, and petitioner promised that he would discuss selling the gun if his arrangement with another potential buyer fell through.

Unfortunately for petitioner, Hoag had contacts not only with narcotics traffickers but also with law enforcement officials. In fact, she was a confidential informant. Consistent with her post, she informed the Broward County Sheriff's Office of petitioner's activities. The Sheriff's Office responded quickly, sending an undercover officer to Hoag's motel room. Several others were assigned to keep the motel under surveillance. Upon arriving at Hoag's motel room, the undercover officer presented himself to petitioner as a pawnshop dealer. Petitioner, in turn, presented the officer with a proposition: He had an automatic MAC-10 and silencer with which he might be willing to part. Petitioner then pulled the MAC-10 out of a black canvas bag and showed it to the officer. The officer examined the gun and asked petitioner what he wanted for it. Rather than asking for money, however, petitioner asked for drugs. He was willing to trade his MAC-10, he said, for two ounces of cocaine. The officer told petitioner that he was just a pawnshop dealer and did not distribute narcotics. Nonetheless, he indicated that he wanted the MAC-10 and would try to get the cocaine. The officer then left, promising to return within an hour.

Rather than seeking out cocaine as he had promised, the officer returned to the Sheriff's Office to arrange for petitioner's arrest. ... Petitioner eventually was apprehended. ...

A grand jury sitting in the District Court for the Southern District of Florida returned an indictment charging petitioner with, among other offenses, two drug trafficking crimes—conspiracy to possess cocaine with intent to distribute and attempt to possess cocaine with intent to distribute in violation of 21 USC §§ 841(a)(1), 846, and 18 USC § 2. App. 3-9. Most important here, the indictment alleged that petitioner knowingly used the MAC-10 and its silencer during and in relation to a drug trafficking crime. *Id.*, at 4-5. Under 18 USC § 924(c)(1), a defendant who so uses a firearm must be sentenced to five years' incarceration. And where, as here, the firearm is a "machinegun" or is fitted with a silencer, the sentence is 30 years. See § 924(c)(1) ("If the firearm is a machinegun, or is equipped with a firearm silencer," the sentence is "thirty years"); § 921(a)(23), 26 USC § 5845(b) (term "machinegun" includes automatic weapons). The jury convicted petitioner on all counts. ...

Section 924(c)(1) requires the imposition of specified penalties if the defendant, "during and in relation to any crime of violence or drug trafficking crime[,] uses or carries a firearm." By its terms, the statute requires the prosecution to make two showings. First, the prosecution must demonstrate that the defendant "use[d] or carrie[d] a firearm." Second, it must prove that the use or carrying was "during and in relation to" a "crime of violence or drug trafficking crime."

A

Petitioner argues that exchanging a firearm for drugs does not constitute "use" of the firearm within the meaning of the statute. He points out that nothing in the record indicates that he fired the MAC-10, threatened anyone with it, or employed it for self-protection. In essence, petitioner argues that he cannot be said to have "use[d]" a firearm unless he used it as a weapon, since that is how firearms most often are used. See 957 F2d at 837 (firearm often facilitates drug offenses by protecting drugs or protecting or emboldening the defendant) ... we confine our discussion to what the parties view as the dispositive issue in this case: whether trading a firearm for drugs can constitute "use" of the firearm within the meaning of § 924(c)(1).

When a word is not defined by statute, we normally construe it in accord with its ordinary or natural meaning. ... In the search for statutory meaning, we give non-technical words and phrases their ordinary meaning. ... Surely petitioner's treatment of his MAC-10 can be described as "use" within the everyday meaning of that term. Petitioner "used" his MAC-10 in an attempt to obtain drugs by offering to trade it for cocaine. *Webster's* defines "to use" as "to convert to one's service" or "to employ." *Webster's New International Dictionary* 2806 (2d ed. 1950). *Black's Law Dictionary* contains a similar definition: "to make use of; to convert to one's service; to employ; to avail oneself of; to utilize; to carry out a purpose or action by means of." *Black's Law Dictionary* 1541 (6th ed. 1990). Indeed, over 100 years ago we gave the word "use" the same gloss, indicating that it means "'to employ'" or "'to derive service from.'" *Astor v. Merritt*, 111 US 202, 213, 28 L Ed. 401, 4 S Ct. 413 (1884). Petitioner's handling of the MAC-10 in this case falls squarely within those definitions. By attempting to trade his MAC-10 for the drugs, he "used" or "employed" it as an item of barter to obtain cocaine; he "derived service" from it because it was going to bring him the very drugs he sought.

In petitioner's view, § 924(c)(1) should require proof not only that the defendant used the firearm, but also that he used it *as a weapon*. But the words "as a weapon" appear nowhere in the statute. Rather, § 924(c)(1)'s language sweeps broadly, punishing any "use" of a firearm, so long as the use is "during and in relation to" a drug trafficking offense. ... Had Congress intended the narrow construction petitioner urges, it could have so indicated. It did not, and we decline to introduce that additional requirement on our own.

Language, of course, cannot be interpreted apart from context. The meaning of a word that appears ambiguous if viewed in isolation may become clear when the word is analyzed in light of the terms that surround it. Recognizing this, petitioner and the dissent argue that the word "uses" has a somewhat reduced scope in § 924(c)(1) because it appears alongside the word "firearm." Specifically, they contend that the average person on the street would not think immediately of a guns-for-drugs trade as an example of "us[ing] a firearm." Rather, that phrase normally evokes an image of the most familiar use to which a firearm is put—use as a weapon. Petitioner and the dissent therefore argue that the statute excludes uses where the weapon is not fired or otherwise employed for its destructive capacity. ... Indeed, relying on that argument—and without citation to authority—the dissent announces its own, restrictive definition of "use." "To use an instrumentality," the dissent argues, "ordinarily means to use it for its intended purpose." *Post*, at 242.

There is a significant flaw to this argument. It is one thing to say that the ordinary meaning of "uses a firearm" *includes* using a firearm as a weapon, since that is the intended purpose of a firearm and the example of "use" that most immediately comes to mind. But it is quite another to conclude that, as a result, the phrase also *excludes* any other use. Certainly that conclusion does not follow from the phrase "uses ... a firearm" itself. As the dictionary definitions and experience make clear, one can use a firearm in a number of ways. That one example of "use" is the first to come to mind when the phrase "uses ... a firearm" is uttered does not preclude us from recognizing that there are other "uses" that qualify as well. In this case, it is both reasonable and normal to say that petitioner "used" his MAC-10 in his drug trafficking offense by trading it for cocaine; the dissent does not contend otherwise. ...

We are not persuaded that our construction of the phrase "uses ... a firearm" will produce anomalous applications. ... As we already have noted ... § 924(c)(1) requires not only that the defendant "use" the firearm, but also that he use it "during and in relation to" the drug trafficking crime. As a result, the defendant who "uses" a firearm to scratch his head ... or for some other innocuous purpose, would avoid punishment for that conduct altogether: Although scratching one's head with a gun might constitute "use," that action cannot support punishment under § 924(c)(1) unless it facilitates or furthers the drug crime; that the firearm served to relieve an itch is not enough. See *infra*, at 238 (phrase "in relation to" requires, at a minimum, that the use facilitate the crime). ...

In any event, the "intended purpose" of a firearm is not that it be used in any offensive manner whatever, but rather that it be used in a particular fashion—by firing it. The dissent's contention therefore cannot be that the defendant must use the firearm "as a weapon," but rather that he must fire it or threaten to fire it, "as a gun." Under the dissent's approach, then, even the criminal who pistol-whips his victim has not used a firearm within the meaning of § 924(c)(1), for firearms are intended to be fired or brandished, not used as bludgeons. It appears that the dissent similarly would limit the scope of the "other use[s]" covered by USSG § 2B3.1(b)(2)(B). The universal view of the courts of appeals, however, is directly to the contrary. No court of appeals ever has held that using a gun to pistol-whip a victim is anything but the "use" of a firearm; nor has any court ever held that trading a firearm for drugs falls short of being the "use" thereof. ...

Finally, it is argued that § 924(c)(1) originally dealt with use of a firearm during crimes of violence; the provision concerning use of a firearm during and in relation to drug trafficking offenses was added later. *Ibid.* From this, the dissent infers that "use" *originally* was limited to use of a gun "as a weapon." That the statute in its current form employs the term "use" more broadly is unimportant, the dissent contends, because the addition of the words " 'drug trafficking crime' would have been a peculiar way to *expand* its meaning." *Ibid.* Even if we assume that Congress had intended the term "use" to have a more limited scope when it passed the original version of § 924(c) in 1968, but see *supra*, at 229-231, we believe it clear from the face of the statute that the Congress that amended § 924(c) in 1986 did not. Rather, the 1986 Congress employed the term "use" expansively, covering both use as a weapon, as the dissent admits, and use as an item of trade or barter, as an examination of § 924(d) demonstrates. Because the phrase "uses ... a firearm" is broad enough in ordinary usage to cover use of a firearm as an item of barter or commerce, Congress was free in 1986 so to employ it. The language and structure of § 924 indicate that Congress did just that. Accordingly, we conclude that using a firearm in a guns-for-drugs trade may constitute "us[ing] a firearm" within the meaning of § 924(c)(1). ...

Finally, the dissent and petitioner invoke the rule of lenity. ... The mere possibility of articulating a narrower construction, however, does not by itself make the rule of lenity applicable. Instead, that venerable rule is reserved for cases where, "after 'seiz[ing] every thing from which aid can be derived,'" the Court is "left with an ambiguous statute." [Citations omitted.] This is not such a case. Not only does petitioner's use of his MAC-10 fall squarely within the common usage and dictionary definitions of the terms "uses ... a firearm," but Congress affirmatively demonstrated that it meant to include transactions like petitioner's as "us[ing] a firearm" by so employing those terms in § 924(d). ... We have observed that the rule of lenity "cannot dictate an implausible interpretation of a statute, nor one at odds with the generally accepted contemporary meaning of a term." *Taylor v. United States*, 495 US 575, 596, 109 L Ed. 2d 607, 110 S Ct. 2143 (1990). That observation controls this case. Both a firearm's use as a weapon and its use as an item of barter fall within the plain language of § 924(c)(1), so long as the use occurs during and in relation to a drug trafficking offense; both must constitute "uses" of a firearm for § 924(d)(1) to make any sense at all. ... We therefore hold that a criminal who trades his firearm for drugs "uses" it during and in relation to a drug trafficking offense within the meaning of § 924(c)(1). Because the evidence in this case showed that petitioner "used" his MAC-10 machine gun and silencer in precisely such a manner, proposing to trade them for cocaine, petitioner properly was subjected to § 924(c)(1)'s 30-year mandatory minimum sentence. The judgment of the Court of Appeals, accordingly, is affirmed.

It is so ordered.

SCALIA J (Stevens and Souter JJ dissenting): Section 924(c)(1) mandates a sentence enhancement for any defendant who "during and in relation to any crime of violence or drug trafficking crime ... uses ... a firearm." 18 USC § 924(c)(1). The Court begins its analysis by focusing upon the word "use" in this passage, and explaining that the dictionary definitions of that word are very broad. See *ante*, at 228-229. It is, however, a "fundamental principle of statutory construction (and, indeed, of language itself) that the meaning of a word cannot be determined in isolation, but must be drawn from the context in which it is used." *Deal v. United States*, *ante*, at 132. That is particularly true of a word as elastic as "use," whose meanings range all the way from "to partake of" (as in "he uses tobacco") to "to be wont or accustomed" (as in "he used to smoke tobacco"). See *Webster's New International Dictionary* 2806 (2d ed. 1950).

In the search for statutory meaning, we give nontechnical words and phrases their ordinary meaning. See *Chapman v. United States*, 500 US 453, 462, 114 L Ed. 2d 524, 111 S Ct. 1919 (1991); *Perrin v. United States*, 444 US 37, 42, 62 L Ed. 2d 199, 100 S Ct. 311 (1979); *Minor v. Mechanics Bank of Alexandria*, 26 US 46, 7 L Ed. 47 (1 Pet.) 46, 64, 7 L Ed. 47 (1828). To use an instrumentality ordinarily means to use it for its intended purpose. When someone asks, "Do you use a cane?," he is not inquiring whether you have your grandfather's silver-handled walking stick on display in the hall; he wants to know whether you *walk* with a cane. Similarly, to speak of "using a firearm" is to speak of using it for its distinctive purpose, *i.e.*, as a weapon. To be sure, "one can use a firearm in a number of ways," *ante*, at 230, including as an article of exchange, just as one can "use" a cane as a hall decoration—but that is not the ordinary meaning of "using" the one or the other. The Court does not appear to grasp the distinction between how a word *can be* used and how it *ordinarily is* used. It would, indeed, be "both reasonable and normal to say that petitioner 'used' his MAC-10 in his drug trafficking offense by trading it for cocaine." *Ibid*. It would also be reasonable and normal to say that he "used" it to scratch his head. When one wishes to describe the action of employing the instrument of a firearm for such unusual purposes, "use" is assuredly a verb one could select. But that says nothing about whether the *ordinary* meaning of the phrase "uses a firearm" embraces such extraordinary employments. It is unquestionably *not* reasonable and normal, I think, to say simply "do not use firearms" when one means to prohibit selling or scratching with them. ...

Given our rule that ordinary meaning governs, and given the ordinary meaning of "uses a firearm," it seems to me inconsequential that "the words 'as a weapon' appear nowhere in the statute," ... they are reasonably implicit. Petitioner is not, I think, seeking to introduce an "additional requirement" into the text, ... but is simply construing the text according to its normal import. ...

Even if the reader does not consider the issue to be as clear as I do, he must at least acknowledge, I think, that it is eminently debatable—and that is enough, under the rule of lenity, to require finding for the petitioner here. "At the very least, it may be said that the issue is subject to some doubt. Under these circumstances, we adhere to the familiar rule that, 'where there is ambiguity in a criminal statute, doubts are resolved in favor of the defendant.'" *Adamo Wrecking Co. v. United States*, 434 US 275, 284-285, 54 L Ed. 2d 538, 98 S Ct. 566 (1978), quoting *United States v. Bass*, 404 US 336, 348, 30 L Ed. 2d 488, 92 S Ct. 515 (1971). ... For the foregoing reasons, I respectfully dissent.

NOTES AND QUESTIONS

1. Would an "ordinary" reader of s. 924(c)(1) take the view that Smith had "used" his MAC-10 "in relation to" a drug trafficking crime?

2. Carry Scalia J's consequential analysis even further: What if an antique dealer traded an antique pistol (circa 1850) for a large quantity of cocaine? Assume that the antique dealer had no idea whether the antique pistol was still capable of firing bullet—after all, the gun was intended to be used as a showpiece. Further assume that the person to whom the dealer traded the pistol was also a collector of Old West memorabilia, and simply wished to display the pistol as part of her collection. Would the majority decision in *Smith* require a subsequent court to convict the antique dealer and impose the enhanced punishment dealing with the use of weapons?

3. The majority claims to be employing the "ordinary meaning" of the word "use."[2] Is the majority employing an "ordinary meaning" of the phrase "use a firearm"? What image is conjured up (in the mind of an "ordinary person") in response to the phrase "don't use guns"?

4. Could *noscitur a sociis* (discussed in chapter 2) have made a material difference to the majority decision in *Smith*?

5. Note that the court in *Smith* makes use of dictionaries in determining the meaning of the word "use." Is the court's use of dictionaries helpful in this case?

6. In your opinion, does the majority's decision rest on the language of s. 924(c)(1), or does it flow instead from the fact that the court considers Smith a particularly dangerous man? Note that the full report of the case reveals that, in addition to his MAC-10, Mr. Smith also had a truck full of dangerous firearms.

7. Is it possible to interpret the word "use" in a way that catches both "firing" and "pistol whipping" while excluding the use of a gun as consideration?

8. The majority spends a great deal of time dealing with congressional intent. If one were to take a poll of the legislators responsible for the enactment of the legislation at issue in *Smith*, would one find that a majority of lawgivers had specifically intended the relevant text to embrace the use of firearms as consideration? Does this matter? Would this poll constitute evidence of "legislative intent"?

9. Does the majority's decision fall under the heading of the literal rule or the golden rule? How would you classify Scalia J's dissent?

10. Does the word "use" amount to an instance of vagueness, ambiguity, subtext, or analogy in this case? How would the unified theory confront the problem at issue in *Smith*?

C. R v. McIntosh

R v. McIntosh
[1995] 1 SCR 686

LAMER CJ:

I. Factual Background

On February 7, 1991, Basile Hudson, who made his living repairing appliances and electronic equipment, was stabbed to death by the respondent. The circumstances surrounding Hudson's death arose during the summer of 1990 when the respondent, a 26-year-old man, was working as a disc jockey. He gave the deceased, who lived in the same neighbourhood, an amplifier and other equipment to repair. Over the next

---

2   The court states that "[w]hen a word is not defined by statute, we normally construe it in accord with its ordinary or natural meaning. ... In the search for statutory meaning, we give nontechnical words and phrases their ordinary meaning. ... Surely petitioner's treatment of his MAC-10 can be described as a 'use' within the everyday meaning of that term."

eight months, the respondent made several attempts to retrieve his equipment, but the deceased actively avoided him. On one occasion, the respondent, armed with a knife, confronted the deceased and told him he would "get him" if the equipment was not returned. On another occasion, the deceased fled through the back exit of his home when the respondent appeared at the front door.

On the day of the killing, the respondent's girlfriend saw the deceased working outside and informed the respondent. The respondent obtained a kitchen knife and approached the deceased. Words were exchanged. The respondent testified that he told the deceased, "Get my fucking amp because I need it. Go suck your mother and bring my fucking amp." According to the respondent, the deceased pushed him, and a struggle ensued. Then the deceased picked up a dolly, raised it to head level, and came at the respondent. The respondent reacted by stabbing the deceased with the kitchen knife. He then threw the knife down and fled the scene. Later that day, after consulting with a lawyer, the respondent turned himself in.

On November 25, 1991, the respondent appeared in the Ontario Court (General Division) before Moldaver J and a jury on a charge of second degree murder. He entered a plea of not guilty, and took the position at trial that the stabbing of the deceased was an act of self-defence. The jury found the respondent guilty of the lesser and included offence of manslaughter. He was sentenced to two and one-half years' imprisonment.

The respondent appealed his conviction to the Ontario Court of Appeal on the ground that the trial judge erred in instructing the jury that s. 34(2) of the *Criminal Code*, RSC, 1985, c. C-46, was not applicable in the event they found that the respondent had been the initial aggressor, having provoked the deceased. The Court of Appeal allowed the respondent's appeal, set aside the conviction and ordered a new trial: (1993), 15 OR (3d) 450, 84 CCC (3d) 473, 24 CR (4th) 265, 65 OAC 199.

The Crown now appeals to this Court, arguing that the Ontario Court of Appeal erred when it reached the conclusion that self-defence as defined in s. 34(2) of the *Criminal Code* is available to accused persons who are initial aggressors.

II. Relevant Statutory Provisions

Criminal Code, RSC, 1985, c. C-46

"Defence of Person

34(1) Every one who is unlawfully assaulted without having provoked the assault is justified in repelling force by force if the force he uses is not intended to cause death or grievous bodily harm and is no more than is necessary to enable him to defend himself.

(2) Every one who is unlawfully assaulted and who causes death or grievous bodily harm in repelling the assault is justified if

(a) he causes it under reasonable apprehension of death or grievous bodily harm from the violence with which the assault was originally made or with which the assailant pursues his purposes; and

(b) he believes, on reasonable grounds, that he cannot otherwise preserve himself from death or grievous bodily harm.

35 Every one who has without justification assaulted another but did not commence the assault with intent to cause death or grievous bodily harm, or has without justification provoked an assault on himself by another, may justify the use of force subsequent to the assault if

   (a) he uses the force

      (i) under reasonable apprehension of death or grievous bodily harm from the violence of the person whom he has assaulted or provoked, and

      (ii) in the belief, on reasonable grounds, that it is necessary in order to preserve himself from death or grievous bodily harm;

   (b) he did not, at any time before the necessity of preserving himself from death or grievous bodily harm arose, endeavour to cause death or grievous bodily harm; and

   (c) he declined further conflict and quitted or retreated from it as far as it was feasible to do so before the necessity of preserving himself from death or grievous bodily harm arose.

36 Provocation includes, for the purposes of sections 34 and 35, provocation by blows, words or gestures.

37(1) Every one is justified in using force to defend himself or any one under his protection from assault, if he uses no more force than is necessary to prevent the assault or the repetition of it.

   (2) Nothing in this section shall be deemed to justify the wilful infliction of any hurt or mischief that is excessive, having regard to the nature of the assault that the force used was intended to prevent."

. . .

IV. Analysis

A. Introduction

This case raises a question of pure statutory interpretation: Is the self-defence justification in s. 34(2) of the *Criminal Code* available where an accused is an initial aggressor, having provoked the assault against which he claims to have defended himself? The trial judge, Moldaver J, construed s. 34(2) as not applying in such a circumstance. The Ontario Court of Appeal disagreed.

The conflict between ss. 34 and 35 is obvious on the face of the provisions. Section 34(1) begins with the statement, "Every one who is unlawfully assaulted without having provoked the assault ... ." In contrast, s. 34(2) begins, "Every one who is unlawfully assaulted ... ." Missing from s. 34(2) is any reference to the condition, "without having provoked the assault." The fact that there is no non-provocation requirement in s. 34(2) becomes important when one refers to s. 35, which explicitly applies where an accused has "without justification provoked an assault ... ." Therefore, both ss. 34(2) and 35 appear to be available to initial aggressors. Hence, the issue arises in this case of whether the respondent, as an initial aggressor raising self-defence, may avail himself of s. 34(2), or should be required instead to meet the more onerous conditions of s. 35.

As a preliminary comment, I would observe that ss. 34 and 35 of the *Criminal Code* are highly technical, excessively detailed provisions deserving of much criticism. These provisions overlap, and are internally inconsistent in certain respects. Moreover, their relationship to s. 37 (as discussed below) is unclear. It is to be expected that trial judges may encounter difficulties in explaining the provisions to a jury, and that jurors may find them confusing. The case at bar demonstrates this. During counsel's objections to his charge on ss. 34 and 35, the trial judge commented, "Well, it seems to me these sections of the *Criminal Code* are unbelievably confusing." I agree with this observation.

Despite the best efforts of counsel in the case at bar to reconcile ss. 34 and 35 in a coherent manner, I am of the view that any interpretation which attempts to make sense of the provisions will have some undesirable or illogical results. It is clear that legislative action is required to clarify the *Criminal Code*'s self-defence regime.

B. Did the trial judge err in charging the jury that s. 34(2) of the *Criminal Code* is not available to an initial aggressor?

(i) Section 34(2) is not ambiguous

In resolving the interpretive issue raised by the Crown, I take as my starting point the proposition that where no ambiguity arises on the face of a statutory provision, then its clear words should be given effect. This is another way of asserting what is some-times referred to as the "golden rule" of literal construction: a statute should be inter-preted in a manner consistent with the plain meaning of its terms. Where the language of the statute is plain and admits of only one meaning, the task of interpretation does not arise (*Maxwell on the Interpretation of Statutes* (12th ed. 1969), at p. 29).

While s. 34(1) includes the statement "without having provoked the assault," s. 34(2) does not. Section 34(2) is clear, and I fail to see how anyone could conclude that it is, on its face, ambiguous in any way. Therefore, taking s. 34(2) in isolation, it is clearly available to an initial aggressor.

The Crown has asked this Court to read into s. 34(2) the words "without having provoked the assault." The Crown submits that by taking into consideration the common law of self-defence, legislative history, related *Criminal Code* provisions, margin notes, and public policy, it becomes clear that Parliament could not have intended s. 34(2) to be available to initial aggressors. Parliament's failure to include the words "without having provoked the assault" in s. 34(2) was an oversight, which the Crown is asking this Court to correct.

The Crown labels its approach "contextual." There is certainly support for a "con-textual approach" to statutory interpretation. Driedger, in *Construction of Statutes* (2nd ed. 1983), has stated the modern principle of contextual construction as follows (at p. 87):

> "Today there is only one principle or approach, namely, the words of an Act are to be read in their entire context and in their grammatical and ordinary sense harmoniously with the scheme of the Act, the object of the Act, and the intention of Parliament. ..."

Certainly, interpreting statutory provisions in context is a reasonable approach. However, a "contextual approach" lends no support to the Crown's position. First, the contextual approach takes as its starting point the intention of the legislature. However, given the confused nature of the *Criminal Code* provisions related to self-defence, I cannot imagine how one could determine what Parliament's intention was in enacting the provisions. Therefore, it seems to me that in this case one is prevented from embarking on a contextual analysis *ab initio*.

The Crown argues that it was Parliament's intention that neither s. 34(1) nor s. 34(2) be available to initial aggressors, and that it was a mere oversight that the words chosen in s. 34(2) do not give effect to this intention. I would have thought it would be equally persuasive to argue that Parliament intended both ss. 34(1) and (2) to be available to initial aggressors, and that Parliament's mistake was in including the words "without having provoked the assault" in s. 34(1).

Parliament's intention becomes even more cloudy when one refers to s. 45 of the 1892 *Criminal Code*, SC 1892, c. 29, which was the forerunner of ss. 34(1) and 34(2):

> "45. Every one unlawfully assaulted, not having provoked such assault, is justified in repelling force by force, if the force he uses is not meant to cause death or grievous bodily harm, and is no more than is necessary for the purpose of self-defence; and every one so assaulted is justified, though he causes death or grievous bodily harm, if he causes it under reasonable apprehension of death or grievous bodily harm from the violence with which the assault was originally made or with which the assailant pursues his purpose, and if he believes, on reasonable grounds, that he cannot otherwise preserve himself from death or grievous bodily harm."

There is a clear ambiguity in this provision. Does the expression "every one so assaulted" refer to "every one unlawfully assaulted," or to "every one unlawfully assaulted, not having provoked such assault"? This question is academic, since Parliament appears to have resolved the ambiguity in its 1955 revision of the *Criminal Code*, SC 1953-54, c. 51. The first part of the former s. 45 was renumbered s. 34(1), and the second part became s. 34(2). The new s. 34(2) omitted any reference to a non-provocation requirement.

If Parliament's intention is to be implied from its legislative actions, then there is a compelling argument that Parliament intended s. 34(2) to be available to initial aggressors. When Parliament revised the *Criminal Code* in 1955, it could have included a provocation requirement in s. 34(2). The result would then be similar to s. 48(2) of the *New Zealand Crimes Act 1961*, SNZ 1961, No. 43 (repealed and substituted 1980, No. 63, s. 2) which was virtually identical to s. 34(2) save that it included an express non-provocation requirement:

> "48. ...
> (2) Every one unlawfully assaulted, *not having provoked the assault* is justified in repelling force by force although in so doing he causes death or grievous bodily harm, if ..." [Emphasis added.]

The fact that Parliament did not choose this route is the best and only evidence we have of legislative intention, and this evidence certainly does not support the Crown's position.

Second, the contextual approach allows the courts to depart from the common grammatical meaning of words where this is required by a particular context, but it does not generally mandate the courts to read words into a statutory provision. It is only when words are "reasonably capable of bearing" a particular meaning that they may be interpreted contextually. I would agree with Pierre-André Côté's observation in his book *The Interpretation of Legislation in Canada* (2nd ed. 1991), at p. 231, that:

> "Since the judge's task is to interpret the statute, not to create it, as a general rule, interpretation should not add to the terms of the law. Legislation is deemed to be well drafted, and to express completely what the legislator wanted to say. ..."

The Crown is asking this Court to read words into s. 34(2) which are simply not there. In my view, to do so would be tantamount to amending s. 34(2), which is a legislative and not a judicial function. The contextual approach provides no basis for the courts to engage in legislative amendment.

Third, in this case we cannot lose sight of the overriding principle governing the interpretation of penal provisions. In *Marcotte v. Deputy Attorney General for Canada*, [1976] 1 SCR 108, Dickson J (as he then was) stated the principle as follows, at p. 115:

> "Even if I were to conclude that the relevant statutory provisions were ambiguous and equivocal ... I would have to find for the appellant in this case. It is unnecessary to emphasize the importance of clarity and certainty when freedom is at stake. No authority is needed for the proposition that if real ambiguities are found, or doubts of substance arise, in the construction and application of a statute affecting the liberty of a subject, then that statute should be applied in such a manner as to favour the person against whom it is sought to be enforced."

Section 34(2), as a defence, acts as a "subtraction" from the liability which would otherwise flow from the criminal offences contained in the *Criminal Code*. *Criminal Code* provisions concerning offences and defences both serve to define criminal culpability, and for this reason they must receive similar interpretive treatment.

This principle was eloquently stated by La Forest JA (as he then was) in *New Brunswick v. Estabrooks Pontiac Buick Ltd.* (1982), 44 NBR (2d) 201, at p. 210:

> "There is no doubt that the duty of the courts is to give effect to the intention of the Legislature as expressed in the words of the statute. And however reprehensible the result may appear, it is our duty if the words are clear to give them effect. This follows from the constitutional doctrine of the supremacy of the Legislature when acting within its legislative powers. The fact that the words as interpreted would give an unreasonable result, however, is certainly ground for the courts to scrutinize a statute carefully to make abundantly certain that those words are not susceptible of another interpretation. For it should not be readily assumed that the Legislature intends an unreasonable result or to perpetrate an injustice or absurdity.
>
> This scarcely means that the courts should attempt to reframe statutes to suit their own individual notions of what is just or reasonable."

It is a principle of statutory interpretation that where two interpretations of a provision which affects the liberty of a subject are available, one of which is more favourable to an accused, then the court should adopt this favourable interpretation.

By this same reasoning, where such a provision is, on its face, favourable to an accused, then I do not think that a court should engage in the interpretive process advocated by the Crown for the sole purpose of narrowing the provision and making it less favourable to the accused. Section 34(2), on its face, is available to the respondent. It was, with respect, an error for the trial judge to narrow the provision in order to preclude the respondent from relying on it.

I therefore conclude that s. 34(2) is not an ambiguous provision, and is available to an initial aggressor. ...

(ii) Even though s. 34(2) may give rise to absurd results, the Crown's interpretation cannot be adopted

... The Crown alleges that it would be absurd to make s. 34(2) available to initial aggressors when s. 35 so clearly applies. Parliament, the Crown submits, could not have intended such an absurd result, and therefore the provision cannot mean what it says. Essentially, the Crown equates absurdity with ambiguity.

The Crown asks this Court to resolve the absurdity/ambiguity by narrowing s. 34(2) so that it does not apply in the case of an initial aggressor. If the Crown is correct, then an initial aggressor could only rely on s. 35 of the *Criminal Code*, which imposes more onerous requirements. In particular, s. 35(c) only allows an initial aggressor to raise self-defence where

> "(c) he declined further conflict and quitted or retreated from it as far as it was feasible to do so before the necessity of preserving himself from death or grievous bodily harm arose."

The respondent takes the position that if there is ambiguity, it must be resolved in the manner most favourable to accused persons. As a result, s. 34(2) must be made available to initial aggressors.

I am of the view that the Crown's argument linking absurdity to ambiguity cannot succeed. I would adopt the following proposition: where, by the use of clear and unequivocal language capable of only one meaning, anything is enacted by the legislature, it must be enforced however harsh or absurd or contrary to common sense the result may be (*Maxwell on the Interpretation of Statutes*, supra, at p. 29). The fact that a provision gives rise to absurd results is not, in my opinion, sufficient to declare it ambiguous and then embark upon a broad-ranging interpretive analysis.

In *Altrincham Electric Supply Ltd. v. Sale Urban District Council* (1936), 154 LT 379 (HL), Lord Macmillan criticized the view that absurdity alone would justify the rejection of a literal interpretation of a statutory provision. He emphasized that an "absurdity approach" is generally unworkable because of the difficulty of developing criteria by which "to judge whether a particular enactment, if literally read, is so absurd that Parliament cannot have intended it to be so read ..." (p. 388). He then proceeded, at p. 388, to outline what I believe to be the correct approach to statutory interpretation where absurdity is alleged:

> "... if the language of an enactment is ambiguous and susceptible of two meanings, one of which is consonant with justice and good sense while the other would lead to

extravagant results, a court of law will incline to adopt the former and to reject the latter, even although the latter may correspond more closely with the literal reading of the words employed."

Thus, only where a statutory provision is ambiguous, and therefore reasonably open to two interpretations, will the absurd results flowing from one of the available interpretations justify rejecting it in favour of the other. Absurdity is a factor to consider in the interpretation of ambiguous statutory provisions, but there is no distinct "absurdity approach."

However, assuming for the moment that absurdity by itself is sufficient to create ambiguity, thus justifying the application of the contextual analysis proposed by the Crown, I would still prefer a literal interpretation of s. 34(2).

As stated above, the overriding principle governing the interpretation of penal provisions is that ambiguity should be resolved in a manner most favourable to accused persons. Moreover, in choosing between two possible interpretations, a compelling consideration must be to give effect to the interpretation most consistent with the terms of the provision. As Dickson J noted in *Marcotte*, supra, when freedom is at stake, clarity and certainty are of fundamental importance. He continued, at p. 115:

"If one is to be incarcerated, one should at least know that some Act of Parliament requires it in express terms, and not, at most, by implication."

Under s. 19 of the *Criminal Code*, ignorance of the law is no excuse to criminal liability. Our criminal justice system presumes that everyone knows the law. Yet we can hardly sustain such a presumption if courts adopt interpretations of penal provisions which rely on the reading-in of words which do not appear on the face of the provisions. How can a citizen possibly know the law in such a circumstance?

The *Criminal Code* is not a contract or a labour agreement. For that matter, it is qualitatively different from most other legislative enactments because of its direct and potentially profound impact on the personal liberty of citizens. The special nature of the *Criminal Code* requires an interpretive approach which is sensitive to liberty interests. Therefore, an ambiguous penal provision must be interpreted in the manner most favourable to accused persons, and in the manner most likely to provide clarity and certainty in the criminal law.

I would agree that some absurdity flows from giving effect to the terms of s. 34(2). One is struck, for example, by the fact that if s. 34(2) is available to an initial aggressor who has killed or committed grievous bodily harm, then that accused may be in a better position to raise self-defence than an initial aggressor whose assault was less serious. This is because the less serious aggressor could not take advantage of the broader defence in s. 34(2), as that provision is only available to an accused who "causes death or grievous bodily harm." Section 34(1) would not be available since it is explicitly limited to those who have not provoked an assault. Therefore, the less serious aggressor could only have recourse to s. 35, which imposes a retreat requirement. It is, in my opinion, anomalous that an accused who commits the most serious act has the broadest defence.

Even though I agree with the Crown that the interpretation of s. 34(2) which makes it available to initial aggressors may be somewhat illogical in light of s. 35, and may lead to some absurdity, I do not believe that such considerations should lead this Court to narrow a statutory defence. Parliament, after all, has the right to legislate illogically (assuming that this does not raise constitutional concerns). And if Parliament is not satisfied with the judicial application of its illogical enactments, then Parliament may amend them accordingly.

What is most important in this case is that s. 34(2) applies on its face to initial aggressors, and is therefore open to such an interpretation. This interpretation is more favourable to accused persons than the alternative advanced by the Crown. Moreover, this interpretation is consistent with the clear wording of s. 34(2), thus providing certainty for citizens. Although I appreciate the efforts of the Crown to underscore the problems with the *Criminal Code*'s self-defence regime through a broad historical, academic and policy-based analysis, I suspect that very few citizens are equipped to engage in this kind of interpretive approach. Rare will be the citizen who will read ss. 34 and 35, and recognize the logical inconsistencies as between the two provisions. Rarer still will be the citizen who will read the provisions and conclude that they are inconsistent with the common law, or with Parliament's intention in 1892, or with margin notes. Given that citizens have to live with the *Criminal Code*, and with judicial interpretations of the provisions of the Code, I am of the view that s. 34(2) must be interpreted according to its plain terms. It is therefore available where an accused is an initial aggressor, having provoked the assault against which he claims to have defended himself.

C. Section 37 of the Criminal Code

Before concluding, I will briefly address the respondent's argument related to s. 37 of the *Criminal Code*. Section 37, itself a distinct justification, contains a general statement of the principle of self-defence:

> "37(1) Every one is justified in using force to defend himself or any one under his protection from assault, if he uses no more force than is necessary to prevent the assault or the repetition of it.
>
> (2) Nothing in this section shall be deemed to justify the wilful infliction of any hurt or mischief that is excessive, having regard to the nature of the assault that the force used was intended to prevent."

Section 37 adds to the confusion surrounding ss. 34 and 35, since it appears to make the self-defence justification available to an accused in any circumstance where the force used by that accused was (i) necessary, and (ii) proportionate. If s. 37 is available to an initial aggressor (and there is no indication that it is not), then it would appear to be in conflict with s. 35. Moreover, it is difficult to understand why Parliament would enact the specific and detailed justifications in ss. 34 and 35, yet then make available a broad justification in s. 37 which appears to render ss. 34 and 35 redundant.

Although Parliament's intention in enacting s. 37 is unclear, at the very least the provision must serve a gap-filling role, providing the basis for self-defence where ss. 34 and 35 are not applicable. The respondent, though taking the position that Moldaver J erred in not putting s. 37 to the jury at his trial, has been unable to advance a scenario under which ss. 34 (as interpreted above) and 35 would not afford him a defence. Therefore, there appears to be no room left for s. 37 in this case.

The respondent has suggested that s. 37 should be put to the jury in all cases because it outlines the basic principles of self-defence, and this will be helpful to the jury. However, a trial judge can explain these principles without resort to s. 37, since these principles form the foundation of ss. 34 and 35.

D. Conclusion

With respect, Moldaver J erred in instructing the jury at the respondent's trial that s. 34(2) was not available to an initial aggressor. I therefore am in agreement with the Ontario Court of Appeal. The appeal is dismissed, the respondent's conviction set aside and a new trial.

McLACHLIN J (La Forest, L'Heureux-Dubé, and Gonthier JJ dissenting):

Introduction

This case raises the issue of whether a person who provokes another person to assault him can rely on the defence of self-defence, notwithstanding the fact that he failed to retreat from the assault he provoked. The Chief Justice would answer this question in the affirmative. I, with respect, take a different view.

The accused McIntosh was a disc jockey. He had given some sound equipment to the deceased to repair. Over the next eight months, McIntosh tried to get the equipment, without success. On one occasion, McIntosh told the deceased he would "get him" if the equipment were not returned. On another occasion, the deceased fled though the back door when McIntosh appeared at his front door. On the day of the killing, McIntosh, armed with a kitchen knife, ordered the deceased to return the equipment. According to McIntosh, the deceased responded by pushing him. They struggled. The deceased picked up a dolly, raised it to head level, and came at the respondent. McIntosh stabbed him, threw the knife down, and fled.

It was open to the jury to find, in this scenario, that McIntosh had provoked the assault by threatening the deceased while armed with a knife. This raised the question of which of the self-defence provisions of the *Criminal Code* apply to a person who provokes the aggression that led to the killing. The answer depends on the interpretation accorded to ss. 34 and 35 of the *Criminal Code*, RSC, 1985, c. C-46, which codify self-defence in Canada. Section 35 clearly applies where the accused initiated the aggression; however, it contains a requirement that the accused have attempted to retreat, and might not have assisted McIntosh. Sections 34(1) and 34(2), on the other hand, contain no requirement to retreat. Section 34(1) clearly does not apply to the initial aggressor. The debate, in these circumstances, focused on s. 34(2). If McIntosh could avail himself of s. 34(2), he would be entitled to rely on self-defence, notwithstanding findings that he provoked the fight and did not retreat.

The trial judge instructed the jury that s. 34(2) would not apply if they found that McIntosh had provoked the fight in which he killed the deceased. In his view, only s. 35 was available to an initial aggressor. The jury returned a verdict of guilty of man-slaughter. McIntosh appealed on the ground that the trial judge erred in telling the jury that s. 34(2) did not apply to the initial aggressor. The Court of Appeal agreed and ordered a new trial: (1993), 15 OR (3d) 450, 84 CCC (3d) 473, 24 CR (4th) 265, 65 OAC 199. The Crown now appeals to this Court, arguing that the trial judge correctly instructed the jury that s. 34(2) is not available to persons who provoke the attack which led to the killing.

A second issue arose with respect to s. 37 of the *Criminal Code*. The trial judge declined to put it to the jury, on the ground that counsel had not indicated how it could be applied to the evidence in the case. The Court of Appeal agreed.

Analysis

1. Does Section 34(2) of the *Criminal Code* Apply to a Person Who Provokes an Attack?

McIntosh raises one main argument. It is this. Section 34(1) states expressly that it does not apply to people who have provoked the assault from which they defended themselves. Section 34(2), by contrast, does not expressly exclude provokers. There-fore, s. 34(2) must be read as applying to people who have provoked the assault from which they defended themselves. In order to prevent s. 34(2) from applying to initial aggressors, it would be necessary to "read in" to s. 34(2) the phrase found in s. 34(1): "without having provoked the assault." On this basis, it is argued that the provisions contain no ambiguity. It is further argued that even if they did contain an ambiguity, it must be resolved in favour of the accused, following the principle that an ambiguity in penal provisions should be resolved in the manner most favourable to accused persons.

Section 34(1), as mentioned, contains the phrase "without having provoked the assault." ... Section 34(2), on the other hand, contains no such phrase. ... Section 35 specifically refers to initial aggressors or provocateurs. ...

At first blush the argument seems attractive that the absence of the phrase "without having provoked the assault" in s. 34(2) makes it applicable to all cases of self-defence, even those where the accused provoked the attack. Yet, a closer look at the language, history and policy of ss. 34 and 35 of the *Criminal Code* suggests that this argument should not prevail.

The Chief Justice starts from the premise that "the language of the statute is plain and admits of only one meaning" (p. 697). From this he concludes that "the task of interpretation does not arise" (p. 697). I cannot agree. First, the language is not, with respect, plain. The facial ambiguity of s. 34(2) is amply attested by the different interpretations which it has been given by different courts. But even if the words were plain, the task of interpretation cannot be avoided. As *Driedger on the Construction of Statutes* (3rd ed. 1994) puts it at p. 4, "no modern court would consider it appropriate to adopt that meaning, however 'plain,' without first going through the work of interpretation."

The point of departure for interpretation is not the "plain meaning" of the words, but the intention of the legislature. The classic statement of the "plain meaning" rule, in the *Sussex Peerage Case* (1844), 11 C & F 85, 8 ER 1034 (HL), at p. 1057, makes this clear: "the only rule for the construction of Acts of Parliament is, that they should be construed according to the intent of the Parliament which passed the Act." To quote Driedger, supra, at p. 3: "The purpose of the legislation must be taken into account, even where the meaning appears to be clear, and so must the consequences." As Lamer CJ put it in *R v. Z. (D.A.)*, [1992] 2 SCR 1025, at p. 1042: "the express words used by Parliament must be interpreted not only in their ordinary sense but also in the context of the scheme and purpose of the legislation." The plain meaning of the words, if such exists, is a secondary interpretative principle aimed at discerning the intention of the legislator. If the words admit of only one meaning, they may indeed "best declare the intention of the lawgiver" as suggested in the *Sussex Peerage Case* at p. 1057, but even here it is the intention, and not the "plain meaning," which is conclusive. But if, as in the case of s. 34(2), the words permit of doubt as to the intention of Parliament, other matters must be looked to to determine that intention.

I also depart from the Chief Justice on his application of the proposition that "where two interpretations of a provision which affects the liberty of a subject are available, one of which is more favourable to an accused, then the court should adopt this favourable interpretation" (p. 702). This Court in *Marcotte v. Deputy Attorney General for Canada*, [1976] 1 SCR 108, at p. 115, made it clear that this rule of construction applies only where "real ambiguities are found, or doubts of substance arise" (per Dickson J (as he then was)). If the intention of Parliament can be ascertained with reasonable precision, the rule has no place. As La Forest J put it in *R v. Deruelle*, [1992] 2 SCR 663, at pp. 676-77:

> "In the court below, the majority suggested that any ambiguity in a penal provision should be resolved in favour of the accused. ... While it is true that s. 254(3) is not a model of clarity, in this instance the intent of Parliament is sufficiently clear that there is no need for the aid of that canon of statutory construction."

In summary, then, I take the view that this Court cannot evade the task of interpreting s. 34(2). The Court's task is to determine the intention of Parliament. The words of the section, taken alone, do not provide a clear and conclusive indication of Parliament's intention. It is therefore necessary to look further to determine Parliament's intention to the history of the section and the practical problems and absurdities which may result from interpreting the section one way or the other. These considerations lead, in my respectful view, to the inescapable conclusion that Parliament intended s. 34(2) to apply only to unprovoked assaults. This in turn leads to the conclusion that the trial judge was correct in declining to leave s. 34(2) with the jury.

The History of Section 34(2)

Self-defence at common law rested on a fundamental distinction between cases where no fault was attributable to the killer, and cases where the killing was partly induced by some fault of the killer. Where the killer was not at fault—that is where he had not provoked the aggression—the homicide was called "justifiable homicide." Where blame could be laid on the killer, as where he had provoked the aggression, on the other hand, the homicide was called "excusable homicide." (See E. H. East, *A Treatise of the Pleas of the Crown* (1803), vol. 1; William Blackstone, *Commentaries on the Laws of England* (1769), Book IV.)

Justifiable homicide and excusable homicide attracted different duties. In the case of justifiable homicide, or homicide in defending an unprovoked attack, the killer could stand his ground and was not obliged to retreat in order to rely on the defence of self-defence. In the case of excusable homicide, on the other hand, the killer must have retreated as far as possible in attempting to escape the threat which necessitated homicide, before he could claim self-defence. In other words, unprovoked attacks imposed no duty to retreat. Provoked attacks did impose a duty to retreat.

The two situations recognized at common law—justifiable homicide and excusable homicide—were codified in the first Canadian *Criminal Code* in 1892, SC 1892, c. 29, in ss. 45 and 46. Section 45 when enacted in 1892 differed from its modern equivalent, s. 34, in that it was not divided into two subsections. Rather, it consisted of two parts divided by a semicolon. The wording too was slightly different. Its wording indicated that the phrase at the heart of this appeal—"not having provoked the assault"—was applicable to both halves of the section. Section 45 read:

> Every one unlawfully assaulted, not having provoked such assault, is justified in repelling force by force, if the force he uses is not meant to cause death or grievous bodily harm, and is no more than is necessary for the purpose of self defence; and every one so assaulted is justified, though he causes death or grievous bodily harm, if he causes it under reasonable apprehension of death or grievous bodily harm from the violence with which the assailant pursues his purpose, and if he believes, on reasonable grounds, that he cannot otherwise preserve himself from death or grievous bodily harm.

The 1892 Code was clear and conformed to the common law on which it was based. An accused who had not provoked the assault was a person "unlawfully assaulted." He was entitled to stand his ground and need not retreat. An accused who had provoked the assault, on the other hand, was covered by s. 46 and could not claim to have acted in self-defence unless he retreated.

In 1906 the *Criminal Code* underwent a general revision. One of the policies of the revision was to divide longer provisions into subsections. In accordance with this policy, s. 45 became s. 53(1) and (2). The wording, however, remained identical. The marginal note to s. 53(1) read "Self defence. Assault.," and the marginal note to s. 53(2) read "Extent justified." In 1927, while the section remained identical in wording and numbering, the marginal note to s. 53(1) reverted to "Self-defence against unprovoked assault."

In 1955, in the course of another general revision, SC 1953-54, c. 51, s. 53 became s. 34. The words "Every one so assaulted is justified, though he causes" in the second subsection were removed, and the words "Every one who is unlawfully assaulted and who causes" were substituted. The second subsection was further divided into two paragraphs, but all else remained the same. Section 35, like the former s. 46, dealt with provoked assault. As might be expected, s. 34 imposed no requirement of retreat; s. 35 did. Thus the common law distinction between justifiable homicide and excusable homicide was carried forward.

One incongruity, however, emerged with the 1955 revision. The phrase "so assaulted" in the second part of the old s. 45 had clearly referred back to the phrase in the first part "unlawfully assaulted, not having provoked such assault." In 1955, however, when "Every one so assaulted" was replaced in the severed subsection by "Every one who is unlawfully assaulted," the clear reference back that had been present in the older versions became less clear. The phrase "not having provoked such assault," which in the old s. 45 had modified or explained the term "unlawfully assaulted" in both the first and second part of the section, was thus effectively deleted from s. 34(2).

History provides no explanation for why the explanatory phrase was omitted from s. 34(2). Certainly there is no suggestion that Parliament was attempting to change the law of self-defence. The more likely explanation, given the history of the changes, is inadvertence. In the process of breaking the old s. 45 into two subsections and later substituting new words for the old connector "so assaulted," and in the context of the significant task of a general revision of the entire Code, the need to insert the modifying phrase "not having provoked such assault" in the newly worded subsection was overlooked.

The marginal notes accompanying ss. 34 and 35 support the view that the omission of the phrase "without having provoked the assault" in the 1955 Code was inadvertent and that Parliament continued to intend that s. 34 would apply to unprovoked assaults and s. 35 to provoked assaults. The note for s. 34 is "Self-defence against unprovoked assault/Extent of justification," for s. 35 "Self-defence in case of aggression," namely assault or provocation. While marginal notes are not part of the legislative act of Parliament, and hence are not conclusive support in interpretation, I agree with the view of Wilson J in *R v. Wigglesworth*, [1987] 2 SCR 541, at pp. 556-58, that they may be of some limited use in gleaning the intention of the enactment. Inasmuch as they do indicate an intention, they clearly support the interpretation suggested by the above discussion.

Parliament's retention of the phrase "unlawfully assaulted" in both s. 34(1) and s. 34(2) provides yet further confirmation of the view that Parliament did not intend to remove the long-standing distinction between provoked and unprovoked assault. The meaning of that phrase, in the context of the two sections, is indicated by its conjunction with the phrase "not having provoked such assault" which modified "unlawfully assaulted" in the 1892 codification. This phrase in the 1892 codification suggests that "unlawfully assaulted" in the context of that section meant "not having provoked such assault." There is no reason to suppose that the meaning of the phrase "unlawfully assaulted" changed in the intervening years. If so, then on its plain wording s. 34(2) applies only to an unprovoked assault, even in the absence of the phrase "without having provoked the assault."

Parliament's intention to retain the long-standing distinction between provoked and unprovoked assault in the context of self-defence is also confirmed by the fact that neither s. 34(1) nor s. 34(2) imposes a duty to retreat, indicating that these provisions deal with the common law category of justifiable homicide, contrasted with the excusable homicide of s. 35.

Taking all this into account, can it be said that Parliament intended to change the meaning of s. 34(2) in the 1955 codification, thus abrogating sixty years of statutory criminal law, based on hundreds of years of the common law? I suggest not. To effect such a significant change, Parliament would have made its intention clear. This it did not do. If the word "unlawful" is given its proper meaning, it is unnecessary to read anything into the section to conclude that it does not apply to provoked assaults. Alternatively, if it were necessary to read in the phrase "without having provoked the assault," this would be justified. Driedger, at p. 106, states that a court will be justified in making minor amendments or substituting one phrase for another where a drafting error is evidenced by the fact that the provision leads to a result that cannot have been intended. Redrafting a provision, it suggests at p. 108, is acceptable where the following three factors are present: (1) a manifest absurdity; (2) a traceable error; and (3) an obvious correction. All three conditions are filled in the case at bar. In a similar vein, Pierre-André Côté, *The Interpretation of Legislation in Canada* (2nd ed. 1991), suggests that words may be read in to "express what is already implied by the statute" (p. 232). This condition too is met in the case of s. 34(2).

The argument that Parliament intended to effect a change to the law of self-defence in 1955 rests finally on the presumption that a change in wording is intended to effect substantive change. But this presumption is weak and easily rebutted in Canada, where making formal improvements to the statute book is a minor industry. This is particularly the case where, as in this case, there is evidence of a drafting error: Driedger, at pp. 450-51.

I conclude that the intention of Parliament is clear and that s. 34(2), read in its historical context, applies only to unprovoked assaults. ...

Policy Considerations

The interpretation of ss. 34 and 35 which I have suggested is supported by policy considerations. The Crown argues that it would be absurd to make s. 34(2) available to aggressors when s. 35 so clearly applies. Parliament, it argues, could not have intended such a result. More practically, as the Chief Justice notes, the sections read as McIntosh urges may lead to absurd results. If s. 34(2) is available to an initial aggressor who has killed or committed grievous bodily harm, then that accused may be in a better position to raise self-defence than an initial aggressor whose assault was less serious; since s. 34(2) is only available to an aggressor who "causes death or grievous bodily harm," the less serious aggressor would not fall under its ambit. The less serious aggressor, forced to rely on s. 35, would have no defence in the absence of retreat. It is anomalous, to use the Chief Justice's word, that an accused whose conduct is the more serious has the broader defence.

Common sense suggests that ss. 34 and 35 set out two situations, each with its corresponding defence. The broader defence of s. 34, not requiring retreat, goes naturally with the less serious category of conduct by the accused, namely, the situation where the accused is unlawfully attacked, not having provoked the assault. The narrower defence of s. 35 similarly goes naturally with the more serious conduct by the accused, the situation where the accused as aggressor provoked the assault.

While I agree with the Chief Justice that Parliament can legislate illogically if it so desires, I believe that the courts should not quickly make the assumption that it intends to do so. Absent a clear indication to the contrary, the courts must impute a rational intent to Parliament. As Lord Scarman put it in *Stock v. Frank Jones (Tipton) Ltd.*, [1978] 1 WLR 231 (HL), at p. 239: "If the words used by Parliament are plain, there is no room for the 'anomalies' test, unless the consequences are so absurd that, without going outside the statute, one can see that Parliament must have made a drafting mistake." That, in my view, describes this case. Indeed, as noted earlier, the law goes so far as to permit a missing provision to be read in where absurdity, traceable error and obvious correction combine.

Not only is the result McIntosh argues for anomalous; to my mind it is unwise and unjust. The common law has for centuries insisted that the person who provokes an assault and subsequently kills the person he attacks when that person responds to the assault must retreat if he wishes to plead self-defence. Otherwise, a person who wished to kill another and escape punishment might deliberately provoke an attack so that he might respond with a death blow. People who provoke attacks must know that a response, even if it is life-threatening, will not entitle them to stand their ground and kill. Rather, they must retreat. The obligation to retreat from provoked assault has stood the test of time. It should not lightly be discarded. Life is precious; the justification for taking it must be defined with care and circumspection.

Conclusion on Section 34(2)

In summary, the history, the wording and the policy underlying s. 34(2) all point to one conclusion: Parliament did not intend it to apply to provoked assault. It follows that the trial judge did not err in limiting s. 34(2) in this way in his instructions to the jury. ...

Appeal dismissed,
La Forest, L'Heureux-Dubé, Gonthier, and McLachlin JJ dissenting.

NOTES AND QUESTIONS

1. Note that Lamer CJ refers to the "'golden rule' of literal construction." Is this evidence of confusion on the part of the chief justice, or does this reference make sense?

2. What maxim is Lamer CJ essentially applying when he relies on (a) the presence of the words "without having provoked the assault" in s. 34(1) and (b) the absence of those words in s. 34(2)? Does the application of that maxim make sense in this instance?

3. The majority finds that both s. 34(2) and s. 35 are available to "initial aggressors" who wish to raise self-defence. Does the majority's interpretation of these provisions violate the "no extraneous words" presumption? Does the interpretation put forward by the dissent violate this presumption?

4. Lamer CJ repeatedly states that the relevant legislation is not, "on its face, ambiguous in any way." Do you agree with this observation? What does the chief justice mean by "ambiguous"? Compare this with the definition of "ambiguity" found in chapter 4 of *Theory and Practice* (at 120).

5. In his decision, Lamer CJ states that he "cannot imagine how one could determine what Parliament's intention was in enacting the provisions." Does this conflict with his earlier claim that the relevant language is not "ambiguous in any way"? If the chief justice can see no way of determining legislative intent, what is he doing when he interprets the relevant language?

6. Lamer CJ deals with the argument that the absence of the words "without having provoked the assault" in s. 34(2) was a simple drafting error. Lamer CJ counters this argument by saying "I would have thought it would be equally persuasive to argue that Parliament intended both ss. 34(1) and (2) to be available to initial aggressors, and that Parliament's mistake was in including the words 'without having provoked the assault' in s. 34(1)." Is Lamer CJ's argument "equally persuasive"? Is a legislature more likely to accidentally add words to legislation, or to accidentally leave words out?

7. Lamer CJ relies on the presumption that "[l]egislation is deemed to be well drafted." Is it safe to rely on that presumption in this particular case? What should a court do when it is faced with legislation that appears to have been drafted incorrectly?

8. Note that the quotation from *New Brunswick v. Estabrooks Pontiac Buick Ltd.* (1982), 44 NBR (2d) 201 (CA) (relied on by Lamer CJ) is an eloquent statement of the literal rule. Does this statement of the literal rule leave any room for the application of the golden rule?

9. Lamer CJ admits that his interpretation of s. 34(2) gives rise to absurd results. In particular, Lamer CJ admits that "[o]ne is struck ... by the fact that if s. 34(2) is available to an initial aggressor who has killed or committed grievous bodily harm, then that accused may be in a better position to raise self-defence than an initial aggressor whose assault was less serious." Is it likely that Parliament intended to give a defence to "initial aggressors" who caused death, while providing no defence to "initial aggressors" who merely inflicted minor wounds? Is this absurd result evidence of "legislative intent"?

10. Note that Lamer CJ claims that "only where a statutory provision is ambiguous, and therefore reasonably open to two interpretations, will the absurd results flowing from one of the available interpretations justify rejecting it in favour of the other. Absurdity is a factor to consider in the interpretation of ambiguous statutory provisions, but there is no distinct absurdity approach." Compare this with the classical statement of the golden rule, set out in *Grey v. Pearson* (1857), 6 HL Cas. 60, at 104-5:

> I have been long and deeply impressed with the wisdom of the rule, now, I believe, universally adopted ... that in construing wills and indeed statutes, and all written instruments, the grammatical and ordinary sense of the words is to be adhered to, unless that would lead to some absurdity, or some repugnance or inconsistency with the rest of the instrument, in which case the grammatical and ordinary sense of the words may be modified, so as to avoid that absurdity and inconsistency, but no farther.

Also compare this with the words of Pigeon J in *Wellesley Hospital v. Lawson*, [1978] 1 SCR 893, at 902, where His Lordship held that "the literal meaning should not be departed from *except* in the case of ... absurdity" (emphasis added). Finally, in *Grand Trunk Pacific Railway Co. v. Dearborn* (1919), 58 SCR 315, at 320-21, the Supreme Court of Canada noted that the courts have the right "to practically amend [statutes] by either eliminating words or inserting limiting words [where] the grammatical and ordinary sense of the words as enacted leads to some absurdity ... and in those cases only to the extent of avoiding that absurdity." In light of these judicial statements, is Lamer CJ correct to claim that there is no "absurdity approach"?

11. McLachlin J characterizes her judgment as one which takes a "closer look at the language, history and policy of ss. 34 and 35 of the *Criminal Code.*" As a result of her analysis of language, history, and policy, McLachlin J determines that s. 34(2) of the *Criminal Code* should not be available to initial aggressors. Is this fair to the "average reader," who is unlikely to have access to the history and policy of the relevant provision when determining what s. 34(2) means?

12. According to McLachlin J, "[t]he plain meaning of the words, if such exists, is a secondary interpretative principle aimed at discerning the intention of the legislator." Does this mean that the "law" is found in the mind of the lawgiver, rather than in the words found in a statute? If so, what is the "law"? Are statutory words the law, or are they merely evidence of what the law entails?

13. Why does McLachlin J review the common law of self-defence before embarking upon her interpretation of s. 34(2)? Given the fact that statutes override the common law, are ancient common law principles relevant to the interpretation of statutory language?

14. McLachlin J contends that the courts have jurisdiction to make "minor amendments" to a statute where it leads to a "manifest absurdity" or "traceable error." Is McLachlin J's method of demonstrating "absurdities" and "errors" convincing?

15. Which judgment is more persuasive: the decision of the chief justice, or the decision of McLachlin J in dissent? Why?

16. Does the problem at issue in *McIntosh* involve vagueness, ambiguity, subtext, or analogy? How would the unified theory address the problem in this case?

III. THE MISCHIEF RULE

A. Introduction

Contrary to popular belief, the mischief rule of interpretation is not a recent judicial creation. Indeed, the mischief rule has existed since at least 1584, when the court in *Heydon's Case*, 3 Co. Rep. 7a, at 637, propounded the following rule for the interpretation of legislative language:

> [For] the sure and true interpretation of all statutes in general (be they penal or beneficial, restrictive or enlarging of the common law), four things are to be discerned and considered:
>
> 1st.   What was the common law before the making of the Act.
> 2nd.   What was the mischief and defect for which the common law did not provide.
> 3rd.   What remedy the Parliament hath resolved and appointed to cure the disease of the commonwealth, and
> 4th.   The true reason of the remedy ... .
>
> And then the office of all the Judges is always to make such construction as shall suppress the mischief, and advance the remedy, and to suppress subtle inventions and evasions for continuance of the mischief, and *pro privato commodo*, and to add force and life to the cure and remedy, according to the true intend of the makers of the Act *pro bono publico*.

This ancient rule of construction has been distilled and re-expressed as the "purposive" method of statutory construction, which holds that a statute must be interpreted in a manner that ensures that the statute achieves its intended purpose. Where the language of a statute leads to two or more potential interpretations, the interpretation which best achieves the statute's "purpose" or "objective" is preferred.

The purposive method of interpretation is discussed at length at 21-31 of *Theory and Practice*. Students should review that portion of *Theory and Practice* before reading the cases discussed in the remainder of this chapter.

B. Legislation

Section 12 of the federal *Interpretation Act*, RSC 1985, c. I-21, which governs the interpretation of all federal statutes, provides as follows:

> Every enactment is deemed remedial, and shall be given such fair, large and liberal construction and interpretation as best ensures the attainment of its objects.

This provision effectively requires the courts to interpret federal statutes in accordance with the mischief rule. This does not mean that the courts are required to ignore the literal rule or the golden rule. On the contrary, s. 12 simply means that, whatever other methods of construction the court employs when interpreting legislation, the court must always interpret the law with a view to ensuring that the law is able to achieve its purpose or objectives.

As noted above, s. 12 of the federal *Interpretation Act* governs the interpretation of *federal* statutes. Provincial statutes are governed by provincial interpretation acts that have adopted provisions that closely parallel s. 12 of the federal Act. See, for example, s. 9(5) of the Nova Scotia *Interpretation Act*, RSNS 1989, c. 235,[3] s. 10 of the Ontario *Interpretation Act*, RSO 1990, c. I.11, and s. 17 of the New Brunswick *Interpretation Act*, RSNB, c. 114. In every jurisdiction in Canada, the courts and legislative assemblies have made it clear that "purposive interpretation" is the appropriate way to interpret a statute's language.

C. R v. Sharpe

The decision of the court in *R v. Sharpe*, [2001] 1 SCR 45, is an excellent example of purposive interpretation. In *Sharpe*, the Supreme Court of Canada was asked to consider the constitutionality of s. 163.1 of the *Criminal Code*. The relevant section prohibits the possession of child pornography, and has obvious implications for the guarantee of freedom of expression set out in s. 2(b) of the *Charter of Rights and Freedoms*.

In determining that s. 163.1 was (largely) saved from constitutional invalidity by the operation of s. 1 of the Charter, the court in *Sharpe* found it necessary to interpret many of the terms found in s. 163.1. In so doing, the court repeatedly relied on "purposive

---

3   Act also quoted in *R v. A.N. Koskolos Realty Ltd.* (1995), 27 WCB (2d) 162 (NS Prov. Ct.), in chapter 2.

interpretation" or the mischief rule of statutory construction. When reading the court's decision, consider the following questions: (1) How did the court determine the purpose of the relevant legislation? (2) Could the court have expressed the legislation's purpose at a different level of generality, thereby changing the meaning of the law and making it more or less likely to withstand constitutional scrutiny? and (3) Did the court's repeated references to purpose truly make a difference to the court's interpretation of s. 163.1?

R v. Sharpe
[2001] 1 SCR 45

McLACHLIN CJ:

I. Introduction

Is Canada's law banning the possession of child pornography constitutional or, conversely, does it unjustifiably intrude on the constitutional right of Canadians to free expression? That is the central question posed by this appeal. ...

II. Provisions of the Legislation and the Charter

In 1993, Parliament enacted s. 163.1 of the *Criminal Code*, creating a number of offences relating to child pornography. The provision supplemented laws making it an offence to make, print, publish, distribute, or circulate obscene material (s. 163), and to corrupt children (s. 172). With the enactment of s. 163.1, the *Criminal Code* contains a comprehensive scheme to attack child pornography at every stage—production, publication, importation, distribution, sale and possession. Subsections (2) and (3) of s. 163.1 criminalize possession of child pornography for the purpose of publication and possession for the purpose of distribution or sale. Section 163.1(4) extends the prohibition to possession simpliciter:

> "163.1 ...
>   (4) Every person who possesses any child pornography is guilty of
>   (a) an indictable offence and liable to imprisonment for a term not exceeding five years; or
>   (b) an offence punishable on summary conviction."

The scope of this offence depends on the definition of "child pornography" in subs. (1):

> "(1) In this section, "child pornography" means
>   (a) a photographic, film, video or other visual representation, whether or not it was made by electronic or mechanical means,
>   (i) that shows a person who is or is depicted as being under the age of eighteen years and is engaged in or is depicted as engaged in explicit sexual activity, or

(ii) the dominant characteristic of which is the depiction, for a sexual purpose, of a sexual organ or the anal region of a person under the age of eighteen years; or

(b) any written material or visual representation that advocates or counsels sexual activity with a person under the age of eighteen years that would be an offence under this Act."

. . .

V. Analysis

. . .

B. The Nature and Scope of the Infringement of the Charter

While the Crown concedes that s. 163.1(4) limits freedom of expression, this does not eliminate the need to consider the nature and scope of the infringement in determining whether or not it is justified. Until we know what the law catches, we cannot say whether it catches too much. This Court has consistently approached claims of overbreadth on this basis. It is not enough to accept the allegations of the parties as to what the law prohibits. The law must be construed, and interpretations that may minimize the alleged overbreadth must be explored: see *Keegstra*, supra, *Butler*, supra, and *Mills*, supra. So we must begin by asking what s. 163.1(4) truly catches as distinguished from some of the broader interpretations alleged by the respondent and some of the interveners in support. The interpretation of the section is a necessary precondition to the determination of constitutionality, although it is understood, of course, that courts in future cases may refine the analysis in light of the facts and considerations that emerge with experience. ...

Parliament's main purpose in passing the child pornography law was to prevent harm to children by banning the production, distribution and possession of child pornography, and by sending a message to Canadians "that children need to be protected from the harmful effects of child sexual abuse and exploitation and are not appropriate sexual partners": *House of Commons Debates*, 3rd Sess., 34th Parl., vol. XVI, June 3, 1993, at p. 20328. However, Parliament did not cast its net over all material that might conceivably pose any risk to children or produce any negative attitudinal changes. Mindful of the importance of freedom of expression in our society and the dangers of vague, overbroad legislation in the criminal sphere, Parliament set its targets principally on clear forms of "child pornography": depictions of explicit sex with children, depictions of sexual organs and anal areas of children and material advocating sexual crimes with children. Through qualifications and defences Parliament indicated that it did not seek to catch all material that might harm children, but only material that poses a reasoned risk of harm to children and, even then, only where the countervailing right of free expression or the public good does not outweigh that risk of harm. With this aim in mind, I turn to s. 163.1.

Section 163.1(1) defines child pornography in terms of two categories: (1) visual representations (s. 163.1(1)(a)); and (2) written and visual advocacy and counselling material (s. 163.1(1)(b)). Visual representations include "a photographic, film, video or other visual representation, whether or not it was made by electronic or mechanical means." This is broad enough to include drawings, paintings, prints, computer graphics, and sculpture: in short, any non-textual representation that can be perceived visually.

A visual representation can constitute child pornography in three ways:

1. By showing a person who is, or is depicted as, being under the age of 18 years and is engaged in, or is depicted as engaged in, explicit sexual activity (s. 163.1(1)(a)(i));
2. By having, as its dominant characteristic, the depiction, for a sexual purpose, of a sexual organ or the anal region of a person under the age of 18 years (s. 163.1(1)(a)(ii)); or
3. By advocating or counselling sexual activity with a person under the age of 18 years that would be an offence under the *Criminal Code* (s. 163.1(1)(b)).

Written material can constitute child pornography in only the last of these ways (s. 163.1(1)(b)). The ambit of these provisions depends on the meaning of the terms used.

1. *"Person"*

In order to constitute child pornography, a visual representation must show, depict, advocate or counsel sexual activity with a "person." Two issues arise here: (1) does "person" apply only to actual, as opposed to imaginary persons; and (2) does it include the person who possesses the material?

The first issue is important because it governs whether the prohibition on possession is confined to representations of actual persons, or whether it extends to drawings from the imagination, cartoons, or computer generated composites. The available evidence suggests that explicit sexual materials can be harmful whether or not they depict actual children. Moreover, with the quality of contemporary technology, it can be very difficult to distinguish a "real" person from a computer creation or composite. Interpreting "person" in accordance with Parliament's purpose of criminalizing possession of material that poses a reasoned risk of harm to children, it seems that it should include visual works of the imagination as well as depictions of actual people. Notwithstanding the fact that "person" in the charging section and in s. 163.1(1)(b) refers to a flesh-and-blood person, I conclude that "person" in s. 163.1(1)(a) includes both actual and imaginary human beings.

This definition of child pornography catches depictions of imaginary human beings privately created and kept by the creator. Thus, the prohibition extends to visual expressions of thought and imagination, even in the exceedingly private realm of solitary creation and enjoyment. As will be seen, the private and creative nature of this expression, combined with the unlikelihood of its causing harm to children, creates problems for the law's constitutionality.

The second issue is whether "person," as the term is used in s. 163.1(1)(a), includes the person who possesses the material. That is, does the definition of "child pornography" catch "auto-depictions"—for example, sexually explicit photographs a person has taken of him- or herself alone? Given that Parliament has not qualified or limited the definition of "person" in s. 163.1(1)(a), I conclude that Parliament intended to catch such auto-depictions, even where the person making the depiction, although under 18, does not appear to be a child, and intends to keep the depiction entirely in his or her own possession. This too creates constitutional problems, as we will see.

The legislation defines children to include all those under the age of 18. This doubtless reflects Parliament's concern that older teenagers may look or be made to look like children. However, this age limit extends the reach of the law to material beyond the ordinary conception of child pornography. For example, it raises the possibility that teenagers, perhaps even married teenagers, could be charged and imprisoned for taking and keeping photos or videos of themselves engaged in law-ful sexual acts, even if those materials were intended exclusively for their own personal use. This prohibition engages the value of self-fulfilment and may be difficult to link to a reasoned risk of harm to children, again raising particularly troubling constitutional concerns.

2. "Depicted"

Section 163.1(1)(a)(i) brings within the definition of child pornography a visual rep-resentation of a person "who is or is *depicted* as being under the age of eighteen years and is engaged in or is *depicted* as engaged in explicit sexual activity" (emphasis added). Does "depicted" mean: (a) intended by the maker to depict; (b) perceived by the possessor as depicting; or (c) seen as being depicted by a reasonable observer?

The first and second interpretations are inconsistent with Parliament's objective of preventing harm to children through sexual abuse. The danger associated with the representation does not depend on what was in the mind of the maker or the possessor, but in the capacity of the representation to be used for purposes like seduction. It is the meaning which is conveyed by the material which is critical, not necessarily the meaning that the author intended to convey. Moreover, it would be virtually impossi-ble to prove what was in the mind of the producer or possessor. On the second alter-native, the same material could be child pornography in the possession of one person and innocent material in the hands of another. Yet the statute makes it an offence for anyone to possess such material, not just those who see it as depicting children. The only workable approach is to read "depicted" in the sense of what would be con-veyed to a reasonable observer. The test must be objective, based on the depiction rather than what was in the mind of the author or possessor. The question is this: would a reasonable observer perceive the person in the representation as being under 18 and engaged in explicit sexual activity?

3. "Explicit Sexual Activity"

Section 163.1(1)(a)(i) catches visual representations of "explicit sexual activity." Sexual activity spans a large spectrum, ranging from the flirtatious glance at one end, through touching of body parts incidentally related to sex, like hair, lips and breasts, to sexual intercourse and touching of the genitals and the anal region. The question is where on this spectrum Parliament intended to place the boundary between material that may be lawfully possessed and material that may not be lawfully possessed. A number of indications suggest that Parliament intended to draw the line at the extreme end of the spectrum concerned with depictions of intimate sexual activity represented in a graphic and unambiguous manner.

The first indication is Parliament's use of the word "explicit" to describe the activity depicted. Parliament could have simply referred to "sexual activity." Instead, it chose "explicit sexual activity." "Explicit" must be given meaning. According to the *Canadian Oxford Dictionary* (1998), "explicit" in the context of sexual acts means "describing or representing nudity or intimate sexual activity." Similarly, "explicit" according to the *New Oxford Dictionary of English* (1998) means "describing or representing sexual activity in a graphic fashion." This suggests that the law catches only depictions of sexual intercourse and other non-trivial sexual acts.

This restricted meaning is supported by the fact that in creating other offences, like sexual assault, Parliament uses the word "sexual" without any modifiers. To constitute sexual assault, the sexual aspect of the contact must be clear. The addition of the modifier "explicit" in s. 163.1 suggests that this at least is required.

A restrained interpretation of "explicit sexual activity" is also supported by reading s. 163.1(1)(a)(i) and s. 163.1(1)(a)(ii) together. They are designed to cover two types of depiction: (i) the depiction of explicit sexual activity; and (ii) the static depiction of the sexual organs or anal regions of children. Subparagraph (ii) clearly indicates that Parliament's concern was with visual representations near the extreme end of the spectrum. While it is possible in the abstract to argue that Parliament intended a much broader sweep for subpara. (i) than for (ii), it seems more likely that Parliament was seeking to catch in subpara. (i) the activity-related counterpart to subpara. (ii).

Finally, Parliament's goal of preventing harm to children related to child pornography supports a restrained interpretation of "explicit sexual activity." The evidence suggests that harm to children produced by child pornography arises from depictions of explicit sexual acts with children at the extreme end of the spectrum. The literature on harm focuses mainly on depictions of sexual activity involving nudity and portrayal of the sexual organs and anal region. It is reasonable to conclude that this sort of material was uppermost in Parliament's mind when it adopted this law.

I conclude that "explicit sexual activity" refers to acts which viewed objectively fall at the extreme end of the spectrum of sexual activity—acts involving nudity or intimate sexual activity, represented in a graphic and unambiguous fashion, with persons under or depicted as under 18 years of age. The law does not catch possession of visual material depicting only casual sexual contact, like touching, kissing, or hugging, since these are not depictions of nudity or intimate sexual activity. Certainly, a photo of teenagers kissing at summer camp will not be caught. At its furthest reach, the section might catch a video of a caress of an adolescent girl's naked breast, but only if the activity is graphically depicted and unmistakably sexual. (For a discussion of such concerns see B. Blugerman and L. May, "The New Child Pornography Law: Difficulties of Bill C-128" (1995), 4 MCLR 17.)

4. "Dominant Characteristic" and "Sexual Purpose"

The objective approach should also be applied to the term "dominant characteristic" in s. 163.1(1)(a)(ii), which targets possession of visual material whose "dominant characteristic" is "the depiction, for a sexual purpose, of a sexual organ or the anal region of a person under the age of eighteen years." The question is whether a reasonable viewer, looking at the depiction objectively and in context, would see its "dominant characteristic" as the depiction of the child's sexual organ or anal region. The same applies to the phrase "for a sexual purpose," which I would interpret in the sense of reasonably perceived as intended to cause sexual stimulation to some viewers.

Family photos of naked children, viewed objectively, generally do not have as their "dominant characteristic" the depiction of a sexual organ or anal region "for a sexual purpose." Placing a photo in an album of sexual photos and adding a sexual caption could change its meaning such that its dominant characteristic or purpose becomes unmistakably sexual in the view of a reasonable objective observer: see *R v. Hurtubise*, [1997] BCJ No. 40 (QL) (SC), at paras. 16-17. Absent evidence indicating a dominant prurient purpose, a photo of a child in the bath will not be caught. To secure a conviction the Crown must prove beyond a reasonable doubt that the "dominant characteristic" of the picture is a depiction of the sexual organ or anal region "for a sexual purpose." If there is a reasonable doubt, the accused must be acquitted.

5. "Sexual Organ"

Section 163.1(1)(a)(ii) catches static depictions for a sexual purpose of the "sexual organ" or "anal region" of a person under 18 years, provided this is the dominant characteristic of the representation. This raises the question of the meaning of "sexual organ."

Prudence suggests leaving the precise content of "sexual organ" to future case-law. However, no one suggests that s. 163.1(1)(a)(ii) was designed to catch depictions of eyes or lips. Parliament's purpose of targeting possession of material associated with a reasoned risk of harm to children suggests a restrained interpretation of "sexual organ" in sub-para. (ii), similar to that discussed above with respect to subpara. (i).

6. Written Material: "Advocates or Counsels"

The second category of child pornography caught by s. 163.1(1) is "any written material or visual representation that advocates or counsels sexual activity with a person under the age of eighteen years that would be an offence under this Act."

This section is more limited than the definition of visual pornography in s. 163.1(1)(a), which captures sexual "representation[s]" of children. Section 163.1(1)(b) is confined to material relating to activity that would be a crime under the *Criminal Code*. Moreover, it is confined to material that "counsels" or "advocates" such crimes. On its face, it appears to be aimed at combating written and visual material that actively promotes the commission of sexual offences with children.

At stake is not whether the maker or possessor of the material intended to advocate or counsel the crime, but whether the material, viewed objectively, advocates or counsels the crime. "Advocate" is not defined in the *Criminal Code*. "Counsel" is dealt with only in connection with the counseling of an offence: s. 22 of the *Criminal Code*, where it is stated to include "procure, solicit or incite." "Counsel" can mean simply to advise; however in criminal law it has been given the stronger meaning of actively inducing: see *R v. Dionne* (1987), 38 CCC (3d) 171 (NBCA), at p. 180, per Ayles JA. While s. 22 refers to a person's actions and s. 163.1(1)(b) refers to material, it seems reasonable to conclude that in order to meet the requirement of "advocates" or "counsels," the material, viewed objectively, must be seen as "actively inducing" or encouraging the described offences with children. Again, Parliament's purpose of capturing material causing a reasoned risk of harm to children may offer guidance. The mere description of the criminal act is not caught. Rather, the prohibition is against material that, viewed objectively, sends the message that sex with children can and should be pursued.

Without suggesting that the distinction is easy to apply in practice, a purposive approach appears to exclude many of the alleged examples of the law's overbreadth. For instance, works aimed at description and exploration of various aspects of life that incidentally touch on illegal acts with children are unlikely to be caught. While Nabokov's *Lolita*, Boccaccio's *Decameron*, and Plato's *Symposium* portray or discuss sexual activities with children, on an objective view they cannot be said to advocate or counsel such conduct in the sense of actively inducing or encouraging it. Nor would the section catch political advocacy for lowering the age of consent because such advocacy would not promote the commission of an offence but the amendment of the law. Likewise, an anthropological work discussing the sexual practices of adolescents in other cultures and describing such adolescents as well-adjusted and healthy would not be caught because it would be merely descriptive as opposed to advocating or counselling illegal acts. I note that in any event these examples would likely fall within the artistic merit, medical, educational, scientific, or public good defences, discussed below.

It must also be remembered that it is only the advocating or counselling of sexual activity with a person under the age of 18 that would be an offence under the *Criminal Code* that is captured by this part of the definition of child pornography. Many of the sexual offences in the Code apply only to sexual activity involving an individual under the age of 14. For instance, the offences of sexual interference (s. 151) and invitation to sexual touching (s. 152) apply only when individuals 13 or under are involved, unless the person doing the touching or inviting is in a position of trust or authority (s. 153). Advocating the consensual sexual touching of a 16-year-old is not an offence under s. 151 and therefore would not be caught by this part of the child pornography definition. However, advocating such touching by, for example, a teacher or hockey coach, is an offence and would be caught. Similarly, inviting a 14-year-old to consensually sexually touch another person is not an offence under s. 152 and would also not be caught (subject to the same position of trust or authority exception). Finally, advocating consensual vaginal intercourse with a 15-year-old is not an offence, as the age of consent is 14. Written materials or visual representations that advocate or counsel such acts of intercourse are therefore also not caught by s. 163.1(1)(b).

However, it must be observed that the provision is broad enough to capture written works created by the author alone, solely for his or her own eyes. For example, the law could arguably extend to a teenager's favourable diary account of a sexual encounter. The interpretations of "advocates or counsels" and the fact that the description must be of an unlawful act reduce the likelihood of this happening. Nevertheless, the possibility remains that a teenager's private account of a sexual encounter could be caught. This example, like that of a drawing made and kept exclusively by the accused, engages the value of private self-fulfilment and appears to pose little real risk of harm to children, rendering it constitutionally problematic. ...

NOTES AND QUESTIONS

1. McLachlin CJ initially characterizes the purpose of s. 163.1 as "prevent[ing] harm to children." Later, the chief justice tempers this purpose by describing Parliament's purpose as the prohibition of material that "poses a reasoned risk of harm to children ... where the countervailing right of free expression or the public good does not outweigh that risk of harm." How might McLachlin CJ's analysis have changed had she simply characterized the law's purpose as "the prevention of harm to children"? Upon what evidence did McLachlin CJ rely when she "watered down" this purpose by reference to "the countervailing right of free expression or the public good"?

2. McLachlin CJ characterizes Parliament's objective as "preventing harm to children through sexual abuse." Is this formulation of Parliament's objective compatible with the objectives described in question (1), above, or does the addition of the words "through sexual abuse" effectively narrow the definition of Parliament's objective? Does this have implications for McLachlin CJ's interpretation of s. 163.1?

3. McLachlin CJ relies on "the goal of preventing harm to children" in support of a "restrained interpretation" of the phrase "explicit sexual activity." As a result, McLachlin CJ holds that the phrase "explicit sexual activity" prohibits only depictions of "explicit sexual acts with children at the extreme end of the spectrum ... involving nudity and portrayal of the sexual organs and anal region." Wouldn't a broader definition of "explicit sexual activity," perhaps including intimate touching through clothing, do a better job of preventing harm to children? How can McLachlin CJ contend that this particular objective supports a narrow interpretation of the section's language?

4. McLachlin CJ relies on "Parliament's purpose of capturing material causing a reasoned risk of harm to children" in holding that the phrase "advocates or counsels" (in s. 163.1) does *not* catch mere descriptions of sexual activity involving children. Instead, McLachlin CJ holds that the relevant words catch only "material that, viewed objectively, sends the message that sex with children can and should be pursued." Once again, is the "purpose" established by McLachlin CJ compatible with her interpretation of the relevant language? Would a broader prohibition be *more* or *less* protective of children? Is McLachlin CJ's interpretation of "advocates or counsels" grounded in the purposes of the section, or merely in the language of the provision?

5. Is McLachlin CJ's "restrained reading" based solely on the purpose of "protecting children," or is part of her reading designed to simply allow the law to withstand a Charter challenge? How are these two objectives related? Note that it seems quite unlikely that a legislator would seek to pass a law that was obviously doomed to be struck down in a Charter challenge.

D. Rizzo & Rizzo Shoes

The decision in *Re Rizzo & Rizzo Shoes Ltd.*, [1998] 1 SCR 27, is dealt with at length at 25-31 of *Theory and Practice*. Review that portion of *Theory and Practice* and consider the following questions:

1. Based on the approach taken in *Rizzo*, is the "purpose" of a provision capable of overriding the express language of that provision? In what circumstances?

2. Does the decision of the court in *Rizzo* effectively overturn the interpretive approach put forward by the majority in *McIntosh* (above)?

3. Note that most post-*Rizzo* decisions from the Supreme Court of Canada cite *Rizzo* as establishing the court's current approach to interpreting the language of legislation. Does this sound the death knell for the literal rule and the golden rule?

4. Is the Supreme Court of Canada correct to hold that the language at issue in *Rizzo* was "literally" incapable of catching cases involving bankruptcy? In other words, was it *necessary* to extend the section's reach by reference to purpose, or was the language of the provision sufficiently broad to achieve the same result?

5. Is the holding of the court in *Rizzo* compatible with the logic underlying *casus omissus* (described in chapter 2)? Is it compatible with *expressio unius est exclusio alterius*?

6. Did the court's decision in *Rizzo* respect the division of power between the judiciary and the legislature? Why or why not?

7. Note that, prior to the court's decision in *Rizzo*, the transcript of legislative debates had never been used by the Supreme Court of Canada in order to establish the specific meaning of a disputed legislative passage. Prior to *Rizzo*, legislative debates were used primarily to establish a law's purpose or objective. Does the court in *Rizzo* go too far with its use of legislative debates? Are the transcripts of legislative debates (commonly known as *Hansard*) convincing evidence of legislative intention?[4]

8. Review the literal language of the statute interpreted in *Rizzo*. In light of the court's decision, how should that provision be rewritten? Is judicial "rewriting" of legislation permissible? Is it fair to expect employers, employees, or creditors to be aware of the decision in *Rizzo* when they read the relevant statutory provision?

9. Is the problem at issue in *Rizzo* a problem of vagueness, ambiguity, subtext, or analogy? How would the unified theory of statutory interpretation (developed in *Theory and Practice*) deal with the *Rizzo* case?

10. Should the legislature amend the *Employment Standards Act* in order to incorporate the decision in *Rizzo*? If the legislature has not done so within five years of the *Rizzo* decision, will that be a sign that the legislature did not approve of the decision?

---

4   The use of legislative debates as interpretive aids is dealt with in chapter 4.

E. R v. Egger

The decision of the Supreme Court of Canada in *R v. Egger*, [1993] 2 SCR 451, is another example of a decision in which the court openly holds that the purpose of a provision allows the court to depart from the statute's literal language. When reading the decision in *Egger*, consider whether the court is applying the mischief rule or the golden rule to the relevant legislation. Does it matter which rule the court applies, so long as the ultimate result "makes sense"?

R v. Egger
[1993] 2 SCR 451

SOPINKA J: This drinking and driving case concerns the availability of the statutory presumption in s. 258(1)(d) of the *Criminal Code*, RSC, 1985, c. C-46, that the accused's blood alcohol level at the time a sample of the accused's blood was tested is proof of the accused's blood alcohol level at the time of the alleged offence of driving "over 80." Section 258(1)(d) imposes several conditions on the availability of the presumption. The present appeal focuses only on some of these, namely ... whether a request by the accused for the second blood sample (taken at the same time as the sample tested by the prosecution) and its release to the accused are prerequisites for the availability of the presumption.

Facts

On March 24, 1990, the car the appellant was driving was involved in a motor vehicle accident. At the scene of the accident, the police formed the opinion that the appellant was impaired, and demanded samples of his blood for analysis. ... The appellant agreed to the blood sample demand and was taken to a hospital where a nurse took the blood samples. At the hospital the appellant asked why blood samples were being taken; the investigating constable told him that two blood samples would be taken and that one was for police use while the other was kept for him in case he wanted to analyze it later on. The appellant was not charged with any offence at this time, although the investigating officer told the appellant that he would be charged with impaired driving in due course. ...

On May 22, 1990, some two months after the accident, the appellant was charged with two counts of impaired driving causing bodily harm (*Criminal Code*, s. 255(2)) and one "over 80" count (driving with a blood-alcohol content of more than 80 mg per 100 ml of blood—*Criminal Code*, s. 253(b)). At the same time he was served with a Certificate of Analyst (CA) which revealed that he had had four times the statutory limit of concentration of alcohol in his blood at the time the samples were taken. The Certificate of Analyst did not mention the existence of a second blood sample.

He was tried on September 21, 1990. In the six months between the time he gave blood samples and his trial, he neither requested the extra sample of his blood nor applied to any court for its release. The appellant was served with a Certificate of

Qualified Technician (CQT) the day before his trial. The CQT stated, among other things, that the taking of the two samples complied with the *Criminal Code*, and that a second sample was taken to permit an analysis to be made by or on behalf of the accused. The delay in serving the CQT was apparently because of inadvertence, and the Crown called the technician (the nurse who had taken the samples) as a witness at trial. The appellant was acquitted of all counts when the trial judge refused to admit the CQT and the CA into evidence. With that the "over 80" charge fell. The trial judge also dismissed the other two charges for other reasons. The respondent's appeal was allowed by the Court of Appeal which ordered a new trial on all counts.

Relevant Statutory Provisions

The statutory presumption that the blood alcohol concentration at the time of testing the blood samples is the same as at the time of driving is found in s. 258(1)(d) of the *Criminal Code*. The provisions in Part VIII of the Code dealing with the use of evidence of breath and blood samples are, as McClung JA in the court below described, "long, convoluted and in some instances, obscure" (*R v. Egger* (1991), 120 AR 360 (CA), at p. 362). Section 258(1)(d) provides as follows:

> "258(1) In any proceedings under subsection 255(1) in respect of an offence committed under section 253 or in any proceedings under subsection 255(2) or (3),
>
> ...
>
> (d) where a sample of the blood of the accused has been taken pursuant to a demand made under subsection 254(3) or otherwise with the consent of the accused or pursuant to a warrant issued under section 256, if
>
> (i) at the time the sample was taken, the person taking the sample took an additional sample of the blood of the accused and one of the samples was retained, to permit an analysis thereof to be made by or on behalf of the accused and, at the request of the accused made within three months from the taking of the samples, one of the samples was ordered to be released pursuant to subsection (4), ...
>
> evidence of the result of the analysis is, in the absence of evidence to the contrary, proof that the concentration of alcohol in the blood of the accused at the time when the offence was alleged to have been committed was the concentration determined by the analysis ..."

Subparagraph (i) refers to the request of the accused, within three months from the taking of the sample, for the release of the second sample. The accused may apply for the release of the sample by right within the three months. Subsection (4) provides:

> "(4) A judge of a superior court of criminal jurisdiction or a court of criminal jurisdiction shall, on the summary application of the accused made within three months from the day on which samples of the blood of the accused were taken, order the release of one of the samples for the purpose of an examination or analysis thereof, subject

to such terms as appear to be necessary or desirable to ensure the safeguarding of the sample and its preservation for use in any proceedings in respect of which it was retained."

The admissibility in evidence of the CA and CQT are unrelated to the availability of the presumption, and are governed by other provisions in s. 258(1). ...,

Point in Issue

The issue in this appeal is the proper interpretation of subpara. (i) of s. 258(1)(d). [In particular], what, if any, action by the accused to obtain the second sample is necessary before the presumption is available? ...

The appellant submits ... that the presumption is not available unless a court has ordered the release of the second sample at the request of the accused made within the three-month period: *Aujla, supra,* per Lambert JA, at p. 490. This submission must, in my opinion, fail. The language of s. 258(1)(d)(i) is problematic in this regard. To repeat the subparagraph for convenience, it provides:

> "258(1) ...
>
> (d) ...
>
> (i) at the time the sample was taken, the person taking the sample took an additional sample of the blood of the accused and one of the samples was retained, to permit an analysis thereof to be made by or on behalf of the accused and, at the request of the accused made within three months from the taking of the samples, one of the samples was ordered to be released pursuant to subsection (4). ...."

It has been observed that this provision is "at best, poorly drafted, and at worst, potentially out of [harmony] with the legislative framework in which it appears": Renee M. Pomerance, "'Over 80' and Under Scrutiny: Selected Charter Issues in Drinking and Driving Cases" (1992), 4 JMVL 121, at p. 167. Indeed, this is a case where the plain and ordinary meaning of a portion of the statutory language would defeat the legislative purpose and therefore, an interpretation consistent with the legislative intent which goes against the literal meaning of the statute must be adopted.

The structure of s. 258(1)(d)(i) suggests that there are three requirements for the presumption to arise (ignoring for the moment the requirements in the other subparagraphs):

> 1. at the time the sample was taken, the person taking the sample took an additional sample, AND
>
> 2. one of the samples was retained to permit an analysis thereof by or on behalf of the accused, AND
>
> 3. at the request of the accused made with the three month period, one of the samples was ordered to be released pursuant to subs. (4).

This is not a case of ambiguity, as the appellant contends in the alternative. The meaning is clear, and it is just as clear that this meaning frustrates the purpose of the legislative scheme enacted by the *Criminal Law Amendment Act, 1985,* SC 1985, c. 19. I would adopt McClung JA's holding in the court below that the principal objective of the legislative scheme for the gathering and receipt of blood and breath sample evidence is to facilitate, with appropriate safeguards, the admission of the evidence and not to exclude it. At a more basic level, the intent of the legislative reforms of 1985, which introduced the provision currently under consideration, was to allow the more effective prosecution of drunk driving offences. The legislation should be given a reasonable interpretation in line with the legislative intent. If the plain meaning of the words of subpara. (i) were given effect, the accused would always be in a position to deprive the Crown of the evidentiary advantage the legislation intended to give it, and every well advised accused would do just that by choosing not to demand a sample. The accused would, in effect, be given a "silent veto" over the Crown's use of the statutory presumption.

In my view, this legislation fits into the principle of construction enunciated by Professor Elmer A. Driedger in the following terms in *Construction of Statutes* (2nd ed. 1983), at p. 105:

> "... If, notwithstanding that the words are clear and unambiguous when read in their grammatical and ordinary sense, there is disharmony within the statute, ... then an unordinary meaning that will produce harmony is to be given the words, if they are reasonably capable of bearing that meaning."

The purpose of s. 258(1)(d) is to give the Crown the benefit of an evidentiary presumption where certain conditions are met in order to facilitate the prosecution of offences which involve driving while under the influence of alcohol. Such a purpose is inconsistent with making the presumption subject to the caprice of the accused. Even Lambert JA, the sole authority relied on by the appellant in this regard, recognized that his interpretation may not have been intended by Parliament (*Aujla, supra*, at p. 490). I would agree with one commentator's remarks in a comment on *Aujla, supra*, that

> "such an interpretation would obviously render nugatory the purpose of the legislation. To put it shortly, if compliance with s. 258(1)(d)(i) is dependent upon accused persons requesting production of their blood samples, one may query what would motivate an accused to do so. [Rick Libman, Annotation—*R v. Aujla* (1989), 13 MVR (2d) 276, at p. 279.]"

The interpretation most in line with the objective of the legislation and the Crown's disclosure obligations is that ... the accused must have notice of the existence and availability of the second sample to permit reasonable time for an informed choice as to the exercise of the right to demand production of the sample. Requiring positive action by the accused to exercise this right before the statutory presumption becomes available would further neither the legislative intent nor the accused's right to make full answer and defence. Nor would it help to enforce the Crown's disclosure obligation since that is accomplished by notifying the accused of the existence and availability of the sample. Under the interpretation that I propose, the availability of the presumption would be tied (as the reference to the right in the subparagraph appears to indicate) to the accused's opportunity to exercise his or her right, without being hamstrung by it.

One might object that this allows the presumption to stand whenever the requisite notice is given, regardless of other circumstances making the accused's right meaningless. This is not necessarily the case. To give one example, in *R v. Redmond* (1990), 37 OAC 133 (CA), the blood samples were accidentally destroyed before the accused requested production of one of them. The Court of Appeal quite rightly denied the Crown the benefit of the presumption. That was a situation where the accused could not exercise his right because of factors out of his control, and the court can always step in to deny the application of the presumption in such circumstances. The result in *Redmond, supra*, was that the Crown was required to adduce viva voce expert testimony extrapolating the accused's blood alcohol concentration and level of impairment at the time of driving. Being denied the benefit of the presumption clearly does not derail "over 80" prosecutions. It simply requires the Crown to prove them by recourse to the evidential tools on which it would ordinarily have to rely in the absence of the presumption. ... [The court went on to acquit the accused for other reasons.]

NOTES AND QUESTIONS

1. Does Sopinka J have sufficient grounds to conclude that s. 258 of the Code contains one or more drafting errors? When should a court feel confident in reaching that conclusion?

2. What should a court do when it discovers a drafting error? Should the court apply the provision as written, "judicially amend" the provision in accordance with the enactment's perceived purpose, or simply refuse to apply the provision at all? Which is the least "intrusive" judicial remedy?

3. Is the problem at issue in *Egger* a problem of vagueness, ambiguity, subtext, or analogy? How would the unified theory (developed in *Theory and Practice*) deal with the *Egger* case?

4. Sopinka J notes that "the plain and ordinary meaning of a portion of the statutory language would defeat the legislative purpose." His Lordship goes on to find that "an interpretation consistent with the legislative intent which goes against the literal meaning of the statute must be adopted." Note that *Egger* was decided two years before the court's decision in *McIntosh*, above. Are the two decisions compatible?

5. In *McIntosh*, Lamer CJ took the view that the court could *not* depart from the literal language of a provision, even where that literal language gave rise to an absurdity. When statutory language "defeats the legislative purpose" of a particular provision, does that constitute an "absurdity"? In other words, would it be "absurd" for Parliament to enact a law which defeats its own purpose?

6. Is the decision in *Egger* an example of the mischief rule, the golden rule, or both? If the decision could be framed either way, is there any reason to choose one rule over the other?

7. Sopinka J holds that "the principal objective of the legislative scheme for the gathering and receipt of blood and breath sample evidence is to facilitate ... the admission of the evidence and not to exclude it." Upon what evidence does Sopinka J rely in arriving at this conclusion?

IV. EXERCISES

A. Auditions

Suggested length: 10-15 pages

Julie and John were aspiring actors trying to build careers in film and television. Everything seemed to be going well for Julie and John, until they applied for the acting jobs described in the following advertisement, placed in the *Peterborough Globe* on February 1, 2001:

OPEN AUDITIONS

Male and Female actors required for Government Sponsored anti-smoking ads. Send Resumé and Photo to the attention of Terrence McGee, Ministry of Propaganda, Peterborough, Ontario.

Julie and John sent their application packages to the specified address, and were granted auditions on February 12, 2001.

On the appointed day, Julie and John showed up at a studio for their auditions. Famed director Justin Mohan walked about the studio glancing at each of the hopeful actors, while Terrence McGee (a provincial government official) walked alongside, giving advice to Mr. Mohan concerning each applicant's qualifications.

As Mohan and McGee approached Julie and John, McGee whispered in Mohan's ear while Mohan shook his head. Having been turned down for parts before, Julie and John both realized that this wasn't a good sign. John stepped forward and asked Mr. Mohan if anything was wrong.

"I'm sorry," Mohan replied, "but we only need two actors—one male and one female. You are far too tall for the male role, and your friend looks too young for the female part. Besides, I saw both of you smoking cigarettes outside, and this is an anti-smoking ad." Mr. McGee then approached Julie and explained that the government, in sponsoring these commercials, was looking to spread its anti-smoking message to a particular demographic—"yuppies" in their early 30s. McGee went on to explain that, as Julie was a rather young-looking 25, and John's height gave him a menacing appearance, the two actors were simply unsuited for the parts.

As an avid reader of law-related novels, John sensed the spectre of illegality. This was a government job—the actors would be paid by the provincial government, who sponsored the commercial and advised the director on all casting decisions. In John's view, the government's action (in failing to hire Julie and John for the reasons noted above) amounted to discrimination contrary to s. 232 of the Ontario *Code of Employment Rights* (1986) (a fictional piece of legislation). Section 232 appears under the heading "Discrimination" and provides as follows:

232(1) No employer may engage in a discriminatory practice.

232(2) For the purposes of subsection (1), "discriminatory practice" includes any act of discrimination, including discrimination based on race, national or ethnic origin, colour, religion, sex, age or mental or physical disability, but does not include any form of discrimination that relates directly to *bona fide* occupational requirements.

After reviewing this section, Julie and John retained Stephanie Merritt to launch a discrimination claim against the government. During the course of her first meeting with Julie and John, however, Stephanie pointed out that the government of Ontario had recently passed a new *Anti-Discrimination Act*, (1998) (another fictional piece of legislation), the preamble of which states:

> *Whereas* the Government of Ontario is committed to the principles of equality and justice, and seeks to ensure that all individuals are treated fairly without undue discrimination,
>
> *And Whereas* certain acts of discrimination may adversely effect the dignity and self-worth of individuals,
>
> *Now Therefore* Her Majesty, by and with the advice and consent of the legislature of the province, enacts as follows:

Stephanie also pointed out s. 9 of the *Anti-Discrimination Act*, which appears under the heading "Employment Discrimination" and provides as follows:

> 9(1) No employer may engage in a discriminatory practice.
>
> 9(2) For the purposes of this Act, "discriminatory practice" means any act of discrimination based on race, sex, age, sexual preference, disability or other personal characteristics.

Both the Ontario *Code of Employment Rights* and the *Anti-Discrimination Act* contain provisions requiring any employer found to have committed discrimination to pay compensatory damages to the victim of the discriminatory practice. It should also be noted that both statutes explicitly apply to the government of Ontario where the government is acting as an employer.

You are an articling student at Stephanie's firm. Stephanie has asked you to prepare a brief memorandum outlining any claim that Julie and John may have against the government of Ontario. In particular, your memorandum should address any issues of interpretation that may effect the likelihood of the claim's success. Be sure to canvass arguments on both sides of each issue.

Notes: The provisions set out above are the *only* provisions relevant to Julie and John's situation. Do not raise any arguments related to other provisions (including the Charter), unless you are simply using them as analogies.

You must assume that neither of the statutes raised in this case has been *expressly* repealed or amended by the government of Ontario.

B. Subway Repair

Suggested length: 10-15 pages

Grant Crough was the assistant chief mechanic for the Downsview Transit Commission (DTC). On September 22, 1997, Grant was lying in bed at home attempting to get over a nasty cold. Grant had stayed home from work for three days, and was finally starting to feel a little better. Just to make sure that he would be fully recovered and able to work in the morning, Grant took a dose of Drowz-all (a well-known cough suppressant and cold medicine) before going to bed for the evening. It should be noted that Drowz-all is 30 percent alcohol and is widely known to cause drowsiness (hence the name). The Drowz-all bottle bears a warning informing users not to drive or operate heavy machinery while under the influence of the product.

At approximately 11:30 p.m., two hours after Grant had gone to bed, Grant received a telephone call from his supervisor at the Downsview Transit Commission, Scott McGee. Apparently, the brakes on one of the DTC's subway cars had failed earlier that evening, causing a minor accident. As a safety precaution, all DTC mechanics were being called in to work through the night, inspecting the brakes on all of the DTC trains and making any necessary repairs.

Grant informed Mr. McGee that he was still a little under the weather and that he had just consumed a dose of Drowz-all, which was likely to impair his judgment and make him too sleepy to perform his job properly. Mr. McGee assured Grant that the work would not be particularly difficult, and that Grant would probably be a member of a team of several mechanics working together, so that were Grant to make any mistakes in his drowsy state, the mistakes would be caught and corrected by other mechanics. Mr. McGee also informed Grant that the job would be paying three times Grant's usual hourly rate as it qualified as "emergency overtime work" pursuant to union rules.

Grant reluctantly agreed to go into work for the evening in exchange for Mr. McGee's promise that Grant could take the remainder of the week off to recover from his cold. As Grant was still feeling a little groggy from the Drowz-all, he woke up his wife and asked her to drive him to work.

After his wife dropped him off at work, Grant set about the task of inspecting the brakes on the DTC trains. After approximately an hour, police officers arrived on the scene to take a statement from Grant's co-workers regarding the accident that had taken place earlier that evening. One of the officers conducting the investigation noticed Grant performing repairs on one of the DTC trains. He also noticed that Grant appeared to be staggering slightly, as if he was under the influence of alcohol or narcotics. At the time that the officer saw Grant repairing the brakes, Grant was the only DTC employee working on that particular train.

The officer called Grant aside and performed a sobriety test. Sure enough, the Drowz-all had taken its toll and Grant failed the sobriety test miserably. As a result, Grant was charged with an offence under s. 253 of the *Criminal Code*. At the time (1997) that section provided as follows:

> 253. Every one commits an offence who operates a motor vehicle or vessel or operates or assists in the operation of an aircraft or of railway equipment or has the care or control of a motor vehicle, vessel, aircraft or railway equipment, whether it is in motion or not,
>
> (a) while the person's ability to operate the vehicle, vessel, aircraft or railway equipment is impaired by alcohol or a drug; or
>
> (b) having consumed alcohol in such a quantity that the concentration in the person's blood exceeds eighty milligrams of alcohol in one hundred millilitres of blood.

Grant admitted at trial that his condition on the night in question was such that he could not have operated a motor vehicle or a train. As a result, Grant was convicted and fined $300.

In addition to fining Grant, the trial judge made an order pursuant to s. 259 of the *Criminal Code* prohibiting Grant from operating a motor vehicle for a period of three months. Section 259 of the *Criminal Code* provided (in part) as follows:

(1) Where an offender is convicted of an offence committed under section 253 or 254 or discharged under section 730 of an offence committed under section 253 and, at the time the offence was committed or, in the case of an offence committed under section 254, within the two hours preceding that time, was operating or had the care or control of a motor vehicle, vessel, aircraft or railway equipment or was assisting in the operation of an aircraft or of railway equipment, the court that sentences the offender shall, in addition to any other punishment that may be imposed for that offence, make an order prohibiting the offender from operating a motor vehicle on any street, road, highway or other public place, or from operating a vessel, aircraft or railway equipment, as the case may be,

    (a) for a first offence, during a period of not more than three years and not less than three months;

    (b) for a second offence, during a period of not more than three years and not less than six months; and

    (c) for each subsequent offence, during a period of not more than three years and not less than one year.

When speaking on the issue of sentencing, Grant's counsel noted that the order under s. 259 was particularly harsh, because Grant lives a long way from his place of work, in an area that (ironically) is not serviced by public transit. The trial judge answered this submission by making the following comments:

> My hands are tied. Although Mr. Crough may not be the type of offender at whom such orders are supposed to be directed, he does stand convicted under s. 253 of the Code. Based on the clear and unambiguous language of s. 259, the order is mandatory in this situation. I have no discretion in the matter.

As a result, the trial judge made the order upon entering the conviction.

Grant has appealed his conviction and his sentence (including the order under s. 259) to the Canadian Court of Justice (Appeal Division). You are a judge on that court: write a judgment either upholding, setting aside, or varying the terms of the judgment below. (Don't concern yourself with procedural issues beyond those contained in the sections produced above.) Note that your court is not bound by any prior judicial decisions. Ensure that your judgment deals only with "interpretive issues" (that is, issues relating to the meaning of words or phrases found within the relevant statute). Also note that the *Criminal Code* is a real statute—any interpretive assistance that you can derive by reference to other *Criminal Code* provisions may be helpful. Finally, be aware that Grant's case is governed by the *Criminal Code* as it existed in 1997—the relevant provisions may have been amended since that time. You may wish to consider whether any recent amendments cast light upon the meaning of the 1997 version.[5]

---

5   The admissibility of prior and subsequent versions of a statute is considered in chapter 4. For now, you may simply assume that such "evidence" is admissible for whatever interpretive assistance you think that it may offer.

C. Current Judicial Approaches

Suggested length: 15-20 pages

Discuss the following statement:

> Statutory interpretation has undergone a significant transformation since its genesis as a series of positivistic rules upon which judges could blindly rely. In the current era of increased judicial activism, judges faced with interpretive problems are more inclined to reject archaic maxims and rules of interpretation, and instead render decisions based on vague notions of social justice and legislative intent.

Without limiting your freedom to choose an appropriate format for this assignment, the following methods of addressing the foregoing statement may be useful:

1. Find a pre-1940 judicial decision that raises several issues of statutory interpretation and addresses them in a "technical" manner through the use of interpretive maxims and concrete rules. Overrule the decision through the use of purposive interpretation, stating why the "old schools of thought" should be rejected.
2. Write an essay explaining why the statement set out above is completely wrong, completely correct, or somewhere in between.
3. Find a confusingly worded statute or a confusing series of legislative provisions. By interpreting the unclear example(s), demonstrate how both the "old" and "new" approaches to statutory interpretation can be used to lead to whatever result the judge desires. What does this say about the evolution of statutory interpretation?

CHAPTER FOUR

Evidence of the Statute's Meaning

I. INTRODUCTION

As we have seen in previous chapters, courts draw on a wide variety of interpretive aids when attempting to determine the meaning of statutory language. We have seen courts refer to a statute's preamble, previous versions of the same enactment, the transcripts of legislative debates and countless other sources in their quest to unearth a statute's meaning. The purpose of this chapter is to consider the use that courts may make of various pieces of "evidence" in attempting to interpret legislation.

Generally speaking, there are two broad categories of evidence that may reveal a statute's meaning—namely, (1) "intrinsic aids" or elements of the statute being considered, and (2) "extrinsic aids" or pieces of evidence found beyond the four corners of the enactment. Usually, internal elements of a statute will be considered admissible and relevant evidence for the purpose of demonstrating an act's meaning. The use that can be made of extrinsic aids has historically been much more contentious, although the modern trend in Canadian courts is to simply admit and give consideration to every piece of evidence that may illuminate the meaning of a statute.

To further complicate matters, interpretation acts throughout Canada set out rules that govern the evidentiary use that may be made of certain "parts" of a statute (such as headings, preambles, titles, and marginal notes), and these rules often vary between jurisdictions. Lawyers should consult the interpretation act of their own jurisdiction before attempting to rely on a heading within a statute (for example) as evidence of the meaning of a provision within that enactment.

This chapter is arranged in sections that deal with specific pieces of evidence that a court may consider when assessing a statute's meaning. There are sections dealing with (1) the statute's title, (2) headings within the statute, (3) marginal notes, (4) punctuation, (5) previous versions of the statute being considered, and (6) legislative debates. This is by no means an exhaustive list of items that judges may refer to when construing legislation. Instead, it is merely a broad sampling of the sources that may be consulted by a court that is asked to construe a statute's language. As noted above, the current trend in Canadian courts is to consider whatever aids may shed light on the meaning of an enactment: in matters of statutory interpretation, courts seem to be growing less concerned with considerations of weight and admissibility.

When reviewing the cases that follow, consider what it is that the court is trying to "prove" by reference to the piece of evidence being considered. Is the court attempting to establish "legislative intent"? Is that useful, given that (as we have seen in chapter 1 of Randal N. Graham, *Statutory Interpretation: Theory and Practice* (Toronto: Emond Montgomery, 2001) (*"Theory and Practice"*)) legislative intent may be nothing more than a legal fiction? What is the point of looking for "evidence" of something that does not really exist? Conversely, is it possible that the courts are merely relying on this "evidence" as rhetorical support for the courts' own arguments concerning a statute's meaning?

II. TITLE

A. Legislation

The evidentiary value of a statute's title is dealt with explicitly in the interpretation acts of some jurisdictions. For example, s. 9 of British Columbia's *Interpretation Act*, RSBC 1996, c. 238, provides that a statute's title is "part of" the enactment, intended to "assist in explaining [the Act's] meaning and object." Section 10 of the *Interpretation Act* of Prince Edward Island, RSPEI 1988, c. I-8, is similar, stating that the title of an enactment "shall be construed as part thereof intended to assist in explaining its purport and object."

The interpretation acts of other jurisdictions (including the federal Act) do not make reference to the evidentiary value of a title. This does not, however, mean that courts in those jurisdictions are precluded from looking to the title of an enactment for evidence of a statute's meaning. As the cases in the following section demonstrate, it is now settled that courts may rely on a statute's title as evidence when attempting to interpret the meaning of that statute's text.

B. R v. Lane

R v. Lane, Ex p. Gould
[1937] 1 DLR 212 (NB SC, App. Div.)

BAXTER, CJ: This case involves the constitutionality of the Provincial Statute 1936, c. 48 "An Act for the Suppression of Slot Machines and Other Gambling Devices," ... "Slot Machine" is defined by the Act in such terms as to include the instrument which is the subject of the present litigation. The Act declares that no slot machine shall be capable of ownership nor shall the same be the subject of property rights within the Province, and no Court of civil jurisdiction shall recognize or give effect to any property rights in any slot machine. Provision is also made for the seizure without warrant by a peace officer of any machine which such officer believes to be a slot machine within the meaning of the Act. He is directed to bring the contrivance before a Magistrate who then issues a summons to the person in whose apparent possession the same was at the time of seizure, requiring such person at a time and place therein named to show cause why the same should not be confiscated. Unless such person satisfies the Magistrate that the contrivance is not a slot machine within the meaning of the Act, the Magistrate orders the same confiscated to His Majesty in the right of the Province, and it is thereupon disposed of as the Attorney-General may direct.

It was argued that the Act invaded the province of criminal law and that the title was evidence of this intended infringement. The title is now a part of an Act. Originally it was not so. In constitutional theory an Act is enacted by the King though, of course, by and with the consent of the representatives of his people. The King always was, at first in actual practice, and later in theory, the maker of the statute law. At first he was invoked to exercise his power by petition though the law might emanate from his own initiative. In the petitory form the bills were entered on the rolls of parliament with the King's answer and at the end of the session the judges drew up those records into statutes to which they gave title: *Maxwell on Statutes*, 4th ed., p. 59.

So, originally, it appears a title was not enacted by the royal assent. It was simply a descriptive sentence attached to the bill after the latter had become law by the expression of the King's will.

In *Jeffries v. Alexander*, 8 HLC 594, at p. 603, note (h), 11 ER 562, Lord Cranworth said that "though the question as to the title of an Act is put from the Chair in the House of Commons it was never put in" the House of Lords. Craies' *Hardcastle*, 4th ed., p. 179 says that under the present procedure in both Houses titles are now the subject of amendment and that the full title is always on the roll. In New Brunswick the title is always put to the House and specially adopted. It becomes part of the roll which is signed by the Lieutenant-Governor when he assents to the legislation. Its office is somewhat similar to that of a preamble, for it may "be looked at in order to remove any ambiguity in the words of the Act." *Coomber v. Justices of Berks* (1882), 9 QBD 17, at p. 33, per Huddleston, B, and see *O'Connor v. NS Telephone Co.* (1893), 22 SCR 276, at p. 292. Also *Fenton v. Thorley & Co.*, [1903] AC 443.

It is alleged that the Act is unconstitutional because it trenches upon the field of the criminal law and that its title evidences this purpose. I cannot accept this view. Assuming that the title is a part of the Act for every possible purpose, what is there to prevent a Provincial Legislature from assisting the Dominion jurisdiction by adopting legislation within its competence? I can see nothing. It is clear that the Provincial Legislature cannot shelter itself under the "Property and Civil Rights" clause if its legislation is, in essence, that of the criminal law. But in order to prosecute for a criminal offence it is necessary to have an accused.

Under the Act in question there is no possibility that any person can be charged with any offence nor is any punishment specified. There are no limits to the powers of a provincial Legislature when dealing with "Property and Civil Rights" except the restraining power of disallowance. Property can be taken from one person and given to another, or, as by the Act in question, it can be vested in the Crown. Nor does "confiscation" necessarily connote crime. It simply means the bringing of something into the treasury of a Government ...

It is not necessary to pursue this interesting subject further because it is sufficient to say that the Crown has acquired the machine in question in this case under the confiscatory provisions of s. 5 of the Act but not as a confiscation for a crime of which any person has been accused. ...

NOTES AND QUESTIONS

1. The court in *R v. Lane* makes it clear that a title is *admissible* as evidence. What "weight" (or level of importance) does the court give to the title of the statute being considered?

2. The court concludes that the relevant act does not deal with criminal law because "there is no possibility that any person can be charged with any offence nor is any punishment specified." Is this persuasive? Could the loss of one's (potentially rather expensive) slot machine count as a "punishment" under the Act? Why or why not?

C. Committee for the Commonwealth of Canada

Committee for the Commonwealth of Canada v. Canada
[1991] 1 SCR 139

[At an airport, an RCMP officer asked the defendants to stop accosting passersby with information about the respondent committee and to cease their attempts to recruit new members. The respondents L and D were told by the airport's assistant manager that such political information activities were not permitted according to ss. 7(a) and 7(b) of the Government Airport Concession Operations Regulations. These sections prohibited the conducting of any business or undertaking, commercial or otherwise, and any advertising or soliciting at an airport unless permission had been granted (in writing) by the minister. At a trial, the judge granted the defendants' action for a declaration that the appellant had violated the respondents' fundamental freedoms. The judgment was affirmed by the Federal Court of Appeal. The Supreme Court had to determine whether ss. 7(a) and 7(b) of the regulations were inconsistent with the guarantee of free expression in s. 2(b) of the Charter and, if so, whether these sections amounted to a reasonable limit under s. 1 of the Charter.]

LAMER CJ: … The appellant argues that the wording of s. 7 of the Regulations is wide enough to embrace political propaganda. Both Dubé J at trial and the majority on appeal (MacGuigan and Hugessen JJA) concluded that s. 7(b) of the Regulations applies only to commercial rather than purely political activities and that accordingly the respondents' conduct did not fall within the scope of this provision. Pratte JA, dissenting, concluded that s. 7(b) did not apply only to commercial activities and that the respondents' political propaganda was covered by the said paragraph. Section 7 reads as follows:

> "7. Subject to section 8, except as authorized in writing by the Minister, no person shall
>
>> (a) conduct any business or undertaking, commercial or otherwise, at an airport;
>>
>> (b) advertise or solicit at an airport on his own behalf or on behalf of any person; or
>>
>> (c) fix, install or place anything at an airport for the purpose of any business or undertaking."

In my opinion, this question must be answered by applying the rules of statutory interpretation, and in particular by considering the exact meaning of the language of s. 7 and the legislative context in which the latter is placed.

The appellant's argument that the wording of para. (a) of the foregoing section is broad enough to embrace the political propaganda offered by the respondents must be dismissed. First, there is no doubt that the respondents' actions were not strictly speaking an "undertaking." Second, although the expression "business ... commercial or otherwise" is theoretically wide enough to cover the dissemination of political ideas, I am, as a matter of logic, convinced that the legislature did not intend to give this language such a wide scope. The words "business ... otherwise" would on that basis be wide enough to encompass virtually any "business" of any nature whatever. Indeed, I do not believe that the legislature intended to make the Minister's authorization necessary for every "business" occurring within an airport. Such a result would be absurd. Despite the broad language of this provision, I conclude from it that para. (a) of s. 7 of the Regulations prohibits businesses or undertakings of a commercial nature, and that the qualifier "or otherwise" cannot extend the scope of this paragraph so as to make it apply to the actions of the respondents in the case at bar. ...

In considering the context in which s. 7 of the Regulations appears, I shall examine first the full title of the Regulations and then the short title. Both form an integral part of the text of the Regulations and may validly be used by anyone interpreting them in order to clarify the meaning of other provisions of the Regulations. (See in this regard *O'Connor v. Nova Scotia Telephone Co.* (1893), 22 SCR 276; *DeWare v. The Queen*, [1954] SCR 182.) The full title of the Regulations reads as follows: "*Regulations Respecting the Control of Commercial and Other **Operations** at Government Airports*" (emphasis added). Although the words "and Other" give the preceding words a rather broad scope, I note that the title indicates that the Regulations apply to "operations." The very idea of an operation, in my opinion, carries with it a connotation of industry or profit; this term seems to me to have intrinsically commercial overtones.

The short title of the said Regulations reads as follows: "*Government Airport **Concession Operations** Regulations*" (emphasis added). It will be seen from reading this version of the title that the commercial emphasis given to the application of the Regulations is still more clearly defined by the reference to the operation of concessions. I cannot imagine a concession being operated for any purpose other than a commercial or lucrative one. Though the short title of necessity ... "sacrifices precision for concision," it is an indication of the federal legislature's intention to limit the scope of the Regulations to commercial matters (on the use of the title for interpretation purposes, reference may be made to Côté, op. cit., at pp. 36-40).

A brief review of the other provisions of the Regulations also indicates that the latter deal first and foremost with services providing transportation for passengers by means of commercial vehicles operated in airports and with the terms and conditions to which such operations are subject. [The remainder of the judgment has been omitted.]

NOTES AND QUESTIONS

1. Is the court's use of the regulation's title persuasive? Why or why not?

2. Note that the court refers both to the "short title" and the "long title" of the enactment being considered. According to Driedger, "[a]lthough a distinction is sometimes made between the long and short title, with the latter receiving less weight, often the courts ignore this distinction and treat the short title as if it were the sole title of the legislation" (Elmer Driedger, *Driedger on the Construction of Statutes*, 3d ed., Ruth Sullivan, ed. (Toronto: Butterworths, 1994). Does it make sense to give a short title "less weight" (or evidentiary impact) than the statute's long title? Why or why not?

3. How might the unified theory assist the court in this case?

III. PREAMBLE

A. Introduction

The preamble of a statute is a statement of the policies underlying the statute or the circumstances that led to its enactment. As Elmer Driedger notes in *Construction of Statutes*, an act's preamble "appears at the beginning of the Act, between the long title and the enacting clause" (Driedger, at 294).

We have already seen examples of the court employing a preamble for the purpose of revealing the meaning of a legislative passage. For example, in *Quebec v. Boisbriand*, [2001] 1 SCR 665 (discussed in chapter 1), the Supreme Court of Canada referred to the preamble of Quebec's *Charter of Human Rights and Freedoms*, RSQ, c. C-12, for the purpose of establishing that statute's purpose. This is typical of the manner in which courts rely on a statute's preamble: generally speaking, the court will rely on the preamble in order to clarify the objective or the purpose of the legislation in question. As previously noted, an analysis of a statute's purpose or objective often plays a critical role in the interpretation of a statute's language. For this reason, a preamble can often be a valuable tool in the interpretation of legislative text.

B. Legislation

The evidentiary value of a statute's preamble is dealt with in the interpretation acts of most jurisdictions. Section 13 of Canada's *Interpretation Act*, RSC 1985, c. I-21, for example, provides that "[t]he preamble of an enactment shall be read as a part of the enactment intended to assist in explaining its purport and object." Section 8 of Ontario's *Interpretation Act*, RSO 1990, c. I.11, is quite similar, providing that "[t]he preamble of an Act shall be deemed a part thereof and is intended to assist in explaining the purport and object of the Act." Other provincial interpretation acts contain parallel provisions.[1] As a result, a preamble must be considered a part of the statute in which it is found, and is accordingly admissible for the purposes of construing the statute's language.

---

1   See, for example, s. 14 of Newfoundland's *Interpretation Act*, RSN 1990 c. I-19 and s. 13 of Manitoba's *Interpretation Act*, RSM 1987, c. I-80, which provides that "[t]he preamble of an Act forms part of it and is intended to assist in explaining its meaning and intent."

C. The Anti-Inflation Act

Re Anti-Inflation Act
[1976] 2 SCR 373

[The question before the court in this case was whether the *Anti-Inflation Act* fell within the jurisdiction of the Parliament of Canada. In particular, the court was asked to determine whether or not the Act fell within Parliament's power to legislate matters for the "Peace, Order and Good Government" of Canada (found in the opening words of s. 91 of the *Constitution Act, 1867*). In answering this question, the court was required to determine whether inflation amounted to a matter of "serious national concern." The court addressed this question by (among other things) reference to the statute's preamble.]

LASKIN CJ (Judson, Spence, and Dickson JJ concurring): By Order in Council PC 1976-581 dated March 11, 1976, the Governor General in Council invoked the authority conferred by s. 55 of the *Supreme Court Act*, RSC 1970, c. S-19 and referred the following [question] to this Court for its opinion:

"1. Is the *Anti-Inflation Act*, Statutes of Canada 1974-75-76, Chapter 75 (a copy of which Act and the Anti-Inflation Guidelines made thereunder are attached hereto as Annex "A") ultra vires the Parliament of Canada either in whole or in part, and, if so, in what particular or particulars and to what extent?" ...

The Bill which became the *Anti-Inflation Act* was introduced into the House of Commons on October 16, 1975 (notice having been given on October 14), and was passed on December 15, 1975, but with effect to a degree from October 14, 1975. Its long title and preamble are as follows:

"An Act to provide for the restraint of profit margins, prices, dividends and compensation in Canada

WHEREAS the Parliament of Canada recognizes that inflation in Canada at current levels is contrary to the interests of all Canadians and that the containment and reduction of inflation has become a matter of serious national concern;

AND WHEREAS to accomplish such containment and reduction of inflation it is necessary to restrain profit margins, prices, dividends and compensation;" ...

The Act as supplemented by the Guidelines, which were promulgated on December 22, 1975 and amended on February 3, 1976, establishes supervision, control and regulation of prices, profits, wages, salaries, fees and dividends by way of monitoring and limiting increases in order to combat inflation. Flexibility in administration is built into the Guidelines by making allowance for such matters as cost increases and productivity factors. The Guidelines are complex in their detail as well as in their language, and it is consoling that an elaboration of their terms is not a prerequisite to the determination of the answers to the two questions referred to this Court. ...

The Attorney-General of Canada relied upon the preamble to the *Anti-Inflation Act* both in respect of his primary argument and in respect of his alternative argument.

He emphasized the words therein "that the containment and reduction of inflation has become a matter of *serious* national concern" and as well the following words that "to accomplish such containment and reduction of inflation it is *necessary* to restrain profit margins, prices, dividends and compensation" (the [italicized] words were especially emphasized). I do not regard it as telling against the Attorney-General's alternative position that the very word "emergency" was not used. Forceful language would not carry the day for the Attorney-General of Canada if the circumstances attending its use did not support the constitutional significance sought to be drawn from it. Of course, the absence of any preamble would weaken the assertion of crisis conditions, and I have already drawn attention to the fact that no preamble suggesting a critical economic situation, indeed no preamble at all was included in the legislation challenged in the Board of Commerce case.

The preamble in the present case is sufficiently indicative that Parliament was introducing a far reaching programme prompted by what in its view was a serious national condition. The validity of the *Anti-Inflation Act* does not, however, stand or fall on that preamble, but the preamble does provide a base for assessing the gravity of the circumstances which called forth the legislation. ...

NOTES AND QUESTIONS

1. What weight does the court give to the preamble of the *Anti-Inflation Act*?

2. Why would Parliament insert the phrases "serious national concern" and "necessary to restrain profit margins" into the preamble of the *Anti-Inflation Act*? Was Parliament genuinely trying to explain the purpose and scope of the Act, or was Parliament preparing for a predictable constitutional challenge? In answering this question, consider how useful the Act's preamble might be as an aid to the interpretation of the Act itself.

3. If preambles can be used for self-serving purposes (that is, to stave off a constitutional challenge), how reliable are preambles as indicators of legislative intent?

4. Review the decision of the court in *Quebec v. Boisbriand*, set out in chapter 1. Is the preamble at issue in that case more or less useful than the preamble at issue in the *Anti-Inflation* reference? Is the court's use of the preamble in *Boisbriand* persuasive?

IV. HEADINGS

A. Legislation

Most statutes are divided up into discrete "parts" or "subdivisions" that are separated from one another by headings. Provincial interpretation acts are fairly uniform in their treatment of headings as interpretive aids. The following are typical examples:

Ontario *Interpretation Act*, s. 9. "The marginal notes and headings in the body of an Act and references to former enactments form no part of the Act but shall be deemed to be inserted for convenience of reference only."

Manitoba *Interpretation Act*, s. 14. "Tables of contents, headings, notes, and historical references that appear at the end of a provision are included in an Act or regulation for convenience of reference only and form no part of it."

It should be noted, however, that the acts of some jurisdictions conspicuously fail to mention the evidentiary value of headings, despite the fact that they contain provisions dealing explicitly with marginal notes and historical references. Section 13 of the federal *Interpretation Act* is a typical example. According to s. 13:

> Marginal notes and references to former enactments that appear after the end of a section or other division in an enactment form no part of the enactment, but are inserted for convenience of reference only.

Several provinces follow the federal model.[2] What is the status of headings in these jurisdictions? Does the explicit reference to marginal notes and historical references imply that, since headings are *not* expressly excluded as interpretive aids, headings can be relied upon for the purposes of interpreting legislation (*expressio unius est exclusio alterius*)? This argument is not particularly compelling, because other sections of the same enactments expressly state that preambles *are* to be considered interpretive aids, but fail to specifically give the same treatment to headings. It seems that no inferences can be drawn concerning the use of headings in jurisdictions whose interpretation acts fail to deal with them expressly. As Elmer Driedger notes in *Construction of Statutes* (at 268), "This treatment is unsatisfactory." Indeed, Driedger advocates the use of headings as interpretive tools, because headings "form an obvious part of the context in which the provisions of an Act are read" (at 268).

Despite the ambiguous legislative treatment given to headings, in many cases Canadian courts have found headings to be quite useful in the interpretation of legislative language. The decision of the Supreme Court of Canada in *R v. Lohnes*, [1992] 1 SCR 167, is a typical example. That case is the topic of the following section.

B. R v. Lohnes

R v. Lohnes
[1992] 1 SCR 167

McLACHLIN J: This case requires this Court for the first time to consider what constitutes a public disturbance under s. 175(1)(a) of the *Criminal Code*, RSC, 1985, c. C-46, which makes it an offence to cause a disturbance in or near a public place by, inter alia, fighting, screaming, shouting, swearing, singing or using insulting or obscene language. Shouting or swearing or singing are not in themselves criminal offences. They become criminal only when they cause a disturbance in or near a public place. What constitutes such a disturbance? For example, does mere annoyance or emotional disturbance of the complainant suffice? Or is something more required?

---

2   See, for example, the *Interpretation Act* of Prince Edward Island, RSPEI 1998, c. I-8, s. 11.

The Facts

The case began as a disagreement between two neighbours in the town of Milton, Nova Scotia. The appellant, Donald Lohnes, lived across the street from a certain Mr. Porter. Mr. Porter, it seems, was given to collecting equipment on his premises and running motors which made loud noises. This disturbed Mr. Lohnes. It disturbed him so much that on two occasions a year apart he went onto the veranda of his house and shouted obscenities at Mr. Porter. The essence of Mr. Lohnes' remarks was that he did not want Mr. Porter "to run that chain saw or that lawn mower or to leave that or have that God-damned junk heap." This was embellished by a string of epithets revealing an impressive command of the obscene vernacular. On the second occasion Mr. Lohnes concluded his oration with the assertion that he would shoot Mr. Porter if he had a gun.

Mr. Porter filed a complaint. He was the only Crown witness. There was no evidence that anyone else heard Mr. Lohnes' statements or that Mr. Porter's conduct was affected by them.

Mr. Lohnes was convicted on the ground that his conduct in itself constituted a disturbance within s. 175(1)(a) of the *Criminal Code*; the trial judge found, as well, that Mr. Porter was "disturbed" by the impugned conduct. The convictions were upheld by the summary conviction appeal court. The Nova Scotia Supreme Court, Appeal Division refused leave from that decision: (1990), 100 NSR (2d) 268, 272 APR 268. He now appeals to this Court.

Legislation

Section 175 of the *Criminal Code*, states:

> "175(1) Every one who
>   (a) not being in a dwelling-house, causes a disturbance in or near a public place,
>   (i) by fighting, screaming, shouting, swearing, singing or using insulting or obscene language,
>
>   ...
>
> is guilty of an offence punishable on summary conviction.
>
>   (2) In the absence of other evidence, or by way of corroboration of other evidence, a summary conviction court may infer from the evidence of a peace officer relating to the conduct of a person or persons, whether ascertained or not, that a disturbance described in paragraph (1)(a) or (d) was caused or occurred."

Analysis

Section 175(1)(a) creates a two-element offence consisting of: (1) commission of one of the enumerated acts; which, (2) causes a disturbance in or near a public place. There is no doubt on the facts of this case that one of the enumerated acts was committed. The only question is whether the evidence establishes that it caused a disturbance in or near a public place.

The word "disturbance" encompasses a broad range of meanings. At one extreme, it may be something as innocuous as a false note or a jarring colour; something which disturbs in the sense of annoyance or disruption. At the other end of the spectrum are incidents of violence, inducing disquiet, fear and apprehension for physical safety. Between these extremes lies a vast variety of disruptive conduct. The question before us is whether all conduct within this broad spectrum elicits criminal liability under s. 175(1), and if not, where the line should be drawn.

The Nova Scotia Supreme Court, Appeal Division in dismissing Mr. Lohnes' application for leave to appeal, agreed with the finding implicit to the judgments below: all that is required to establish an offence under s. 175(1)(a) is one of the forms of prohibited conduct (fighting, screaming, shouting, swearing, singing or using insulting or obscene language) which one ought to know would disturb others. The appellant contends that this interpretation is too broad; there must be some overtly manifested disturbance of the public's use and enjoyment of the public place where the act takes place. The main issue thus turns on how "disturbance" in s. 175(1)(a) is defined; does foreseeable emotional upset suffice, or must there be an externally manifested disturbance of a public nature? ...

I propose to consider these issues from the perspectives of the authorities, the principles of statutory construction, and the underlying policy issues. On my reading, these considerations point to the conclusion that s. 175(1)(a) of the *Criminal Code* requires an externally manifested disturbance in or near a public place, consisting either in the act itself or in a secondary disturbance. ...

Principles of Statutory Construction

The word "disturbance" is capable of many meanings. The task is to choose the meaning which best accords with the intention of Parliament.

The following arguments support the conclusion that "disturbance" in s. 175(1)(a) involves more than mere mental or emotional annoyance or disruption.

First, the noun "disturbance" may have a different connotation than the verb "to disturb." Not everything that disturbs people results in a disturbance (e.g., smoking). A definition which posits identity between "disturb" and "disturbance" is contrary to ordinary usage, the most fundamental principle of statutory construction. This is not to say that one cannot speak of a purely emotional disturbance, but rather that "disturbance" has a secondary meaning which "disturb" does not possess; a meaning which suggests interference with an ordinary and customary conduct or use.

Second, the context of "disturbance" in s. 175(1)(a) suggests that Parliament did not intend to protect society from mere emotional disturbance. Had Parliament sought to protect society from annoyance and anxiety, the section would not be confined to acts occurring in or near a public place, nor would it single out particular forms of objectionable conduct—many other types of conduct disturb us. Parliament could have expressly protected against emotional disturbance, as was done in the *Public Order Act 1986* (UK), 1986, c. 64. But, to borrow the language of MacKeigan CJNS in *Swinimer*, ... Parliament chose to speak of a disturbance in or near a public place, not in someone's mind. By addressing "disturbance" in the public context, Parliament signalled that its objective was not the protection of individuals from emotional upset, but the protection of the public from disorder calculated to interfere with the public's normal activities.

Third, interpretative aids suggest that s. 175(1)(a) is directed at publicly exhibited disorder. As noted in *Skoke-Graham*, ... headings and preambles may be used as intrinsic aids in interpreting ambiguous statutes. Section 175(1)(a) appears under the section "Disorderly Conduct." Without elevating headings to determinative status, the heading under which s. 175(1)(a) appears supports the view that Parliament had in mind, not the emotional upset or annoyance of individuals, but disorder and agitation which interfere with the ordinary use of a place. ...

NOTES AND QUESTIONS

1. Do you agree with McLachlin J's contention that "not everything that disturbs people results in a disturbance"? What evidence does McLachlin J put forward to establish that "a definition which posits identity between 'disturb' and 'disturbance' is contrary to ordinary usage, the most fundamental principle of statutory construction"?

2. Is "ordinary usage" really the "most fundamental principle of statutory construction," as McLachlin J states? Should it be?

3. Is it possible to characterize the provision at issue in *Lohnes* as an instance of vagueness, ambiguity, subtext, or analogy? Should the relevant provision be interpreted by reference to historical expectation or by reference to current social concerns?

4. Note that the court's use of context is an example of the logic underlying *noscitur a sociis*. Is the court's use of that logic persuasive in this case?

5. McLachlin J makes it clear that she is unwilling to elevate "headings to determinative status." How much weight does the court give to the heading at issue in *Lohnes*? Does the heading in *Lohnes* (that is, "Disorderly Conduct") actually support McLachlin J's decision? Does the presence of that heading provide any indication of legislative intent? Could that heading be used to justify a result other than the outcome preferred by McLachlin J?

6. Driedger notes in *Construction of Statutes* (at 269) notes that various cases have established that "headings are a valid indicator of legislative meaning and should be taken into account in interpretation." This appears to be the case even in those provinces that have explicitly excluded the use of headings as aids to interpretation. Is this a sensible approach? Should courts be permitted to ignore the interpretation acts when the courts feel that headings are a useful source of meaning?

7. Does the usefulness of headings depend upon the extent to which they are actively debated when the relevant legislation is being enacted? Would your answer change if you were told that very few of the *operative* provisions of most statutes are ever actively debated?

8. In assessing the weight to be given to headings, Driedger points to the decision of the Supreme Court of Canada in *Law Society v. Skapinker*, [1984] 1 SCR 357, in which Estey J made the following comments:

> The extent of the influence of a heading ... will depend upon many factors including ... the degree of difficulty by reason of ambiguity or obscurity in construing the section; the length

and complexity of the provision; the apparent homogeneity of the provision appearing under the heading; the use of generic terminology in the heading; the presence or absence of a system of headings which appear to segregate the component elements of the [legislation] and the relationship of the terminology employed in the heading to the substance of the headlined provision. [As quoted by Driedger, at 272.]

V. MARGINAL NOTES

A. Legislation

The legislative printers of most jurisdictions add small, descriptive notations above or beside the operative provisions of legislation. For example, in the margin beside s. 11 of the *Interpretation Act* of Prince Edward Island, the words "Reference aids not part of enactments" can be found in small print. Section 11 itself provides as follows:

> In an enactment marginal notes and historical reference to other enactments after the end of a section form no part of the enactment, but shall be construed as being inserted for convenience of reference only.

As this section makes clear, the purpose of marginal notes is to enhance "convenience of reference"—the notes help readers find the appropriate section quickly and easily, as anyone who has written a provincial bar exam can verify.[3] Because s. 11 states that the marginal notes "form no part of the enactment," it appears that PEI's *Interpretation Act* would counsel against the overzealous use of marginal notes as interpretive aids.[4]

All Canadian jurisdictions give marginal notes the same treatment that they are given in PEI's *Interpretation Act*—as we saw (in section IV(A), above), federal and provincial interpretation acts make it clear that marginal notes form no part of an enactment.

Despite the uniform legislative treatment of marginal notes, Canadian courts appear to be becoming more willing to refer to marginal notes in the interpretation of legislative language. This is consistent with the trend, noted above, of admitting more and more "evidence" of a statute's meaning for the purpose of clarifying the meaning intended by the legislation's author. The next two cases discussed in this chapter demonstrate the vast difference between the traditional view of marginal notes (revealed in *R v. Basaraba*, [1975] 3 WWR 481 (Man. QB)) and the current view established by the Supreme Court of Canada (revealed in *R v. Wigglesworth*, [1987] 2 SCR 541).

---

3   It is interesting to note that the marginal note beside s. 11 seems to be somewhat broader than the section itself. While the section declares marginal notes and historical references to be convenient reference aids that are not part of the enactment, the marginal note appears to imply that anything that can be construed as a reference aid (such as headings, perhaps) should not be regarded as part of the Act. This demonstrates the potential danger (or utility) of employing marginal notes as interpretive aids.

4   Of course, the fact that something is *not* part of the statute does not automatically mean that it cannot be used as an interpretive aid. This idea will be explored in the sections dealing with "Previous Versions of the Statute" and "Debates and Parliamentary Materials," below.

B. R v. Basaraba

R v. Basaraba
[1975] 3 WWR 481 (Man. QB)

HUNT J: I deal here with six originating notices of motion which concern three charges laid against one Leslie Basaraba. ... [A discussion of the first two charges against the accused has been omitted.]

3. That Leslie Basaraba on the 27th day of June AD 1974, at the City of Brandon, in the Province of Manitoba, did wrongfully and without lawful authority for the purpose of compelling Sylvester Puchailo, and Everett Puchailo and Frank Puchailo, to transfer land to Dry Creek Livestock Inc., Gilbert Plains, Manitoba which Sylvester Puchailo and Frank Puchailo and Everett Puchailo had a lawful right to abstain from doing, use threats of violence to the said people, contrary to the provisions of the *Criminal Code*: s. 381 ...

In regard to [the charge] under s. 381, it is argued that there is a heading preceding ss. 380, 381 and 382 which reads "*Breach of Contract, Intimidation and Discrimination Against Trade Unionists.*"

There is a difference in the interpretation of statutes between headings and marginal notes. One may be led astray by certain unofficial editions of the Canadian *Criminal Code* where marginal notes are printed so that they appear to be headings, but the above quote is a heading covering these three sections. However, what appear to be headings in front of each of the separate sections are in fact marginal notes, if one refers to the official version.

It is, of course, clear that marginal notes ought not to be relied upon in interpreting a statute. This has been the law for some years and is now embodied in statute. It is also clear that headings may sometimes be usefully referred to to determine the sense of any doubtful expression in a section following under a particular heading. I place special emphasis on the words "sometimes" and "doubtful expression."

In my opinion, the words used in s. 381 are not "doubtful expressions." They are perfectly clear. They refer in no way to trade unionists and must be held to apply generally to anyone who acts contrary to the provisions of that section, whether he be a trade unionist, an employer, or anyone involved in other intimidating activities. ...

NOTES AND QUESTIONS

1. Note that, according to the court, the "heading" considered in *Basaraba* was an actual heading, rather than a mere marginal note. Also note that the heading at issue in *Basaraba* contains information not found in the operative provisions found below it (that is, the operative provisions merely dealt with "intimidation," and the heading referred to "intimidation against trade unionists"). Given the decisions discussed in the section on "Headings," was *Basaraba* rightly decided? Was it open to the court in *Basaraba* to hold that the heading, which referred explicitly to trade unionists, cast light on the meaning of the provisions with which the heading was associated?

2. If the heading at issue in *Basaraba* truly does conflict with the legislative intention underlying the relevant operative provisions, what does this say about the persuasive value of headings as interpretive aids?

3. Perhaps the most important feature of *Basaraba* (to anyone other than Leslie Basaraba) is the court's admonition to counsel to be wary of the distinction between headings and marginal notes. The court correctly points out that, in many unofficial consolidations of legislation, items that are merely marginal notes have been taken from the margins of the official enactment and placed above the language of the operative provisions, such that they appear to be headings or subheadings. To the extent that headings and marginal notes are given different treatment by the judiciary, it is important to verify (by referring to official statutory sources) whether a particular "heading" is really a heading or a mere marginal note.[5]

4. As noted above, *Basaraba* demonstrates the traditional view of the evidentiary value of marginal notes. With the decision of the Supreme Court of Canada in *R v. Wigglesworth*, [1987] 2 SCR 541, the status of marginal notes appears to have changed. The decision in *Wigglesworth* is the topic of the next section of this chapter.

C. R v. Wigglesworth

R v. Wigglesworth
[1987] 2 SCR 541

WILSON J: The central issue on this appeal is whether the appellant's conviction of a "major service offence" under the *Royal Canadian Mounted Police Act*, RSC 1970, c. R-9, precludes subsequent proceedings under the *Criminal Code* for the same misconduct. The resolution of this issue requires a decision as to whether such a major service offence constitutes an "offence" within the meaning of s. 11 of the *Canadian Charter of Rights and Freedoms* and, if so, whether proceedings under the *Criminal Code* would violate the appellant's right under s. 11(h) of the Charter not to be tried and punished again for the same offence. Before turning to a consideration of these issues it is necessary to examine briefly the facts of the case.

1. The Facts

The appellant was at all material times a Constable of the Royal Canadian Mounted Police. On August 21, 1981, one Donald Kerr was brought to the RCMP detachment in Yorkton, Saskatchewan for a breathalyzer test. Kerr was taken into a room where he met the appellant.

The appellant started to question Kerr concerning the incident giving rise to his arrest. He asked Kerr who was driving the car at the time. Kerr indicated that his

---

5   This is particularly important when one is conducting online research. Most online versions of legislation are printed with marginal notes in "heading position," rather than in the margins of the text.

sister was driving. The appellant suspected he was lying. He repeated the question a couple of times, receiving the same response each time. The appellant then grabbed Kerr, who was seated in a chair at the time, by the throat and pushed him against a wall. The grab around the throat was sufficient to cause a choking sensation to Kerr.

After a few seconds the appellant questioned Kerr again as to who was driving the car. Kerr continued to maintain that his sister was driving. The appellant slapped Kerr across the face with his open hand and repeated the question. Kerr gave the same answer. However, after three or four slaps Kerr admitted that he had been driving the car. At no time did Kerr respond physically to the appellant's slaps. The defence has admitted, on these facts, that the appellant committed a common assault as defined in the *Criminal Code*. As a result of the assault Kerr suffered a sore throat, a ringing in his ears, and several minor marks on his face.

Two charges were laid following this incident. On August 21, 1981 the appellant was charged with common assault contrary to s. 245(1) of the *Criminal Code*, RSC 1970, c. C-34. The appellant was also charged under the *Royal Canadian Mounted Police Act* as follows:

"That at or near Yorkton, in the Province of Saskatchewan, on the 21st day of August, 1981, that you were unnecessarily violent towards a prisoner, to wit: Donald Kerr, by forcibly grabbing him and slapping him in the face, contrary to Section [sic] (L), Section 25 of the *Royal Canadian Mounted Police Act*."

. . .

3. The Issue

Section 11 of the Charter reads as follows:

"11. Any person charged with an offence has the right … :
  (h) if finally acquitted of the offence, not to be tried for it again and, if finally found guilty and punished for the offence, not to be tried or punished for it again; …

As mentioned above, the first question to be considered is whether the appellant has been "charged with an offence" within the meaning of the opening words of s. 11. The proper approach to Charter interpretation was set out by this Court in *R v. Big M Drug Mart Ltd.*, [1985] 1 SCR 295. At page 344, Dickson CJ stated:

"The meaning of a right or freedom guaranteed by the Charter [is] to be ascertained by an analysis of the purpose of such a guarantee; it was to be understood, in other words, in the light of the interests it was meant to protect." …

I turn first to the text of s. 11. The Ontario Court of Appeal in *Trumbley and Pugh v. Metropolitan Toronto Police (sub nom. Re Trumbley and Fleming)* (1986), 55 OR (2d) 570, in concluding that s. 11 is concerned with only criminal or penal matters, properly observed that "the clear impression created by s. 11, read as a whole, is that it is intended to provide procedural safeguards relating to the criminal law process." Section 11 contains terms which are classically associated with criminal proceedings: "tried," "presumed innocent until proven guilty," "reasonable bail," "punishment for the offence," "acquitted of the offence" and "found guilty of the offence." Indeed, some of the rights guaranteed in s. 11 would seem to have no meaning outside the criminal or quasi-criminal context. As Hugessen ACJSC stated in *Belhumeur v. Discipline Committee of Quebec Bar Association, supra*, at p. 281, s. 11 [TRANSLATION] "is directed exclusively at procedure in criminal and penal matters." This same observation was made by Stevenson JA in *Re Barry and Alberta Securities Commission* (1986), 25 DLR (4th) 730 (Alta. CA), at p. 734, and by Monnin CJ in *Re Law Society of Manitoba and Savino, supra*, at p. 292. ...

The marginal note to s. 11 seems to support this interpretation of the section. It reads "Proceedings in criminal and penal matters." The Attorney General for Ontario and the respondent submitted, however, that the Court ought not to place any emphasis on the marginal note to s. 11 in interpreting the section. There is no doubt that the traditional view was that marginal notes could not be used as aids to interpretation as they formed no part of the Act which was passed by Parliament: see E. A. Driedger, *Construction of Statutes* (2nd ed. 1983), at p. 133; P. B. Maxwell, *Maxwell on the Interpretation of Statutes* (12th ed. 1969), at p. 10; W. F. Craies, *Craies on Statute Law* (7th ed. 1971), at p. 195. But reference to marginal notes has been made in some English authorities: see, for example, *Eastern Counties and London and Blackwall Railway Cos. v. Marriage* (1860), 9 HL Cas. 31, at p. 41; *Sheffield Waterworks Co. v. Bennett* (1872), LR 7 Ex. 409, at p. 421; *Stephens v. Cuckfield Rural District Council*, [1960] 2 All ER 716 (CA), at p. 720. And this Court has used statutory headings to assist in interpreting sections of the Charter: see *Law Society of Upper Canada v. Skapinker*, [1984] 1 SCR 357. In that case, Estey J, writing for a unanimous Court, held that the headings were deliberately included as part of the Charter and formed part of the resolution which Parliament debated. At pages 376-77 he stated:

> "It is clear that these headings were systematically and deliberately included as an integral part of the Charter for whatever purpose. At the very minimum, the Court must take them into consideration when engaged in the process of discerning the meaning and application of the provisions of the Charter. The extent of the influence of a heading in this process will depend upon factors including (but the list is not intended to be all-embracing) the degree of difficulty by reason of ambiguity or obscurity in construing the section; the length and complexity of the provision; the apparent homogeneity of the provision appearing under the heading; the use of generic terminology in the heading; the presence or absence of a system of headings which appear to segregate the component elements of the Charter; and the relationship of the terminology employed in the heading to the substance of the headlined provision.
>
>   ...
>
> I conclude that an attempt must be made to bring about a reconciliation of the heading with the section introduced by it. If, however, it becomes apparent that the section when read as a whole is clear and without ambiguity, the heading will not operate to change that clear and unambiguous meaning. Even in that midway position, a court should not, by the adoption of a technical rule of construction, shut itself off from whatever small assistance might be gathered from an examination of the heading as part of the entire constitutional document."

It must be acknowledged, however, that marginal notes, unlike statutory headings, are not an integral part of the Charter: see *Canadian Pacific Ltd. v. Attorney General of Canada*, [1986] 1 SCR 678, at p. 682. The case for their utilization as aids to statutory interpretation is accordingly weaker. I believe, however, that the distinction can be adequately recognized by the degree of weight attached to them. I find some support in the marginal note therefore for the proposition that the opening words of s. 11 "charged with an offence" restrict the application of the section to criminal or quasi-criminal proceedings and proceedings giving rise to penal consequences. ... [The court accordingly held that the conviction of the appellant under RCMP regulations (which did not amount to "penal proceedings") did not preclude a subsequent conviction under the *Criminal Code* in relation to the same conduct.]

NOTES AND QUESTIONS

1. The marginal note dealt with in *Wigglesworth* had the peculiar distinction of being a marginal note in a constitutional document. Marginal notes have subsequently been used by the Supreme Court of Canada in the interpretation of "ordinary statutes" as well: see *R v. Moore*, [1999] 3 SCR 250.

2. Despite the court's contention that a marginal note is a less useful interpretive aid than a heading, did the court truly treat the marginal note at issue in *Wigglesworth* any differently from the way it would have treated a heading containing the same language?

3. Should the courts treat marginal notes and headings differently from each other? Should either (or both) be relied on as items that may cast light on the meaning of obscure legislative text?

4. Review the decision of the court in *R v. McIntosh*, [1995] 1 SCR 686 (see chapter 3). In that case, McLachlin J relies on the marginal notes adjacent to ss. 34 and 35 of the *Criminal Code* in order to prove that the "plain language" of the relevant sections does not reflect the true intent of the statute's drafters. Is this a legitimate use of marginal notes?

VI. PUNCTUATION

A. Introduction

It seems counterintuitive to question a court's reliance on punctuation as an interpretive aid. Punctuation is an important component of written language: ignoring the punctuation found in a written passage seems about as sensible as ignoring the vowels. Consider the following passage:

BILL FED HIS DOG. TO MARY, THIS SEEMED LIKE A SENSIBLE IDEA.

With a minor change in punctuation, the meaning of the passage is radically transformed:

BILL FED HIS DOG TO MARY. THIS SEEMED LIKE A SENSIBLE IDEA.

Obviously, we rely heavily on punctuation when transmitting and interpreting information that is contained in written text. Indeed, punctuation is *part* of the text being considered, rather than a mere "non-textual" interpretive aid.

Despite the obvious importance of punctuation in the generation of a text's meaning, ancient courts refused to consider punctuation when interpreting the language of legislation. Indeed, this odd judicial habit can still be seen from time to time in current cases.

B. R v. Jaagusta

R v. Jaagusta
[1974] 3 WWR 766 (BC Prov. Ct.)

GOULET DJ: The facts of this case are very simple and not in dispute. A peace officer stopped the vehicle driven by the accused and told the accused he was searching for prohibited drugs under authority of the *Narcotic Control Act*. ... After searching the vehicle, he attempted to search the accused person who reacted by pushing the peace officer away.

At trial on a charge of "Resisting a Peace Officer in the lawful execution of his duty," the policeman admitted he had no grounds whatsoever to believe that the accused had any prohibited drugs in his vehicle or on his person.

If the attempted search by the peace officer of the accused person was illegal, then the accused is clearly not guilty of the charge. ... Conversely if the peace officer was conducting a legal search, I am satisfied on the evidence that the accused should be convicted.

The Crown has urged upon me that if the *Narcotic Control Act*, s. 10(1), is construed according to the rules of grammar, no other meaning can be imported but that a peace officer may enter any place other than a dwelling house, with or without reasonable grounds to believe that there is a narcotic to be found, and search any persons found in such place. The section is as follows:

> "10(1) A peace officer may, at any time,
>
> (a) without a warrant enter and search any place other than a dwelling-house, and under authority of a writ of assistance or a warrant issued under this section, enter and search any dwelling-house in which he reasonably believes there is a narcotic by means of or in respect of which an offence under this Act has been committed;
>
> (b) search any person found in such place; and
>
> (c) seize ..."

I must agree that if one applies the ordinary rules of punctuation, the requirement that a police officer must have reasonable belief appears to apply only to entry into a dwelling house and does not qualify the right to enter and search any place other than a dwelling house. An examination of the French language version of s. 10(1), again applying the ordinary punctuation rules, results in the same conclusion.

It is also apparent that if there were no commas at all in para. (a), or if the comma following the word "section" were to be moved to follow "dwelling-house" in the fifth line, the requirement to have reasonable belief could qualify both entry and search in dwelling houses and places other than dwelling houses.

At common law a peace officer could conduct a search of a person only as an incidental part of an arrest, and then only to assure the safeguarding of evidence or to prevent further criminal acts by such persons. … Furthermore, all statutory enactments providing for the search of a person, that have come to my attention, require the peace officer to have reasonable belief that the person being searched was somehow involved in an offence. …

It seems very strange to me, almost incredible, that the Parliament of Canada would have introduced into legislation an abrogation of the traditional rights of privacy of the individual to permit peace officers to search any person or numbers of persons in any place whatsoever, without a scintilla of evidence or even suspicion that such person or persons were in possession of any drug or had committed any offence, without using more specific language to that effect.

Maxwell on The Interpretation of Statutes … quotes *Craies on Statute Law* … as follows:

> "Punctuation is disregarded in the construction of statutes, since there was generally no punctuation in old statutes as engrossed on the Parliament Roll, and not all of the modern vellum prints of statutes are punctuated."

The interpretation advanced by the Crown in this case, which would in effect legalize the most unreasonable and arbitrary searches of individuals by peace officers, depends entirely upon the placement of a comma. In the absence of any statutory precedent vesting such power in a peace officer or of clear and unambiguous language to effect such a change, I am not prepared to accept it as the law in Canada at the present time. Accordingly, I hold that the attempted search of the accused in this case was illegal and that his resistance to it was justified. The accused is acquitted of the charge.

NOTES AND QUESTIONS

1. The court in *Jaagusta* ignored the punctuation of the *Narcotic Control Act* in order to acquit the accused. Does this carry implications for the use of punctuation as an interpretive aid, or is it better to regard *Jaagusta* as an application of the golden rule[6] (discussed in chapter 3)?

2. Is it unfair to expect police officers to know that the punctuation found in a statute may be ignored by appellate courts, taking away authority that the "plain meaning" of the text (including the punctuation) appears to convey?

3. What linguistic problem lies at the heart of *Jaagusta*? Is it an instance of vagueness, ambiguity, subtext, or analogy?

---

6   The golden rule, it will be remembered, allows the court to depart from the "literal meaning" of an enactment to the extent that such a departure is required in order to avoid an absurd outcome. The court in *Jaagusta* appears to accept that allowing police to search individuals on the basis of a "whim," rather than a suspicion that such a person is carrying narcotics, would constitute an absurd result. The golden rule would accordingly allow the court in *Jaagusta* to ignore the comma in order to avoid this absurd result.

C. R v. Popoff

R v. Popoff
(1985), 14 WCB 290 (BC Co. Ct.)

McTAGGART Co. Ct. J: In England in 1916 Sir Roger Casement was convicted and executed for high treason, (1917) 1 KB 98. At issue was the interpretation of a statute passed nearly 600 years earlier. One of the factors considered was the effect to be given to a comma in the relevant wording. Sir Roger is reported to have said that his death turned on that comma (see *Hanged by a Comma* by E. Stewart Fay-Lovat, Dickson Limited 1937).

The present appeal turns on the absence of a colon. Mr. Popoff was convicted of a ".08" charge under Code Section 236(1) and fined $550.00. He now submits (on a ground raised at the trial) that there is no evidence as to when the qualified technician took the two tests. The Certificate of Analyses (Exhibit 1) states that one of the samples commenced at "2112:50 hours" and was concluded at "2113:03 hours." The other sample was commenced at "2131:10 hours" and concluded at "2131:22 hours." The appellant says they should read "21:12:50 hours," and so on (my underlining). Otherwise, the times are meaningless. He relies on *Regina v. Gosby* (1974) 26 CRNS 161 (NSSC App. Div.). Further, he submits that the accused should not be made to speculate or to require expert interpretation of the certificate given to him. ...

My research indicates a number of reported cases dealing with the use of punctuation marks (see *Canadian Abridgement* (2d), Volume 36, p. 11; *Regina v. Jaagusta* (1974) 3 WWR 766; and "Legal Drafting," Robert C. Dick, QC, 1972, p. 109. One authority, *Medicine Hat v. Hawson* (1920) 2 WWR 810, states: "The rule adopted in the courts is, I think, to pay little, if any, attention to punctuation" per Stuart J. [The Court went on to uphold the conviction of the accused.]

NOTES AND QUESTIONS

1. Elmer Driedger provides an excellent summary of the historical and current positions regarding the use of punctuation. According to Driedger in *Construction of Statutes* (at 276):

> At one time courts were unwilling to look at punctuation as an indicator of legislative meaning. Originally this reluctance was justified because the punctuation appearing in the printed version of an Act was not included in the bill as examined and voted on by Parliament but was added to the legislation by the printer after royal assent. In modern practice, of course, the printer does not add punctuation to legislation. This is done by the drafter when the bill is first prepared; subsequent changes are either included in amendments to the bill or, in the case of a mere correction, made by the legislative Clerk.

The court in *Cardinal v. R*, [1980] 1 FC 149 made it clear that modern courts will inevitably consider punctuation when interpreting the text of legislation. This is, of course, the only sensible position on the matter. As a result, cases in which courts *ignore* the punctuation in an enactment are best regarded as applications of the golden rule (the court departs from the text of the legislation in order to avoid an absurd result).

VII. PREVIOUS VERSIONS OF THE STATUTE

A. Introduction

When interpreting the text of legislation, courts will often consider previous versions of the statute being considered.[7] This seems to be a sensible procedure. After all, when determining what a law *means*, it seems useful to determine how the law came to exist in its current form: this is a part of the overall legal context that led to the enactment of the legislation in question.

Courts have consistently held that earlier[8] versions of an enactment are admissible evidence of the current statute's meaning.[9] The difficulty arises in determining the *use* that courts will make of this evidence. Consider an example.

> Section 5 of the *Animals Act, 1990* (a fictitious statute) provides that "[n]o person may possess a cat." Your client has been charged with "cat possession" because your client owns a Siberian tiger. Clearly, the interpretive battle in this case centres upon the meaning of the word "cat": if "cat" includes domestic cats only, then your client (who possessed a Siberian tiger) will not be caught by the legislation.
>
> Now suppose that an earlier version of the relevant provision had stipulated that "[n]o person may possess a *domestic* cat." Two years before your client was charged, the relevant Act was amended through the deletion of the word "domestic." What would this imply about the meaning of "cat" in the current enactment (where the word "domestic" does not appear)? Consider the following possibilities:
>
> 1. *Housekeeping or "formal" changes.* Perhaps the legislature was simply engaged in a little "housekeeping" by removing extraneous words from the legislation. Perhaps it felt that cats were, by definition, "domestic animals," and that the word "domestic" added nothing to the Act (in violation of the "no extraneous words" principle). Accordingly, the legislature deleted the extra word and, as a result, "cat" in the new version continues to apply only to domestic cats.
> 2. *Substantive changes.* Perhaps the legislature saw a deficiency in the *Animals Act*, and felt that the old Act (which applied explicitly to "domestic" cats) should be amended in

---

7   Courts and commentators often refer to this practice as reviewing the "legislative history" of a statute. The phrase "legislative history" is also sometimes used to refer to the debates and proceedings that led to the enactment of a law. In order to avoid confusion between these two ideas, I prefer to avoid the phrase "legislative history" altogether, and to refer to the practice of reviewing old versions of the statute being considered as "the practice of reviewing previous versions of the same statute." For more on this distinction, see Driedger, at 449.

8   Note that courts have also approved of the use of *subsequent* (rather than prior) versions of a statute in the interpretation of an enactment (see, for example, *R v. Hasselwander*, [1993] 2 SCR 398). The use of subsequent versions of an enactment, while less common than the use of prior versions, seems to be no less sensible: the manner in which a legislature deals with an enactment before, during, and after the time that that enactment is in force will shed light on the legislature's view concerning the statute's meaning. To the extent that the legislature's view is relevant, these "pieces of evidence" may be useful interpretive aids.

9   See, for example, *Gravel v. City of St. Leonard*, [1978] 1 SCR 660, where the Supreme Court of Canada noted (at 667) that prior versions of a statute "may be used to interpret a statute because prior enactments may throw some light on the intention of the legislature in repealing, amending, replacing or adding to it."

order to catch the owners of lions, tigers, cougars, and other large felines. As a result, the legislature deleted the word "domestic" in order to expand the meaning of the *Act*.

Determining whether a change is "substantive" or merely "formal" is the task of the interpreter. According to Laskin J in *Bathurst Paper Ltd. v. New Brunswick Minister of Municipal Affairs*, [1972] SCR 471, at 477, courts will cautiously presume that an amendment has been made for substantive reasons. In the words of Laskin J, "[l]egislative changes may reasonably be viewed as purposive,[10] unless there is internal or admissible external evidence to show that only language polishing was intended."

B. Legislation

The use of prior (or subsequent) versions of an enactment as interpretive aids is dealt with in federal and provincial interpretation acts. All of the acts that deal with this issue[11] are built on the federal *Interpretation Act*, which provides (in s. 45) as follows:

> (2) The amendment of an enactment shall not be deemed to be or to involve a declaration that the law under that enactment was or was considered by Parliament or other body or person by whom the enactment was enacted to have been different from the law as it is under the enactment as amended.
>
> (3) The repeal or amendment of an enactment in whole or in part shall not be deemed to be or to involve any declaration as to the previous state of the law.

It is important to read these sections carefully. Specifically, it should be noted that the sections say that amendments "shall not be deemed" to constitute a parliamentary declaration that a substantive change was intended. The sections *do not* say that amendments "shall be deemed not" to involve substantive change. A court is perfectly able to infer that a particular amendment *was* designed to change the law: even in the face of s. 45 (and its provincial equivalents),[12] a court is permitted to hold that an amendment was made in order to change the meaning of a provision. What s. 45 prohibits is the automatic, conclusive presumption that amendment *always* means substantive change. Section 45 effectively draws our attention to the "formal change" or "housekeeping" option, and reminds us that we are not compelled to assume that all amendments involve substantive changes in the meaning of legislation.

In the cases that follow, the courts demonstrate the typical uses that are made of prior versions of the enactment being interpreted. When reading each case, consider the

---

10 From the context of Laskin J's comments, it is clear that by "purposive" Laskin J did not merely mean that we can presume that the legislation was not amended "accidentally." Instead, His Lordship's comments clearly equate "purposive" with "substantive." See Driedger, at 454, where the author has simply replaced the word "purposive" with "substantive" (in square brackets) during the editorial process.

11 Only Nova Scotia and Quebec fail to deal with this issue.

12 See, for example, ss. 17-18 of Ontario's *Interpretation Act*, RSO 1990, c. I.11.

following questions: (1) What motivated the legislature to make the relevant change, and (2) How does the evolution of the relevant language change our understanding of the statute's meaning?

C. Re Simon Fraser University

Re Simon Fraser University and District of Burnaby
(1968), 67 DLR (2d) 638 (BC SC), aff'd. 1 DLR (3d) 427 (BC CA)

DOHM, J: Simon Fraser University came into existence as a body politic and corporate by way of the *Universities Act*, 1963 (BC), c. 52. This university then acquired approximately 1,200 acres of land from the Corporation of the District of Burnaby by way of deed and at the date of this application Simon Fraser University is the owner of the said land.

When the university acquired the land it was encumbered with certain charges including easements in favour of the British Columbia Power Authority, Imperial Oil Limited and Trans-Mountain Oil Pipeline Company as well as leases in favour of a rifle range club, two transmission towers and a second rifle range.

In order to consolidate the titles, surrenders were taken of the aforementioned leases and new leases were executed by the university in favour of the holders of the old leases and subsequently the university granted new leases to some further tenants including a bank, a barber shop, an archery range and a gas station. All of these lessees pay rents to Simon Fraser University and of course none of them are colleges affiliated with Simon Fraser University.

The Corporation of the District of Burnaby now desires to know whether the lands leased out by the university are liable to taxation under the *Municipal Act*, RSBC 1960, c. 255, the *Public Schools Act*, RSBC 1960, c. 319, and the *Taxation Act*, RSBC 1960, c. 376.

The pertinent section which requires interpretation by the Court is s. 40 of the *Universities Act* which reads as follows:

> 40. *The property, real and personal, vested in a University is exempt from taxation under the Municipal Act, the Public Schools Act, and the Taxation Act*; and any real property so vested which is disposed of by lease to a college affiliated with the University, so long as it is held for college purposes, continues to be entitled to the exemption from taxation provided in this section. (The italicizing is mine.)

These first italicized words are all-encompassing general words and are absolutely clear.

The additional words which refer to leases to affiliated colleges bring about the present ambiguity which gives rise to the different interpretations placed on this section by the Corporation of the District of Burnaby and by Simon Fraser University. It is urged by Burnaby that the clause referring to the affiliated colleges' leases limits the general immunity granted by the first general words. Burnaby argues that by referring to affiliated colleges the Legislature intended to exclude any other properties leased to others.

The university takes the position that the clear and unequivocal general words grant an exemption to the university from the taxation under the three statutes regardless of whether they have leased out parts of the property and are receiving rents therefrom. The university takes the position that the additional words were intended by the Legislature as merely a safeguard to see that the leases previously granted to any affiliated colleges by any British Columbia university under this statute "continues" [*sic*] to be entitled to the exemption.

Both counsel have agreed I should look at the history of this legislation in order to ascertain the intention of the Legislature when it enacted the present s. 40 and of course there is ample authority for my so doing. In the year 1908 [by c. 53] a similar section (then numbered s. 47) read as follows:

> The property, real and personal, vested in the University, being actually occupied or used by the University in the conduct of any part of its educational system, shall not be liable to taxation for Provincial, Municipal or School purposes, but shall be exempt from every description of taxation.

In the year 1916 [by c. 70, s. 2] this section (also numbered s. 47) read as follows:

> The property, real and personal, vested in the University shall not be liable to taxation for Provincial, municipal, or school purposes, but shall be exempt from every description of taxation *until disposed of by sale, lease, or otherwise*. (The italicizing is mine.)

In the year 1925 [by c. 60, s. 3] this section (also numbered s. 47) was amended as follows:

> Section 47 of said chapter 265 is amended by adding thereto the words "and any real property so vested which is disposed of by lease to a college affiliated with the University shall, *so long as it is held for college purposes*, continue to be entitled to the exemption from taxation provided in this section." (The italicizing is mine.)

In the year 1960 [RSBC 1960, c. 38] this section (then numbered s. 51) read as follows:

> The property, real and personal, vested in the University is not liable to taxation for Provincial, municipal, or school purposes, but is exempt from every description of taxation *until disposed of by sale, lease, or otherwise*; and any real property so vested which is disposed of by lease to a college affiliated with the University, so long as it is held for college purposes, continues to be entitled to the exemption from taxation provided in this section. (The italicizing is mine.)

The italicized words in the 1960 section were removed by the Legislature in 1963 in the section with which I am here concerned.

The pattern of the above legislative enactments demonstrates quite clearly that the Legislature originally in 1908 enacted by clear and unambiguous language that all property, real and personal, vested in a university should "be exempt from every description of taxation," providing that the land was actually occupied or used by a university in the conduct of any part of its educational system. In 1916 a change was made, again in clear and unambiguous language, and the Legislature at that time exempted the property vested in a university whether actually occupied or used by a university in the conduct of its educational system or not, from any description of taxation until a university disposed of any of the property so vested by sale, lease or otherwise.

It is difficult to understand why the word "sale" was used because a sale of property would divest the university of any interest in the property.

It was in the year 1916 that property disposed of by sale, lease or otherwise was no longer protected from the incidence of taxation.

In 1925 the section as enacted in 1916 was continued but amended to exclude from property disposed of by sale, lease or otherwise, any property specifically disposed of by lease to an affiliated college.

In 1925 therefore the Legislature in simple language enacted:

> (a) that property vested in a university was completely exempt from taxation, and property leased out to an affiliated college in the terms set forth in the section as amended in that year "continued" to be exempt, and
>
> (b) that property disposed of by sale or lease (except to an affiliated college) or otherwise should not be excluded from taxation but specifically subject to the taxation laws of the Province.

In 1960 the same concept was retained in clear and unambiguous language.

It would appear therefore that since 1916 the legislation specifically excluded from the tax exempt provisions, lands disposed of by a university by sale, lease or otherwise (except lands leased to an affiliated college) as described in the section. It was obvious that during the said period the Legislature spelled out and used specific words to declare what disposition of property vested in a university should be subject to taxation in order to exclude such lands from the general and unequivocal language used to declare that all property, real and personal, vested in a university should be tax exempt.

Mr. Hinkson in his very able argument on behalf of Burnaby states that if this section in the 1963 statute is construed according to its plain meaning then I shall be imputing to the Legislature that they passed a law inconsistent with previous legislation and inconsistent with the history of this matter.

Mr. Hebenton with equal vigour argues that this is not a sufficient reason for not giving to the section the plain meaning of the words used.

In deciding the intention of the Legislature I keep in mind the following:

> (a) the section itself has the object of exempting from taxation and this being so the wording should be interpreted to effect that object;
>
> (b) any change in language is some indication of the change of intention on the part of the Legislature: *Grey et al. v. Inland Revenue Com'rs*, [1958] Ch. 690; affd [1960] AC 1.

Why were the words "disposed of by sale, lease, or otherwise" deleted from this section by the Legislature? If the historic pattern of words used were considered necessary to express the true intent of the Legislature during the 47-year period referred to, why then would the words be deleted, unless the clear intention of the Legislature was to completely exempt from taxation all property, both real and personal, vested in a university including affiliated colleges? To say that because lands leased to an affiliated college in the conditions set forth in s. 40 of the present Act gives rise to an implication that other leases are therefore subject to tax, is to ask this Court to interpret the section in its wording as it was during the preceding 47 years. How can a Court do so in view of the legislative enactments analysed? It is said that where words used in a statute are not ambiguous or confusing, its interpretation should not be affected by a comparison of language used with that of previous legislation on the subject. However because of the submission made that there is an implied right to tax, with which submission I do not agree, and because I was urged by both counsel to do so I have allowed myself to review the legislative enactments passed as set forth above since the year 1908. I am of the opinion that the Legislature of British Columbia when departing from the language used previously did so intentionally and deliberately: see Schroeder, JA, in *R v. American News Co. Ltd.*, 118 CCC 152 at pp. 180-1, [1957] OR 145. ...

The general wording used in the present s. 40 together with the deletion of the previous words which appeared in the 1960 section lead me to the opinion that the Legislature intended to exempt the British Columbia universities from all provincial forms of taxation. Had the Legislature intended the exemption to be restricted it could have inserted the previous words which clearly restricted the exemption: *R v. Lowden*, [1914] 1 KB 144.

Accordingly I am of the opinion that the real property vested in the Simon Fraser University does not cease to be exempt from taxation under the Municipal Act, Public Schools Act and Taxation Act by reason of the university having granted leases to some one other than a college affiliated with the university. I find that the Simon Fraser University has not disposed of real property but has granted leases to the companies and organizations set forth in the notice filed herein. Section 40 as presently worded gives to Simon Fraser University exemption from taxation by the Corporation of the District of Burnaby under the Municipal Act, the Public Schools Act and Taxation Act in relation to real property leased to the persons or associations hereinbefore referred to.

NOTES AND QUESTIONS

1. Is it possible that the amendments being considered in *Re Simon Fraser University* were intended as mere "housekeeping" or "formal" changes?

2. Is the problem at issue in *Re Simon Fraser University* a problem of vagueness, ambiguity, subtext, or analogy? How would the unified theory deal with the problem in this case?

3. When a "typical reader" attempts to order his or her affairs based on the language of an enactment, he or she is likely to rely on "plain language." Is it fair for a court to depart from plain language when relying on materials, such as prior enactments, to which the typical reader is unlikely to have access? Was any unfairness caused in *Re Simon Fraser University*?

4. Note that the principal argument brought against the court's decision was based on an application of the logic underlying *expressio unius est exclusio alterius* (see chapter 2).

Because the relevant section extended the tax exemption to "any real property ... disposed of *by lease to a college affiliated with the University*" (emphasis added), the court was asked to infer that the exemption did not extend to real property leased to anything other than an affiliated college: the expression "a college affiliated with the university" implied the exclusion of other lessees. Is the application of the maxim persuasive in this case?

5. Based on the "plain language" of the statute being considered, consider the following question: where an affiliated college (a) leases land from the university, but (b) stops using the land for "college purposes," is the land still entitled to the tax exemption? Is this clarified through the prior enactments considered by the court?

6. The pattern of amendments exhibited in *Re Simon Fraser University* is intriguing. The legislature (a) enacted a general principle, (b) enacted an exception to that principle, and then (c) enacted an exception to the exception. Finally, the legislature eliminated the original exception (item (b), above), leaving items (a) and (c) intact. Consider a parallel example:

> In 1980, the legislature enacts a statute providing that "Pets are permitted in all public parks." In 1985, the statute is amended through the addition of an exception—the statute now reads that "Pets are permitted in all public parks, *except for dogs and canaries*." In 1990, the legislature amends the statute again in order to permit guide dogs, such that the statute provides as follows: "Pets are permitted in all public parks, except for dogs and canaries, *but guide dogs may enter a park if accompanying a visually impaired individual*." In 1995 the legislature no longer supports the "dogs and canaries" exception, so the words creating that exception (that is, "except for dogs and canaries") are deleted. The legislation finally reads as follows: "Pets are permitted in all public parks, but guide dogs may enter a park if accompanying a visually impaired individual."

Based on the final version of the statute, are guide dogs permitted in parks when not accompanying a visually impaired individual? Does the result coincide with the legislature's intention?

7. Does the court's decision violate the "no extraneous words" principle? If so, is that violation justified?

D. R v. Ulybel Enterprises Ltd.

R v. Ulybel Enterprises Ltd.
[2001] SCJ no. 55

[A Canadian vessel, registered and owned by the respondent, was observed fishing without the required registration or licence card, in the NAFO Convention Area, contrary to the *Atlantic Fisheries Regulations, 1985*. The respondent's vessel and its cargo were seized and the Crown took physical possession of the vessel. The respondent was indicted on charges to be tried before the Newfoundland Supreme Court, Trial Division. During this same time, the vessel was still in the possession of the Crown, who was incurring storage and maintenance costs. The Crown intervened in one of the Federal Court actions in 1996 and successfully sought an order permitting the sale of the vessel. The receiver general collected the proceeds of the sale for the benefit of the Federal Court. The respondent was convicted of the charges in 1997 and the sentence included the forfeiture of $50,000 from the profit of the vessel's sale. The Newfoundland Court of Appeal upheld the respondent's conviction and concluded that the sentence was not excessive. However, the court held that the Supreme Court, Trial Division had no jurisdiction or authority to order the forfeiture of the proceeds from the sale of the fishing vessel. Concluding that continued physical detention of an object seized under the *Fisheries Act* is a necessary precondition to an order of forfeiture, the court overturned the order of forfeiture against the defendant.]

IACOBUCCI J: ...

II. Relevant Legislation

Fisheries Act, RSC 1985, c. F-14, as amended by SC 1991, c. 1 ...

70(1) A fishery officer or fishery guardian who seizes any fish or other thing under this Act may retain custody of it or deliver it into the custody of any person the officer or guardian considers appropriate. ...

(3) A fishery officer or fishery guardian who has custody of any fish or other perishable thing seized under this Act may dispose of it in any manner the officer or guardian considers appropriate and any proceeds realized from its disposition shall be paid to the Receiver General.

72(1) Where a person is convicted of an offence under this Act, the court may, in addition to any punishment imposed, order that any thing seized under this Act by means of or in relation to which the offence was committed, or any proceeds realized from its disposition, be forfeited to Her Majesty. ...

III. Issue and Principal Arguments of the Parties

The basic issue on appeal is whether the Newfoundland Court of Appeal erred in reversing the sentencing judge's order for forfeiture of proceeds of the vessel. The focus of argument is on the proper interpretation of the scope of the power to order the forfeiture of proceeds under s. 72(1) of the *Fisheries Act*: can it cover proceeds from the sale of a ship or is it limited to those proceeds realized from a sale of perishables pursuant to s. 70(3) of the Act?

The appellant submits that the Court of Appeal erred by interpreting the power to make an order of forfeiture under s. 72(1) of the *Fisheries Act* too narrowly. She argues that the plain language of s. 72(1) supports a broader interpretation, one that permits the court to make an order of forfeiture against the proceeds of sale of a vessel, even where the sale of the vessel was made under the authority of another court. The appellant says that such an interpretation is necessary to harmonize the *Fisheries Act*, with the *Federal Court Act*, RSC 1985, c. F-7, and the *Federal Court Rules*.

The respondent adopts the position taken by the Newfoundland Court of Appeal in this case. The respondent argues that the only proceeds that are subject to forfeiture under the *Fisheries Act* are the proceeds of perishables sold pursuant to s. 70(3).

The respondent says that the *Fisheries Act* should be interpreted as requiring the continued physical detention of a thing seized as a necessary precondition to an order of
forfeiture of that thing. Thus, in this case, the sale of the vessel under the authority of
the Federal Court precluded the sentencing court from imposing a valid order of forfeiture against the proceeds of the vessel as part of the sentence in this case. The respondent says that such an interpretation is consistent with the scheme of the *Fisheries
Act* and the presumption of innocence.

IV. Analysis

...

1. Grammatical and Ordinary Meaning

In interpreting the scope of the power to order forfeiture of proceeds under the
Fisheries Act, it is natural to begin by considering the grammatical and ordinary
meaning the words of s. 72(1). As already noted, s. 72(1) provides:

> 72(1) Where a person is convicted of an offence under this Act, the court may, in
> addition to any punishment imposed, order that any thing seized under this Act by means
> of or in relation to which the offence was committed, or *any proceeds realized from its
> disposition*, be forfeited to Her Majesty. [Emphasis added.]

The possessive pronoun in the phrase "any proceeds realized from its disposition"
clearly refers to the antecedent "any thing seized under the Act" in the preceding
clause. Section 51 is the exclusive source of the power to seize property under the
Fisheries Act. It provides for the seizure of "any fishing vessel, vehicle, fish or other
thing that [a fishery] officer or guardian believes on reasonable grounds was obtained
by or used in the commission of an offence under this Act... ." Therefore, in light of
the kinds of property subject to seizure under s. 51, reading the words in s. 72(1) in
their ordinary and grammatical sense, the provision clearly contemplates the making
of an order of forfeiture of the proceeds of disposition of a vessel seized under the
Fisheries Act. Furthermore, it is notable that the proceeds subject to forfeiture are not
limited to those proceeds realized through dispositions made under the *Fisheries Act*.

2. Legislative History and the Intention of Parliament

To understand the scope of s. 72(1), it is useful to consider its legislative evolution.
Prior enactments may throw some light on the intention of Parliament in repealing,
amending, replacing or adding to a statute: *Gravel v. City of St-Leonard*, [1978] 1
SCR 660, at p. 667, per Pigeon J, cited approvingly by Major J in *Amos v. Insurance
Corp. of British Columbia*, [1995] 3 SCR 405, at para. 13. As noted above, a former
version of the forfeiture provision did limit the scope of the power to order forfeiture
of proceeds to the proceeds of a disposition of perishables made under s. 71(3) of the
Act (now s. 70(3)). However, in 1991, s. 72(1) was amended and the language limiting
the scope of the power to order forfeiture of proceeds was removed. Indeed, this was

the only meaningful change made to s. 72(1). A review of the Minutes of Proceedings of the Legislative Committee and the Parliamentary debates in Hansard offers little insight into the intention of Parliament in making this change in the forfeiture provision. In fact, no references were made to this specific provision in either the Committee hearings or the Parliamentary debate that preceded its amendment. However, it is clear that as a whole, the 1991 amendments to the *Fisheries Act* were intended to modernize the legislation, and to increase the flexibility and severity of penalties for *Fisheries Act* offences.

It is possible that the removal of the reference to the proceeds of a disposition of perishables, in favour of a general reference to the proceeds of "any thing seized under the Act," was intended by the drafters merely to streamline the language of the section, and not to broaden the scope of forfeiture as it relates to proceeds. However, there is a presumption that amendments to the wording of a legislative provision are made for some intelligible purpose, such as to clarify the meaning, to correct a mistake, or to change the law: [citations omitted]. Laskin J (as he then was) applied this presumption in *Bathurst Paper Ltd. v. Minister of Municipal Affairs of New Brunswick*, [1972] SCR 471, at p. 477. Writing for the Court, he held that "[l]egislative changes may reasonably be viewed as purposive, unless there is internal or admissible external evidence to show that only language polishing was intended." In this case, through its wholesale removal of specific limiting language, the effect of the 1991 amendment to s. 72(1) is to broaden the scope of the forfeiture provision to include the power to forfeit proceeds of the sale of a vessel. This effect is consistent with the intention of Parliament, as recorded in Hansard, to increase the flexibility and severity of available penalties for *Fisheries Act* offences.

Before this Court, counsel did not initially refer to the legislative history of the forfeiture provision. It appears that the Court of Appeal did not benefit from argument on the effect of the 1991 amendments on the proper interpretation of the scope of the power to order forfeiture. Nevertheless, in combination, the grammatical and ordinary meaning of the words in s. 72(1) and the intention of Parliament as indicated by the legislative history of the provision do support a broader interpretation of the scope of the forfeiture power than was given by the Court of Appeal.

NOTES AND QUESTIONS

1. Is it possible that the amendments referred to in *Ulybel* were the result of mere "housekeeping"? Apart from those discussed by Iacobucci J, are there any "substantive reasons" for the amendment?

2. How much evidentiary "weight" was given to the prior enactment referred to in *Ulybel*?

3. Do you agree with Iacobucci J's assessment of the "grammatical and ordinary" meaning of the provision?

4. Is the language at issue in *Ulybel* plagued by vagueness, ambiguity, subtext, or analogy? Is there any reason that the legislative drafter might have intentionally inserted the relevant obscurity into the statute?

E. R v. McIntosh

Review the decision of the Supreme Court of Canada in *R v. McIntosh*, [1995] 1 SCR 686 (the decision is set out in chapter 3). In that case, both the majority and the dissent made reference to previous versions of the *Criminal Code* when attempting to interpret the self-defence provisions of the Code. Compare the two judgments in the case and consider the following questions:

1. Which judgment makes better use of the previous versions of the *Criminal Code*?
2. Is Lamer CJ correct in his apparent assessment of the relative weight of (a) a statute's "plain meaning," and (b) the intention revealed when one examines the previous versions of the Code?
3. Does McLachlin J place too much weight on the previous versions of the *Criminal Code*? Is she justified in determining that certain changes to the Code were drafting errors, rather than intentional changes in the statute's meaning?

VIII. DEBATES AND PARLIAMENTARY MATERIALS

A. Introduction

The enactment of legislation is a fairly long and arduous process. During this process, the proposed legislation is drafted and rewritten numerous times. Memoranda are written concerning changes that should be made to the proposed legislation. Legislative drafters spend endless hours debating particular words, phrases, and provisions found within the proposed enactment.

Once the proposed enactment is introduced in the relevant legislative assembly, the language of the enactment is debated by members of the assembly. It may be accepted, defeated, or returned to the drafters for substantive changes or formal clarifications.

If "legislative intent" is truly the key to statutory interpretation, it seems sensible that any materials generated during the drafting, debating, and enacting process should be admissible for the purpose of establishing the meaning of a statute. If, for example, the transcript of legislative debates reveals that a particular word in a statute was being used in a rather peculiar sense, it may be useful (for those who are guided by historical legislative intent) to rely on that evidence when interpreting the legislation in question. If authorial intent is our guide to interpretation, we must surely be entitled to rely on any evidence that may reveal the author's historical understanding.

Surprisingly, the "parliamentary history" of an enactment (that is, the transcripts of debates and preparatory materials generated during the creation of a statute) has traditionally been considered inadmissible for the purpose of proving the lawmaker's intention. Pierre-André Côté (*The Interpretation of Legislation in Canada*, 2d ed. (Cowansville, QC: Yvon Blais, 1992), at 354) describes the rationale for this exclusionary rule in the following terms:

> The rule had its heyday in the nineteenth century, a period dominated by emphasis on the form of Parliament's intention, by the Literal Rule. Lord Halsbury's surprising remarks, that the person least able to interpret a statute is the drafter, because he is unconsciously influenced by what he meant rather than by what he said, must be appreciated in this context. If the drafter's opinions are unreliable, all the more so are those of parliamentarians.

As a result, the traditional "rule" in Anglo-Canadian jurisprudence has been to exclude evidence of an enactment's "parliamentary history" when attempting to determine the statute's meaning.

This tradition (which has long since been abandoned in the United States) was grounded in rather important policy concerns regarding the reliability of such evidence.[13] Consider legislative debates: when a provision is debated in the House of Commons, do those who actively debate the relevant language have any more authority over the statute's meaning than those who sit quietly in the backbenches and simply vote in favour of the law? What if the meaning reflected in the debates is not the meaning that was in the minds of the backbenchers who voted for the law? What if a majority of those who voted for the law disagreed with statements made in the debates? In a bicameral system (where two houses of Parliament are involved in the passage of legislation), what if each house has a different view of a statute's meaning? Are these differences in opinion always reflected in the legislative debates?

Many of these concerns relate to our understanding of who "the lawgiver" really is. Clearly, no individual member of Parliament can be looked upon as "the lawgiver." In Canada, "the lawgiver" is a theoretical, composite entity composed of all members of the legislative assembly. No one member of Parliament has the authority or the ability to speak for the composite entity. As a result, statements made in legislative debates can properly be regarded as the speaker's own views, rather than those of "the lawgiver."

In truth, most of the concerns regarding parliamentary history seem to flow from the weaknesses of "legislative intent." As we have seen (in chapter 1 of *Theory and Practice*), legislative intent is a rather ephemeral legal fiction. The weaknesses of legislative intent, together with the difficulties involved in *proving* legislative intent by resort to parliamentary history, are discussed at 18-20 of *Theory and Practice*.

Regardless of the many policies weighing against the use of parliamentary history in statutory interpretation, the traditional rule (requiring the exclusion of such evidence) has now been abandoned in Canada. The trend began in constitutional cases, when courts would refer to the transcripts of debates surrounding the drafting and enactment of the Charter when attempting to construe the Charter's language (see, for example, *R v. Big M Drug Mart*, [1985] 1 SCR 295). Following these Charter cases, it was only a small step for courts to conclude that, when a statute was undergoing Charter scrutiny, the debates regarding the passage of that statute (like the debates regarding the passage of the constitution) were admissible for the purpose of establishing the relevant act's objective.[14] The final death knell for the traditional, exclusionary rule came in 1998, when the Supreme Court of Canada finally used the transcripts of legislative debates (commonly known as *Hansard*) for the purpose of demonstrating the specific meaning of a phrase within an "ordinary" statute in a non-constitutional case. The case that resulted in this radical leap is set out below.

---

13   In Côté, at 358-61, the author gives an excellent recitation of the policies for and against the use of parliamentary history.

14   See, for example, *R v. Morgentaler*, [1993] 3 SCR 463, in which the court stated (at 484) that evidence of parliamentary history (often referred to as *Hansard* evidence) "should be admitted as relevant to both the background and the purpose of legislation."

B. Re Rizzo & Rizzo Shoes Ltd.

Re Rizzo & Rizzo Shoes Ltd.
[1998] 1 SCR 27

IACOBUCCI J: This is an appeal by the former employees of a now bankrupt employer from an order disallowing their claims for termination pay (including vacation pay thereon) and severance pay. The case turns on an issue of statutory interpretation. Specifically, the appeal decides whether, under the relevant legislation in effect at the time of the bankruptcy, employees are entitled to claim termination and severance payments where their employment has been terminated by reason of their employer's bankruptcy. ...

Analysis

The statutory obligation upon employers to provide both termination pay and severance pay is governed by ss. 40 and 40a of the ESA [*Employment Standards Act*, RSO 1990, c. E.4], respectively. The Court of Appeal noted that the plain language of those provisions suggests that termination pay and severance pay are payable only when the employer terminates the employment. For example, the opening words of s. 40(1) are: "No employer shall terminate the employment of an employee... ." Similarly, s. 40a(1a) begins with the words, "Where ... fifty or more employees have their employment terminated by an employer... ." Therefore, the question on which this appeal turns is whether, when bankruptcy occurs, the employment can be said to be terminated "by an employer."

The Court of Appeal answered this question in the negative, holding that, where an employer is petitioned into bankruptcy by a creditor, the employment of its employees is not terminated "by an employer," but rather by operation of law. Thus, the Court of Appeal reasoned that, in the circumstances of the present case, the ESA termination pay and severance pay provisions were not applicable and no obligations arose. ...

Although the Court of Appeal looked to the plain meaning of the specific provisions in question in the present case, with respect, I believe that the court did not pay sufficient attention to the scheme of the ESA, its object or the intention of the legislature; nor was the context of the words in issue appropriately recognized. I now turn to a discussion of these issues. ...

In my view ... the severance pay obligation does in fact extend to bankrupt employers. ... This interpretation is ... consistent with statements made by the Minister of Labour at the time he introduced the 1981 amendments to the ESA. With regard to the new severance pay provision he stated:

> "The circumstances surrounding a closure will govern the applicability of the severance pay legislation in some defined situations. For example, a bankrupt or insolvent firm will still be required to pay severance pay to employees to the extent that assets are available to satisfy their claims.

...

... the proposed severance pay measures will, as I indicated earlier, be retroactive to January 1 of this year. That retroactive provision, however, will not apply in those cases of bankruptcy and insolvency where the assets have already been distributed or where an agreement on a proposal to creditors has already been reached."

(Legislature of Ontario Debates, 1st sess., 32nd Parl., June 4, 1981, at pp. 1236-37.)

Moreover, in the legislative debates regarding the proposed amendments the Minister stated:

"For purposes of retroactivity, severance pay will not apply to bankruptcies under the *Bankruptcy Act* where assets have been distributed. However, once this act receives royal assent, employees in bankruptcy closures will be covered by the severance pay provisions."

(Legislature of Ontario Debates, 1st sess., 32nd Parl., June 16, 1981, at p. 1699.)

Although the frailties of Hansard evidence are many, this Court has recognized that it can play a limited role in the interpretation of legislation. Writing for the Court in *R v. Morgentaler*, [1993] 3 SCR 463, at p. 484, Sopinka J stated:

"... until recently the courts have balked at admitting evidence of legislative debates and speeches. ... The main criticism of such evidence has been that it cannot represent the "intent" of the legislature, an incorporeal body, but that is equally true of other forms of legislative history. Provided that the court remains mindful of the limited reliability and weight of Hansard evidence, it should be admitted as relevant to both the background and the purpose of legislation." ...

[The court went on to interpret the provision in accordance with the views expressed in *Hansard*.]

NOTES AND QUESTIONS

1. Do you agree with Iacobucci J's assessment of the "plain meaning" of the relevant provision, or is the language broader than Iacobucci J indicated? Is it possible that "terminated by an employer" could mean "terminated as a result of the employer's actions"? If so, could an employer's financial failure (leading to bankruptcy) constitute "termination" by the employer?

2. Is the language at issue in *Rizzo* an instance of vagueness, ambiguity, subtext, or analogy? How would the unified theory deal with the problem at issue in *Rizzo*?

3. The court in *Rizzo* relied on *Morgentaler* for the proposition that *Hansard* was admissible evidence. Note, however, that in *Morgentaler* the court held that *Hansard* was admissible to establish the "background and the purpose" of legislation. Does Iacobucci J use *Hansard* to establish the background and purpose of the relevant provision, or to establish the specific meaning of a specific term in the legislation? Is this distinction important?

4. Do you agree with the court's reliance on *Hansard* in *Rizzo*? Are the policies weighing against the use of *Hansard* properly regarded as a matter supporting the weight of the evidence, or should such evidence be excluded?

5. Review the decision of the Supreme Court of Canada in *Quebec v. Boisbriand*, [2000] 1 SCR 665 (set out in chapter 1). In that case, L'Heureux-Dubé J combines the use of (a) previous versions of a statute, and (b) the transcripts of the legislative debates regarding amendments to the statute. Does L'Heureux-Dubé J attribute the appropriate amount of weight to these forms of evidence? Is her use of that evidence persuasive?

C. The Firearms Reference

Reference re Firearms Act (Can.)
[2000] 1 SCR 783

I. Introduction

In 1995, Parliament amended the *Criminal Code*, RSC 1985, c. C-46, by enacting the *Firearms Act*, SC 1995, c. 39, commonly referred to as the gun control law, to require the holders of all firearms to obtain licences and register their guns. In 1996, the Province of Alberta challenged Parliament's power to pass the gun control law by a reference to the Alberta Court of Appeal. The Court of Appeal by a 3:2 majority upheld Parliament's power to pass the law. The Province of Alberta now appeals that decision to this Court.

The issue before this Court is not whether gun control is good or bad, whether the law is fair or unfair to gun owners, or whether it will be effective or ineffective in reducing the harm caused by the misuse of firearms. The only issue is whether or not Parliament has the constitutional authority to enact the law.

The answer to this question lies in the Canadian Constitution. The Constitution assigns some matters to Parliament and others to the provincial legislatures: *Constitution Act, 1867*. The federal government asserts that the gun control law falls under its criminal law power, s. 91(27), and under its general power to legislate for the "Peace, Order and good Government" of Canada. Alberta, on the other hand, says the law falls under its power over property and civil rights, s. 92(13). All agree that to resolve this dispute, the Court must first determine what the gun control law is really about—its "pith and substance"—and then ask which head or heads of power it most naturally falls within.

. . .

V. Analysis

The ... first task is to determine the "pith and substance" of the legislation. To use the wording of ss. 91 and 92, what is the "matter" of the law? What is its true meaning or essential character, its core? To determine the pith and substance, two aspects of the law must be examined: the purpose of the enacting body, and the legal effect of the law.

A law's purpose is often stated in the legislation, but it may also be ascertained by reference to extrinsic material such as Hansard and government publications: see *Morgentaler*, supra, at pp. 483-84. While such extrinsic material was at one time inadmissible to facilitate the determination of Parliament's purpose, it is now well accepted that the legislative history, Parliamentary debates, and similar material may be quite properly considered as long as it is relevant and reliable and is not assigned undue weight: see *Global Securities*, supra, at para. 25; *Rizzo & Rizzo Shoes Ltd. (Re)*, [1998] 1 SCR 27, at para. 35; and *Dore v. Verdun (City)*, [1997] 2 SCR 862, at para. 14. Purpose may also be ascertained by considering the "mischief" of the legislation—the problem which Parliament sought to remedy: see *Morgentaler*, supra, at pp. 483-84. ...

The statements of the Honourable Allan Rock, Minister of Justice at the time, in his second-reading speech in the House of Commons, reveal that the federal government's purpose in proposing the law was to promote public safety. He stated: "The government suggests that the object of the regulation of firearms should be *the preservation of the safe, civilized and peaceful nature of Canada*" (*House of Commons Debates*, vol. 133, No. 154, 1st Sess., 35th Parl., February 16, 1995, at p. 9706 (emphasis added)). Mr. Rock went on to describe the contents of the bill in more detail (at p. 9707):

> "First, tough measures to deal with the *criminal misuse of firearms*; second, specific *penalties to punish those who would smuggle illegal firearms*; and third, measures overall to provide a context in which the legitimate use of firearms can be carried on in a manner consistent with *public safety*. [Emphasis added.]"

(See also the judgment of Fraser CJA, at paras. 169-72.)

Later, the Minister referred to the problems of suicide, accidental shootings, and the use of guns in domestic violence, and detailed some of the shooting tragedies that had spurred public calls for gun control. Russell MacLellan, the Parliamentary Secretary of Justice at the time, underscored the government's concerns, noting that the Act pursues "three fundamental policies: the deterrence of the misuse of firearms, general controls on persons given access to firearms, and controls placed on specific types of firearms" ("Canada's firearms proposals" (1995), 37 Can. J Crim. 163, at p. 163). ...

We conclude that the impugned sections of the *Firearms Act* contain prohibitions and penalties in support of a valid criminal law purpose. The legislation is in relation to criminal law pursuant to s. 91(27) of the *Constitution Act, 1867* and hence *intra vires* Parliament. It is not regulatory legislation and it does not take the federal government so far into provincial territory that the balance of federalism is threatened or the jurisdictional powers of the provinces are unduly impaired. ...

NOTES AND QUESTIONS

1. If a federal minister knows that a proposed bill is (a) controversial, and (b) likely to be subjected to constitutional attack, are the comments that the minister makes regarding the purpose of that law reliable? Assuming that Mr. Rock knew that the *Firearms Act* was likely to be challenged, did he not have an incentive (as a federal minister) to make strategic comments designed to provide evidence of a legitimate "federal" purpose? What does this say about the reliability of legislative debates?

2. Would Allan Rock's comments have been as persuasive if he were a backbencher, rather than the minister responsible for the administration of the relevant act? What if

Rock had been a member of the opposition (who nevertheless voted in favour of the law)? Do the statements of one parliamentarian carry more weight than the statements of another parliamentarian?

3. Is there really a reason *not* to admit legislative debates, or any other piece of evidence that may or may not cast light on the meaning of an enactment? Why not just admit everything and then consider the relative weight of each piece of evidence?

IX. EXERCISES

A. Spy Mission

Suggested length: 10-20 pages

Colleen Traub is a spy employed by the American Central Intelligence Agency (CIA). As part of her complex "cover," Colleen is also employed by an American communications company (ACC) as a telephone service technician.

Colleen's latest CIA assignment was to observe Sanjay Akai, a Canadian physicist suspected of being involved in the development of advanced tactical weaponry. The American government feels that Canada, already dangerously advanced in Zamboni and snowplow technology, could become a potential threat if permitted to develop high-tech weapons. As a result, Colleen has been sent to determine the nature of Sanjay's research, and to put an end to it if it conflicts with American interests.

On the evening of July 24, 1997, Colleen was sitting in her black Corvette across the street from Sanjay's home. Through Sanjay's window, Colleen could observe Dr. Akai watching television. After several hours, Sanjay eventually walked across the room and picked up his cordless phone.

Colleen opened her glove compartment searching frantically for her electronic telephone receiver, which she could use to record transmissions passing to and from cordless phones. Unfortunately, Colleen had left the receiver in her hotel. Somewhat discouraged by her lack of forethought, the ever-resourceful Colleen reached for her high-tech electronic binoculars, and used them to "zoom in" on Dr. Akai.

As a highly skilled lip-reader, Colleen was able to transcribe everything said by Sanjay during a series of telephone conversations. As luck would have it, most of the conversations dealt with Sanjay's secret research, which indeed involved the invention of high-tech weapons.

While Colleen sat spying on the hapless Dr. Akai, local security guard Jarrod Robertson was making his way home after an arduous night of guarding a shopping mall. Jarrod, who was an avid Corvette enthusiast, wandered over to Colleen's car to check it out. While admiring the Corvette, Jarrod spotted Colleen spying on Dr. Akai.

Ever vigilant, Jarrod quickly opened the door to Colleen's Corvette and made a citizen's arrest. Colleen, whose legs had fallen asleep from sitting in her car for such an extended period, was unable to defend herself against Jarrod's expert choke hold. Jarrod easily overpowered the American spy, and dragged her to the local police station.

Colleen was charged with "intercepting a private communication," contrary to s. 184 of the *Criminal Code* (as it existed at the time of the offence). At the relevant time (1997), that section of the Code provided as follows:

(1) Everyone who, by means of any electro-magnetic, acoustic, mechanical or other device, willfully intercepts a private communication is guilty of an indictable offence and liable to imprisonment for a term not exceeding five years.

(2) Subsection (1) does not apply to

(a) a person who has the consent to intercept, express or implied, of the originator of the private communication or of the person intended by the originator thereof to receive it;

(b) a person who intercepts a private communication in accordance with an authorization or pursuant to section 184.4 or any person who in good faith aids in any way another person who the aiding person believes on reasonable grounds is acting with an authorization or pursuant to section 184.4;

(c) a person engaged in providing a telephone, telegraph or other communication service to the public who intercepts a private communication,

(i) if the interception is necessary for the purpose of providing the service,

(ii) in the course of service observing or random monitoring necessary for the purpose of mechanical or service quality control checks, or

(iii) if the interception is necessary to protect the person's rights or property directly related to providing the service; or

(d) an officer or servant of Her Majesty in right of Canada who engages in radio-frequency spectrum management, in respect of a private communication intercepted by that officer or servant for the purpose of identifying, isolating or preventing an unauthorized or interfering use of a frequency or of a transmission.

Colleen elected to represent herself at trial, and did an awful job. As a result, Colleen was convicted and sentenced to five years in prison. To add insult to injury, the trial judge also ordered the forfeiture of Colleen's binoculars and Corvette pursuant to s. 192 of the *Criminal Code*, which provided as follows:

(1) Where a person is convicted of an offence under section 184 or 191, any electro-magnetic, acoustic, mechanical or other device by means of which the offence was committed or the possession of which constituted the offence, on the conviction, in addition to any punishment that is imposed, may be ordered forfeited to Her Majesty whereupon it may be disposed of as the Attorney General directs.

(2) No order for forfeiture shall be made under subsection (1) in respect of telephone, telegraph or other communication facilities or equipment owned by a person engaged in providing telephone, telegraph or other communication service to the public or forming part of the telephone, telegraph or other communication service or system of that person by means of which an offence under section 184 has been committed if that person was not a party to the offence.

It should be noted that Colleen personally owned the high-tech binoculars and the Corvette that were forfeited under s. 192.

Colleen, who has wisely retained a lawyer, is now appealing both the conviction and the forfeiture order to the Canadian Court of Justice (Appeal Division). The Honourable Chief Justice MacKenzie has denied Colleen leave to raise any arguments concerning international relations. As a result, Colleen has raised the following arguments:

1. As a result of her employment with ACC, Colleen is a "person engaged in providing telephone service to the public."
2. Colleen did not "intercept" a communication: she merely transcribed what was said by *one party* in a telephone conversation.
3. Neither the binoculars nor the Corvette constitutes an "electro-magnetic, acoustic, mechanical or other device" within the meaning of s. 184 or s. 192.
4. The interception of the communication was necessary to protect Colleen's rights within the meaning of s. 184(2)(c)(iii) (that is, if Canadians develop high-tech weaponry, Colleen's right to security will be compromised). Note that this argument has been granted leave by the chief justice, despite its slightly "international" tone.

Colleen is also willing to accept acquittal on whatever grounds the court may deem just.

You are presiding over Colleen's appeal. Write a judgment that deals with the appeal of the conviction, as well as the appeal regarding the forfeiture. A good judgment will deal with each of the four arguments noted above. A *great* judgment should deal with any other relevant interpretive issues found within the legislation. Note, of course, that the *Criminal Code* is a *real* piece of legislation: any interpretive assistance that you can draw from any part of the Code will be most helpful. As always, deal only with interpretive issues (that is, those issues that relate to the meaning of words or phrases found in the legislation).

B. Human Rights Legislation

Suggested length: 7-15 pages

The Homosexual and Bisexual Society of the Yukon ("HABSY") is an unincorporated, social association of homosexual and bisexual residents of the Yukon Territory. HABSY's activities include the promotion of gay, lesbian, and bisexual rights throughout the Yukon, as well as various social gatherings. Participation in the activities is open to HABSY members only.

The most important and well-known service offered by HABSY is the provision of counselling and community support services to individuals who have been affected by discrimination. HABSY provides these services free of charge to *any* individual in need (regardless of race, sexual preference, gender, etc.).

Lionel Persaud is a heterosexual resident of the Yukon, who has been active in the promotion of gay rights. Lionel's younger brother Jeremy is a homosexual man who has frequently suffered from the effects of discrimination. Hoping to improve the lives of other individuals who find themselves in his brother's situation, Lionel has taken an active role in promoting the rights of homosexuals in the Yukon.

Last month, Lionel offered to take a position as one of HABSY's volunteer counsellors. Lionel has a PhD in sociology as well as extensive experience as a social worker. Lionel felt that his experience would make him an asset to HABSY and allow him to contribute to the valuable work of the HABSY organization. Unfortunately, HABSY did not accept Lionel's offer.

In a short rejection letter, HABSY informed Lionel that only members of HABSY were permitted to act as counsellors on behalf of the organization. Membership in HABSY is restricted to homosexuals and bisexuals. Because Lionel is heterosexual, HABSY refused to offer him membership in the organization. Lionel is accordingly ineligible for the counselling position.

Lionel was upset by HABSY's rejection, and is thinking of making a complaint under s. 8 of the Yukon Territory's *Human Rights Act* (RSY 1986 (Supp.), c. 11). At the relevant time, that section provided as follows:

> 8. No person shall discriminate
>
>   (a) when offering or providing services, goods, or facilities to the public,
>
>   (b) in connection with any aspect of employment or application for employment,
>
>   (c) in connection with any aspect of membership in or representation by any trade union, trade association, occupational association, or professional association,
>
>   (d) in connection with any aspect of the occupancy, possession, lease, or sale of property offered to the public,
>
>   (e) in the negotiation or performance of any contract that is offered to or for which offers are invited from the public.

Will Lionel be successful if he brings forward a claim under this section? Prepare a legal memorandum outlining Lionel's chances of success. When preparing your memorandum, you must assume the following:

1. There are no paid positions in HABSY. All members are volunteers.
2. HABSY is a prestigious organization. HABSY social gatherings and activities are very popular.
3. HABSY feels that only those who have suffered from discrimination are capable of identifying with HABSY's clientele, which is necessary for the provision of high-quality counselling services.
4. Lionel does not want to make his complaint under the Charter. (While you may use Charter-related arguments to help you interpret the Yukon Territory's *Human Rights Act*, you may not recommend the pursuit of a remedy under the Charter.)
5. No judgment of any court should be considered binding for the purposes of this assignment: while you should consult decisions that relate to similar issues, those decisions should be considered "persuasive authorities" only.

When invoking evidence of the legislature's intention, be sure to address the issues of weight and admissibility. You should also address any differences that arise between the interpretation of human rights statutes and the interpretation of "ordinary" legislation (refer to *Quebec v. Boisbriand*, [2000] 1 SCR 665 (set out in chapter 1) for a discussion of this issue).

C. Dynamism and Evidentiary Rules

Suggested length: 15-20 pages

Discuss the following statement:

> The rules regarding "evidence of a statute's meaning" are strictly originalist in nature, designed to ascertain the intention of the legislative author. As a result, a truly "dynamic"

approach to statutory construction should avoid reliance on headings, preambles, legislative debates, and other so-called indicators of legislative intent when attempting to determine a statute's meaning. Indeed, the dynamic interpreter must rely solely on current social policy when assigning a meaning to legislative language.

CHAPTER FIVE

Interpreting Criminal Legislation

I. INTRODUCTION

The purpose of this chapter is to describe and evaluate the interpretive doctrines governing the interpretation of criminal legislation. The nature, history, and rationale of these interpretive doctrines are described in chapter 7 of Randal N. Graham, *Statutory Interpretation: Theory and Practice* (Toronto: Emond Montgomery, 2001) (*"Theory and Practice"*).[1] Students should review that chapter before dealing with the cases set out below.

II. R v. MAC

A. Introduction

In *R v. Mac* (2001), 152 CCC (3d) 1 (Ont. CA),[2] the Ontario Court of Appeal was asked to interpret the *Criminal Code* provision governing "the possession of forgers' tools." The provision was found in s. 369(b) of the Code, and read in part:

> Every one who ... (b) ... knowingly has in his possession any plate, die, machinery, instrument or other writing or material that is adapted and intended to be used to commit forgery ... is guilty of an indictable offence.

For the purposes of the decision in *Mac*, the most important word in s. 369(b) was the word "adapted." The interpretation of the word "adapted" became important because the "forgers' tools" possessed by the accused were *originally designed* as forgers' tools and had never been "adapted" in any way: they were forgers' tools from the moment of their creation and had never been altered. As a result, the court in *Mac* was asked to determine whether or not the word "adapted" was capable of embracing forgers' tools that had never been altered in any way.

---

1   Chapter 7 of *Theory and Practice* also deals with the interpretation of tax statutes.

2   The Court of Appeal's decision was overturned by the Supreme Court of Canada on March 14, 2002, based on the French version of the relevant provision. See [2002] SCJ no. 26.

B. The Court's Decision

R v. Mac
(2001), 152 CCC (3d) 1 (Ont. CA)

DOHERTY JA:

I

The appellant was tried with two other accused on a 31-count indictment. He was charged in seven of the counts (counts 1, 26, 27, 28, 29, 30, and 31). The charges were laid after an investigation of what the police alleged was a widespread and sophisticated criminal enterprise involving various criminal activities, including the large scale manufacture and sale of forged credit cards.

After a lengthy trial, the appellant was convicted on five counts and acquitted on two counts (counts 1, 31). The five convictions (counts 26-30) arose out of charges laid under s. 369(b) of the *Criminal Code*. These charges alleged that the appellant was in possession of various machines and materials adapted for and intended to be used to create forged credit cards. The trial judge imposed a total sentence of 11 months to be followed by one year probation. The appellant appeals his convictions and seeks leave to appeal his sentence. ...

The appellant ... argues that the trial judge erred in instructing the jury that the word "adapted" in s. 369(b) meant "suitable for." The appellant submits that it means "altered so as to be suitable for." The material and machines referred to in counts 26, 28, 29, and 30 were suitable for use in the making of forged credit cards but had not been altered in any way. If the appellant's submission is correct, he should have succeeded on his motion for a directed verdict of acquittal on those counts. ...

III

The meaning to be given to the word "adapted" in s. 369(b) is a matter of statutory interpretation. I need not review the evidence.

It is sufficient to say that there was evidence from which it could be inferred that the material and machines referred to in the relevant counts were suitable for use in the manufacture of forged credit cards. There was also evidence from which it could be inferred that the appellant intended to use the materials and machines to manufacture forged credit cards. Finally, as observed above, there was no evidence that the material or machines referred to in counts 26, 28, 29, and 30 had been changed or altered in any way so as to make them suitable for the manufacture of forged credit cards. They could serve that purpose without any alteration. There was evidence that some of the material referred to in count 27 had been altered by embossment so as to make it suitable for the manufacture of forged credit cards. ...

Each count alleged an offence under s. 369(b) of the *Criminal Code*. The relevant parts of that provision read: 369. Every one who ... (b) ... knowingly has in his possession any plate, die, machinery, instrument or other writing or material that is adapted and intended to be used to commit forgery ... is guilty of an indictable offence. ...

The conduct component of the offence created by s. 369(b) consists of possession of any plate, die, machinery, instrument, writing, or other material that is adapted for use in the commission of forgery. The fault component of the crime requires proof of:

> knowledge that the plate, die, machinery, instrument, writing, or other material is in the accused's possession and adapted for use in the commission of forgery; and an intention to commit forgery.

Section 369(b) renders conduct criminal that is preparatory to the commission of forgery. It is colloquially described as possession of "forgers' tools." Section 369(b) is akin to the crime of attempt or more exactly what Professor Ashworth describes as an "incomplete attempt": A. Ashworth, *Principles of Criminal Law*, 2nd ed. (Oxford: Clarendon Press, 1995) at 443-44. The rationale for the offence created by s. 369(b), like the rationale for attempt, is preventative. By criminalizing conduct short of actual forgery engaged in by a person who intends to commit forgery, the state is able to intervene before the harm caused by the completed crime occurs.

The argument that "adapted" in s. 369(b) means "altered so as to be suitable for" was made at trial on a motion for a directed verdict. The trial judge, after referring to various dictionaries, acknowledged that the word "adapted" had two recognized meanings. It could mean "suited for" or it could mean "modified or altered so as to be suited for": see also *R v. Formosa* (1991), 92 Cr. App. R 11 (CA) at 13.

After referring to other sections of the *Criminal Code* in which the word "adapted" is used to make the point that the word could have different meanings in different contexts, the trial judge concluded:

> In my view, where machines or other materials for forgery are usable for both illegal and for legal purposes without any modification or alteration, then the most logical and rational meaning to be given to the word "adapted" in s. 369(b) is "suited" and not "altered." As noted above, this word does add something to the section in that meaning because it limits the eligible machines to those that are suited for forgery, which limits the machines, dies or other material that would qualify. Counsel have provided the recent Supreme Court decision in *R v. McIntosh* (1995), 95 CCC (3d) 481, which deals with the principles of statutory interpretation of the *Criminal Code* provisions. I am satisfied that my analysis herein is consistent with the principles set out in that case. I therefore find that there is no requirement that any of the charged material be modified or altered in order to form the basis for a conviction under the section. ...

Section 369(b) refers to "plate, die, machinery, instrument or other writings or material." These words have a very wide compass: *R v. Griffith* (1969), 7 CR (NS) 196 (Que. CA) at 208. If, as the trial judge held, "adapted" means simply "suitable for," then the prohibition created by s. 369(b) is potentially very broad. An intention to commit forgery, combined with the possession of mundane objects like a piece of paper or a pen would come within the reach of s. 369(b). The criminalization of such innocuous and harmless conduct, albeit joined with a criminal intent, comes perilously close to imposing criminal liability based solely on the existence of a criminal intention. It has been a fundamental principle of the criminal law for many centuries that criminal liability should not rest solely on an accused's intention, no matter how worthy of censure that intention might be: D. Stuart, *Canadian Criminal Law*, 3rd ed. (Toronto: Carswell, 1995) at 71-72.

The ambit of s. 369(b) is significantly narrower on the appellant's interpretation. On that interpretation, something must be done to the "plate, die, machinery, instrument, material or other writing" to make it suitable for use in the commission of forgery. The appellant contends that the alteration provides a manifestation of the criminal intention to commit forgery and moves an accused's conduct beyond the realm of mere intention. Counsel demonstrates his position by reference to the facts in this case. He submits that criminalizing the possession of a piece of plastic, albeit accompanied by an intention to commit forgery, is in reality punishing an intention to commit forgery. However, if that piece of plastic is altered, as for example by embossment, so as to make it suitable for use in the making of a forged credit card, and the accused knows that it has been so altered, then the accused's possession of the altered piece of plastic manifests his intention to commit the crime of forgery. The accused is no longer punished for mere intention, but for doing something towards the achievement of that intention.

If the word "adapted" in s. 369(b) is ambiguous, then the significant difference in the reach of that section, depending on which interpretation of the word "adapted" is accepted, becomes important in determining the meaning to be given to s. 369(b). Ambiguity in the meaning of criminal statues has always been resolved by choosing the meaning which is most favourable to the accused. In *Marcotte v. Canada (Deputy Attorney General)* (1974), 19 CCC (2d) 257 (SCC) at 261-62, Dickson J put it this way:

> Even if I were to conclude that the relevant statutory provisions were ambiguous and equivocal—a conclusion one could reach without difficulty on reading [Citations omitted.]—I would have to find for the appellant in this case. It is unnecessary to emphasize the importance of clarity and certainty when freedom is at stake. No authority is needed for the proposition that if real ambiguities are found, or doubts of substance arise, in the construction and application of a statute affecting the liberty of a subject, then that statute should be applied in such a manner as to favour the person against whom it is sought to be enforced. If one is to be incarcerated, one should at least know that some Act of Parliament requires it in express terms, and not, at most, by implication.

In *R v. Pare* (1987), 38 CCC (3d) 97 (SCC) at 106, Wilson J described the principle that true ambiguities in penal statutes must be construed in favour of the person whose liberty is at stake as "one of ancient lineage." After observing that the rule had originally served to soften the impact of draconian criminal laws, Wilson J said:

> … Criminal law remains, however, the most dramatic and important incursion that the state makes into individual liberty. Thus, while the original justification for the doctrine has been substantially eroded, the seriousness of imposing criminal penalties of any sort demands that reasonable doubts be resolved in favour of the accused.

More recently, in *R v. McIntosh* (1995), 95 CCC (3d) 481 (SCC) at 495, Lamer CJC, for the majority, said:

The *Criminal Code* is not a contract or a labour agreement. For that matter, it is qualitatively different from most other legislative enactments because of its direct and potentially profound impact on the personal liberty of citizens. The special nature of the *Criminal Code* requires an interpretative approach which is sensitive to liberty interests. Therefore, an ambiguous penal provision must be interpreted in the manner most favourable to accused persons, and in the manner most likely to provide clarity and certainty in the criminal law.

The principle identified in these three cases and countless others is justified on at least two grounds. Persons who are subject to the coercive and stigmatizing power of the criminal law are entitled to fair notice of the conduct which will subject them to that power. Where a crime is defined in ambiguous terms, fair notice is only given with respect to the conduct which is captured by each of the meanings which are reasonably available upon a reading of the statute: A. Ashworth, *Principles of Criminal Law*, supra, at 76-78.

The second justification underlying the principle arises out of our commitment to individual liberty, particularly where the criminal law power is engaged. Canadian society operates on the basis that individuals are free to do as they choose, subject to constitutionally permissible limits on that liberty imposed by Parliament (and not the courts). Where it is unclear whether Parliament has chosen to prohibit conduct by making it criminal, the commitment to individual liberty commands that the doubt be resolved in favour of the maintenance of individual liberty: D. Stuart, *Canadian Criminal Law*, supra, at 37-40.

The principle that ambiguous penal provisions must be interpreted in favour of an accused does not mean that the most restrictive possible meaning of any word used in the penal statute must always be the preferred meaning. The principle applies only where there is true ambiguity as to the meaning of a word in a penal statute: *R v. Hasselwander* (1993), 81 CCC (3d) 471 (SCC) at 476-77. The meaning of words cannot be determined by examining those words in isolation. Meaning is discerned by examining words in their context. True ambiguities in a statute exist only where the meaning remains unclear after a full contextual analysis of the statute. As Martin JA said in *R v. Goulis* (1981), 60 CCC (2d) 347 (Ont. CA) at 351:

> I do not think, however, that this principle always requires a word which has two accepted meanings to be given the more restrictive meaning. Where a word used in a statute has two accepted meanings, then either or both meanings may apply. The Court is first required to endeavour to determine the sense in which Parliament used the word from the context in which it appears. It is only in the case of an ambiguity which still exists after the full context is considered, where it is uncertain in which sense Parliament used the word, that the above rule of statutory construction requires the interpretation which is the more favourable to the defendant to be adopted. This is merely another way of stating the principle that the conduct alleged against the accused must be clearly brought within the proscription.

Like the trial judge, I find nothing in the language of s. 369(b), nor the rest of s. 369, that helps me discern which of the two meanings of the word "adapted" Parliament intended. Context, however, goes beyond the language of the specific section in issue. In *Re Rizzo & Rizzo Shoes Ltd.*, [1998] 1 SCR 27 at 41, Iacobucci J, for the Court, observed that the process of statutory interpretation cannot rest merely on the wording of the legislation. He quoted with approval the observation of E. Driedger in *Construction of Statutes* 2nd ed. (Toronto: Butterworths, 1983) at 87:

> Today there is only one principle or approach, namely, the words of an Act are to be read in their entire context and in their grammatical and ordinary sense harmoniously with the scheme of the Act, the object of the Act, and the intention of Parliament.

The words of Driedger adopted in *Re Rizzo & Rizzo Shoes Ltd.*, supra, were applied to the interpretation of *Criminal Code* provisions in *R v. Gladue*, [1999] 1 SCR 688 at 704, 133 CCC (3d) 385.

It is impossible to speak in terms of "the object" or "the scheme" of the *Criminal Code*. The Code addresses procedural and substantive matters that run the gamut of the entire criminal law process. To the extent that the *Criminal Code* creates crimes, however, I would describe its objects as the prohibition of activity that could reasonably be regarded as harmful or potentially harmful to society in a way that puts everyone on notice of where the line between criminal and non-criminal conduct has been drawn. These objects favour a restrained reading of *Criminal Code* provisions that create crimes so as to avoid overreaching and uncertainty.

Reference to these "objects" of the *Criminal Code* does little to advance the inquiry beyond the principle that true ambiguities must be resolved in favour of the accused. The objects are obviously identical to the rationale underlying the principle itself.

Legislative history can sometimes help in resolving apparent ambiguities. Unfortunately, the legislative history of s. 369(b) offers no insight into the meaning of the word "adapted" in that section. The word first appeared in s. 312(b) of the *Criminal Code*, SC 1953-54, c. 51. The language of the present section is identical to the language of the former s. 312(b). Prior to the enactment of s. 312(b), there was no general prohibition against the possession of "forgers' tools," although possession of certain specific kinds of material used for certain kinds of forgeries was prohibited. The widening of the criminal law net brought about by s. 312(b) does not appear to have sparked any discussion in Parliament and has been ignored by commentators who, erroneously in my view, saw s. 312(b) as no more than a consolidation of previous forgery-related provisions. The legislative history of the section is traced in G. Rodrigues, ed., *Crankshaw's Criminal Code of Canada*, 8th ed., vol. 2 (Scarborough: Carswell, 1993) at 9-292 to 9-297; see also J.C. Martin, QC, ed., *Martin's Annual Criminal Code 1955* (Toronto: Cartwright and Sons, 1955) at 540-542.3

An apparent ambiguity can sometimes be resolved by reference to other sections in the same enactment. This technique was used by the trial judge and by counsel in this Court. While this comparative process can sometimes be helpful, it must be proceeded with cautiously for at least two reasons. First, different sections of the *Criminal Code* were enacted at different times over the last 110 years. I do not think it can be assumed that a word used in a provision of the *Criminal Code* necessarily has the same meaning as it has in an entirely unrelated provision of the Code introduced many years earlier.

Second, comparisons with other sections of the *Criminal Code* in which the word "adapted" appears are of limited value given that it is accepted that the word can take on one of two meanings depending on the context. As the trial judge noted, the conclusion that "adapted" has one meaning in a particular section of the *Criminal Code* may provide no assistance in determining the meaning to be given to that word in another section.

The trial judge did find some assistance in the use of the word "adapted" in s. 458(d) of the *Criminal Code*. It provides that:

> 458. Every one who without lawful justification or excuse, the proof of which lies on him ... (d) has in his custody or possession, any machine, engine, tool, instrument, material or thing that he knows has been used or that he knows is adapted and intended for use in making counterfeit money or counterfeit tokens of value is guilty of an indictable offence. ...

She reasoned, at para. 8, that the word "adapted" in this section must mean "suitable for":

> ... It would be illogical for the section to be interpreted to require for conviction that machines be altered in some way if they have not yet been used, but not if the same machines were used right out of the box if they have already been used before the arrest of the accused.

I do not share the trial judge's view that the distinction she describes would be illogical. If an accused knows that a machine has been used to create counterfeit money, the possession of that machine may manifest a criminal intention to engage in the production of counterfeit money. Similarly, if an accused knows that a machine has been altered so that it can be used to make counterfeit money, the possession of that machine is arguably a manifestation of a criminal intention. If, however, an accused has possession of a machine that could be used to make counterfeit money without any alteration, then in my view, the accused possession of that machine does not manifest a criminal intention in the same way as does possession of a machine that an accused knows has been used or has been altered to make it suitable for the manufacture of counterfeit money. Unlike the trial judge, I think it is more consistent with the other forms of liability created in s. 458(d) to interpret "adapted" as requiring some alteration of the machine so as to make it suitable for use in the manufacture of counterfeit money.

I find some limited assistance in interpreting s. 369(b) in the other sections of the *Criminal Code* which prohibit the possession of "tools" to be used in the commission of other crimes. Sections 351 and 352 prohibit the possession of instruments which are "suitable for" the commission of the crimes described in those sections. It is arguable that had Parliament intended to prohibit the possession of things that were suitable for use in the commission of forgery, it would have used those very words in s. 369(b), just as it did in ss. 351 and 352.

In the end, however, I find comparisons with the other provisions of the *Criminal Code* as it stood at the time of trial of little help in discerning the meaning of s. 369(b).

Since the trial, however, the *Criminal Code* has been amended by the addition of s. 342.01(1)(d). The section was introduced into the *Criminal Code* by the *Criminal Law Improvement Act 1996*, SC 1997, c. 18, s. 17, and proclaimed in force on June 16, 1997. A comparison of that section with s. 369(b) does assist in giving meaning to the word "adapted" in s. 369(b). For ease of reference, the two sections are set out below:

> 369. Every one who ... (b) ... knowingly has in his possession any plate, die, machinery, instrument or other writing or material that is adapted and intended to be used to commit forgery ... is guilty of an indictable offence.

> 342.01(1) Every person who, without lawful justification or excuse ... (d) possesses any instrument, device, apparatus, material or thing that the person knows has been used or knows is adapted or intended for use in forging or falsifying credit cards is guilty of an indictable offence and liable to imprisonment for a term not exceeding ten years, or is guilty of an offence punishable on summary conviction.

The similarity between the two sections is self-evident. The conduct alleged in this case falls squarely within s. 342.01(1)(d). Most of the conduct which is criminalized by that section would also be an offence under s. 369(b). While s. 369(b) targets possession of "forgers' tools," in general, the new section is aimed at possession of those "forgers' tools" used for the creation of fraudulent credit cards. Finally, both sections strike at activity which is preliminary to the actual commission of forgery and do so by prohibiting the possession of virtually anything that is "adapted" for use in the commission of either forgery (s. 369(b)) or in forging credit cards (s. 342.01(1)(d)). As both sections address the same subject matter in very similar language, it would make sense for the word "adapted" to have the same meaning in both sections.

Section 342.01(1)(d) is different from s. 369(b) in one important respect. It prohibits possession of anything which a person knows is adapted for use in forging credit cards regardless of whether that person actually intends to use that thing for the purpose of forging credit cards. Section 369(b) requires knowing possession of a thing adapted for use in the commission of forgery combined with an intention to actually commit forgery. If the word "adapted" in s. 342.01(1)(d) means simply "suitable for," then a person who is in possession of a piece of plastic which he knows could be used to make a forged credit card is guilty of a crime even if that person has no intention of using the piece of plastic for that purpose. This interpretation imposes criminal liability for conduct which is not morally blameworthy, causes no harm, and poses no risk. In my view, interpreting "adapted" as meaning "suitable for" in s. 342.01(1)(d) stretches the criminal law beyond all acceptable limits. Although the parties did not raise any constitutional arguments, it is well understood that Charter principles should guide statutory interpretation. An interpretation of s. 342.01(1)(d) that purported to criminalize innocuous conduct absent any criminal intent would seem to be inconsistent with the minimum fault requirements protected by s. 7 of the Charter: see *R v. Wholesale Travel Group Inc.*, [1991] 3 SCR 154, 67 CCC (3d) 193; *R v. Clay* (2000), 146 CCC (3d) 276 (Ont. CA) at 288-291.

If, however, "adapted" is interpreted as meaning "altered so as to be suitable for," criminal liability is imposed by s. 342.01(1)(d) on those who are in possession of something that they know has been altered to make it suitable for use in forging credit cards. Possession with knowledge of the nature of the alteration is arguably sufficiently culpable to warrant criminalization. "Adapted" in s. 342.01(1)(d) must mean "altered so as to be suitable for."

The meaning of the word "adapted" in s. 342.01(1)(d), combined with the close connection between that provision and s. 369(b), pushes me close to the conclusion that there is no ambiguity in s. 369(b) and that "adapted" means "altered so as to be suitable for." I stop short of that conclusion only because it assumes a consistency in the drafting of different sections of the *Criminal Code* which seems to me to be more fiction than fact.

My contextual search for the meaning of "adapted" in s. 369(b) ends where it began after a reading of the section. The word has two possible meanings and it cannot be said with any confidence which of the two Parliament intended. The section is truly ambiguous. According to well-established authority, the interpretation which favours the accused must be adopted. I would interpret "adapted" in s. 369(b) as meaning "altered so as to be suitable for." It follows that the trial judge erred in law in telling the jury that "adapted" meant "suitable for." ...

NOTES AND QUESTIONS

1. Does the word "adapted" truly have more than one meaning? Consider the following sentence: "The female pelvis is adapted for childbirth." In this sentence, does the word "adapted" mean "suitable for," or does it imply that the female pelvis is *currently* suitable for childbirth due to some "adaptation" that has taken place over time?

2. Does the problem in *Mac* involve vagueness, ambiguity, subtext, or analogy? How would the unified theory (developed in *Theory and Practice*) apply in *Mac*?

3. According to Doherty JA: "If, as the trial judge held, 'adapted' means simply 'suitable for,' then the prohibition created by s. 369(b) is potentially very broad. An intention to commit forgery, combined with the possession of mundane objects like a piece of paper or a pen would come within the reach of s. 369(b)." Is this an accurate statement? Given the language of s. 369(b), would the police (or prosecutor) have to point out the *specific* pen and piece of paper that a forger intended to use as "forgers' tools"? Is it likely that the prosecution could successfully do so? Absent the presence of "obvious" forgers' tools (as opposed to pens and papers), how is the prosecution likely to know that the forger has an intention to commit forgery?

4. Is it likely that Parliament intended to criminalize the possession of "adapted" forgers' tools, while failing to criminalize the possession of tools that were suitable for forging when they were first created or purchased? Why would Parliament do that?

5. When must an "adaptation" take place? Presumably, forgers' tools are rarely found in nature: they must be created from raw materials such as steel, plastic, wood, etc. If one were to take a piece of plastic and make a "credit card forging machine," could it be said that the machine had been altered or "adapted," so as to make it suitable for forgery?

6. According to Doherty JA, "[a]mbiguity in the meaning of criminal statutes has always been resolved by choosing the meaning which is most favourable to the accused." Is this accurate, given the decision of the Supreme Court of Canada in *R v. Hasselwander*, [1993] 2 SCR 398, at 411, in which the court held that the "pro-accused" rule had been

"modified and indeed transformed over the last fifty years"? (The *Hasselwander* decision is discussed in detail at 213-15 of *Theory and Practice*.)

7. Doherty JA holds that it is "impossible to speak in terms of 'the object' or 'the scheme' of the *Criminal Code*." Is this statement correct? If it *is* impossible to attribute a single objective to the entire *Criminal Code*, should the court nonetheless attempt to discern the "object" or the "scheme" of the specific provisions being considered? Note that the court in *R v. Hasselwander* takes this approach, which appears to be required in light of s. 12 of the federal *Interpretation Act*.[3]

8. Doherty JA refers to other sections of the *Criminal Code* in order to cast light on the meaning of s. 369(b). Recall that s. 342.01 of the Code (which is referred to by Doherty JA) deals with "credit card falsification" and provides (in part) as follows:

> Every person who ... possesses any instrument, device, apparatus, material or thing that ...
> is *adapted or intended* for use in forging or falsifying credit cards. ... [Emphasis added.]

Does the phrase "adapted *or* intended" make more sense than "adapted *and* intended"? What is the difference between these two phrases? Is it possible that when drafting s. 369(b), the legislature meant to use the word "or" but committed a drafting error?

9. How would the golden rule (discussed in chapter 3) apply to the interpretation of s. 369(b)? Do any absurd results flow from the interpretations put forward by the parties in *Mac*?

10. How do the policies underlying "strict construction" apply to the provision at issue in *R v. Mac*?[4] Does a "strict" construction of s. 369(b) coincide with a "purposive" construction of the provision? If not, which construction is more appropriate?

11. What is the purpose of s. 369(b)? Presumably, one purpose of the section is to facilitate the prosecution of forgers (that is, the section makes it easier to convict persons involved in forgery). Does the court's interpretation fulfill this purpose?

III. R v. RUSSELL

A. The Court's Decision

R v. Russell
[2001] SCJ no. 53

McLACHLIN CJ: ... The substantive question is whether s. 231(5) of the *Criminal Code*, RSC 1985, c. C-46, which states that murder is first degree if the accused caused the death of another person "while committing or attempting to commit" an offence enumerated under that provision, requires that the victim of the murder and

---

3   As we have seen several times, s. 12 of the federal *Interpretation Act*, RSC 1985, c. I-21, provides that
     "[e]very enactment is deemed remedial, and shall be given such fair, large and liberal construction and
     interpretation as best ensures the attainment of its objects."

4   Strict construction is discussed in detail in *Theory and Practice* at 195-99.

the victim of the enumerated offence be the same person. For the following reasons, I conclude that ... s. 231(5) may apply even where the victim of the murder and the victim of the enumerated offence are not the same.

I. Facts

The appellant was charged with the first degree murder of John Whittaker. He was also charged with the sexual assault, sexual assault with a weapon, forcible confinement, and robbery of the complainant, Janet Secombe. The appellant did not contest his committal to trial for all charges listed in the information except for the charge of first degree murder. The only issue at the preliminary inquiry was whether he could be committed to trial for first degree murder rather than second.

Secombe's testimony at the preliminary inquiry was to the following effect. Secombe met the appellant in 1992, while he was serving a jail term, and began a romantic relationship with him that continued after his release from jail in March of 1997. When Secombe first met the appellant, Whittaker had been a tenant in her home for approximately 14 years and was "like a brother" to her. Whittaker and the appellant did not get along and were openly hostile toward one another. Whenever the appellant visited Secombe, Whittaker avoided him by going downstairs to the basement to work on his computer. Whittaker indicated to Secombe that he would move out if the appellant moved in. Accordingly, the appellant did not move in with Secombe after his release from jail. Secombe attributed the hostility between the appellant and Whittaker to the fact that the appellant is black and Whittaker was racist.

The relationship between Secombe and the appellant deteriorated, apparently because the appellant refused to make payments on a car that Secombe had purchased on his behalf. They had a disagreement on December 24, 1997. On December 28, the appellant called Secombe and she agreed to go to dinner and exchange Christmas gifts.

The appellant arrived at Secombe's home at around 4:30 p.m. on December 28. Whittaker was at home and in the basement. There is no evidence that the appellant knew Whittaker was in the house. After sharing a bottle of beer with Secombe, drinking a shot of rum, and giving Secombe two Christmas gifts, the appellant told Secombe that he had also purchased a dress for her. He asked her to go upstairs and put it on to wear to dinner. Secombe went upstairs, sat on her bed and started to undress.

The appellant followed her into the bedroom, put his arm around her neck, and threatened her with a knife. The appellant told her that he was in an "awful lot of trouble" and needed her car keys, credit card, and PIN number. The appellant tied her up on the bed with an extension cord and shoelaces and gagged her. He then went downstairs, returned with a bottle of rum, undressed, untied Secombe's feet, and allegedly sexually assaulted her. Afterward, he released Secombe so that she could go to the bathroom. The appellant then tied her up again, this time using a telephone cord. He drank more rum, brought her a beer (removing the gag but threatening Secombe with the knife), inserted a pornographic movie into the VCR, masturbated, and then again asked for Secombe's PIN and her daily withdrawal limit. After Secombe gave him the information, the appellant left the room.

For five to ten minutes the house seemed "really quiet" before Secombe suddenly heard Whittaker screaming "Oh, my God, oh, no, oh no." After ten to fifteen minutes, the appellant returned to the bedroom, out of breath, with water or sweat pouring down his face. He wiped his knife on Secombe's night dress, which was on the bed. The doorbell then began to ring continuously. The appellant asked Secombe if the neighbours were home; she indicated that she did not know. The appellant left the bedroom. Three to four minutes later, a female police officer entered Secombe's room and untied her.

Secombe's neighbours testified that they heard a violent struggle taking place in the basement of Secombe's home. After hearing Whittaker saying, "Stop, you're going to kill me" or "going to kill me," they called the police, and an officer was dispatched at 7:14 p.m. Officers arrived at 7:18 p.m.

The appellant met police at the door with a large bump on his forehead. Police found Whittaker in the basement beaten and stabbed to death. He had approximately forty stab wounds from the chest upward on the front and back and had been beaten with a blunt instrument. A wooden mallet was found on the floor near Whittaker's body. The knife was found upstairs in the hall. Secombe was found tied to the bed. Upon his arrest at the scene, the appellant told the officers, "You guys better call an ambulance ... because I stabbed him ... he hit me with a hammer so I stabbed him."

· · ·

III. Legislation

Criminal Code, RSC 1985, c. C-46

"231(1) ...

(2) Murder is first degree murder when it is planned and deliberate.

...

(5) Irrespective of whether a murder is planned and deliberate on the part of any person, murder is first degree murder in respect of a person when the death is caused by that person while committing or attempting to commit an offence under one of the following sections:

(a) section 76 (hijacking an aircraft);

(b) section 271 (sexual assault);

(c) section 272 (sexual assault with a weapon, threats to a third party or causing bodily harm);

(d) section 273 (aggravated sexual assault);

(e) section 279 (kidnapping and forcible confinement); or

(f) section 279.1 (hostage taking).

· · ·

V. Analysis

. . .

2. Section 231(5)

I turn now to the question of whether the preliminary inquiry judge erred in holding that s. 231(5) may apply even if the victim of the murder and the victim of the enumerated offence are not the same.

The question is first and foremost one of statutory interpretation. As such, the governing principles are well settled: the words in question should be considered in the context in which they are used, and read in a manner consistent with the purpose of the provision and the intention of the legislature: see *R v. Heywood*, [1994] 3 SCR 761, at p. 784 (citing Elmer A. Driedger, *Construction of Statutes* (2nd ed. 1983), at p. 87; *R v. Hasselwander*, [1993] 2 SCR 398). "If the ordinary meaning of the words is consistent with the context in which the words are used and with the object of the act, then that is the interpretation which should govern": *Heywood*, supra, at p. 784.

The language of s. 231(5) is clear. The provision does not state that the victim of the murder and the victim of the enumerated offence must be one and the same. It requires only that the accused have killed "while committing or attempting to commit" one of the enumerated offences. Nothing in that phrase suggests that the provision's application is limited to cases in which the victim of the murder and the victim of the enumerated offence are the same. An interpretation of the provision that recognized such a limitation would effectively read into the provision a restriction that is not stated.

Other provisions of the *Criminal Code* indicate that, where Parliament intends to limit the phrase "while committing or attempting to commit," it does so in express language. Section 231(6), for example, provides that

> "Irrespective of whether a murder is planned and deliberate on the part of any person, murder is first degree murder when the death is caused by that person while committing or attempting to commit an offence under section 264 [Criminal Harassment] and the person committing that offence intended to cause *the person murdered* to fear for the safety of *the person murdered* or the safety of anyone known to *the person murdered*. [Emphasis added.]"

Without the limitation, s. 231(6) would apply to a person who had murdered one person while criminally harassing another. The limitation restricts the application of the provision to those who murder the person they are criminally harassing. No analogous limitation is stated in s. 231(5).

Still other provisions of the *Criminal Code* suggest that Parliament's use of the phrase "while committing or attempting to commit" does not in itself reflect an intention to create a same-victim requirement. Section 231(6.1), for example, provides that

> "[M]urder is first degree when the death is caused while committing or attempting to commit an offence under section 81 [using explosives] for the benefit of ... a criminal organization."

Section 81 proscribes conduct that includes using explosives against property: see s. 81(1)(c) ("Every one commits an offence who ... with intent to destroy or damage property without lawful excuse, places or throws an explosive substance anywhere ..."). Parliament must have contemplated, therefore, that s. 231(6.1) might be applied even where there is no "victim" at all to the underlying crime. It would be senseless to say that the victim of the murder and the explosives offence must be one and the same where the latter crime might have no victim at all. Section 231(6.1) suggests that the use of the phrase "while committing or attempting to commit" does not itself create a same-victim requirement.

If Parliament had intended to restrict the scope of s. 231(5), it could have done so explicitly, as it did in s. 231(6). That Parliament did not incorporate such a restriction suggests that it intended "while committing or attempting to commit" to apply even where the victim of the murder and the victim of the enumerated offence are not the same. Indeed, several of the offences enumerated in s. 231(5) quite clearly raise the possibility that the person murdered will not be the same as the victim of the enumerated crime, and it would be difficult to conclude that this possibility did not occur to the drafters of the provision. A hijacker might kill a person on the runway; a kidnapper might kill the parent of the child he means to kidnap; a hostage-taker might kill an innocent bystander or a would-be rescuer. It is difficult to conclude that Parliament did not envision such possibilities.

The fact that s. 231(5) reaches not only successfully executed offences but also attempts raises similar concerns. Many attempt charges stem from crimes that were thwarted or aborted, often because of the intervention of a third party. Parliament surely envisioned such scenarios when it drafted the provision. Had Parliament not wanted the provision to reach these circumstances, it could easily have attached an explicit restriction to the provision's language. ...

In my view the appellant states the organizing principle of s. 231(5) too narrowly. The provision reflects Parliament's determination that murders committed in connection with crimes of domination are particularly blameworthy and deserving of more severe punishment. "While committing or attempting to commit" requires the killing to be closely connected, temporally and causally, with an enumerated offence. As long as that connection exists, however, it is immaterial that the victim of the killing and the victim of the enumerated offence are not the same.

In oral argument, the appellant relied heavily on the fact that murder is not itself an offence enumerated under s. 231(5). On the appellant's theory, if Parliament had contemplated that the provision might be applied to multiple-victim scenarios, it would surely have included murder on the list of offences, because murder committed to facilitate another, or other, murder is obviously as morally blameworthy as murder committed to facilitate any of the enumerated offences. In the appellant's view, the absence of murder from the list of offences can only be explained by the fact that Parliament did not contemplate that the provision might be applied to situations in which the victim of the murder and the victim of the enumerated offence are not the same.

I think the more likely explanation for the exclusion of murder from the list of enumerated offences under s. 231(5) is simply that, in most situations in which an accused has killed two or more people and there is a temporal and causal nexus between the killings, s. 231(2) will apply. That provision states that "[m]urder is first degree murder when it is planned and deliberate." While one can imagine situations in which an accused might have killed two or more people spontaneously, without planning or deliberation, such scenarios are surely the exception rather than the rule. In all likelihood, the reason that Parliament did not include murder as an enumerated offence under s. 231(5) is that it concluded that most multiple murders would engage s. 231(2).

The appellant rightly points out that s. 231(5) imposes a severe penalty—indeed, the most severe penalty imposed under our *Criminal Code*—and accordingly it is particularly important that the provision be strictly construed. While this principle is unimpeachable, it cannot in itself justify restricting the ordinary meaning of the provision's words. The cases of this Court dealing with s. 231(5) make clear that an accused commits a murder "while committing or attempting to commit" an enumerated offence only if there is a close temporal and causal connection between the murder and the enumerated offence: see, e.g., *Pare*, ... at p. 632 (stating that a murder is committed "while committing" an enumerated offence only "where the act causing death and the acts constituting [the enumerated offence] all form part of one continuous sequence of events forming a single transaction"); *R v. Kirkness*, [1990] 3 SCR 74, at p. 86. In my view this requirement appropriately restricts the application of s. 231(5) to contexts within the intended scope of the provision. ...

NOTES AND QUESTIONS

1. Note that the court's comparison of s. 231(6) (which contains an explicit "same-victim" requirement) and s. 231(5) (which contains no explicit "same-victim" requirement) is essentially an application of the presumption of consistent expression (that is, where Parliament intends to have a same-victim requirement, it says so explicitly). This closely parallels the logic underlying *expressio unius est exclusio alterius*.[5] Is that logic persuasive in this case?

2. Does the court make appropriate use of the "purpose" underlying s. 231(5)? What is the "mischief" that s. 231(5) was aimed at preventing?

3. Review the arguments concerning the absence of "murder" from the list of crimes set out in s. 231(5). Is the court's response to that argument convincing? Is there a better way to respond to that argument? Is it possible that the failure to include "murder" in the relevant list was simply a drafting error?

4. How does the court in *Russell* balance the principles of "strict construction" against the purpose or objective of s. 231(5)?

5. The problem in *Russell* involves an issue of (alleged) subtextual language, which is addressed in chapter 5 of *Theory and Practice*. What is the "subtext" that the accused asks the court to "read into" the relevant section? How would the unified theory (described in chapter 6 of *Theory and Practice*) assist the court in resolving the relevant problem?

---

5   This maxim is discussed in chapter 2 of this text and in *Theory and Practice* at 104-9.

IV. CARON v. UNITED STATES

A. The Court's Decision

Caron v. United States
524 US 308 (1998)

KENNEDY J: Under federal law, a person convicted of a crime punishable by more than one year in prison may not possess any firearm. 18 USC § 922(g)(1). If he has three violent felony convictions and violates the statute, he must receive an enhanced sentence. § 924(e). A previous conviction is a predicate for neither the substantive offense nor the sentence enhancement if the offender has had his civil rights restored, "unless such ... restoration of civil rights expressly provides that the person may not ... possess ... firearms." § 921(a)(20). This is the so-called "unless clause" we now must interpret. As the ellipses suggest, the statute is more complex, but the phrase as quoted presents the issue for our decision.

The parties, reflecting a similar division among various Courts of Appeals, disagree over the interpretation of the unless clause in the following circumstance. What if the State restoring the offender's rights forbids possession of some firearms, say pistols, but not others, say rifles? In one sense, he "may not ... possess ... firearms" under the unless clause because the ban on specified weapons is a ban on "firearms." In another sense, he can possess firearms under the unless clause because the state ban is not absolute [citations omitted].

The Government contends the class of criminals who "may not ... possess ... firearms" includes those forbidden to have some guns but not others. On this reading, the restoration of rights is of no effect here, the previous offenses are chargeable, and petitioner's sentence must be enhanced. On appeal, the Government's position prevailed in the Court of Appeals for the First Circuit, and we now affirm its judgment.

I

Petitioner Gerald Caron has an extensive criminal record, including felonies. In Massachusetts state court, he was convicted in 1958 of attempted breaking and entering at night and, in 1959 and 1963, of breaking and entering at night. In California state court, he was convicted in 1970 of assault with intent to commit murder and attempted murder.

In July 1993, petitioner walked into the home of Walter Miller, carrying a semi-automatic rifle. He threatened Miller, brandished the rifle in his face, and pointed it at his wife, his daughters, and his 3-year-old grandson. Police officers disarmed and arrested petitioner.

In September 1993, a federal agent called on petitioner at home to determine if he had other unlawful firearms. Petitioner said he had only flintlock or other antique weapons (not forbidden by law) and owned no conventional firearms. Federal law, the agent told him, forbade his possession of firearms and was not superseded by state law. In December 1993, agents executed a search warrant at petitioner's house, seizing six rifles and shotguns and 6,823 rounds of ammunition.

A federal jury convicted petitioner of four counts of possessing a firearm or ammunition after having been convicted of a serious offense. See 18 USC § 922(g)(1). The District Court enhanced his sentence because he was at least a three-time violent felon, based on his one California and three Massachusetts convictions. See § 924(e). Petitioner claimed the Court should not have counted his Massachusetts convictions because his civil rights had been restored by operation of Massachusetts law. Massachusetts law allowed petitioner to possess rifles or shotguns, as he had the necessary firearm permit and his felony convictions were more than five years old. Mass. Gen. Laws §§ 140:123, 140:129B, 140:129C (1996). The law forbade him to possess handguns outside his home or business. See §§ 140:121, 140:131, 269:10. ...

On remand, the District Court, interpreting the unless clause of the federal statute, disregarded the Massachusetts convictions. It ruled Massachusetts law did not forbid petitioner's possession of firearms because he could possess rifles. 941 F Supp. 238, 251-254 (Mass. 1996). Though Massachusetts restricted petitioner's right to carry a handgun, the District Court considered the restriction irrelevant because his case involved rifles and shotguns. See *ibid*. The First Circuit reversed, counting the convictions because petitioner remained subject to significant firearms restrictions. We granted certiorari. 522 US (1998).

II

A federal statute forbids possession of firearms by those convicted of serious offenses. An abbreviated version of the statute is as follows:

"It shall be unlawful for any person—

"(1) who has been convicted in any court of, a crime punishable by imprisonment for a term exceeding one year;

. . . . .

"to ship or transport in interstate or foreign commerce, or possess in or affecting commerce, any firearm or ammunition; or to receive any firearm or ammunition which has been shipped or transported in interstate or foreign commerce." 18 USC § 922(g).

Three-time violent felons who violate § 922(g) face enhanced sentences of at least 15 years' imprisonment. § 924(e)(1). "Violent felony" is defined to include burglary and other crimes creating a serious risk of physical injury. § 924(e)(2)(B)(ii). This term includes petitioner's previous offenses discussed above. ...

Aside from the unless clause, the parties agree Massachusetts law has restored petitioner's civil rights. As for the unless clause, state law permits him to possess rifles and shotguns but forbids him to possess handguns outside his home or business. The question presented is whether the handgun restriction activates the unless clause, making the convictions count under federal law. We note these preliminary points. First, Massachusetts restored petitioner's civil rights by operation of law rather than by pardon or the like. This fact makes no difference. Nothing in the text of

§ 921(a)(20) requires a case-by-case decision to restore civil rights to this particular offender. While the term "pardon" connotes a case-by-case determination, "restoration of civil rights" does not. Massachusetts has chosen a broad rule to govern this situation, and federal law gives effect to its rule. All Courts of Appeals to address the point agree [citations omitted].

Second, the District Court ruled, and petitioner urges here, that the unless clause allows an offender to possess what state law permits him to possess, and nothing more. Here, petitioner's shotguns and rifles were permitted by state law, so, under their theory, the weapons would not be covered by the unless clause. While we do not dispute the common sense of this approach, the words of the statute do not permit it. The unless clause is activated if a restoration of civil rights "expressly provides that the person may not ... possess ... firearms." 18 USC § 921(a)(20). Either the restorations forbade possession of "firearms" and the convictions count for all purposes, or they did not and the convictions count not at all. The unless clause looks to the terms of the past restorations alone and does not refer to the weapons at issue in the present case. So if the Massachusetts convictions count for some purposes, they count for all and bar possession of all guns.

III

The phrase "may not ... possess ... firearms," then, must be interpreted under either of what the parties call the two "all-or-nothing" approaches. Either it applies when the State forbids one or more types of firearms, as the Government contends; or it does not apply if state law permits one or more types of firearms, regardless of the one possessed in the particular case.

Under the Government's approach, a state weapons limitation on an offender activates the uniform federal ban on possessing any firearms at all. This is so even if the guns the offender possessed were ones the State permitted him to have. The State has singled out the offender as more dangerous than law-abiding citizens, and federal law uses this determination to impose its own broader stricture.

Although either reading creates incongruities, petitioner's approach yields results contrary to a likely, and rational, congressional policy. If permission to possess one firearm entailed permission to possess all, then state permission to have a pistol would allow possession of an assault weapon as well. Under this view, if petitioner, in violation of state law, had possessed a handgun, the unless clause would still not apply because he could have possessed a rifle. Not only would this strange result be inconsistent with any conceivable federal policy, but it also would arise often enough to impair the working of the federal statute. Massachusetts, in this case, and some 15 other States choose to restore civil rights while restricting firearm rights in part. The permissive reading would make these partial restrictions a nullity under federal law, indeed in the egregious cases with the most dangerous weapons. Congress cannot have intended this bizarre result.

Under petitioner's all-or-nothing argument, federal law would forbid only a subset of activities already criminal under state law. This limitation would contradict the intent of Congress. In Congress' view, existing state laws "provide less than positive assurance that the person in question no longer poses an unacceptable risk of dangerousness." *Dickerson*, 460 US at 120. Congress meant to keep guns away from all offenders who, the Federal Government feared, might cause harm, even if those persons were not deemed dangerous by *States*. See 460 US at 119. If federal law is to provide the missing "positive assurance," it must reach primary conduct not covered by state law. The need for this caution is borne out by petitioner's rifle attack on the Miller family, in which petitioner used a gun permitted by state law. Any other result would reduce federal law to a sentence enhancement for some state-law violations, a result inconsistent with the congressional intent we recognized in *Dickerson*. Permission to possess one gun cannot mean permission to possess all.

Congress responded to our ruling in *Dickerson* by providing that the law of the State of conviction, not federal law, determines the restoration of civil rights as a rule. While state law is the source of law for restorations of other civil rights, however, it does not follow that state law also controls the unless clause. Under the Government's approach, with which we agree, the federal policy still governs the interpretation of the unless clause. We see nothing contradictory in this analysis. Restoration of the right to vote, the right to hold office, and the right to sit on a jury turns on so many complexities and nuances that state law is the most convenient source for definition. As to the possession of weapons, however, the Federal Government has an interest in a single, national, protective policy, broader than required by state law. Petitioner's approach would undermine this protective purpose.

As a final matter, petitioner says his reading is required by the rule of lenity, but his argument is unavailing. The rule of lenity is not invoked by a grammatical possibility. It does not apply if the ambiguous reading relied on is an implausible reading of the congressional purpose. See *United States v. Shabani*, 513 US 10, 17, 130 L Ed. 2d 225, 115 S Ct. 382 (1994) (requiring use of traditional tools of statutory construction to resolve ambiguities before resorting to the rule of lenity). For the reasons we have explained, petitioner's reading is not plausible enough to satisfy this condition.

In sum, Massachusetts treats petitioner as too dangerous to trust with handguns, though it accords this right to law-abiding citizens. Federal law uses this state finding of dangerousness in forbidding petitioner to have any guns. The judgment of the Court of Appeals is

Affirmed.

THOMAS J (Scalia and Souter JJ dissenting): The only limitation that Massachusetts law imposed on petitioner's possession of firearms was that he could not carry handguns outside his home or business. See *ante*, at 3. In my view, Massachusetts law did not "expressly provide" that petitioner "may not ... possess ... firearms," 18 USC § 921(a)(20), and thus petitioner cannot be sentenced as an armed career criminal under 18 USC § 924(e). Because the Court holds to the contrary, I respectfully dissent.

Petitioner's prior Massachusetts convictions qualify as violent felonies for purposes of § 924(e) only if the "restoration of [his] civil rights" by operation of Massachusetts law "expressly provided that [petitioner] may not ... possess ... firearms." 18 USC

§ 921(a)(20). In 1994, Massachusetts law did not expressly provide that petitioner could not possess firearms. To the contrary: Petitioner was permitted by Massachusetts law to possess shotguns, rifles, and handguns. See *ante*, at 3; Mass. Gen. Stat. §§ 140:123, 140:129B, 140:129C. (1998). Indeed, Massachusetts provided petitioner with a firearm identification card that enabled him to possess such firearms. The only restriction Massachusetts law placed on petitioner's possession of firearms was that he could not carry handguns outside his home or business. See § 269:10(A). By prohibiting petitioner from possessing only certain firearms (handguns) in only certain places (outside his home or office), Massachusetts law did not expressly provide that petitioner could not possess firearms.

The plain meaning of § 921(a)(20) thus resolves this case. The Court, however, rejects this plain meaning on the basis of "a likely, and rational, congressional policy" of prohibiting firearms possession by all ex-felons whose ability to possess certain firearms is in any way restricted by state law. *Ante*, at 7. According to the Court, Congress could not have intended the "bizarre result" that a conviction would not count as a violent felony if a State only partially restricts the possession of firearms by the ex-felon. But this would not be a bizarre result at all. Under § 921(a)(20), state law limitations on firearms possession are only relevant once it has been established that an ex-felon's other civil rights, such as the right to vote, the right to seek and to hold public office, and the right to serve on a jury, have been restored. See 77 F3d 1, 2 (CA1 1996). In restoring those rights, the State has presumably deemed such ex-felons worthy of participating in civic life. Once a State makes such a decision, it is entirely rational (and certainly not bizarre) for Congress to authorize the increased sentences in § 924(e) only when the State additionally prohibits those ex-felons from possessing firearms altogether.

Moreover, as the Court concedes, its own interpretation creates "incongruities." *Ante*, at 7. Under the statute, whether a prior state conviction qualifies as a violent felony conviction under § 924(e) turns entirely on state law. Given the primacy of state law in the statutory scheme, it is bizarre to hold that the *legal* possession of firearms under state law subjects a person to a sentence enhancement under federal law. That, however, is precisely the conclusion the Court reaches in this case. It is simply not true, as the Court reasons, that federal law "must reach primary conduct not covered by state law." *Ante*, at 7. It is entirely plausible that Congress simply intended to create stiffer penalties for weapons possessions that are already illegal under state law. And such a purpose is consistent with the statutory direction that state law controls what constitutes a conviction for a violent felony.

I believe that the plain meaning of the statute is that Massachusetts did not "expressly provide" that petitioner "may not ... possess ... firearms." At the very least, this interpretation is a plausible one. Indeed, both the Government and the Court concede as much. See Brief for United States 16 ("grammatically possible" to read statute to say that its condition is not satisfied if the State does permit its felons to possess some firearms); *ante*, at 8 (this "reading is not plausible enough"). Accordingly, it is far from clear under the statute that a prior state conviction counts as a violent felony conviction for purposes of § 924(e) just because the State imposes some restriction, no matter how slight, on firearms possession by ex-felons. The rule of lenity must therefore apply: "The Court will not interpret a federal criminal statute so as to increase the penalty that it places on an individual when such an interpretation can be based on no more than a guess as to what Congress intended." *Ladner v. United States*, 358 US 169, 178, 3 L Ed. 2d 199, 79 S Ct. 209 (1958). Ex-felons cannot be expected to realize that a federal statute that explicitly relies on state law prohibits behavior that state law allows.

The Court rejects the rule of lenity in this case because it thinks the purported statutory ambiguity rests on a "grammatical possibility" and "an implausible reading of the congressional purpose." *Ante*, at 8. But the alleged ambiguity does not result from a mere grammatical possibility; it exists because of an interpretation that, for the reasons I have described, both accords with a natural reading of the statutory language and is consistent with the statutory purpose.

The plain meaning of § 921(a)(20) is that Massachusetts law did not "expressly provide that [petitioner] may not … possess … firearms." This interpretation is, at the very least, a plausible one, and the rule of lenity must apply. I would therefore reverse the judgment below.

NOTES AND QUESTIONS

1. According to the majority, the interpretation advocated by Mr. Caron "yields results contrary to a likely, and rational, congressional policy." Note that this is simply an application of "consequential analysis," which is closely related to the golden rule of statutory construction (see chapter 3).

2. The court defines the purpose of the "unless clause" as follows: "Congress meant to keep guns away from all offenders who, the Federal Government feared, might cause harm, even if those persons were not deemed dangerous by States." Does the interpretation presented by the majority fulfill this purpose? Does the dissent's interpretation fulfill this purpose?

3. Note that the court's reference to the "rule of lenity" is simply a reference to the American version of the rule of strict construction. Under the "rule of lenity," criminal statutes must receive the interpretation that is the most "lenient." This clearly parallels the rule of strict construction developed in Anglo-Canadian jurisprudence.

4. Does the court's method of weighing the "rule of lenity" against congressional purpose coincide with the balance between purpose and strict construction developed in Canadian jurisprudence?

5. Which is more persuasive, the majority judgment or the dissent? Why?

6. According to the dissent, the majority "rejects [the statute's] plain meaning on the basis of 'a likely, and rational, congressional policy' of prohibiting firearms possession." Do you agree with the dissent's assessment of the plain meaning of the "unless clause"? Is it ever possible to rely on a statute's "plain meaning"?

7. The dissent and the majority come to opposing conclusions regarding the application of the "rule of lenity." Which approach makes more sense given the rationale of the "rule of lenity" (or the rule of strict construction)?

V. OTHER CASES

1. Review the decision of the US Supreme Court in *Smith v. United States*, 508 US 223 (1993) (set out in chapter 3). In this case both the majority and the dissent discuss the "rule of lenity." Which judgment does a better job of: (a) articulating and applying the rule of lenity, (b) balancing that rule against the purposes of the relevant statute, and (c) balancing that rule against the "plain language" of the relevant statute?

2. Review the decision of the Supreme Court of Canada in *R v. McIntosh*, [1995] 1 SCR 686 (set out in chapter 3). In that case, Lamer CJ invokes the rule of strict construction in the following passage:

> the overriding principle governing the interpretation of penal provisions is that ambiguity
> should be resolved in a manner most favourable to accused persons.

Is it accurate to refer to this as the "overriding" principle governing the interpretation of penal provisions? What does this principle override? Compare Lamer CJ's application of the rule of strict construction with the decision of McLachlin J in dissent.

3. How would the unified theory address the problems raised in *McIntosh* and *Smith*? Do the problems raised in those cases relate to vagueness, ambiguity, subtext, or analogy?

VI. EXERCISES

A. The Roller Coaster

Suggested length: 10-20 pages

Shiva Pawar was a proud employee of *Smilin' Sheehy's World of Wonders*, a travelling carnival operated by Ezekiel Sheehy throughout western and southern Ontario. During the carnival's stay in London, Ontario, Mr. Pawar was assigned the fun task of running the "Train of Terror," a metal roller coaster that was the pride of Sheehy's midway. Pawar's task was to collect fares from the riders and operate the "on and off" switch of the coaster.

On September 24, 2001, Trevor Montgomery (a well-known London resident) decided to take the day off work and go to the carnival. Trevor purchased $20 worth of "Sheehy Shekels" (the only currency accepted in Smilin' Sheehy's midway) and proceeded to try out each of Sheehy's rides. After several hours of stomach-churning bliss, Trevor, with only 3 Sheehy Shekels remaining in his pocket, had a burning desire to ride the Train of Terror. Unfortunately, the fare for riding the Train of Terror was 5 Sheehy Shekels.

Trevor approached Mr. Pawar, who was busily collecting fares from the other carnival patrons, and explained his plight. Trevor promised that if Mr. Pawar would let him ride the coaster for 3 Sheehy Shekels, he would recommend *Smilin' Sheehy's World of Wonders* to all of his friends. Pawar, being a rather charitable carny, shrugged his shoulders, collected the 3 Sheehy Shekels, and admitted Trevor onto the Train of Terror.

Unfortunately for Mr. Pawar, his entire exchange with Trevor Montgomery was witnessed by Constable Joan Nickle of the London Police. Joan arrested Mr. Pawar and charged him with an offence under s. 393(1) of the *Criminal Code*, which provided as follows:

393(1) Every one whose duty it is to collect a fare, toll, ticket or admission who wilfully
    (a) fails to collect it,
    (b) collects less than the proper amount payable in respect thereof, or
    (c) accepts any valuable consideration for failing to collect it or for collecting
less than the proper amount payable in respect thereof,
is guilty of an indictable offence and liable to imprisonment for a term not exceeding
two years.

As Joan finished slapping the cuffs on Mr. Pawar, she waited for the Train of Terror to finish its two-minute run in order to arrest Trevor Montgomery as well. Mr. Montgomery was charged with an offence under s. 393(3) of the *Criminal Code*, which provided as follows:

393(3) Every one who, by any false pretence or fraud, unlawfully obtains transportation
by land, water or air is guilty of an offence punishable on summary conviction.

At a joint trial held before Judge Clysdale of the London District Court, both Mr. Pawar and Mr. Montgomery were convicted. Mr. Pawar was sentenced to one year in prison, and Mr. Montgomery was given a fine of $50.

Pawar and Montgomery have appealed their convictions and their sentences to the Canadian Court of Justice (the highest court in the country). In your wisdom, you (as a justice of the court) have decided to hear their appeals together. Will the appeals succeed? Be sure to address any interpretive issues that arise. Be sure to consider the fact that the *Criminal Code* is (a) criminal legislation, and (b) real. Any interpretive assistance that you can draw from other provisions of the *Criminal Code* will be most helpful.

B. Firearms Prohibitions

Suggested length: 15-25 pages

Late in the evening on October 31, 1995, Norman Penney of Winnipeg, Manitoba was making his way home from the local YMCA, where he was employed as a martial arts instructor. Along the way, Norman stopped at a nearby video store to rent a copy of "Nasty Tales of Spooky Horror," his favourite Halloween film. After paying for the movie, Norman left the video store and headed for home.

Being a rather impatient type, Norman could hardly wait to get home and watch his movie. As a result, Norman unwisely took a shortcut through an abandoned railway yard. As Norman proceeded through the yard, he was accosted by three costumed youths intent on relieving Norman of his possessions. Norman instinctively relied on his martial arts training and dealt out a series of brutal karate chops to his assailants. Unfortunately, Norman mistakenly used excessive force in thwarting his attackers, and left the three youths lying battered and unconscious beneath an old caboose. Feeling that the youths had learned their lesson (and realizing that he had used excessive force), Norman refrained from informing the police of the incident.

Three days after the incident, Norman was arrested by the local police and charged with aggravated assault under s. 268(1) of the *Criminal Code*. Norman felt extremely guilty about his use of excessive force, and accordingly entered a plea of guilty to the lesser offence of "assault causing bodily harm," contrary to s. 267 of the Code. Norman was ultimately sentenced to six months incarceration.

While making submissions regarding Norman's sentence, the Crown requested an order under s. 100(1) of the *Criminal Code* prohibiting Norman from owning a firearm. At the material time (1995), s. 100 provided as follows:

(1) Where an offender is convicted or discharged under section 730 of an indictable offence in the commission of which violence against a person is used, threatened or attempted and for which the offender may be sentenced to imprisonment for ten years or more or of an offence under section 85, the court that sentences the offender shall, subject to subsections (1.1) to (1.3), in addition to any other punishment that may be imposed for that offence, make an order prohibiting the offender from possessing any firearm or any ammunition or explosive substance for any period of time specified in the order that commences on the day on which the order is made and expires not earlier than

(a) in the case of a first conviction for such an offence, ten years, and

(b) in any other case, life,

after the time of the offender's release from imprisonment after conviction for the offence or, if the offender is not then imprisoned or subject to imprisonment, after the time of the offender's conviction or discharge for that offence.

(1.1) The court is not required to make an order under subsection (1) where the court is satisfied that the offender has established that

(a) it is not desirable in the interests of the safety of the offender or of any other person that the order be made; and

(b) the circumstances are such that it would not be appropriate to make the order.

(1.2) In considering whether the circumstances are such that it would not be appropriate to make an order under subsection (1), the court shall consider

(a) the criminal record of the offender, the nature of the offence and the circumstances surrounding its commission;

(b) whether the offender needs a firearm for the sustenance of the offender or the offender's family; and

(c) whether the order would constitute a virtual prohibition against employment in the only vocation open to the offender.

(1.3) Where the court does not make an order under subsection (1), the court shall give reasons why the order is not being made.

Norman, who has been a rifle enthusiast since his youth, vehemently opposed the Crown's request. In opposing the Crown's motion, Norman proved the following facts:

1. The YMCA has dismissed Norman from his job as a karate instructor because of his apparent inability to control his aggression.
2. Upon his release from custody, Norman plans to leave Winnipeg and move to northern Saskatchewan to help his uncle work on a trapline. The ability to use and carry a rifle (to put down wounded animals) is a prerequisite for this job.
3. Although Norman has been involved in several barroom brawls, each incident was instigated by other individuals. None of the brawls resulted in criminal charges.

4. Norman has a prior criminal record involving several non-violent offences, including marijuana possession and "theft under."
5. Norman dropped out of high school in grade 9. He had a dismally poor academic
   record, and appears to have no noteworthy job skills aside from his martial arts
   training. Norman has only ever been employed as a martial arts instructor and as a
   dishwasher in a local restaurant. If Norman is unable to work for his uncle, he plans
   to apply for social assistance.

There was no evidence that Norman required (or would ever require) a firearm to ensure
his own safety (to ward off bears or assassins, for example).

The sentencing judge granted the Crown's request and entered an order prohibiting
Norman from possessing a firearm for 20 years following his release from custody. In her
reasons, the judge held that although Norman was unlikely to use a gun in an unlawful
manner, the prohibition order was mandatory under s. 100. Norman has appealed the
prohibition order (but not the six-month sentence).

You are a judge of the Canadian Court of Justice (the highest court in Canada), and
you are presiding over Norman's appeal. Using the information noted above (and
employing techniques of statutory interpretation), write a judgment either dismissing or
allowing Norman's appeal (a good judgment will address both sides of the argument).
Assume that Norman's conviction and six-month sentence were entirely proper.

Be sure to note that (a) the relevant provisions were found in criminal legislation, and
(b) the *Criminal Code* is a real statute. Additional interpretive assistance may be found in
other provisions of the Code and the evidentiary aids discussed in chapter 4. Finally, it is
important to note that the relevant Code provisions have been radically amended since
the time of Norman's conviction. While the original provisions will apply to Norman's
case, you may wish to have a look at the current provisions for any interpretive assistance
that they may offer. Be sure to address the evidentiary value of these new provisions if
you choose to raise those provisions as interpretive aids.

C. Originalism, Dynamism, and Criminal Legislation

Suggested length: 12-20 pages

Discuss the following statement:

> A violation of criminal law carries with it the possibility of a loss of the subject's liberty. As
> a result, it is particularly important that individuals are able to ascertain, in advance,
> whether or not a particular action constitutes a breach of a criminal law. Since dynamic
> interpretation causes the meaning of legislation to shift in accordance with current judicial
> whims, dynamic interpretation must never be applied to criminal laws: only originalist
> construction can ensure the level of certainty that is required of criminal legislation.

CHAPTER SIX

Interpreting Tax Laws

I. INTRODUCTION

The purpose of this chapter is to describe and evaluate judicial approaches to the interpretation of tax statutes. Like criminal laws, tax statutes have historically been interpreted by reference to "special" rules that fail to apply in cases involving the construction of "ordinary" legislation. The history, development, and rationale of these "special" rules are discussed in chapter 7 of Randal N. Graham, *Statutory Interpretation: Theory and Practice* (Toronto: Emond Montgomery, 2001) (*"Theory and Practice"*). Students should review that chapter before reviewing the cases set out below.

The following cases demonstrate the continuing development of the modern approach to the interpretation of tax statutes (discussed at 199-210 of *Theory and Practice*). When reading these cases, consider the following questions: (1) Is there really a single "modern approach" to the interpretation of tax enactments? (2) Are judicial decisions truly driven by the court's selection of a particular interpretive approach, or does the court select an interpretive approach in order to justify decisions that are reached by other means? and (3) Do tax statutes truly need to be addressed through specialized rules, or are "ordinary" methods of construction sufficient to deal with the interpretation of tax legislation?

II. WILL-KARE PAVING & CONTRACTING

A. Introduction

In *Will-Kare Paving & Contracting Ltd. v. Canada*, [2000] 1 SCR 915, the Supreme Court of Canada was asked to interpret s. 127(5) of the *Income Tax Act*, which provides for favourable tax treatment in respect of property used "primarily in the manufacturing or processing of goods for sale or lease." The decision in *Will-Kare* turned upon the meaning of the phrase "sale or lease."

The taxpayer in *Will-Kare* operated a paving business. Most of the taxpayer's business involved the provision of paving services: customers would hire Will-Kare Paving to pave their driveways, parking lots, etc., and in carrying out this service Will-Kare supplied all of the asphalt that would be used in paving the customer's unpaved surface. This asphalt was not explicitly "sold" to the customer through a separate contract of sale. Instead, it was simply provided as an incident of the overall "service contract" between

Will-Kare and its customers.[1] The question before the court in *Will-Kare* was whether or not the asphalt qualified as a good that was "for sale": if it was, the taxpayer would be permitted to take advantage of various tax savings.

The decision in *Will-Kare* deals with capital cost allowances, investment tax credits, and other tax concepts that an uninitiated reader may find confusing. For the purposes of the present discussion, students need only focus on the question of whether Will-Kare's asphalt constituted a "good for sale or lease." More advanced tax concepts can be safely ignored.

B. The Court's Decision

Will-Kare Paving & Contracting Ltd. v. Canada
[2000] 1 SCR 915

MAJOR J: This appeal concerns the appellant's ability to claim two manufacturing and processing tax incentives in respect of its 1988, 1989 and 1990 taxation years based upon the capital cost of an asphalt plant it constructed in 1988. The availability of both incentives, an accelerated capital cost allowance and an investment tax credit, turns upon whether using the plant to produce asphalt to be supplied in connection with paving services constitutes use primarily for the purpose of manufacturing or processing goods for sale.

I. Factual Background

The appellant, Will-Kare Paving & Contracting Limited ("Will-Kare"), paves driveways, parking lots and small public roadways for commercial and residential customers.

Until 1988, Will-Kare purchased all its asphalt from competitors, making it vulnerable in terms of price and availability. That year, Will-Kare constructed its own asphalt plant to remove its reliance upon third-party suppliers. As additional motivation, it anticipated that owning its own plant would allow it to bid on larger contracts. Finally, while Will-Kare's previous asphalt consumption did not justify construction of its own plant, it was confident that third-party sales of excess production would make the plant economically feasible.

After acquiring the plant, Will-Kare's sales and revenues from paving contracts increased as expected. For the taxation years in question, approximately 75 percent of Will-Kare's asphalt output was utilized in its own paving business and approximately 25 percent of its output was sold to third parties.

In the taxation years 1988, 1989 and 1990, Will-Kare included the plant and additions to it in Class 39 of Schedule II of the *Income Tax Regulations*, CRC 1978, c. 945 ("Regulations"), claiming that the plant was property used primarily in the

---

1   Contracts of this nature are referred to as contracts "for work and materials." The materials are provided
     as an incident of the "work" that is supplied.

manufacturing and processing of goods for sale. As such, Will-Kare claimed an accelerated capital cost allowance under s. 20(1)(a) of the *Income Tax Act*, SC 1970-71-72, c. 63 ("Act"). Will-Kare also claimed the s. 127(5) investment tax credit on the basis that the plant was "qualified property" within the meaning of s. 127(9) of the Act. Finally, Will-Kare claimed the s. 125.1(1) manufacturing and processing profits deduction for its 1988 and 1989 taxation years with respect to the whole of its income in accordance with s. 5201 of the Regulations, the so-called "Small Manufacturers' Rule."

The Minister of National Revenue reassessed Will-Kare, reclassifying the plant as Class 8 property for capital cost allowance purposes and denying the investment tax credit, in both cases on the basis that the plant was not being used primarily for the manufacturing or processing of goods for sale. As a consequence of the reassessment, Will-Kare's active business income was raised above $200,000, necessitating that the manufacturing and processing profits deduction be calculated based upon the general pro-rata formula set out in s. 5200 of the Regulations rather than applying the deduction to Will-Kare's entire income in accordance with s. 5201 of the Regulations.

. . .

V. Analysis

Will-Kare's ability to claim both the s. 127(5) investment tax credit and the Class 39 accelerated capital cost allowance depends on an interpretation of a statutory requirement common to both incentives.

It was not disputed that Will-Kare was entitled to depreciate its asphalt plant for tax purposes by claiming a capital cost allowance in accordance with s. 20(1)(a) of the Act. What is disputed, however, is into which of the asset pools enumerated in Schedule II of the Regulations Will-Kare's plant was to be placed.

Will-Kare clearly prefers that its plant be characterized as Class 39 property and, as such, be depreciated at an accelerated rate vis-à-vis the plant's alternate characterization as Class 8 property. Schedule II of the Regulations defines Class 39 property essentially as Class 29 property acquired after 1987. Therefore, for the plant to qualify as Class 39 property, Will-Kare must have acquired it "to be used directly or indirectly ... in Canada primarily in the manufacturing or processing of goods for sale or lease."

Will-Kare's ability to claim the s. 127(5) investment tax credit is contingent upon the plant being characterized as "qualified property" within the meaning of s. 127(9) of the Act, generally defined as prescribed machinery and equipment to be used by the taxpayer in Canada primarily for the purpose of manufacturing or processing goods for sale or lease. Pursuant to s. 4600(2)(k) of the Regulations, property is prescribed machinery and equipment if it is property included in, *inter alia*, Class 39 of Schedule II.

Therefore, for Will-Kare to receive the benefit of the above incentives, it must establish that it acquired the asphalt plant primarily for the purpose of manufacturing or processing goods for sale or lease. ...

Manufacturing or Processing Goods for Sale

Canadian jurisprudence to this point has adopted two divergent interpretations of the activities that constitute manufacturing and processing goods for sale. Without canvassing these authorities exhaustively, it may be helpful to outline briefly those cases which delineate these two distinct approaches.

One point of view is expressed in *Crown Tire Service Ltd. v. The Queen*, [1984] 2 FC 219 (TD), where the court imports common law and provincial sale of goods law distinctions in defining the scope of the manufacturing and processing incentives' application. Only capital property used to manufacture or process goods to be furnished through contracts purely for the sale of such goods qualifies. Property used to manufacture or process goods to be supplied in connection with the provision of a service, namely through a contract for work and materials, is not viewed as being used directly or indirectly in Canada primarily in the manufacturing or processing of goods for sale, and as such, does not qualify for either the accelerated capital cost allowance or the investment tax credit.

The *Crown Tire* case related to whether the application of treads manufactured by the taxpayer to tires brought in by customers for repair constituted the manufacture or processing of goods for sale. Strayer J (later JA) disallowed the taxpayer's claim to the s. 125.1 manufacturing and processing profits deduction as the manufactured tread was supplied through a contract for work and materials, a characterization based upon the method through which property transferred to the buyer. See p. 223:

> "In *Benjamin's Sale of Goods* (London, 1974), in considering the distinction between a contract of sale of goods and a contract for work and materials, it is stated:
>
>> Where work is to be done on the land of the employer or on a chattel belonging to him, which involves the use or affixing of materials belonging to the person employed, the contract will ordinarily be one for work and materials, the property in the latter passing to the employer by accession and not under any contract of sale. ...
>
> I believe that the situation here fits within the general principle as stated in *Benjamin*. With respect to the retreading of tires owned by customers, it appears to me that the customers retain ownership throughout the process."

A second line of authority departs from the point of view in *Crown Tire* and declines to apply statutory and common law sale of goods rules in delineating that capital property to which the manufacturing and processing incentives apply. Rather, these cases advocate a literal construction of "sale" such that the provision of a service incidental to the supply of a manufactured or processed good does not preclude receiving the benefit of the incentives. Any transfer of property for consideration would suffice. See *Halliburton Services Ltd. v. The Queen*, 85 DTC 5336 (FCTD), aff'd 90 DTC 6320 (FCA), and *The Queen v. Nowsco Well Service Ltd.*, 90 DTC 6312 (FCA).

Halliburton and *Nowsco* considered the form of contract entered into between the taxpayer and customer to be irrelevant. In both cases the Federal Court of Appeal quoted with approval language from Reed J's decision in *Halliburton* at the Trial

Division that appears to suggest an alternative test based upon the source of the tax-payer's profit. As stated by Reed J, at p. 5338:

"… I do not find any requirement that the contract which gives rise to the taxpayer's profit must be of a particular nature, eg: one for the sale of goods and not one of a more extensive nature involving work and labour as well as the goods or material supplied. In my view it is the source of the profit, (arising out of processing) that is important … not the nature of the taxpayer's contract with its customers."

Rolls-Royce (Canada) Ltd. v. The Queen, 93 DTC 5031 (FCA), attempted to reconcile these diverging lines of authority by restricting *Crown Tire's* reasoning to circum-stances that do not evidence the manufacture of a discrete and identifiable good prior or contemporaneous to the provision of a service. As stated by MacGuigan JA at p. 5034:

"The crucial distinction between *Crown Tire* and *Halliburton* seems to me to be … that the processing in *Crown Tire* 'did not involve the creation of a good antecedent to its use in the provision of a service.' … The rubber strip in *Crown Tire* was not on the evidence manufactured or processed by the taxpayer, whereas the cement in Halliburton was made by the taxpayer, indeed was custom-made according to very exact specifications."

In *Hawboldt Hydraulics, supra*, the respondent taxpayer relied upon the *Rolls-Royce* interpretation of *Crown Tire* to claim a Class 29 accelerated capital cost allowance and s. 127(5) investment tax credit with respect to property used to manufacture parts for use in repair services. Rejecting the taxpayer's claim, the court reverted to the original *Crown Tire* approach. Isaac CJ wrote at p. 847:

"We are invited by the modern rule of statutory interpretation to give those words their ordinary meaning. But we are dealing with a commercial statute and in commerce the words have a meaning that is well understood. … Strayer J was right, in my respectful view, to say in Crown Tire, at page 225 that:

one must assume that Parliament in speaking of "goods for sale or lease" had reference to the general law of sale or lease to give greater precision to this phrase in particular cases."

In this appeal, Will-Kare admits that asphalt supplied in connection with its paving services is provided pursuant to a contract for work and materials. Nevertheless, Will-Kare requests that we adopt the *Halliburton* and *Nowsco* ordinary meaning interpre-tation such that the manufacturing of goods for sale includes all manufactured goods supplied to a customer for consideration, regardless of whether paving services are provided in connection with that supply. To the contrary, the respondent asserts that, as noted in *Crown Tire* and *Hawboldt Hydraulics*, use of the term sale in the manu-facturing and processing incentives necessarily imports common law and statutory sale of goods concepts.

Both parties make extensive reference to Hansard as support for their respective interpretations of Parliament's intent in utilizing the words "goods for sale" in con-nection with the manufacturing and processing incentives. I do not propose to review

this legislative material as I generally agree with the characterization ascribed to it by
Isaac CJ in *Hawboldt Hydraulics*, *supra*, at pp. 846-47:

> "… it is clear from the total context of the legislation, including the passages from the
> *House of Commons Debates* to which I have referred, that Parliament's objective in
> enacting the legislation was encouragement of increased production of manufactured
> and processed goods to be placed on the domestic and international markets in competi-
> tion with foreign manufacturers. That that is the activity which Parliament sought to
> encourage is, to my mind, plain from the Debates. It is equally plain that Parliament
> intended to benefit manufacturers and processors who engaged in those activities. In
> other words, the relevant statutory provisions were designed to give Canadian manu-
> facturers and processors an advantage over their foreign competitors in the domestic
> and foreign markets. It is also clear that Parliament had in mind specific target groups
> and specific target activities. The legislation was not intended to benefit every manu-
> facturing activity or every manufacturer. The language of the statute is clear that the
> activity to be benefited was the manufacture of goods for sale or lease. …"

From the legislative material accompanying the manufacturing and processing
incentives, it is clear that Parliament's objective was to encourage the manufacturing
and processing sector's ability to address foreign competition in the domestic and
international markets and foster increased employment in that sector of the Canadian
economy. Furthermore, it is clear that Parliament did not wish to define exhaustively
the scope of manufacturing or processing, words which do not have distinct legal
meanings, but left it to the courts to interpret this language according to common
commercial use. The language in Hansard is not helpful as to the meaning which
Parliament intended to subscribe to the words "for sale or lease." It neither dictates,
nor precludes, the application of common law sale of goods distinctions.

Notwithstanding this absence of direction, the concepts of a sale or a lease have
settled legal definitions. As noted in *Crown Tire* and *Hawboldt Hydraulics*, Parliament was cognizant of these meanings and the implication of using such language. It
follows that the availability of the manufacturing and processing incentives at issue
must be restricted to property utilized in the supply of goods for sale and not extended to property primarily utilized in the supply of goods through contracts for
work and materials.

It is perhaps true, as Will-Kare submitted and as noted in *Halliburton*, *supra*, at
p. 5338, that the use of sale of goods law distinctions sometimes yields the anomalous result that the provision of services in connection with manufactured and
processed goods will disqualify property that would, but for the services, qualify
for the incentives. Nevertheless, it remains that in drafting the manufacturing processing incentives to include reference to sale or lease, Parliament has chosen to use
language that imports relatively fine private law distinctions. Indeed, the Act is
replete with such distinctions. Absent express direction that an interpretation other
than that ascribed by settled commercial law be applied, it would be inappropriate to do so.

To apply a "plain meaning" interpretation of the concept of a sale in the case at bar
would assume that the Act operates in a vacuum, oblivious to the legal characterization

of the broader commercial relationships it affects. It is not a commercial code in addition to a taxation statute. Previous jurisprudence of this Court has assumed that reference must be given to the broader commercial law to give meaning to words that, outside of the Act, are well-defined. See *Continental Bank Leasing Corp. v. Canada*, [1998] 2 SCR 298. See also P. W. Hogg, J. E. Magee and T. Cook, *Principles of Canadian Income Tax Law* (3rd ed. 1999), at p. 2, where the authors note:

> "The *Income Tax Act* relies implicitly on the general law, especially the law of contract and property. ... Whether a person is an employee, independent contractor, partner, agent, beneficiary of a trust or shareholder of a corporation will usually have an effect on tax liability and will turn on concepts contained in the general law, usually provincial law."

Referring to the broader context of private commercial law in ascertaining the meaning to be ascribed to language used in the Act is also consistent with the modern purposive principle of statutory interpretation. As cited in E. A. Driedger, *Construction of Statutes* (2nd ed. 1983), at p. 87:

> "Today there is only one principle or approach, namely, the words of an Act are to be read in their entire context and in their grammatical and ordinary sense harmoniously with the scheme of the Act, the object of the Act, and the intention of Parliament."

See *Rizzo & Rizzo Shoes Ltd. (Re)*, [1998] 1 SCR 27, at para. 21. The modern approach to statutory interpretation has been applied by this Court to the interpretation of tax legislation. See *65302 British Columbia Ltd. v. Canada*, [1999] 3 SCR 804, at para. 5, per Bastarache J, and at para. 50, per Iacobucci J; *Stubart Investments Ltd. v. The Queen*, [1984] 1 SCR 536, at p. 578.

The technical nature of the Act does not lend itself to broadening the principle of plain meaning to embrace popular meaning. The word sale has an established and accepted legal meaning.

Will-Kare's submissions essentially advocate the application of an economic realities test to the interpretation of what constitutes a sale for the purpose of the manufacturing and processing incentives. However, as noted above, in the absence of express legislative direction to the contrary, I view the incentives' reference to the concepts of sale and lease as importing private law distinctions. As such, the provisions at issue are clear and unambiguous and reference to economic realities is not warranted. See *Shell Canada Ltd. v. Canada*, [1999] 3 SCR 622, at para. 40.

It would be open to Parliament to provide for a broadened definition of sale for the purpose of applying the incentives with clear language to that effect. Given, however, the provisions merely refer to sale, it cannot be concluded that a definition other than that which follows from common law and sale of goods legislation was envisioned.

For the taxation years in issue, approximately 75 percent of the asphalt produced by the Will-Kare's plant was supplied in connection with Will-Kare's paving services. Thus the plant was used primarily in the manufacturing or processing of goods supplied through contracts for work and materials, not through sale. Property in the asphalt transferred to Will-Kare's customers as a fixture to real property.

The principles enunciated in *Crown Tire* and *Hawboldt Hydraulics*, to the extent they dictate reference to a common law and statutory definition of sale, offer a guide preferable to the broader interpretation of sale described in *Halliburton* and *Nowsco*.

Therefore I would dismiss the appeal with costs throughout.

BINNIE J (Gonthier and McLachlin JJ dissenting): The fundamental issue in this case is the interpretation of everyday words used by Parliament in the context of a tax regime based on self-assessment. In 1997, the last year for which precise statistics are available, 20,453,540 tax returns were filed with Revenue Canada. Most taxpayers are not (and likely have no desire to be) learned in the law. When confronted as here with the phrase "primarily in the manufacturing or processing of goods for sale or lease" under s. 127(9) of the *Income Tax Act*, SC 1970-71-72, c. 63 ("Act"), he or she is entitled, in my opinion, to the benefit of the plain meaning of an everyday word like "sale." The taxpayer was denied that benefit by the Minister in this case. The millions of taxpayers who are *not* lawyers cannot be expected to reach for *Benjamin's Sale of Goods* to research the difference between a contract for the sale of goods and a contract for work and materials and to apply these distinctions in the assessment of their own income tax liability. I would therefore allow the appeal.

The taxpayer appellant, who was originally in the paving business, expanded his operation to include the manufacture of asphalt, and thereafter claimed an accelerated capital cost allowance under s. 20(1)(a) of the Act. (The appellant also seeks an investment tax credit pursuant to s. 127(5) of the Act.) Entitlement to the accelerated capital cost allowance ("fast tax write-off") turns on the taxpayer's ability to demonstrate that its investment in the asphalt plant was made to acquire property

> "to be used directly or indirectly by him in Canada primarily in the manufacturing or processing of *goods for sale* or lease [emphasis added]"

within the meaning of s. 20(1)(a) of the Act and Classes 39 and 29 in Schedule II of the *Income Tax Regulations*, CRC 1978, c. 945. Entitlement to the investment tax credit turns on similar wording in s. 127(9)(c)(i).

The asphalt plant produced a manufactured product in a saleable condition. The asphalt came fully into existence prior to any paving services being rendered, obviously. The evidence is that about 25 percent of the product was appropriated by the taxpayer and sold as is to customers. It disposed of the balance of the asphalt under various paving contracts for work and materials. None of the asphalt was retained by the taxpayer. The Minister denied the fast tax write-off because, while the asphalt plant produced a saleable product, the taxpayer chose to dispose of it primarily under contracts for work and materials rather than under contracts of sale within the meaning of the *Sale of Goods Act, 1893* (UK), 56 & 57 Vict., c. 71, and various derivative provincial statutes.

It is common ground that if the taxpayer had sold to its paving customers the asphalt in one contract and the installation of it in another, it would be entitled to the deduction.

In this case, the Tax Court of Canada and the Federal Court of Appeal upheld the Minister's decision based on an interpretation developed by Strayer J in *Crown Tire*

Service Ltd. v. The Queen, [1984] 2 FC 219 (TD), where he said at p. 225:

> "While the distinctions employed here may seem somewhat technical and remote from revenue law, one must assume that Parliament in speaking of goods 'for sale or lease' had reference to the general law of sale or lease to give greater precision to this phrase in particular cases."

As applied to the facts of this case, however, the asphalt at the plant door was in fact "for sale." The Minister's interpretation requires that the statutory text be supplemented with additional words so that, as extended, it would read "goods to be disposed of under contracts for sale or lease." I agree in this respect with the approach of Reed J speaking of a comparable provision of the Act in *Halliburton Services Ltd. v. The Queen*, 85 DTC 5336 (FCTD), at p. 5338, aff'd 90 DTC 6320 (FCA):

> "It seems to me to be quite clear that what was intended was a tax deduction with respect to profit arising out of the manufacturing and processing of goods, not a requirement that the goods had to be sold in a particular fashion."

Considerable argument was addressed to us and in the courts below about the percentage of asphalt that was disposed of under contracts of work and materials as opposed to contracts of sale. This debate was precipitated by the word "primarily" in the definition. In my view, the taxpayer's case, if it is to succeed, does not turn on these percentages, but on the proposition that all of the asphalt produced at the plant was for sale and asphalt disposed of under a contract for work and materials was a "sale" of the manufactured asphalt within the plain meaning of the Act.

Contracts for Work and Material

The appellant's standard form customer contract was "for furnishing all labour, materials and equipment required for the performance" of the work. In the sample contract provided in the appellant's record, the handwritten notation undertook to "excavate unsuitable material, supply necessary gravel, grade, compact and pave with 2 1/2" of asphalt." The global price for the job is then stipulated. The evidence was that about half of the contract price was for materials, of which about half was for asphalt. These percentages are not significant because the tax benefit relates not to a percentage of the paving contract price but to the $433,535 wholly spent to acquire the asphalt plant.

I note at the outset that this case differs from the "repair cases" such as *Rolls-Royce (Canada) Ltd. v. The Queen*, 93 DTC 5031 (FCA), application for leave to appeal to the Supreme Court of Canada refused, [1993] 2 SCR x, where it was held that the overhauling of aircraft engines constituted "manufacturing or processing" but not "for sale" because the engines in issue were throughout owned by customers of the taxpayer. *Crown Tire, supra*, is to the same effect. No such issue arises here. In the beginning, the taxpayer owned the asphalt. At the end, the customer did. The only issue on this appeal is whether the asphalt as manufactured was for sale.

La Forest J pointed out in *H. W. Liebig & Co. v. Leading Investments Ltd.*, [1986] 1 SCR 70, at p. 83, that "the primary meaning of sale is the transfer of property to another for a price." Referring to the definition in the *Oxford English Dictionary* of "sale" as "the action or an act of selling or making over to another for a price; the exchange of a commodity for money or other valuable consideration," La Forest J said of the word "sale," in the admittedly different context of a real estate purchase agreement, "I do not think the technical meaning that lawyers may attach to a word for certain purposes should be substituted for the ordinary meaning of that word in everyday speech unless there is evidence that the parties intended to use it in that special or technical sense" (p. 84). In my view, ordinary words in the Act like "for sale" should also be interpreted in light of "the ordinary meaning of the word in everyday speech." Here, the supply of asphalt was specified, although the price was not allocated in the contract as between work and materials. The customer's objective was to obtain an asphalt driveway, and the services provided by the taxpayer were incidental to realization of that objective. The price was paid, and the customer became the owner of the asphalt in his driveway. The taxpayer and its customers were likely oblivious to the fact (relied on by the Minister) that, in the eye of the law, title to the steaming stretch of asphalt passed by accession.

This Court has frequently endorsed the "plain meaning" rule of interpretation in relation to the Act. A recent instance is *Shell Canada Ltd. v. Canada*, [1999] 3 SCR 622, per McLachlin J, as she then was, for the Court, at para. 40:

"Where the provision at issue is clear and unambiguous, its terms must simply be applied. ..."

For this proposition, McLachlin J cited *Continental Bank Leasing Corp. v. Canada*, [1998] 2 SCR 298, at para. 51, per Bastarache J; *Tennant v. MNR*, [1996] 1 SCR 305, at para. 16, per Iacobucci J; *Friesen v. Canada*, [1995] 3 SCR 103, at para. 11, per Major J; *Alberta (Treasury Branches) v. MNR*, [1996] 1 SCR 963, at para. 15, per Cory J.

This is not to say that the "plain meaning" is to be applied by a court oblivious to the context. In *Stubart Investments Ltd. v. The Queen*, [1984] 1 SCR 536, at p. 578, Estey J emphasized that "courts today apply to this statute [the *Income Tax Act*] the plain meaning rule, but in a substantive sense," which he elaborated by reference to the oft-quoted passage from E. A. Driedger, *Construction of Statutes* (2nd ed. 1983), at p. 87 (which Driedger styled "the modern rule"):

"Today there is only one principle or approach, namely, the words of an Act are to be read in their entire context and in their grammatical and ordinary sense harmoniously with the scheme of the Act, the object of the Act, and the intention of Parliament."

"Words, like people, take their colour from their surroundings," observed Professor J. Willis at p. 6 in "Statute Interpretation in a Nutshell" (1938), 16 *Can. Bar Rev.* 1, the classic article cited by Estey J at p. 577 of *Stubart Investments, supra*. More recently, Professor J. M. Kernochan has made a similar point: "The precise words which are in issue in relation to the facts must be weighed in the light of successive circles of context" ("Statutory Interpretation: An Outline of Method" (1976), 3 *Dalhousie LJ* 333, at pp. 348-49). The *Stubart Investments* principles were further addressed by Cory J in *Alberta (Treasury Branches) v. MNR, supra*, at para. 15:

"Even if the ambiguity were not apparent, it is significant that in order to determine the clear and plain meaning of the statute it is always appropriate to consider the 'scheme of the Act, the object of the Act, and the intention of Parliament.'"

In *Quebec (Communaute urbaine) v. Corp. Notre-Dame de Bon-Secours*, [1994] 3 SCR 3, Gonthier J, for the Court, cited and applied the *Stubart Investments* principles and, at p. 17, adopted the following statement as summarizing his conclusion on the issue of ambiguity in the legislative text:

"There has been one distinct change [after Stubart] however, in the resolution of ambiguities. In the past, resort was often made to the maxims that an ambiguity in a taxing provision is resolved in the taxpayer's favour and that an ambiguity in an exempting provision is resolved in the Crown's favour. *Now an ambiguity is usually resolved openly by reference to legislative intent.* [Emphasis added by Gonthier J.]"

The emphasis on purposive interpretation in *Notre-Dame de Bon-Secours*, *supra*, is occasionally portrayed as somewhat out of step with the modern plain meaning rule: see, e.g., B. J. Arnold, "Statutory Interpretation: Some Thoughts on Plain Meaning", in *Report of Proceedings of the Fiftieth Tax Conference* (1999), 6:1, at p. 6:20, but I don't think this observation is correct. The *Notre-Dame de Bon-Secours* judgment was directed against excessive resort to "predetermined presumptions" and advocated greater focus on the actual "legislative provision in question" (p. 20). The Court held that where, after going through the *Stubart Investments* analysis, a court concludes that the words themselves do not disclose a "plain meaning," other interpretive tools must necessarily gain in influence, including "the context of the statute, its objective and the legislative intent" (p. 20). Far from downplaying the "plain meaning," Gonthier J, at p. 21, was at pains to explore the statutory text, finally concluding at p. 27 that:

"If the legislature had intended that the tax exemption of a reception centre should be subject to the existence of a permit issued by the proper authority, it would have said so expressly as it did for day-care centres. The same textual argument can be drawn from s. 204(15). ..."

The first rule identified in the *Notre-Dame de Bon-Secours* summary at p. 20 is that "the interpretation of tax legislation should follow the ordinary rules of interpretation." The "ordinary rules" include the modern plain meaning rule, as noted by J. E. Fulcher, a tax counsel with the Department of Justice, in "The Income Tax Act: The Rules of Interpretation and Tax Avoidance. Purpose vs. Plain Meaning: Which, When and Why?" (1995), 74 *Can. Bar Rev.* 563. Commenting at p. 578 on the later case of *Canada v. Antosko*, [1994] 2 SCR 312, he says:

"The case never gets beyond the first rule in *Bon-Secours*. The ordinary rule of interpretation here is that unambiguous provisions are to be interpreted as written, and while finding ambiguity is a subjective undertaking, why come to the Finance Department's aid when the provision is drafted with such blinding certainty?"

The primary rule of statutory interpretation is to ascertain the intention of Parliament. Where the meaning of the words used is plain and no ambiguity arises from context, then the words offer the best indicator of Parliament's intent: *R v. McIntosh*, [1995] 1 SCR 686, at p. 697, per Lamer CJ, and at p. 712, per McLachlin J, dissenting. No doubt the statement that words have a "plain meaning" is itself a conclusion based on a contextual analysis. However, once the tools of interpretation have been deployed and the issue considered from the different perspectives identified by Professor Driedger, if the result of that exercise is the conclusion that the meaning of the words used by Parliament is plain, then effect must be given to them. The *Stubart Investments* gloss on "plain meaning" was thus reaffirmed by Major J in *Friesen*, *supra*, at para. 10. He said that, if, after examining the context and purpose of the tax provision, the Court nevertheless concludes that "a provision is couched in specific language that admits of no doubt or ambiguity in its application to the facts, then the provision must be applied regardless of its object and purpose": *Friesen*, *supra*, at para. 11, quoting P. W. Hogg and J. E. Magee, *Principles of Canadian Income Tax Law* (1995), at p. 454.

The strength of the "plain meaning" rule is its recognition that it is the words of the provision themselves that constitute the vehicle used by Parliament to convey its intent to the people who are trying to assess their rights and tax liabilities under the Act. As the Court said in *Antosko*, *supra*, at pp. 326-27:

> "While it is true that the courts must view discrete sections of the *Income Tax Act* in light of the other provisions of the Act and of the purpose of the legislation, and that they must analyze a given transaction in the context of economic and commercial reality, such techniques cannot alter the result where the words of the statute are clear and plain and where the legal and practical effect of the transaction is undisputed. ..."

Even less attractive, I think, is the attempt in the present case to narrow the words "sale or lease" by reference to technical legal distinctions among various types of disposal contracts which are totally extraneous to the Act and are not easily accessible to the self-assessing taxpayer. Apart from everything else, such imported technical distinctions may frustrate not only the plain meaning, but the legislative purpose of the tax provision. Where (as here) Parliament has spoken in language that continues to speak plainly despite "successive circles of context," I think the taxpayer is entitled to the benefit voted by Parliament. It is the Minister (or the Minister's colleague, the Minister of Finance) who recommended the particular wording to Parliament, and it is the Minister or his colleague who may recommend amendments to the Act if it is thought desirable to narrow the tax benefit.

Commentary by the Tax Bar

The "plain meaning" approach as defined in *Stubart Investments*, *supra*, has been much discussed in the recent tax literature, including S. W. Bowman, "Interpretation of Tax Legislation: The Evolution of Purposive Analysis" (1995), 43 *Can. Tax J* 1167; Fulcher, *supra*; K. Sharlow, "The Interpretation of Tax Legislation and the Rule of Law—Rejoinder" (1996), 75 *Can. Bar Rev.* 151; R. Taylor, "The Interpretation of Fiscal Statutes: The 'Plain Meaning' Approach in Recent Supreme Court of Canada Decisions," in *Report of Proceedings of the Forty-Eighth Tax Conference* (1997),

64:1; Arnold, *supra*. More recently still, the "plain meaning" rule has been discussed in detail and criticized by Professor D. G. Duff in two articles titled "Interpreting the Income Tax Act" (1999), 47 *Can. Tax J* 464 and 741. At p. 770, Professor Duff says that by over-simplifying the interpretive task, the plain meaning rule in its pure form (i.e., before Estey J married the "plain meaning" rule to Driedger's "modern rule" in *Stubart Investments, supra*)

"obscures the process of statutory interpretation, artificially limits its scope, produces decisions contrary to legislative intentions and statutory purposes, permits substantial judicial discretion, and places an unreasonable burden on legislative drafters."

Whatever might have been said about the original "plain meaning" rule, I do not think that the modern plain meaning rule spelled out in *Stubart Investments* is fairly subject to these criticisms.

To take Professor Duff's points in reverse order, I do not think it unreasonable to require the legislative drafter to make it plain (if such be the intent) that the product must not only be manufactured for sale, but must be disposed of under a specific type of contract, e.g., excluding contracts for work and materials. It would be a simple matter to signal to the taxpayer in ordinary language that if he or she supplies services along with the manufactured product, the fast write-off and the investment tax credit will be forfeited.

Secondly, adoption of the plain meaning in this case reduces rather than enlarges judicial discretion. The Court respects the very words Parliament has used, and operates on the assumption that Parliament meant what it said: *Friesen, supra*, at para. 53. It does not complicate the Act with ideas borrowed from the *Sale of Goods Act, 1893*.

Thirdly, a review of the related text in the Act and the legislative history confirms the fact that the "plain meaning" accords with Parliament's intent expressed by the responsible Minister and senior officials, a type of evidence the Court has ruled admissible as part of the interpretive exercise: *Symes v. Canada*, [1993] 4 SCR 695, at pp. 749-50; *Thibaudeau v. Canada*, [1995] 2 SCR 627, at para. 173; *Friesen, supra*, at para. 63. While the criticism may occasionally be made that "judges have considerable freedom in formulating their descriptions of legislative purpose" (R. Sullivan, *Driedger on the Construction of Statutes* (3rd ed. 1994), at p. 60), the fact is that in this case there is a wealth of authoritative guidance on point.

On May 8, 1972, the Minister of Finance, the Honourable John Turner, introduced to the House of Commons a tax amendment to permit machinery and equipment required for manufacturing operations to be written off within two years ("the fast write-off") to provide "a substantial incentive for the establishment in Canada of new manufacturing enterprises and the expansion of existing enterprises by increasing the return that can ultimately be realized on capital investment" (*House of Commons Debates*, vol. III, 4th Sess., 28th Parl., at p. 2002). A major emphasis was on creating jobs. Asphalt plants create jobs irrespective of the form of the asphalt disposal contract.

The Minister of Finance returned to the theme of encouraging investment in manufacturing facilities in his budget address of February 19, 1973 (*House of Commons Debates*, vol. II, 1st Sess., 29th Parl., at p. 1428), and in the post-budget debate on

June 13, 1973, when he pointed out that "increasing the after-tax rate of return on investment, these measures will help to achieve these national objectives by encouraging the establishment in many parts of the country of new manufacturing and processing industries and of supporting service industries" (*House of Commons Debates*, vol. V, 1st Sess., 29th Parl., at p. 4725). Whatever else may be said of the taxpayer's activities in this case, it acquired a new manufacturing plant and it worked the plant in conjunction with its paving service business.

On June 23, 1975, the Finance Minister returned to the same theme, explaining that "I am therefore proposing to introduce an investment tax credit as a temporary extra incentive for investment in a wide range of new productive facilities" (*House of Commons Debates*, vol. VII, 1st Sess., 30th Parl., at p. 7028).

In the same year, he explained to the Canadian Tax Foundation that:

> "We want the application of the policy to be clear as well. Grey areas in tax administration are no more popular with governments than with taxpayers.
>
> To apply the reduced rate, a taxpayer must be able to answer two questions:
>
> Am I carrying on a manufacturing or processing activity?
>
> If I am, how much of my business income is subject to the reduced rate?"

("Banquet Address," in *Report of Proceedings of the Twenty-Fourth Tax Conference* (1973), 278, at p. 281.)

In the following year, R. D. Weil, CA, of the Technical Interpretations Division of the Department of National Revenue, further explained the tax changes in an address to the Canadian Tax Foundation and gave an example which is apposite in the present appeal:

> "Where a company enters into a *supply and erect* contract, the *off-site* manufacturing of building products is not considered to be construction, whereas the activities of erecting and installing these products in place at the construction site are considered to be construction. Where a building product such as ready-mix concrete *or asphalt* is manufactured or processed off site *and then is installed* at the place of construction by the same company, *some concern may exist that there is no sale of the concrete or asphalt*. In these and similar circumstances, the product *is considered to be sold at the time the completed structure is sold and therefore such activities will qualify* [Italics in original; [bold] added.]"

("Manufacturing and Processing Tax Incentives," in *Report of Proceedings of the Twenty-Fifth Tax Conference* (1974), 124, at p. 127.)

Administrative policy and interpretation are not determinative but are entitled to weight and can be an important factor in case of doubt about the meaning of legislation: *Harel v. Deputy Minister of Revenue of Quebec*, [1978] 1 SCR 851, at p. 859, per de Grandpre J; *Nowegijick v. The Queen*, [1983] 1 SCR 29, at p. 37, per Dickson J. Bulletin No. IT-145 issued by the Department of National Revenue on February 5, 1974, incorporated Mr. Weil's interpretation as follows:

> "9. Where a building product such as ready-mix concrete or *asphalt* is manufactured or processed off site and then *is installed at the place of construction by*

the same corporation, some concern may exist that there is no sale of the concrete or asphalt. In these and similar circumstances, *the product is considered to be sold* at the time the completed structure is sold and therefore such activities will qualify. [Emphasis added.]"

These comments seem directed to construction projects which are a traditional heartland of work and materials contracts, and, I think, undermine the Minister's narrow interpretation urged here.

Moreover, this legislative history makes it clear that the distinction drawn from the niceties of contract law adopted by the Minister and the courts below to defeat the taxpayer's claim is unrelated to the purpose of the deductions. By basing the availability of the tax incentives on the distinction between a contract for the sale of goods and a contract for work and materials, the Minister applies doctrines developed in a non-tax context aimed at the totally different (and irrelevant) law governing the rights and obligations of buyers and sellers. There are, no doubt, provisions in the *Income Tax Act* which require for their proper understanding resort to commercial law or accounting practice, but the provisions at issue in the present appeal are not among them.

Notre-Dame de Bon-Secours, supra, at p. 18, recognized that, while at one time tax legislation was arguably limited to raising funds to cover government expenses, "in our time it has been recognized that such legislation serves other purposes and functions as a tool of economic and social policy. ... Both are legitimate purposes which equally embody the legislative intent and it is thus hard to see why one should take precedence over the other." In my view, the legislative purpose here is to give positive encouragement to manufacturing and processing plants. This corroborates and reinforces the "plain meaning" of the Act.

While the plain meaning principle to some extent limits the scope of the interpretive exercise, it does not do so "artificially." It arrives at the intent of Parliament by the most direct route, namely by giving effect to the words Parliament has used where Parliament has made its meaning plain. While there is little danger that the Act will ever become user-friendly or self-explanatory, it is of particular importance in a self-assessment tax system to promote an interpretation of provisions, where possible, that is comprehensible to the taxpayers themselves.

Disposition

I would therefore allow the appeal and remit the matter to the Minister to be dealt with in accordance with these reasons.

Appeal dismissed with costs, Gonthier, McLachlin, and Binnie JJ dissenting.

NOTES AND QUESTIONS

1. Both the majority and the dissent address Parliament's purpose in enacting the provision being considered in *Will-Kare*. How do the two judgments differ in their assessment and use of legislative purpose?

2. Is it fair for the court to rely on "settled legal definitions" of arcane terms of art found in statutes that apply to ordinary people? Should citizens be expected to know the general law concerning the sale of goods?

3. In the majority's decision, Major J discusses the "anomalous result" that flows from the majority's interpretation of the relevant legislation. Does the court adequately address this anomaly? Is this anomaly sufficiently "absurd" to call for the application of the golden rule of statutory construction?

4. Is Major J's approach to "plain meaning" consistent with the approach that he takes in the decisions discussed in chapter 7 of *Theory and Practice*?

5. Major J distinguishes "plain meaning" from "popular meaning." Is this a sensible distinction? When is a meaning "plain" but "unpopular"? Is it possible for a "popular meaning" not to be "plain"?

6. According to Binnie J, the words "sale or lease" are "everyday words." Would an average reader of the *Income Tax Act* generally assume that words in the Act were used in an "everyday" sense, or would the reader suspect that the words were used in a more formal sense?

7. How would Will-Kare's average customer characterize the contract with Will-Kare? Would the consumer say that Will-Kare had "sold" asphalt to him or her and then spread it on the driveway? Would the consumer be surprised to hear the contract described in this way?

8. Consider the following situation: On Friday night you go to a tattoo parlour where you have your mother's name tattooed on your right shoulder. At the conclusion of the procedure, the tattoo artist applies a gauze strip to your arm, attaching it with a bandage. There is no extra charge for the gauze strip or the bandage. After paying the tattoo artist $30 for the services, would you say that the tattoo artist had just "sold" you tattoo dye, bandages, and a gauze strip? Is this analogy useful in the interpretation of the language at issue in *Will-Kare*? Why or why not?

9. Binnie J notes that "it is common ground that if the taxpayer had sold to its paving customers the asphalt in one contract and the installation of it in another, it would be entitled to the deduction." Is it likely that Parliament intended to treat Will-Kare's case differently from a case in which two separate contracts (one for the sale of asphalt and one for paving services) are entered into by the parties? Why would Parliament legislate an incentive for taxpayers to write contracts in a peculiar way?

10. Is the provision at issue in *Will-Kare* "clear and unambiguous"?

11. According to Binnie J, "[t]he primary rule of statutory interpretation is to ascertain the intention of Parliament." In light of the cases and materials that you have read in this course, is this an accurate portrayal of statutory interpretation?

12. Is it possible to characterize the problem at issue in *Will-Kare* as a problem of vagueness, ambiguity, subtext, or analogy? How would the unified theory (developed in *Theory and Practice*) address the issue raised in the *Will-Kare* case?

13. According to Professor David Duff (cited in the dissent), the original "plain meaning" rule

obscures the process of statutory interpretation, artificially limits its scope, produces decisions contrary to legislative intentions and statutory purposes, permits substantial judicial discretion, and places an unreasonable burden on legislative drafters.

Do the current methods of statutory interpretation avoid these problems? In particular, does the "modern approach" to the interpretation of tax statutes truly limit judicial discretion?

III. LUDCO ENTERPRISES LTD. v. CANADA

A. Introduction

In *Ludco Enterprises Ltd. v. Canada*, 2001 SCC 62, the Supreme Court of Canada was asked to interpret s. 20(1)(c)(i) of the *Income Tax Act*. That section provides (in part) that in computing a taxpayer's "income from business or property," the taxpayer may deduct from income the amount of interest that the taxpayer paid in respect of "borrowed money used for the purpose of earning income from a business or property." In simplified terms, where the taxpayer borrows money "for the purpose of earning income from business or property," the taxpayer may deduct from his or her income the amount of interest that the taxpayer paid on that borrowed money.

In *Ludco*, the taxpayer borrowed a huge sum of money in order to purchase shares in two corporations. The money was borrowed "for the purpose" of purchasing those shares. Over the relevant time period, the taxpayer paid over $6 million in interest on that borrowed money.

Eventually, the taxpayer sold the shares and generated a whopping capital gain of $9.24 million. It is important to recognize that a capital gain is not "income from a business or property." During the time that the taxpayer held the shares, the shares paid dividends of $600,000 (which was roughly 10 percent of the amount of interest that was paid on the borrowed money). Dividends, unlike capital gains, do constitute "income from a business or property."

The question in *Ludco* was whether or not the $6 million in interest was incurred "for the purpose" of generating $600,000 in income. Obviously, the taxpayer's main purpose in borrowing the money was to generate a capital gain through the eventual sale of the shares. The taxpayer knew from the outset that the amount of dividends paid on the shares would be far less than the amount of interest that the taxpayer would have to pay on the borrowed money. As a result, it seemed unusual to argue that the taxpayer had borrowed a vast sum of money "for the purpose" of generating an amount of income that would pale by comparison to the amount of interest that the taxpayer would have to pay.

Once again, the decision in *Ludco* deals with several advanced tax concepts. For present purposes, it is only important for students to focus on one question: where a taxpayer (a) borrows money, and (b) realizes that the interest that he or she will pay on that loan will far exceed any "income" that the borrowed money will generate for the taxpayer, can the taxpayer be said to have borrowed the money "for the purpose" of generating income?

B. The Court's Decision

Ludco Enterprises Ltd. v. Canada
2001 SCC 62

IACOBUCCI J:

I. Introduction

In this appeal, we are asked to decide whether interest charges incurred with respect to money the appellants borrowed to purchase shares in two foreign companies are deductible from their income from other sources pursuant to s. 20(1)(c)(i) of the *Income Tax Act*, RSC 1985, c. 1 (5th Supp.). ... The main issue [is] whether the money borrowed by the taxpayers was "used for the purpose of earning income from property" within the meaning of s. 20(1)(c)(i) of the *Income Tax Act*.

· · ·

II. Facts

A. The Companies

The two companies at issue in this case, Justinian Corporation SA ("Justinian") and Augustus Corporation SA ("Augustus"), operated investment funds that were carefully structured to avoid the application of the Foreign Accrual Property Income rules (the "FAPI" rules), and to provide other tax advantages to investors such as deferral of taxes and the conversion of income into capital gains. It was the policy of Justinian and Augustus (together the "Companies") to invest in debt-securities and reinvest almost all profits, retaining only a relatively small portion for the purpose of dividend distribution. In the eight years the appellants held shares in the Companies, they received approximately $600,000 in dividends, but incurred approximately $6 million in interest charges. After the FAPI rules were amended to eliminate the tax advantages of these investment funds, the appellants disposed of their shares and earned capital gains of approximately $9.2 million.

· · ·

D. The Share Redemption and the Tax Consequences

In 1984, the FAPI rules were amended to discourage the type of off-shore investment at issue in this case by eliminating the tax benefits and advantages it generated. These amendments, known as the "FAPI amendments," led to the winding up of the Companies' businesses.

In 1985, upon the coming into force of the FAPI amendments, the taxpayers disposed of their shares and realized a capital gain of $9.24 million. Over the eight years during which the shares had been held by the appellants, they received some $600,000 in dividends. Over the same period they incurred interest costs of $6 million.

For the taxation years 1981-1985, the appellants deducted their interest costs against other reported income pursuant to s. 20(1)(c)(i) of the *Income Tax Act*. In 1986 and 1987, the Minister of National Revenue reassessed the appellants and disallowed those deductions. The Minister took the position that the amount borrowed had not been used "for the purpose of earning income from property" as stipulated in s. 20(1)(c)(i), rather the real purpose of the investment was to defer taxes and convert income into capital gains.

. . .

III. Relevant Statutory Provisions

Subparagraph 20(1)(c)(i) of the *Income Tax Act*, RSC 1985, c. 1 (5th Supp.), provides:

"20 (1) Notwithstanding paragraphs 18(1)(a), 18(1)(b) and 18(1)(h), in computing a taxpayer's income for a taxation year from a business or property, there may be deducted such of the following amounts as are wholly applicable to that source or such part of the following amounts as may reasonably be regarded as applicable thereto

...

(c) an amount paid in the year or payable in respect of the year (depending on the method regularly followed by the taxpayer in computing the taxpayer's income), pursuant to a legal obligation to pay interest on

(i) borrowed money used for the purpose of earning income from a business or property (other than borrowed money used to acquire property the income from which would be exempt or to acquire a life insurance policy).

. . .

VI. Analysis

A. The Preliminary Issue: Fact or Law?

As a preliminary matter, it was argued that the trial judge made a finding of fact when he determined that the appellants' true purpose in making the investments at issue was not to earn income but to defer taxes and acquire capital gains. It was further argued that this Court is prevented from revisiting the trial judge's finding in this regard by the principle that, absent a palpable and overriding error, findings of fact made at trial are not subject to appellate court interference. However, whether or not a taxpayer's purpose in making an investment falls within the ambit of s. 20(1)(c)(i) of the Act is properly viewed as a question of mixed fact and law. For the reasons set out below, the main issue in this appeal is to determine and apply the proper test under s. 20. That is a question of law. Moreover, in my view, with respect, the trial judge did not apply the correct legal test to determine the appellants' purpose in this case. Therefore, it is open to this Court to interfere with the finding of the trial judge in this regard.

The identification of the correct legal test in this case centres on a question of statutory interpretation. As a result, before discussing the legal test for interest deductibility under s. 20(1)(c)(i), and whether interest costs are deductible in this case, it may be helpful to review briefly the principles of statutory interpretation that apply in this case.

B. Principles of Statutory Interpretation

The modern rule of statutory interpretation was put succinctly by E.A. Driedger in *Construction of Statutes* (2nd ed., 1983), at p. 87:

> "Today there is only one principle or approach, namely, the words of an Act are to be read in their entire context and in their grammatical and ordinary sense harmoniously with the scheme of the Act, the object of the Act, and the intention of Parliament... ."

This passage from Driedger "best encapsulates" the preferred approach to statutory interpretation: *Rizzo & Rizzo Shoes (Re)*, [1998] 1 SCR 27, at paras. 21 and 23. This is the case for the interpretation of any statute, and it is noteworthy that Driedger's famous passage has been cited with approval by our Court on numerous occasions both in the non-tax and in the tax context [citations omitted].

Furthermore, when interpreting the *Income Tax Act* courts must be mindful of their role as distinct from that of Parliament. In the absence of clear statutory language, judicial innovation is undesirable: *Royal Bank of Canada v. Sparrow Electric Corp.*, [1997] 1 SCR 411, at para. 112. Rather, the promulgation of new rules of tax law must be left to Parliament: *Canderel Ltd. v. Canada*, [1998] 1 SCR 147, at para. 41. As McLachlin J (now CJ) recently explained in *Shell Canada Ltd. v. Canada*, [1999] 3 SCR 622, at para. 43:

> "The Act is a complex statute through which Parliament seeks to balance a myriad of principles. This Court has consistently held that courts must therefore be cautious before finding within the clear provisions of the Act an unexpressed legislative intention... . Finding unexpressed legislative intentions under the guise of purposive interpretation runs the risk of upsetting the balance Parliament has attempted to strike in the Act. [Citations omitted.]"

See also *Antosko, supra*, at p. 328. Having said this, it is within the jurisdiction of courts to interpret the rules enacted by Parliament, including the elucidation of otherwise undefined concepts such as "income" or "profit": see *Canderel, supra*, at para. 42. ...

With these principles in mind, I turn to consider the legal test for interest deductibility under s. 20(1)(c)(i).

C. The Legal Test for Interest Deductibility Under Section 20(1)(c)(i)

(1) Introduction

The deductibility of interest under s. 20(1)(c)(i) of the *Income Tax Act* has given rise to considerable litigation and has been the topic of much legal commentary, as pointed out by the parties. Many of the features of the interest deductibility provision are matters of settled law. However, as explained below, the appeal at bar raises two novel issues related to the concepts of "purpose" and "income" contained within s. 20(1)(c)(i).

Recently, in *Shell Canada*, *supra*, at para. 28, McLachlin J, writing for the Court, described the four elements of s. 20(1)(c)(i) that must be present before interest can be deducted:

> "The provision has four elements: (1) the amount must be paid in the year or be payable in the year in which it is sought to be deducted; (2) the amount must be paid pursuant to a legal obligation to pay interest on borrowed money; (3) the borrowed money must be used for the purpose of earning non-exempt income from a business or property; and (4) the amount must be reasonable, as assessed by reference to the first three requirements."

The first two elements are not in dispute here. As noted above, the focus of the inquiry in this case is clearly on the third element, namely, whether the borrowed money was used for the purpose of earning non-exempt income from business or property.

In this connection, Dickson CJ, writing for the Court in *Bronfman Trust*, *supra*, closely analysed the third element of the interest deductibility provision and classified the various possible uses of borrowed money as: eligible and ineligible, original and current, and direct and indirect. Dickson CJ outlined the inquiry into the third element at pp. 45-46:

> "Not all borrowing expenses are deductible. Interest on borrowed money used to produce tax exempt income is not deductible. Interest on borrowed money used to buy life insurance policies is not deductible. Interest on borrowings used for non-income earning purposes, such as personal consumption or the making of capital gains is similarly not deductible. The statutory deduction thus requires a characterization of the use of borrowed money as between the eligible use of earning non-exempt income from a business or property and a variety of possible ineligible uses. The onus is on the taxpayer to trace the borrowed funds to an identifiable use which triggers the deduction.
>
> ...
>
> The interest deduction provision requires not only a characterization of the use of borrowed funds, but also a characterization of "purpose." Eligibility for the deduction is contingent on the use of borrowed money for the purpose of earning income. It is well-established in the jurisprudence, however, that it is not the purpose of the borrowing itself which is relevant. What is relevant, rather, is the taxpayer's purpose in using the borrowed money in a particular manner: *Auld v. Minister of National Revenue*, 62 DTC 27 (TAB) Consequently, the focus of the inquiry must be centered on the use to which the taxpayer put the borrowed funds."

In short, a determination of whether borrowed money has been put to an eligible use requires a characterization of the use of the borrowed funds and a characterization of the taxpayer's purpose in using the funds in a particular manner. Dickson CJ went on to deny the interest deduction in that case on the ground that, properly characterized, the taxpayer's "use" of borrowed funds was a directly ineligible one. Thus, the law relating to the matter of the taxpayer's "purpose" was not fully elaborated on in that case.

In the case at bar, and in contrast to *Singleton, supra*, there is no dispute as to the particular use that the borrowed funds were put to: they were directly used to purchase shares in the Companies. Rather, the focus of the inquiry is on whether the taxpayers' purpose in so using the funds was to earn income within the meaning of s. 20(1)(c)(i). Consequently, in the present appeal, the Court is asked for the first time to explicate the law on two of the central concepts in s. 20(1)(c)(i): "purpose" and "income."

(2) When Is Borrowed Money "Used for the Purpose of Earning Income" Within the Meaning of Section 20(1)(c)(i)?

In this case, three different tests have been advanced for determining whether the requisite income earning purpose is present, they are: the bona fide purpose test, the dominant purpose test, and the reasonable expectation of income test. In several decisions, including those of the lower courts in the case at bar, courts have simply adopted the bona fide purpose test on the strength of some obiter dicta by Dickson CJ in *Bronfman Trust, supra*.

It is worth repeating what Dickson CJ in *Bronfman Trust, supra*, stated on this point. At p. 54, the former Chief Justice explained:

> "Even if there are exceptional circumstances in which, on a real appreciation of a taxpayer's transactions, it might be appropriate to allow the taxpayer to deduct interest on funds borrowed for an ineligible use because of an indirect effect on the taxpayer's income-earning capacity, I am satisfied that those circumstances are not presented in the case before us. It seems to me that, at the very least, the taxpayer must satisfy the Court that his or her bona fide purpose in using the funds was to earn income. In contrast to what appears to be the case in *Trans-Prairie*, the facts in the present case fall far short of such a showing. Indeed, it is of more than passing interest that the assets which were preserved for a brief period of time yielded a return which grossly fell short of the interest costs on the borrowed money. In 1970, the interest costs on the $2,200,000 of loans amounted to over $110,000 while the return from an average $2,200,000 of Trust assets (the amount of capital "preserved") was less than $10,000. The taxpayer cannot point to any reasonable expectation that the income yield from the Trust's investment portfolio as a whole, or indeed from any single asset, would exceed the interest payable on a like amount of debt. The fact that the loan may have prevented capital losses cannot assist the taxpayer in obtaining a deduction from income which is limited to use of borrowed money for the purpose of earning income."

It appears to me that Dickson CJ's suggestion that a bona fide purpose test should apply was made as a passing comment and did not result from an analysis of the text of the provision. In my opinion, Dickson CJ's comments fall short of elevating the bona fide purpose test to a rule of law. Indeed, as discussed below, the importation of the bona fide purpose test into s. 20(1)(c)(i) is not supported by the principles of statutory interpretation outlined above, especially as applied in our recent tax law jurisprudence.

With respect to the plain meaning of s. 20(1)(c)(i), the only express requirement related to "purpose" is that borrowed money must have been "used for the purpose of earning income." Apart from the use of the definite article "the," which on closer analysis is hardly conclusive of the issue before us, nothing in the text of the provision indicates that the requisite purpose must be the exclusive, primary or dominant purpose, or that multiple purposes are to be somehow ranked in importance in order to determine the taxpayer's "real" purpose. Therefore, it is perfectly consistent with the language of s. 20(1)(c)(i) that a taxpayer who uses borrowed money to make an investment for more than one purpose may be entitled to deduct interest charges provided that one of those purposes is to earn income.

In this connection, the adjectives that have been heretofore used by courts to characterize the requisite purpose in s. 20(1)(c)(i), such as "bona fide," "actual," "real" or "true," are to my mind ultimately useful only when describing whether the transaction at issue was a mere sham or window-dressing designed to obtain the benefit of interest deductibility. Absent a sham or window dressing or other vitiating circumstances, a taxpayer's ancillary purpose may be nonetheless a bona fide, actual, real and true objective of his or her investment, equally capable of providing the requisite purpose for interest deductibility in comparison with any more important or significant primary purpose. …

Having determined that an ancillary purpose to earn income can provide the requisite purpose for interest deductibility, the question still remains as to how courts should go about identifying whether the requisite purpose of earning income is present. What standard should be applied? In the interpretation of the Act, as in other areas of law, where purpose or intention behind actions is to be ascertained, courts should objectively determine the nature of the purpose, guided by both subjective and objective manifestations of purpose: see *Symes, supra*, at p. 736; *Continental Bank, supra*, at para. 45; *Backman, supra*, at para. 25; *Spire Freezers, supra*, at para. 27. In the result, the requisite test to determine the purpose for interest deductibility under s. 20(1)(c)(i) is whether, considering all the circumstances, the taxpayer had a reasonable expectation of income at the time the investment is made.

Reasonable expectation accords with the language of purpose in the section and provides an objective standard, apart from the taxpayer's subjective intention, which by itself is relevant but not conclusive. It also avoids many of the pitfalls of the other tests advanced and furthers the policy objective of the interest deductibility provision aimed at capital accumulation and investment, as discussed in the next section of these reasons.

In conclusion, of the three tests proposed in this case, in my view only the reasonable expectation of income test is consistent with the wording of the section in light of all of the applicable principles of statutory interpretation. In this respect, I agree with both Letourneau and Desjardins JJA, who formed the majority at the Federal Court of Appeal on this point.

(3) What Is Income for the Purposes of Section 20(1)(c)(i)?

The *Income Tax Act* does not define the term "income." The Act speaks of "net income," "taxable income," and income from different sources, but it neither identifies nor describes the legal characteristics of "income"; it only speaks of what is to be included or excluded from income. Similarly, tax theorists have proposed many different definitions of "income" distinguishable by their varying degrees of inclusiveness. The common feature of all the definitions of income, whether derived from tax law, economic theory or the dictionary, is that "income" is a measure of gain: see V. Krishna, *The Fundamentals of Canadian Income Tax* (6th ed., 2000), at pp. 97-100.

In the case at bar, both the Tax Court of Canada and the Federal Court—Trial Division ostensibly applied this Court's decision in *Moldowan v. The Queen*, [1978] 1 SCR 480, in equating "income" with "profit." However, that case was concerned not with the meaning of the term "income" as such, but with identifying the source of income in play and, more specifically, with differentiating between business activities as distinct from personal or hobby activities. It is clear that *Moldowan, supra*, does not stand for the absolute proposition that "income" necessarily means "profit."

Because it is left undefined in the Act, this Court must apply the principles of statutory interpretation to discern what is meant by "income" in the context of s. 20(1)(c)(i). The plain meaning of s. 20(1)(c)(i) does not support an interpretation of "income" as the equivalent of "profit" or "net income." Nowhere in the language of the provision is a quantitative test suggested. Nor is there any support in the text of the Act for an interpretation of "income" that involves a judicial assessment of sufficiency of income. Such an approach would be too subjective and certainty is to be preferred in the area of tax law. Therefore, absent a sham or window dressing or similar vitiating circumstances, courts should not be concerned with the sufficiency of the income expected or received.

As noted by Letourneau JA, Bowman JTCC (as he then was) lucidly dealt with the argument that the word "income" in s. 20(1)(c)(i) necessarily means "profit" in *Mark Resources Inc. v. The Queen*, 93 DTC 1004, at p. 1015. Most importantly, Bowman JTCC dismissed that argument at p. 1015 in these terms:

> "Interest on money that is borrowed to invest in common shares, or property, or a business or corporation is deductible because it is laid out to earn amounts that must be included in the computation of income. Amounts of income such as dividends which must be included in income under paragraphs 12(1)(j) and (k) do not cease to be income merely because they are exceeded by the cost of their production."

I agree. Indeed, when one looks at the immediate context in which the term "income" appears in s. 20(1)(c)(i), it is significant that within the provision itself the concept of "income" is used in contradistinction from the concept of tax-exempt income. Viewed in this context, the term "income" in s. 20(1)(c)(i) does not refer to net income, but to income subject to tax. In this light, it is clear that "income" in s. 20(1)(c)(i) refers to income generally, that is an amount that would come into income for taxation purposes, not just net income.

I am bolstered in this conclusion by the other evidence of Parliamentary intention. If Parliament had intended interest to be deductible only in circumstances where borrowed money was used for the purpose of earning "net income," it could have expressly said so. Indeed, as noted by Letourneau JA, in both 1981 and 1991, amendments to the Act that would have restricted interest deductibility to circumstances where borrowed money is used for the purpose of making a profit were proposed but never enacted.

Furthermore, reading "income" in s. 20(1)(c)(i) to mean income generally, as described above, is more consistent with the objective of the interest deductibility provision. In most circumstances, ss. 9 and 18(1)(b) of the Act prohibit the deduction of amounts expended on account of capital. Section 20(1)(c)(i) is an exception to this prohibition, designed to encourage the accumulation of capital which would produce income: see *Shell Canada, supra,* at para. 28, per McLachlin J; *Tennant v. MNR,* [1996] 1 SCR 305, at para. 16, per Iacobucci J; *Bronfman Trust, supra,* at p. 45, per Dickson CJ Thus, the object of s. 20(1)(c)(i) is to create an incentive to accumulate capital with the potential to produce income by allowing taxpayers to deduct interest costs associated with its acquisition. The accumulation of income producing capital is seen as desirable because it creates wealth and increases the income tax base. It is clearly sufficient for the purpose of the provision that an investor have a reasonable expectation of gross income as described above when investing borrowed money. In contrast, the incentive would be much less effective if the investor bore the additional burden of establishing a reasonable expectation of net income or profit.

Finally, in defining the taxpayer's real or true purpose by emphasizing the relatively nominal amount of income earned in this case compared to the capital gains realized and interest deductions sought, the respondent effectively asks the Court to take an "economic realities" view of the investments at issue. However, there are limits to the economic realities approach to the assessment of a particular transaction: see *Shell Canada, supra,* at para. 39. In particular, a court should not place so much reliance on "economic realities" so as to cause it to stray from the express terms of s. 20(1)(c)(i) and supplement the provision with extraneous policy concerns that are said to form part of its purpose. Rather, where the provision at issue is clear and unambiguous, the court's duty is to simply apply its terms to the transaction at issue: see *Shell Canada, supra,* at para. 43, per McLachlin J; *Continental Bank, supra,* at para. 51, per Bastarache J; *Tennant, supra,* at para. 16, per Iacobucci J; *Antosko, supra,* at pp. 326-27 and 330, per Iacobucci J; *Friesen, supra,* [1995] 3 SCR 103, at para. 11, per Major J; *Alberta (Treasury Branches), supra,* [1996] 1 SCR 963, at para. 15, per Cory J.

In conclusion, where a taxpayer uses borrowed money for a purpose yielding a reasonable expectation of income from business or property as I have described above, the interest charges incurred will fall within the ambit of s. 20(1)(c)(i) and are deductible.

D. Application of the Foregoing Principles: Are the Interest Charges Incurred by the Appellants Deductible in This Case?

(1) Interest Charges for Initial Investments in Shares of the Companies

The question now to be determined is whether, in using borrowed money to purchase shares of the Companies, the appellants had a reasonable expectation of income? If the answer is affirmative, and the amount of interest paid was reasonable within the meaning of the provision, the interest charges are deductible.

Here, the objective documentary evidence indicates that the appellants did have a reasonable expectation of income. Owing to the nature of the investments and the Companies' investment strategy, it was reasonable to expect income would be available for distribution. In addition, given the terms of the Dividend Policy, it is clear that the appellants had a reasonable expectation of receiving dividends.

Although earning income was not the principal factor that motivated Mr. Ludmer to invest in the Companies, upon reading the relevant documents he did anticipate the receipt of dividend income. In my view, Mr. Ludmer's expectation of dividend income was reasonable. Indeed, the judge at the Federal Court, Trial Division came to the same conclusion at p. 6056.

Furthermore, it is notable that income was actually received in the amount of $600,000 of dividends. Although this amount may be small in comparison to the capital gains realized and the interest charges incurred, absent a sham or window dressing or similar vitiating circumstances (none of which was argued before this Court), we are not concerned with the sufficiency of the income expected or received. There is no sham in this case: the purchase of the shares were genuine investments. Neither can the amount of dividends actually paid be properly be characterized as window dressing. Six hundred thousand dollars is a significant sum and there was some expert evidence indicating that the actual rate of return on the shares of Justinian was within the norm of most of the companies publicly traded on the Toronto and Montreal Stock Exchanges.

I conclude that the appellants did have a reasonable expectation of income when they used the borrowed money to purchase shares in the Companies. Therefore, the requisite purpose is present in the circumstances of this case. ...

NOTES AND QUESTIONS

1. According to Iacobucci J, "judicial innovation" (through the use of statutory interpretation) "is undesirable." Based on the cases that you have studied thus far, do courts truly shy away from "judicial innovation" when interpreting the text of legislation?

2. Consider the following situation: Assume that a taxpayer borrows $1,000 in order to build a lemonade stand for the taxpayer's child. The taxpayer's principal motivation for building the lemonade stand is to provide his or her child with a summer activity that will introduce the child to basic business concepts. The taxpayer is aware, when building the stand, that a child's lemonade stand is likely to generate approximately $50 in income over the course of the summer. The amount of $50 will be less than the interest incurred on the $1,000 loan that the taxpayer used to build the stand. Based on the "ordinary

meaning" of the language used in the *Income Tax Act*, did the taxpayer truly borrow $1,000 "for the purpose" of generating $50 of "income"? Should the interest paid on the taxpayer's debt be deductible?[2]

3. Does the court in *Ludco* deal with "statutory purpose" in a sensible manner? Does the court's interpretation of the Act (in light of that purpose) fulfill the obligation set out in s. 12 of the federal *Interpretation Act*?[3]

4. Did the taxpayer in *Ludco* truly earn "income," given the fact that the taxpayer's interest expense was much greater than any "income" that was generated as a result?

5. Would the unified theory (developed in *Theory and Practice*) support or preclude a particular result in the *Ludco* case?

IV. O'GILVIE v. UNITED STATES

A. The Court's Decision

O'Gilvie v. United States
519 US 79 (1996)

BREYER J: *Internal Revenue Code* § 104(a)(2), as it read in 1988, excluded from "gross income" the

> "amount of any *damages received* (whether *by suit* or agreement and whether as lump sums or as periodic payments) *on account of personal injuries or sickness*." 26 USC § 104(a)(2) (emphasis added).

The issue before us is whether this provision applies to (and thereby makes nontaxable) punitive damages received by a plaintiff in a tort suit for personal injuries. We conclude that the punitive damages received here were not received "*on account of*" personal injuries; hence the provision does not apply, and the damages are taxable.

---

2   Note that the taxpayer's "main purpose" in *Ludco* was to profit from the resale of shares. Ordinarily, where a taxpayer purchases property for the purpose of profiting from its resale, the taxpayer is said to be engaging in "an adventure in the nature of trade." Profits made in an "adventure" of this nature are taxed as income, rather than as capital gains. If the sale of Ludco's shares had been treated as an "adventure in the nature of trade," the profits would have been taxed as income (rather than a capital gain) and it would have been obvious that the $6 million of interest would have been deductible. For various practical reasons, however, profits made on the sale of shares are rarely treated as adventures in the nature of trade, despite the fact that the lion's share of investors purchase shares for the primary purpose of selling the shares at a profit. Arguably, it is the failure of the tax authorities to tax the sale of shares as an "adventure in the nature of trade" that gave rise to the problem in *Ludco*, rather than any ambiguity in the *Income Tax Act*.

3   As we have seen, s. 12 of the federal *Interpretation Act*, RSC 1985, c. I-21, provides that "[e]very enactment is deemed remedial, and shall be given such fair, large and liberal construction and interpretation as best ensures the attainment of its objects."

I

Petitioners in this litigation are the husband and two children of Betty O'Gilvie, who died in 1983 of toxic shock syndrome. Her husband, Kelly, brought a tort suit (on his own behalf and that of her estate) based on Kansas law against the maker of the product that caused Betty O'Gilvie's death. Eventually, he and the two children received the net proceeds of a jury award of $1,525,000 actual damages and $10 million punitive damages. Insofar as the proceeds represented punitive damages, petitioners paid income tax on the proceeds but immediately sought a refund. ...

II

Petitioners received the punitive damages at issue here "by suit"—indeed "by" an ordinary "suit" for "personal injuries." ... These legal circumstances bring those damages within the gross-income-exclusion provision, however, only if petitioners also "received" those damages "*on account of*" the "personal injuries." And the phrase "on account of" does not unambiguously define itself.

On one linguistic interpretation of those words, that of petitioners, they require no more than a "but-for" connection between "any" damages and a lawsuit for personal injuries. They would thereby bring virtually all personal injury lawsuit damages within the scope of the provision, since: "but for the personal injury, there would be no lawsuit, and but for the lawsuit, there would be no damages."

On the Government's alternative interpretation, however, those words impose a stronger causal connection, making the provision applicable only to those personal injury lawsuit damages that were awarded by reason of, or because of, the personal injuries. To put the matter more specifically, they would make the section inapplicable to punitive damages, where those damages

> "'are not compensation for injury [but] instead ... are private fines levied by civil juries to punish reprehensible conduct and to deter its future occurrence.'" *Electrical Workers v. Foust*, 442 US 42, 48, 60 L Ed. 2d 698, 99 S Ct. 2121 (1979), quoting *Gertz v. Robert Welch*, Inc., 418 US 323, 350, 41 L Ed. 2d 789, 94 S Ct. 2997 (1974) (footnote omitted).

The Government says that such damages were not "received ... on account of" the personal injuries, but rather were awarded "on account of" a defendant's reprehensible conduct and the jury's need to punish and to deter it. Hence, despite some historical uncertainty about the matter, ... the Government now concludes that these punitive damages fall outside the statute's coverage.

We agree with the Government's interpretation of the statute. For one thing, its interpretation gives the phrase "on account of" a meaning consistent with the dictionary definition. See, *e.g.*, *Webster's Third New International Dictionary* 13 (1981) ("for the sake of: by reason of: because of").

More important, ... in *Schleier, supra*, we came close to resolving the statute's ambiguity in the Government's favor. That case did not involve damages received in an ordinary tort suit; it involved liquidated damages and backpay received in a settlement of a lawsuit charging a violation of the ADEA. Nonetheless, in deciding one of the issues there presented (whether the provision now before us covered ADEA liquidated damages), we contrasted the elements of an ordinary tort recovery with ADEA liquidated damages. We said that pain and suffering damages, medical expenses, and lost wages in an ordinary tort case are covered by the statute and hence excluded from income

> "not simply because the taxpayer received a tort settlement, but rather because each element ... satisfies the requirement ... that the damages were received 'on account of personal injuries or sickness.' " *Id.*, at 330.

In holding that ADEA liquidated damages are not covered, we said that they are not "designed to compensate ADEA victims," *id.*, at 332, n. 5; instead, they are " 'punitive in nature,' " *id.*, at 332, quoting *Trans World Airlines, Inc. v. Thurston*, 469 US 111, 125, 83 L Ed. 2d 523, 105 S Ct. 613 (1985).

Applying the same reasoning here would lead to the conclusion that the punitive damages are not covered because they are an element of damages not "designed to compensate ... victims," *Schleier*, 515 US at 332; rather they are " 'punitive in nature,' " *ibid*. Although we gave other reasons for our holding in *Schleier* as well, we explicitly labeled this reason an "independent" ground in support of our decision, 515 US at 334. We cannot accept petitioners' claim that it was simply a dictum.

We also find the Government's reading more faithful to the history of the statutory provision as well as the basic tax-related purpose that the history reveals. That history begins in approximately 1918. At that time, this Court had recently decided several cases based on the principle that a restoration of capital was not income; hence it fell outside the definition of "income" upon which the law imposed a tax. [Citations omitted.] The Attorney General then advised the Secretary of the Treasury that proceeds of an accident insurance policy should be treated as nontaxable because they primarily

> "substitute ... capital which is the source of *future* periodical income ... merely tak[ing] the place of capital in human ability which was destroyed by the accident. They are therefore [nontaxable] 'capital' as distinguished from 'income' receipts." 31 Op. Atty. Gen. 304, 308 (1918).

The Treasury Department added that

> "upon similar principles ... an amount received by an individual as the result of a suit or compromise for personal injuries sustained by him through accident is not income [that is] taxable. ..." TD 2747, 20 Treas. Dec. Int. Rev. 457 (1918).

Soon thereafter, Congress enacted the first predecessor of the provision before us. That provision excluded from income

> "amounts received, through accident or health insurance or under workmen's compensation acts, as compensation for personal injuries or sickness, plus the amount of any damages received whether by suit or agreement on account of such injuries or sickness." Revenue Act of 1918, ch. 18, § 213(b)(6), 40 Stat. 1066.

The provision is similar to the cited materials from the Attorney General and the Secretary of the Treasury in language and structure, all of which suggests that Congress sought, in enacting the statute, to codify the Treasury's basic approach. A contemporaneous House Report, insofar as relevant, confirms this similarity of approach, for it says:

> "Under the present law it is doubtful whether amounts received through accident or health insurance, or under workmen's compensation acts, as compensation for personal injury or sickness, and damages received on account of such injuries or sickness, are required to be included in gross income. The proposed bill provides that such amounts shall not be included in gross income." HR Rep. No. 767, pp. 9-10 (1918).

This history and the approach it reflects suggest there is no strong reason for trying to interpret the statute's language to reach beyond those damages that, making up for a loss, seek to make a victim whole, or, speaking very loosely, "return the victim's personal or financial capital."

We concede that the original provision's language does go beyond what one might expect a purely tax-policy-related "human capital" rationale to justify. That is because the language excludes from taxation not only those damages that aim to substitute for a victim's physical or personal well-being—personal assets that the Government does not tax and would not have taxed had the victim not lost them. It also excludes from taxation those damages that substitute, say, for lost wages, which would have been taxed had the victim earned them. To that extent, the provision can make the compensated taxpayer better off from a tax perspective than had the personal injury not taken place.

But to say this is not to support cutting the statute totally free from its original moorings in victim loss. The statute's failure to separate those compensatory elements of damages (or accident insurance proceeds) one from the other does not change its original focus upon damages that restore a loss, that seek to make a victim whole, with a tax-equality objective providing an important part of, even if not the entirety of, the statute's rationale. All this is to say that the Government's interpretation of the current provision (the wording of which has not changed significantly from the original) is more consistent than is petitioners' with the statute's original focus.

Finally, we have asked *why* Congress might have wanted the exclusion to have covered these punitive damages, and we have found no very good answer. Those damages are not a substitute for any normally untaxed personal (or financial) quality, good, or "asset." They do not compensate for any kind of loss. The statute's language does not require, or strongly suggest, their exclusion from income. And we can find no evidence that congressional generosity or concern for administrative convenience stretched beyond the bounds of an interpretation that would distinguish compensatory from noncompensatory damages.

Of course, as we have just said, from the perspective of tax policy one might argue that noncompensatory punitive damages and, for example, compensatory lost wages are much the same thing. That is, in both instances, exclusion from gross income provides the taxpayer with a windfall. This circumstance alone, however, does not argue strongly for an interpretation that covers punitive damages, for coverage of compensatory damages has both language and history in its favor to a degree that coverage of noncompensatory punitive damages does not. Moreover, this policy argument assumes that coverage of lost wages is something of an anomaly; if so, that circumstance would not justify the extension of the anomaly or the creation of another. See Wolfman, "Current Issues of Federal Tax Policy," 16 *U Ark. Little Rock L J* 543, 549-550 (1994) ("To build upon" what is, from a tax policy perspective, the less easily explained portion "of the otherwise rational exemption for personal injury," simply "does not make sense").

Petitioners make three sorts of arguments to the contrary. First, they emphasize certain words or phrases in the original, or current, provision that work in their favor. For example, they stress the word "any" in the phrase "any damages." And they note that in both original and current versions Congress referred to certain amounts of money received (from workmen's compensation, for example) as "amounts received ... as compensation," while here they refer only to "damages received" without adding the limiting phrase "as compensation." 26 USC § 104(a); Revenue Act of 1918, § 213(b)(6), 40 Stat. 1066. They add that in the original version, the words "on account of personal injuries" might have referred to, and modified, the kind of lawsuit, not the kind of damages. And they find support for this view in the second sentence of the Treasury Regulation first adopted in 1958 which says:

> "The term 'damages received (whether by suit or agreement)' means an amount received (other than workmen's compensation) through prosecution of a legal suit or action based upon tort or tort type rights, or through a settlement agreement entered into in lieu of such prosecution." 26 CFR § 1.104-1(c) (1996).

These arguments, however, show only that one can reasonably read the statute's language in different ways—the very assumption upon which our analysis rests. They do not overcome our interpretation of the provision in *Schleier*, nor do they change the provision's history. The help that the Treasury Regulation's second sentence gives the petitioners is offset by its *first* sentence, which says that the exclusion applies to damages received "on account of personal injuries or sickness," and which we have held sets forth an independent requirement. *Schleier*, 515 US at 336. ...

Second, petitioners argue that to some extent the purposes that might have led Congress to exclude, say, lost wages from income would also have led Congress to exclude punitive damages, for doing so is both generous to victims and avoids such administrative problems as separating punitive from compensatory portions of a global settlement or determining the extent to which a punitive damages award is itself intended to compensate.

Our problem with these arguments is one of degree. Tax generosity presumably has its limits. The administrative problem of distinguishing punitive from compensatory elements is likely to be less serious than, say, distinguishing among the compensatory elements of a settlement (which difficulty might account for the statute's treatment of, say, lost wages). And, of course, the problem of identifying the elements of an ostensibly punitive award does not exist where, as here, relevant state law makes clear that the damages at issue are not at all compensatory, but entirely punitive. *Brewer v. Home-Stake Production Co.*, 200 Kan. 96, 100, 434 P2d 828, 831 (1967)

("Exemplary damages are not regarded as compensatory in any degree"); accord, *Smith v. Printup*, 254 Kan. 315, 866 P2d 985 (1993); *Folks v. Kansas Power & Light Co.*, 243 Kan. 57, 755 P2d 1319 (1988); *Nordstrom v. Miller*, 227 Kan. 59, 605 P2d 545 (1980).

Third, petitioners rely upon a later enacted law. In 1989, Congress amended the law so that it now specifically says the personal injury exclusion from gross income

"shall not apply to any punitive damages in connection with a case not involving physical injury or physical sickness." 26 USC § 104(a).

Why, petitioners ask, would Congress have enacted this amendment removing punitive damages (in nonphysical injury cases) unless Congress believed that, in the amendment's absence, punitive damages did fall within the provision's coverage?

The short answer to this question is that Congress might simply have thought that the then-current law about the provision's treatment of punitive damages—in cases of physical and nonphysical injuries—was unclear, that it wanted to clarify the matter in respect to nonphysical injuries, but it wanted to leave the law where it found it in respect to physical injuries. The fact that the law was indeed uncertain at the time supports this view. Compare Rev. Rul. 84-108, 1984-2 Cum. Bull. 32, with, *e.g.*, *Roemer v. Commissioner*, 716 F2d 693 (CA9 1983); *Miller v. Commissioner*, 93 TC 330 (1989), rev'd 914 F2d 586 (CA4 1990).

The 1989 amendment's legislative history, insofar as relevant, offers further support. The amendment grew out of the Senate's refusal to agree to a House bill that would have made *all* damages in nonphysical personal injury cases taxable. The Senate was willing to specify only that the Government could tax punitive damages in such cases. Compare HR Rep. No. 101-247, p. 1355 (1989), with HR Conf. Rep. No. 101-386, pp. 622-623 (1989). Congress' primary focus, in other words, was upon what to do about nonphysical personal injuries, not upon the provision's coverage of punitive damages under pre-existing law.

We add that, in any event, the view of a later Congress cannot control the interpretation of an earlier enacted statute. *United States v. Price*, 361 US 304, 4 L Ed. 2d 334, 80 S Ct. 326 (1960); *Higgins v. Smith*, 308 US 473, 84 L Ed. 406, 60 S Ct. 355 (1940). But cf. *Burke*, 504 US at 235, n. 6 (including a passing reference to the 1989 amendment, in dicta, as support for a view somewhat like that of petitioners).

(Although neither party has argued that it is relevant, we note in passing that § 1605 of the Small Business Job Protection Act of 1996, Pub. L 104-188, 110 Stat. 1838, explicitly excepts most punitive damages from the exclusion provided by § 104(a)(2). Because it is of prospective application, the section does not apply here. The Conference Report on the new law says that "no inference is intended" as to the proper interpretation of § 104(a)(2) prior to amendment. HR Conf. Rep. No. 104-737, p. 301 (1996).)

The upshot is that we do not find petitioners' arguments sufficiently persuasive. And, for the reasons set out above, *supra*, at 83-87, we agree with the Government's interpretation of the statute. ... The judgment of the Court of Appeals is *Affirmed*.

SCALIA J (O'Connor and Thomas JJ dissenting): Section 104(a)(2), as it stood at the time relevant to these cases, provided an exclusion from income for "any damages received ... on account of personal injuries or sickness." 26 USC § 104(a)(2) (1988 ed.). The Court is of the view that this phrase, in isolation, is just as susceptible of a meaning that includes only compensatory damages as it is of a broader meaning that includes punitive damages as well. *Ante*, at 82-83. I do not agree. The Court greatly understates the connection between an award of punitive damages and the personal injury complained of, describing it as nothing more than "but-for" causality, *ante*, at 82. It seems to me that the personal injury is as proximate a cause of the punitive damages as it is of the compensatory damages; in both cases it is the *reason* the damages are awarded. That is *why* punitive damages are called *damages*. To be sure, punitive damages require intentional, blameworthy conduct, which can be said to be a coequal reason they are awarded. But negligent (or intentional) conduct occupies the same role of coequal causality with regard to compensatory damages. Both types of damages are "received on account of" the personal injury.

The nub of the matter, it seems to me, is this: If one were to be asked, by a lawyer from another legal system, "What damages can be received on account of personal injuries in the United States?" surely the correct answer would be "Compensatory damages and punitive damages—the former to compensate for the inflicting of the personal injuries, and the latter to punish for the inflicting of them." If, as the Court asserts, the phrase "damages received on account of personal injuries" *can* be used to refer only to the former category, that is only because people sometimes *can* be imprecise. The notion that Congress carefully and precisely used the phrase "damages received on account of personal injuries" to segregate out *compensatory* damages seems to me entirely fanciful. That is neither the exact nor the ordinary meaning of the phrase, and hence not the one that the statute should be understood to intend.

What I think to be the fair meaning of the phrase in isolation becomes even clearer when the phrase is considered in its statutory context. The Court proceeds too quickly from its erroneous premise of ambiguity to analysis of the history and policy behind § 104(a)(2). *Ante*, at 84-87. Ambiguity in isolation, even if it existed, would not end the textual inquiry. Statutory construction, we have said, is a "holistic endeavor." *United Sav. Assn. of Tex. v. Timbers of Inwood Forest Associates, Ltd.*, 484 US 365, 371, 98 L Ed. 2d 740, 108 S Ct. 626 (1988). "A provision that may seem ambiguous in isolation is often clarified by the remainder of the statutory scheme." *Ibid.*

Section 104(a)(2) appears immediately after another provision, § 104(a)(1), which parallels § 104(a)(2) in several respects but does not use the critical phrase "on account of":

> "(a) Gross income does not include—
>
> "(1) amounts received under workmen's compensation acts *as compensation for* personal injuries or sickness;
>
> "(2) the amount of any damages received ... *on account of* personal injuries or sickness." (Emphasis added.)

Although § 104(a)(1) excludes amounts received "as compensation for" personal injuries or sickness, while § 104(a)(2) excludes amounts received "on account of" personal injuries or sickness, the Court reads the two phrases to mean precisely the same thing. That is not sound textual interpretation. "When the legislature uses certain language in one part of the statute and different language in another, the court assumes different meanings were intended." ... N. Singer, Sutherland on Statutory Construction § 46.07 (5th ed. 1992 and Supp. 1996). See, *e.g.*, *Russello v. United States*, 464 US 16, 23, 78 L Ed. 2d 17, 104 S Ct. 296 (1983). This principle of construction has its limits, of course: Use of different terminology in differing contexts might have little significance. But here the contrasting phrases appear in adjoining provisions that address precisely the same subject matter and that even have identical grammatical structure.

The contrast between the two usages is even more striking in the original statute that enacted them. The Revenue Act of 1918 combined subsections (a)(1) and (a)(2) of § 104, together with (a)(3) (which provides an exclusion from income for amounts received through accident or health insurance for personal injuries or sickness), into a single subsection, which provided:

> " 'Gross income' ... does not include ... :
>
> "(6) Amounts received, through accident or health insurance or under workmen's compensation acts, *as compensation for* personal injuries or sickness, plus the amount of any damages received ... *on account of* such injuries or sickness." § 213(b)(6) of the Revenue Act of 1918, 40 Stat. 1065-1066 (emphasis added).

The contrast between the first exclusion and the second could not be more clear. Had Congress intended the latter provision to cover only damages received "as compensation for" personal injuries or sickness, it could have written "amounts received, through accident or health insurance, under workmen's compensation acts, or in damages, as compensation for personal injuries or sickness." Instead, it tacked on an additional phrase "plus the amount of[, etc.]" with no apparent purpose except to make clear that not *only* compensatory damages were covered by the exclusion.

The Court maintains, however, that the Government's reading of § 104(a)(2) is "more faithful to [its] history." *Ante*, at 84. The "history" to which the Court refers is not statutory history of the sort just discussed—prior enactments approved by earlier Congresses and revised or amended by later ones to produce the current text. Indeed, it is not "history" from within even a small portion of Congress, since the House Committee Report the Court cites, standing by itself, is uninformative, saying only that "under the present law it is doubtful whether ... damages received on account of (personal) injuries or sickness are required to be included in gross income." HR Rep. No. 767, 65th Cong., 2d Sess., 9-10 (1918). The Court makes this snippet of legislative history relevant by citing as pertinent an antecedent Treasury Department decision, which concludes on the basis of recent judicial decisions that amounts received from prosecution or compromise of a personal-injury suit are not taxable *because they are a return of capital*. *Ante*, at 85 (citing TD 2747, 20 Treas. Dec. Int. Rev. 457 (1918)).

One might expect the Court to conclude from this that the Members of Congress (on the unrealistic assumption that they knew about the Executive Branch opinion) meant the statutory language to cover only return of capital, the source of the "doubt" to which the Committee Report referred. But of course the Court cannot draw that logical conclusion, since even if it is applied only to compensatory damages the statute obviously and undeniably covers *more* than mere return of "human capital," namely, reimbursement for lost income, which would be a large proportion (indeed perhaps the majority) of any damages award. The Court concedes this is so, but asserts that this inconsistency is not enough "to support cutting the statute totally free from its original moorings," *ante*, at 86, by which I assume it means the Treasury Decision, however erroneous it might have been as to the "capital" nature of compensatory damages. But the Treasury Decision was no more explicitly limited to compensatory damages than is the statute before us. It exempted from taxation "an amount received by an individual as the result of a suit or compromise for personal injuries." TD 2747, *supra*, at 457. The Court's entire thesis of taxability rests upon the proposition that this Treasury Decision, which overlooked the obvious fact that "an amount received ... as the result of a suit or compromise for personal injuries" almost always includes compensation for lost future income, did *not* overlook the obvious fact that such an amount sometimes includes "smart money."

So, to trace the Court's reasoning: The statute must exclude punitive damages because the Committee Report must have had in mind a 1918 Treasury Decision, whose text no more supports exclusion of punitive damages than does the text of the statute itself, but which must have *meant* to exclude punitive damages since it was based on the "return-of-capital" theory, though, inconsistently with that theory, it did *not* exclude the much more common category of compensation for lost income. Congress supposedly knew all of this, and a reasonably diligent lawyer could figure it out by mistrusting the inclusive language of the statute, consulting the Committee Report, surmising that the Treasury Decision of 1918 underlay that Report, mistrusting the inclusive language of the Treasury Decision, and discerning that Treasury *could* have overlooked lost-income compensatories, but could *not* have overlooked punitives. I think not. The sure and proper guide, it seems to me, is the language of the statute, inclusive by nature and doubly inclusive by contrast with surrounding provisions.

The Court poses the question, *ante*, at 86, "*why* Congress might have wanted the exclusion [in § 104(a)(2)] to have covered ... punitive damages." If an answer is needed (and the text being as clear as it is, I think it is not), surely it suffices to surmise that Congress was following the Treasury Decision, which had inadvertently embraced punitive damages just as it had inadvertently embraced future-income compensatory damages. Or if some reason free of human error must be found, I see nothing wrong with what the Court itself suggests but rejects out of hand: Excluding punitive as well as compensatory damages from gross income "avoids such administrative problems as separating punitive from compensatory portions of a global settlement." *Ante*, at 88. How substantial that particular problem is is suggested by the statistics which show that 73 percent of tort cases in state court are disposed of by settlement, and between 92 and 99 percent of tort cases in federal court are disposed of by either settlement or some other means (such as summary judgment) prior to trial. See B. Ostrom & N. Kauder, Examining the Work of State Courts, 1994, p. 34 (1996); Administrative Office of the United States Courts, L. Mecham, Judicial Business of the United States Courts: 1995 Report of the Director 162-164. What is at issue, of course, is not just imposing on the parties the necessity of allocating the settlement between compensatory and punitive damages (with the concomitant suggestion of intentional wrongdoing that *any* allocation to punitive damages entails), but also imposing on the Internal Revenue Service the necessity of reviewing that allocation, since there would always be strong incentive to inflate the tax-free compensatory portion. The Court's only response to the suggestion that this is an adequate reason (if one is required) for including punitive damages in the exemption is that "the administrative problem of distinguishing punitive from compensatory elements is likely to be less serious than, say, distinguishing among the compensatory elements of a settlement." *Ante*, at 88. Perhaps so; and it may also be more simple than splitting the atom; but that in no way refutes the point that it is complicated *enough* to explain the inclusion of punitive damages in an exemption that has already abandoned the purity of a "return-of-capital" rationale.

The remaining argument offered by the Court is that our decision in *Commissioner v. Schleier*, 515 US 323, 132 L Ed. 2d 294, 115 S Ct. 2159 (1995), came "close to resolving"—in the Government's favor—the question whether § 104(a)(2) permits the exclusion of punitive damages. *Ante*, at 83. I disagree. In *Schleier* we were faced with the question whether backpay and liquidated damages under the Age Discrimination in Employment Act of 1967 (ADEA) were "damages received ... on account of personal injuries or sickness" for purposes of § 104(a)(2)'s exclusion. As the dissent accurately observed, 515 US at 342 (opinion of O'CONNOR, J), "the key to the Court's analysis" was the determination that an ADEA cause of action did not necessarily entail "personal injury or sickness," so that the damages awarded for that cause of action could hardly be awarded "on account of personal injuries or sickness." See *id.*, at 330. In the case at hand, we said, "respondent's unlawful termination may have caused some psychological or 'personal' injury comparable to the intangible pain and suffering caused by an automobile accident," but "it is clear that no part of respondent's recovery of back wages is attributable to that injury." *Ibid.* The respondent countered that at least "the liquidated damages portion of his settlement" could be linked to that psychological injury. 515 US at 331. And it was in response to *that* argument that we made the statement which the Court seeks to press into service for today's opinion. ADEA liquidated damages, we said, were punitive in nature, rather than compensatory. 515 US at 331-332, and n 5.

The Court recites this statement as though the point of it was that punitive damages could not be received "on account of" personal injuries, whereas in fact the point was quite different: Since the damages were punishment for the conduct that gave rise to the (non-personal-injury) cause of action, they could not be "linked to" the incidental psychological injury. In the present cases, of course, there is no question that a personal injury occurred and that this personal injury is what entitled petitioners to compensatory and punitive damages. We neither decided nor intimated in *Schleier* whether punitive damages that are indisputably "linked to" personal injuries or sickness are received "on account of" such injuries or sickness. Indeed, it would have been odd for us to resolve that question (or even come "close to resolving" it) without any discussion of the numerous considerations of text, history, and policy highlighted by today's opinion. If one were to search our opinions for a dictum bearing upon the present issue, much closer is the statement in *United States v. Burke*, 504 US 229, 119 L Ed. 2d 34, 112 S Ct. 1867 (1992), that a statute confers "tort or tort type rights" (qualifying a plaintiff's recovery for the § 104(a)(2) exemption) if it entitles the plaintiff to "a jury trial at which 'both equitable and legal relief, including compensatory and, under certain circumstances, punitive damages' may be awarded." *Id.*, at 240 (quoting *Johnson v. Railway Express Agency, Inc.*, 421 US 454, 460, 44 L Ed. 2d 295, 95 S Ct. 1716 (1975)).

But all of this is really by the way. Because the statutory text unambiguously covers punitive damages that are awarded on account of personal injuries, I conclude that petitioners were entitled to deduct the amounts at issue here. This makes it unnecessary for me to reach the question, discussed *ante*, at 90-92, whether the Government's refund action against the O'Gilvie children was commenced within the 2-year period specified by 26 USC § 6532(b). I note, however, that the Court's resolution of these cases also does not demand that this issue be addressed, except to the extent of rejecting the proposition that the statutory period begins to run with the mailing of a refund check. So long as that is not the trigger, there is no need to decide whether the proper trigger is receipt of the check or some later event, such as the check's clearance.

For the reasons stated, I respectfully dissent from the judgment of the Court.

NOTES AND QUESTIONS

1. According to the majority, the government's interpretation of "on account of" is consistent with the dictionary definition, which defines "on account of" as "for the sake of: by reason of: because of." Is the dictionary definition any less ambiguous than the words "on account of"? Is the phrase "because of" inconsistent with the taxpayer's interpretation of "on account of"?

2. Is there a "plain meaning" of the phrase "on account of"?

3. Does the American approach to tax interpretation (revealed in *O'Gilvie*) appear to coincide with the Canadian approach discussed in chapter 7 of *Theory and Practice*? Specifically, consider the manner in which the US Supreme Court balances "legislative purpose" against the "pro-taxpayer" reading of the enactment in *O'Gilvie*.

4. Note that the majority makes extensive use of previous versions of the relevant statutory provisions. Is this court's use of that evidence consistent with the approach demonstrated in chapter 4?

5. The majority notes that the taxpayer relies "upon a later enacted law" (that is, an amendment that was passed after the taxpayer's case arose). Note that "later enacted laws" are dealt with in much the same way as "prior versions of the same enactment" (discussed in chapter 4). Are you persuaded by the manner in which the Court in *O'Gilvie* deals with the "later enacted law"?[4]

---

4   The court simply notes that the amendment may have been passed simply to "clarify" the law, rather than to make a substantive change. Compare this with the approach taken in the cases discussed in chapter 4.

6. The court notes that "the view of a later Congress cannot control the interpretation of an earlier enacted statute." What does this say concerning the weight that may be attributed to "later enacted laws"?

7. According to Scalia J, "[i]f, as the Court asserts, the phrase 'damages received on account of personal injuries' can be used to refer only to [compensatory damages], that is only because people sometimes *can* be imprecise." Do you agree with Scalia J's claim?

8. Scalia J refers to the "fair meaning" of the relevant legislation. How does this compare with "plain meaning," "accurate meaning," and "strict construction"?

9. Scalia J invokes a corollary of the presumption of consistent expression in the following terms: "[w]hen the legislature uses certain language in one part of the statute and different language in another, the court assumes different meanings were intended." Do you agree with Scalia J's application of this interpretive doctrine? Is this a sensible interpretive doctrine?

10. Scalia J is often referred to as a "pure textualist." Assuming that Scalia J's judgment in *O'Gilvie* reflects his "textualist" nature, what *is* textualism?

11. At the end of his dissent, Scalia J concludes that "the statutory text unambiguously covers punitive damages that are awarded on account of personal injuries." Do you agree that the provision being considered is "unambiguous" in its application to punitive damages?

12. Would the modern approach (discussed in chapter 7 of *Theory and Practice*) inevitably lead to a particular result in the *O'Gilvie* case? Would the unified theory (developed in *Theory and Practice*) lead to a specific result?

V. EXERCISE

Suggested length: 12-20 pages

Assume that the United States has become a colony of Canada and the decision of the US Supreme Court in *O'Gilvie v. United States* (519 US 79 (1996)) is being appealed to Canada's highest court. You have recently been appointed chief justice of Canada and you must write a judgment overturning or upholding the American court's decision. The reasoning of your decision should address the modern approach (described in chapter 7 of *Theory and Practice*), together with the reasoning in *Will-Kare* and *Ludco*.[5]

---

5   An alternative version of this assignment would require students to write both a majority and a dissent, together with a "case comment" at the end explaining how the modern approach was employed to justify conflicting interpretations.